# Advance Praise

*Beyond Indenture* is a fitting tribute to the late Brij V. Lal, scholar and individual extraordinaire. It places the history of indentured labourers from India alongside a variety of overseas labour from India. The result is a volume with a good mix of both familiar and unusual topics. The shared theme across the essays is the resilience and grit of people even under exploitative conditions. It makes this a standout volume on the subject.

—**Mrinalini Sinha**, *University of Michigan*

The lives of millions of plantation and domestic workers, traders, moneylenders, teachers, civil servants, sailors and others who migrated from India in the nineteenth and early twentieth centuries to all continents deserve a close and detailed study. This book, with its rigorous, wide-ranging and accomplished scholarship, is exciting to read. It is a monumental contribution to the history of indenture and post-indentureship studies.

—**David Dabydeen**, *University of Cambridge*

An insightful and impressive set of essays on many facets of the social lives of South Asian migrant labourers in the colonial and post-colonial eras. A worthy tribute to Brij Lal.

—**Sugata Bose**, *Harvard University*

*Beyond Indenture* brings together complex tales of agency and resistance by the globally migrant labour force since the days of colonial empires. Instead of focusing on the well-known labour exploitation by officials, planters, and other types of employers, this work explores the stories of workers. It covers a wide range of issues, from resistance to derogatory conditions of employment, including the cases of poisoning of employers by domestic servants. Once a subject of crime thrillers, this has become a domain of exploration by historians. It highlights issues of remigration, a fascinating effort of workers to improve their living conditions. The point of domestic intimacy, new forms of families in plantations, caste mobility and stories of Eurasian labourers add a new dimension to the complex historiography of indentured workers. Finally, the book covers the complex post-colonial political developments in societies with complex demographic mosaics due to indentured workers. As an editor, Crispin Bates weaves a synthetic introduction that captures the huge complexities of indentured migration from its inception to its post-colonial legacies and that demonstrates his mastery over this subaltern narrative. The book is a must-read for all those engaged in studying labour history.

—**Subho Basu**, *McGill University*

*Beyond Indenture* represents an exciting new chapter in the scholarship on Indian indentured migration. Going far beyond earlier debates that saw indentured labourers either purely as victims of exploitation or as wholly free agents, the bracing collection of essays here highlights a range of voices and a diversity of experiences. The book is exemplary in featuring cutting-edge scholarship from scholars at different stages of their careers and from different locations. The collection is expertly edited and hugely compelling.

—**Sunil Amrith**, *Yale University*

# Beyond Indenture

*Beyond Indenture* brings together original essays by a mix of experienced and upcoming scholars. They reflect, as far as possible, the viewpoints and voices of indentured Indians who exercised agency, resisted and manipulated the colonial labour system to their advantage, and went on to build new lives for themselves overseas following the expiry of their contracts. Some remigrated to other colonies to earn a better wage and escape from debt and other burdens. Among those who chose to remain, women played a prominent role in the struggle for rights, freedom and opportunities, achieving them in ways which often defied or redefined South Asian customs and traditions. Alongside the migrant labourers, 'passenger Indians' made their way to the sugar, tea and rubber colonies, and became clerks, teachers and shopkeepers. After independence, the Indian communities overseas faced newer problems, not least of which were discrimination and marginalisation. Some were forced to return home. Others built upon the experience of struggles in the colonial era to collectively mobilise. Another theme explored is that of the broad alliances of diasporic Indians and Pakistani and Bangladeshi migrants who have been recently enabled by the internet to connect with each other and to reconnect with the countries from which they originated.

**Crispin Bates** is Professor of Modern and Contemporary South Asian History at the University of Edinburgh and Honorary Visiting Professor in the Graduate School of African and Asian Studies, Kyoto University. He has authored, co-authored and edited a total of 15 books including a history of South Asia from 1600 to the present, entitled *Subalterns and Raj* (2007), and a series of seven volumes concerning the history of the Indian uprising of 1857, entitled 'Mutiny at the Margins' (2013–2017). In 2015–2018, he led 'Becoming Coolies', an Arts and Humanities Research Council (AHRC)–funded project on the origins of Indian overseas labour migration in the Indian Ocean, for which he conducted research in archives throughout the Indian Ocean region.

# GLOBAL SOUTH ASIANS

Throughout the modern era, South Asia and South Asians have been entangled with global flows of goods, people and ideas. In the context of these globalised conditions, migrants from the subcontinent of India created some of the world's most extensive and influential transnational networks. While operating within the constraints of imperial systems, they nevertheless made distinctive and important contributions to international trade, global cultures and transnational circuits of knowledge. This series seeks to explore these phenomena, placing labourers, traders, thinkers and activists at the centre of the analysis. Beginning with volumes that seek to radically reappraise indenture, the series will continue with books on the mobility of elite actors, including intellectuals, and their contributions to the global circulation of ideas and the evolution of political practice. It will highlight the creativity and agency of diasporic South Asians and illuminate the crucial role they played in the making of global histories. As such it sets out to challenge popular misconceptions and established scholarly narratives that too often cast South Asians as passive observers.

# Beyond Indenture

Agency and Resistance in the Colonial
South Asian Diaspora

*Edited by*
**Crispin Bates**

CAMBRIDGE
UNIVERSITY PRESS

Shaftesbury Road, Cambridge CB2 8EA, United Kingdom

One Liberty Plaza, 20th Floor, New York, NY 10006, USA

477 Williamstown Road, Port Melbourne, VIC 3207, Australia

314–321, 3rd Floor, Plot 3, Splendor Forum, Jasola District Centre, New Delhi – 110025, India

103 Penang Road, #05–06/07, Visioncrest Commercial, Singapore 238467

Cambridge University Press is part of Cambridge University Press & Assessment, a department of the University of Cambridge.

We share the University's mission to contribute to society through the pursuit of education, learning and research at the highest international levels of excellence.

www.cambridge.org
Information on this title: www.cambridge.org/9781009339797

First published 2024

Printed in India by Avantika Printers Pvt. Ltd.

*A catalogue record for this publication is available from the British Library*

ISBN 978-1-009-33979-7 Hardback

*For Brij V. Lal (1952–2021)*

# Contents

# Figures and Tables

## Figures

## Tables

# Acknowledgements

This volume grew out of several conferences, with accompanying exhibitions, held in 2016 that were funded by the Arts and Humanities Research Council (AHRC), Swindon, as part of the 'Becoming Coolies' project on the origins of South Asian overseas labour migration in the Indian Ocean region. The first conference was at the Centre for the Study of Developing Societies (CSDS), New Delhi; the second conference, 'After Slavery', and the 'Coolitudes' exhibition were hosted by the University of Leeds; and the final conference, entitled 'Indentured Lives: Rethinking the Experience of Indian Overseas Labour Migration, 1800–1920', was hosted by the School of History in the University of Edinburgh. The scope of the volume was subsequently expanded to include additional chapters that were commissioned in the Caribbean and Fiji. Enormous gratitude is due to the collaborators in the AHRC project – Andrea Major, Marina Carter and Ashutosh Kumar – and to Danny Amos Flynn for his artwork as well as to all those who participated in the Delhi, Leeds and Edinburgh conferences and who helped make them such a success. Further thanks are due to Jessica Robinson for her assistance in copyediting the initial drafts of the manuscript, and to Sohini Ghosh and Qudsiya Ahmed and latterly Anwesha Rana at Cambridge University Press who patiently shepherded this book through the production process until its publication.

The editor wishes to acknowledge the kind support of publishers who have permitted the reproduction of extracts from various publications in this volume: Enuga Reddy and Kalpana Hiralal's *Pioneers of Satyagraha: Indian South Africans Defy Racist Laws, 1907–1914* (2017), the *Journal of Sikh and Punjab Studies*, *Women's History Review* and the *Colombo Telegraph*.

This book is dedicated to the memory of the distinguished Indo-Fijian historian Brij V. Lal, who contributed to it what he described as his very last non-fiction essay before he retired from academic writing to focus solely on literary work. His decision was motivated by failing eyesight. Most were unaware of his other health problems until his sudden and shocking death on 25 December 2021 at the age of 69.

Brij rose to fame from humble origins in a poor farming family in Tabia, Vanua Levu, via a competitive scholarship to study at the newly founded University of the South Pacific, Suva. He went on to complete his MA at the University of British Columbia, Vancouver, and PhD at the Australian National University, Canberra, where he was Professor of Pacific and Asian History at the School of Culture, History and Language. He is remembered for his pioneering research on the history of indentured migration to Fiji and Fijian history (his own paternal grandfather was a *girmitiya*) and his famous book *Girmitiyas: The Origins of the Fiji Indians* (1983) which used statistical records to challenge assumptions about Indian migrants. He is also remembered for the warm advice and encouragement he gave to many younger scholars around the world who were struggling to follow in his wake. Brij was not just a well-known and hugely admired historian, but also a poet and novelist and an influential public intellectual who, amongst other things, played an important role as a member of the committee that devised Fiji's revised constitution of 1995, an achievement of which he was justly proud. Brij wore lightly the numerous honours heaped upon his shoulders, including Officer of the Order of Fiji (OF) in 1998, the Australian Centenary Medal in 2001 and the Member of the Order of Australia (AM) in 2015. Having been expelled from his beloved home country in 2009, he spent his remaining years residing in Brisbane, Queensland, as Emeritus Professor at the Australian National University. He was a hugely valued and much-loved presence at numerous conferences held over the years devoted to exploring the history of the South Asian diaspora. His work will continue to live on and inspire historians for many generations to come.

Crispin Bates

# Introduction

*Crispin Bates*

The historiography on South Asian overseas migration in the colonial era has focused extensively on the history of indentured labour. This was a system of recruitment of workers on a fixed contract of three to five years with a single employer, at the end of which they could re-indenture, find other employment or have their passage paid home. These contracts were prominently used by private employers to hire plantation labour in sugar, rubber, tea and coffee plantations following the abolition of slavery and by rural Indians to escape from poverty and/or discrimination. They were also used in government public works departments, in railway construction and in the military. Those who signed such an agreement (known as a *girmit* in north India) described themselves as *girmitiyas*. Although guaranteed food, shelter and employment, and subject to periodic inspections, those in the hands of private employers overseas could be exploited as they were often working in remote locations and were legally not free to leave until their contract had expired or they (or their family) had bought their way out of it. Although never allowed in Sri Lanka or Myanmar, and superseded by other forms of migration by the beginning of the twentieth century, more has been written about South Asian indentured labour than any other form of historical migration from India, partly because it was subject to government regulation and is therefore unusually well documented in colonial archives.

Within the literature on indentured labour, most of the writing has revolved around migration statistics and the debates between anti-slavery campaigners, planters, British imperial officials and, latterly, the complaints of Indian nationalist politicians, leading up to the effective abolition of indentured overseas labour contracts by 1920. The voices of the migrants themselves are not so often heard, nor those of the many other Indians who were not on contracts of indenture who migrated at the same time. A classic text, Hugh Tinker's *A New System of Slavery*,[1]

---

[1] Tinker (1974).

drew its inspiration from the early campaigns against indentured migration launched by the anti-slavery movement in Britain. However, in recent years, a new scholarship has been emerging, especially from within the diaspora – most prominently in South Africa – which sheds light on the highly varied social lives of migrants. Rather than depicting migrants as the silent victims of planters and colonial officials, these social histories reveal intimate details of their lives and the diverse and inventive ways in which they managed to survive and even prosper in their new homes. An early pioneer of revisionism was Brij V. Lal, followed by P. C. Emmer, Marina Carter, Ashwin Desai, Goolam Vahed and Ashutosh Kumar.[2] This newer literature has highlighted the pivotal role of Indian intermediaries (*sirdar*s and *kangani*s) in the recruitment of overseas labour,[3] as in the Indian labour market as a whole.[4] It has also revealed the various ways in which migrants exercised agency, manipulating the otherwise often cruel colonial labour system to their advantage. One of these methods was to remigrate to other colonies, to earn a better wage and to escape from debt and other burdens – a phenomenon highlighted in this volume. Among those who chose to build new homes and lives for themselves in the colonies to which they had migrated, women played a prominent role in the struggle for rights, freedom and opportunities, achieving it in ways which often (controversially) defied or redefined South Asian customs and traditions.[5]

The important role of Indian migration in the global history of capitalism and the emergence of modern societies in the Global South in the nineteenth and twentieth centuries have been highlighted in the works of Adam McKeown, Sugata Bose, Thomas Metcalf, Sunil Amrith, Yoshina Hurgobin, Subho Basu, Crispin Bates, Lynn Hollen Lees, Radhika Mongia and Neilesh Bose.[6] These have shown Indians to be part of a global circulation of labour power, which included convicts[7] and was integral to the expansion of empire and imperial enterprises. It has been estimated that as many as 30 million Indians travelled abroad between 1830 and 1930, with some 24 million returning in what Sugata Bose has described as a 'circular migration' rather than 'emigration'.[8] Sunil Amrith has proposed that as

---

[2] Lal (1983); Emmer (1986); Carter (1995, 1996); Ashwin and Vahed (2008); Kumar (2017).

[3] Carter (1995); Peebles (2001).

[4] Bates and Carter (2017).

[5] Carter (1994); Gupta (2015); Bahadur (2014); Pande (2018); Datta (2020).

[6] McKeown (2004); S. Bose (2006); Metcalf (2007); Amrith (2013); Hurgobin and Basu (2015); Bates (2017); Lees (2017); Mongia (2018); N. Bose (2021).

[7] Anderson (2018, 2022); Yang (2021).

[8] S. Bose (2006), p. 73.

many as 28 million may have crossed the Bay of Bengal, in both directions, between 1840 and 1940.[9] They contributed not only through their work on the plantations but also through working as civil servants, schoolteachers, moneylenders, traders, shopkeepers, dockworkers and policemen (especially Sikhs), through serving in the Indian army,[10] by working in the construction industry, road and rail building,[11] mining, shipping and – not least of all – as *ayah*s (nursemaids) and domestic servants.

Indian domestic workers, like Indian *lascars* (sailors), were to be found in every continent. Like many categories of only semi-bonded labour, they have been little studied until recently.[12] Domestic workers were not often indentured but were commonly indebted for their passage and bonded to their employers in the same way as plantation labourers. They laboured under intense supervision and travelled as far as Britain, where even Victoria, the empress of India, paraded her favourite servant, the handsome 24-year-old Abdul Karim.[13] The further they were from home, the more vulnerable they could be. However, there were many ways in which migrants resisted and fought against oppressive working conditions, which could even cause them to be feared, as Prinisha Badassy shows in her contribution to this volume. Both in domestic servitude and in plantations, the workers were far more assertive than is commonly assumed in the infamous trope of the 'meek Hindu'. By the early twentieth century, indentured migrants overseas were joined by many more free migrants, or 'passenger Indians'[14] and old migrants who had served out their contracts and moved on to new occupations. They embraced the concept of civil rights and began to demand equality before the law and political and workplace representation. Many in South Africa, in the early 1900s, were willing to undergo harsh conditions of imprisonment in defence of those rights in one of the earliest anti-colonial struggles. Sikhs who migrated to North America networked internationally at the same time, connecting with comrades in Calcutta and Punjab in order to rebel against colonial rule, as shown by Chhanda Chatterjee later in this book.

Uniquely armed amongst Asian workers with their contract – the *girmit* – an inspectorate, access to courts (however unequal) and a complaints procedure (however flawed), the concepts of their individual, legal and civil rights gradually

---

[9] Amrith (2013), p. 2.

[10] Singha (2019).

[11] Kerr (1995).

[12] See Sen (2009); Datta (2021); Fischer (2004, 2006); Ahuja (2006); and Balachandran (2012).

[13] Basu (2011).

[14] Dhupelia-Mesthrie (2009); Vahed (2016).

grew amongst migrant workers over many decades, as they contested and struggled against their employers and the local colonial governments. New and improved rights were enshrined in a succession of labour ordinances in the 1890s. Thousands, at the end of their contracts of indenture, stayed on and found themselves new employment, sometimes working alongside and even in competition with Europeans with whom – notably in South Africa – they demanded equality. The ideas of equality and civil rights were further reinforced in the politics of early Indian nationalists, egalitarian Hindu reform movements such as the Arya Samaj and pan-Islamism. They were formally internationalised in the work of the League of Nations after 1919[15] and affirmed again at the end of the Second World War in the freedom struggles of multiple nations, beginning with India. However, the equality of South Asian migrants as citizens in their new homes continued to be contested following the collapse of the European empires. Burmese Indian refugees struggled to gain rehabilitation in India, whilst Indians in independent South Africa were thrown into a long and protracted war against the oppressive policies of the apartheid regime. Struggles to achieve democracy and equal rights of citizenship were repeated in nations all over the Global South, with varying outcomes. There was success in countries such as Mauritius, Guyana and Trinidad, where migrants were a large minority or a majority of the population. Elsewhere, such as in Malaysia, complex constitutional arrangements achieved a remarkable sharing of power and a level of social harmony. However, in some places, migrants suffered a dramatic reversal in their conditions, including expulsion (in Uganda) or exclusion from political influence. Perhaps the saddest example of this is Fiji, where Indian migrants played a substantial role in building one of the most prosperous Pacific island economies but have been progressively marginalised in the last half-century. These and other themes are addressed in the essays in this volume, by a mixture of experienced and upcoming scholars – the majority from within the diaspora – who attempt to reflect, as far as possible, the viewpoint and voices of the migrants themselves.

## Agency and Resistance

This book is divided into four sections. To begin, we have a section that looks at various forms of agency and resistance amongst those who migrated overseas for work. This section is eloquently introduced in Chapter 1, by Goolam Vahed, who surveys the historical literature concerning the various forms in which resistance may be encountered. Citing Sherry Ortner, Vahed points out that the aim of

---

[15]  Sturman (2014).

individuals in resisting power is not always clear, nor are the workings of power itself, which creates difficulties in characterising it. It may be expressed in the form of a violent liberation movement, as in the Haiti of Toussaint L'Overture in 1804, or in the everyday forms of resistance, described by James C. Scott, which do not necessarily aim to overthrow an established order at all but merely to exert greater control over daily life. Vahed then goes on to examine the ways in which indentured migrants negotiated structures of power, specifically in colonial Natal in South Africa. Indenture was a complex system, he argues, and the indentured cannot be painted as simply passive victims. Most of them worked on the colony's sugar plantations, where the strange environment, rigid work schedule, overbearing *sirdars* (overseers), draconian laws and strenuous work made life difficult. Yet there were few open rebellions. Instead, the indentured subverted the system indirectly to lessen the impact of an alienated existence and to rebuild their lives. This approach may not have overthrown authority in the workplace or state power, but it allowed the labourers to mitigate the worst effects of indenture. Many had come to Natal to make a new life for themselves and focused on doing so once they completed their contracts. This was not a case of 'false consciousness'. Indenture was not a permanent state, he argues, and most migrants simply wanted to survive and move on to free lives, often showing great initiative and enterprise in the process.

Chapter 2, by Prinisha Badassy, explores the highly contested and often emotionally charged relationships between colonial settlers and their bonded labourers. Both masters and mistresses on the one hand and servants on the other fought to own, shape and define the power relations between them. The experiences and emotional strain associated with being a domestic servant frequently gave rise to a culture of anger, resistance and violence within the ranks of Indian servants and the domestic space in colonial Natal. This chapter posits that poisoning, as a criminal act, reveals a great deal about the feelings and circumstances of those who were accused of it and tried by the colonial courts, unveiling the ubiquitous feelings of inequity and ill-treatment experienced by Indian domestic workers. Poisoning occupies a special place in the history of crime, requiring premeditation, planning and knowledge for its successful execution. The delegation of responsibility for the preparation and cooking of food to these servants frequently caused masters and mistresses to distrust their servants and aroused feelings of suspicion and fear. Between the years 1880 and 1920, there were several high-profile cases that reached the courts. However, because of the calculated and clandestine nature of poisoning, as well as the difficulty of detection, as it produced very little incriminating evidence, the cases that came through the Natal courts probably represent only a small proportion of the actual number of attempted poisonings. These crimes were situated, Badassy argues, at varying points on a continuum of distressed interactions between masters, mistresses and servants, and each possessed its own intimate performative terrain.

In Chapter 3, veteran historian Rana Behal explores labour resistance on indentured plantations in the Assam valley in India. The tea industry was the earliest British commercial enterprise in the Assam valley. From the mid-1860s, it was powered almost entirely by indentured labour. By the end of colonial rule, half a million labourers were employed on over 300,000 acres of cultivated land. The lives of these labourers under the authority of the planters left much to be desired. Annual reports between 1868 and 1906 revealed recruitment abuses and poor living and working conditions. The indentured employees also had to cope with their individual identities being subsumed into the 'coolie' whole. In this chapter, Behal seeks to explore the resistance offered by the labouring community to this treatment. It examines the use of desertions, so-called riots, assaults and unlawful assemblies by both individual and collective workers in opposition to economic and physical coercion and particularly the sexual exploitation of coolie women. The enacting of cultural traditions, including music, as a means of resistance is described. In considering the impact of labour resistance, the chapter concludes with the eventual development of trade unions and their relationship with the Indian Tea Association in the 1940s.

In Chapter 4, Kalpana Hiralal presents a forgotten narrative of the Gandhian-inspired Satyagraha campaign in South Africa in a study of the treatment of Indian political prisoners between 1907 and 1914. The Satyagraha struggle in South Africa was a pioneering political protest movement, spearheaded by the Indian community, against the pervasive injustices and racial discrimination characteristic of colonial rule. Well over 20,000 men, women and children joined the struggle and defied civic laws. Thousands were detained, imprisoned and subjected to harsh treatment and living conditions. Yet in the vast corpus of literature on this struggle, the treatment and impact of prison conditions have not been analysed or documented. This chapter examines the prison conditions experienced by Indian Satyagraha prisoners between 1907–1914. It highlights their diet, physical assaults, living and labouring conditions, and argues that even though some *satyagrahis* (peaceful protestors) were treated less than humanely in prison, this did little to quash their spirit of resistance. On the contrary, they became more defiant amidst the plethora of discriminatory laws. The chapter explores the intersections of migration and political resistance in the diaspora, adding to current debates on the complexity of indentureship and its legacy.

In Chapter 5, Chhanda Chatterjee explores the global networks of resistance that connected Sikhs in the Punjab, Canada and Calcutta in the colonial era. Punjabi Sikhs travelled the world both as migrant workers and as part of the British army within the empire. As they did so, they passed on news of the often better-paid labour to be found in different locations overseas. One promising destination was Canada, which in 1903–1907 had a booming economy and a need for workers in the railways and other industries. However, the growth in immigrant labour caused resentment among white labourers, and tensions between (mainly white) workers' unions, the federal government and Indian immigrants grew. The Sikh workers organised themselves in defence of their interests, forming the Khalsa Diwan Society in 1907 as the first step in their proactive stance towards their position in Canada. This chapter examines the evolving conflict between British authorities and the proponents of 'white Canada' on one side and the Sikh community on the other. Central to its exploration is the significance of the Sikh network that connected Punjab, Calcutta (the point of embarkation for Punjabi immigrants) and Canada in the dissemination of revolutionary Sikh ideas and political opposition to their colonial oppressors.

## Remigration

The second part of this volume concerns the theme of remigration of indentured migrants, an important example of workers' agency that took various forms and has attracted renewed attention of late, most notably with Reshaad Durgahee's introduction of the concept of 'subaltern careering'.[16] In Chapter 6, Chan E. S. Choenni describes the return migration of 'Hindostanis' from Surinam to India between 1878 and 1921. The Dutch colony of Surinam was one of the last colonies to introduce indentured labour from India. The first ship to arrive from Calcutta docked in 1873, and between 1873 and 1916, 34,304 immigrants came to work in Surinam. The Coolie Treaty (*Koelietractaat*) that dictated the practices of indenture in Surinam stated that the labourers had a right to a free return passage after five years of service. More than a third of the Indian immigrants returned to India at the expense of the Dutch government; the rest chose to remain. This chapter analyses the remigration of this group to India, comparing it with the number of returnees from other colonies, exploring the motivations for making the journey back to their country of origin and examining the categories of returnees under the Coolie Treaty. It includes a detailed statistical study of the surprising amounts of jewellery and savings that those remigrating carried with

---

[16] See Bates and Carter (2021); Hurgobin and Basu (2015); and Durgahee (2021).

them and goes on to explore the different receptions they experienced upon their return to India. The tale of Indian indentured labour in Surinam concludes with the last sputterings of the arrangement between 1917 and 1922.

Chapter 7, by Lomarsh Rooparine, analyses the remigration of Indians in the Caribbean during the indenture and the modern period, essentially from the middle of the nineteenth to the twenty-first centuries. Specifically, the chapter examines the period when Indians were under contractual indentured obligations and the period after the abolition of indenture in 1920. Rooparine demonstrates that the remigration of Indians within the Caribbean has received less attention when compared to other migrations. Unfortunately, we are left with a poor understanding of how these once cyclical migrants turned settlers navigated the contours of the Caribbean landscape to achieve better livelihood opportunities. The remigration of Indians was based on illegal and legal motivations and aspirations brought about by their desire to make the best of their transplanted life from India to the tropical sugarcane plantation zones of the Caribbean. The contention is that although a majority of Indians either returned to India or remained in their specific islands, a minority of them remigrated within the Caribbean. These migratory dynamics reveal another side of the Indian experience in the Caribbean, notably that Indians have not been stationary since their arrival to the region. They have instead shown a remarkable degree of determination to participate in the larger migratory flows in the Caribbean. In so doing, their remigration patterns have shown a strong relationship between thought and action as well as negation and affirmation amid bouts of marginalisation and discrimination in sending and receiving destinations. Rooparine predicts that Indian remigration in the Caribbean will continue with greater intensity because of the uneven level of development between nations. The remigration of Indians has also become a way of life. To develop, he says, one must remigrate.

Chapter 8, by Yoshina Hurgobin, uses passenger logs and colonial reports to examine Indian labour remigration within various nodes of the Indian Ocean between 1847 and 1906. Remigration, here, means the process whereby labour migrants moved across colonies (and their dependencies) without returning to India or making the three main ports of embarkation (Calcutta, Madras and Bombay) the main points of departure. The first part of the chapter explores how indentured Indian workers remigrated and engaged in numerous back-and-forth mobilities between Mauritius and nearby islands (Agaléga, Diego Garcia, Réunion, Seychelles and St Brandon) because of their oceanic proximity. In one case, Mauritius became the departure point towards Mombasa. The chapter thereby brings into discussion the historiographies of both indentured Indian labour and the Indian Ocean.

Existing scholarship on indentured labour in Mauritius has revealed how returnee migrants actively journeyed to India to recruit new migrants and thereby increased their information networks allowing them to migrate to places near (Natal, Madagascar and Réunion) and far (Brazil and China).[17] Hurgobin takes this scholarship in additional directions, highlighting how complex circumstances engendered remigration to diverse destinations and marginal spaces such as the small-island dependencies of Mauritius, which rarely feature even in the larger historiographical Indian Ocean-wide canvases.[18] Hurgobin teases out original material incorporating rarely seen nodes such as Lombok and Penang, revealing ever greater complexity and unanticipated levels of agency in the global movements of South Asian labour.

## Gender and Family

The third part of this book explores issues of agency and resistance relating to gender and family and begins with a chapter by Arunima Datta on the lives of 'coolie' women in Malayan plantations. 'Coolie' was an Indian term for a day labourer, often used by the British to describe migrant workers, but which became increasingly seen as pejorative amongst Indians overseas. By the 1890s, colonial rubber planters in Malaya had become convinced of the benefits of locally settled pools of labour and began encouraging the immigration of Indian 'coolie' women and families. As Malaya entered the 1930s, women constituted 39 per cent of the migrant Indian population, but an entrenched gender imbalance remained and permeated everyday life. Against this backdrop, Chapter 9 examines the complex interactions and intimacies between Indian coolie men and women in Malaya, presenting new insights into Indian–Malaysian history and offering a better understanding of the textured realities of plantation life. A selection of reported trials concerning intimate or conjugal problems amongst Indian coolies in Malaya, such as elopement and adultery, are interrogated to reveal the misrepresentation that pervades colonial discourses and uncover evidence of female agency.

Women were indisputably sometimes victims of male violence and kidnapping. However, Datta argues that colonial gender stereotypes, which painted women as perpetual victims and men as perpetual perpetrators, downplayed the active engagement of women in sexual and conjugal relationships. The colonial documentation of these cases systematically ignores the agency of women and the socio-economic realities behind their behaviour. The scarcity of women and

---

[17]  Carter (1994, 1996); Bates and Carter (2021).

[18]  S. Bose (2006); Metcalf (2007).

loopholes in colonial administrative policy, in fact, created new possibilities for intimate relationships between Indian 'coolie' men and women that significantly differed from those back in India. The reportage also overlooks the complex potential motivations behind male conduct, including concerns regarding emasculation, control and status tied to their economic subjugation.

Beyond establishing the realities of 'coolie' life, the chapter probes colonial preoccupations, demonstrating how both judicial administrators and newspapers reporting trials focused on coolie 'moral failings', ranging from lack of modesty, trustworthiness or honesty to a propensity for violence. The re-examination of these cases therefore raises questions about the basis for such stereotyped views, their utilisation in maintaining 'order' among colonial subjects and the integrity of the colonial courts that relied upon them. Ultimately, Datta seeks to re-endow coolie women with power and agency and to expose the dependence of the plantation economic system on the exploitation of gendered workers.[19]

In Chapter 10, Nafisa Essop Sheikh similarly grapples with the agency of indentured Indian women in South Africa and endeavours to reinvest them with a complexity stripped away by previous studies that have described their oppression as totalising and irresistible. The social reproductive role of indentured women, in particular, meant that they were uniquely and advantageously placed in comparison to Indian women who remained on the subcontinent. Sheikh considers the dichotomy between women's productive (waged) and reproductive (unpaid, often household-related) labour in relation to life in Natal and how female indentured workers used existing patriarchal discourses to create spaces of autonomy and opportunities for themselves.

In Chapter 11, Sheetal Bhoola discusses the family enterprises of Gujarati 'passenger Indians' in the Eastern Cape, South Africa, from the early 1900s till the present, exploring the connections between financial mobility, business, caste and community. Bhoola's subjects are the second- and third-generation Gujarati Hindu 'passenger migrants' who travelled to South Africa at their own expense and who chose to relocate to Port Elizabeth (present-day Gqeberha) and Uitenhage (present-day Kariega) instead of colonial Natal from the 1900s onwards. The study is based on narratives that illuminate the way in which their caste-based occupation of shoemaking served them as a migrant populous. Descendants of these migrants also established caste-based businesses and engaged in other entrepreneurial activities to achieve financial mobility. A tight-knit community based around shoemaking developed in Port Elizabeth, and formal caste-based organisations

---

[19] The story continues in her book in this same series (Datta 2020).

sprang up in response, with the aim of engaging in social and financial upliftment. Bhoola identifies and attempts to fill a lacuna in the literature available on the families of this little-known community of Hindu Gujaratis in the Eastern Cape.

Chapter 12, by Rochelle Almeida, studies the domestic Anglo-Indian female workforce in imperial Britain. Almeida seeks to corroborate the existence of women of mixed racial descent as part of the early South Asian workforce in Britain. These women are often invisible to us as today they have European surnames, anglicised first names, westernised dress and lifestyles and speak English. By using pictorial and epistolary evidence, however, they can be identified and their lives explored. Many travelled to Britain with the families that had employed them as *ayah*s in India. Being far from home, they were uniquely vulnerable, and if dismissed upon arrival, they were forced to find new work in a strange and alien environment. The travails involved in this, British attitudes towards these women and the experiences of specific mixed-race individuals are vividly reconstructed within this chapter.

## Legacies

The dispersal of Indian workers across the globe left a long shadow, and their precarious situation was dramatically exposed with the collapse of British rule. In this final part of the book, Chapter 13, by Emma C. Meyer, describes the profound effect of the Japanese military's takeover of British Burma in late 1941 and 1942 on the communities of Indian descent who were living and working there. Many fled across the Bay of Bengal by steamship or aircraft or on foot, and approximately 500,000 reached the borders of British India and settled there for the duration of the war. Scholars of South Asian history have produced a small but growing literature on the evacuation of Burma and the experiences of those who fled during the war. However, there has been very little research conducted on the fates of the Indian refugees who spent the war in India and later made attempts to return to Burma. Using archival evidence from Visakhapatnam district in south-eastern India, which received more wartime evacuees than any other district in British India, Meyer explores the resettlement of Indian evacuees during the war and the failed attempts to 'repatriate' them after the war's conclusion. Meyer provides an analysis of the impact that the Second World War had on the many migratory South Asian populations in the Bay of Bengal and their frustrated attempts in the late 1940s to return to the state of 'normalcy' they had previously enjoyed.

A far longer and pernicious struggle faced the South Asian community in South Africa, who were confronted after the Second World War with a barrage of legislation aimed at entrenching white minority rule. Amongst these, the Group Areas Act (GAA) was one of the key instruments used to reinforce the ideology of apartheid in South Africa by emphasising separate residential areas, educational services and other amenities for the different supposed racial groups. The GAA was a culmination of anti-Indian measures, restricting access to land and trade for almost a century. In Chapter 14, Brij Maharaj focuses on Indian opposition to the GAA and resistance to the forced displacement that resulted from it. In a manner reminiscent of their pioneering struggle for civil rights in the early 1900s, Indian political organisations were vociferous in their condemnation of and opposition to the GAA and racial residential segregation, which was intended to ruin the community economically and force them into ghettoes. However, while the Natal Indian Congress and the Natal Indian Organisation claimed to represent the whole Indian community, there was very little evidence of mobilisation of the working class and the poor, whose interests were neglected by elite political leaders. Segregation represented a double-edged sword for the underclasses – with increasing rents and slum clearance, some would become homeless, while others could possibly be housed in municipal housing schemes. Political action against the GAA consisted mainly of petitions, letters and delegations to the South African government authorities and the occasional mass meeting. However, their numbers were too few, and the coercive apparatus of the apartheid state, as represented by the army and the security branch of the police force was too formidable. Indians struggling to eke out a living were unlikely to court arrest and imprisonment in sufficient numbers to have much impact. Whilst sincere in their efforts, their successes, as in 1907–1914, were severely limited until joined in later years by the power of international boycotts of the apartheid regime.

The penultimate chapter in this volume, Chapter 15, by Brij V. Lal, describes the decline of the Indo-Fijian from a time of pre-eminent agency and achievement to one of abjection. By the time the indenture system was abolished in Fiji on 1 January 1920, 60,000 Indian indentured immigrants had arrived in Fiji. Abolition raised the question of the rights of those Indians who had decided to stay back in the British colony. Would they enjoy rights 'no whit' inferior to those enjoyed by other British subjects as they had been promised? Indians wanted equal and non-racial franchise on the basis of a common roll. However, this demand was resisted by Europeans, who saw in this a threat to their own privileged position, and by Fijian chiefs, who wanted to preserve their traditional hierarchical way of life. The colonial government settled on racial franchise in an arrangement which would preserve the status quo. The call for non-racial franchise fell on deaf ears. Fiji's 1970 independence entrenched a racially elected parliament. Unfortunately, the assumptions that underpinned the political culture were flawed. Among them was the assumption that Fijians would always vote as one to keep power. That was found wanting. When a multiracial coalition won power in 1987, a Fijian-dominated military overthrew the government at the behest of the Fijian establishment. This coup proved to be a pyrrhic victory for Fijian nationalism as Fijians fragmented into competing factions. Nonetheless, in 2000, when a coalition headed by an Indo-Fijian won power, it was overthrown in a putsch by a part-Fijian, ostensibly at the behest of the Fijian nationalists. In 2006, Fiji's fourth military coup started a new era, jettisoning the protocols and parameters of Fiji's twentieth-century past. Racial franchise was abolished, and equal citizenship for all was entrenched by a constitution decreed into existence without any public consultation. Indo-Fijians supported the coup leader, Frank Bainimarama, and his party overwhelmingly, placing their faith in a military leader to protect them from the Fijian nationalists but thinking little of what would happen when Bainimarama would finally go. The 2013 decreed constitution gives the overwhelmingly Fijian military the guardian role over the constitution, endowing it the power both to interpret the constitution as well as to enforce it, usurping power which rightfully belongs to an elected parliament. The majority of the members on the government benches are Indo-Fijians, but they lack political weight and moral authority and are used to rubber-stamp public policy rather than help make it. Indo-Fijians have been voting with their feet since the 1987 coup. Then about half the population, now they are about 30 per cent and declining due to low birth rate and continuing emigration. A true partnership in governance is beyond the reach of Indo-Fijians in Fiji. They will have to content themselves with some participation, living uncertainly on the sufferance of others. Once the movers of political change, they are now its passive recipients.

The final chapter in this volume, Chapter 16, by Darini Rajasingham-Senanayake, compares the new and old diasporas of South Asians and how they are now linked through the internet. The chapter explores what Rajasingham-Senanayake calls the political economy of 'cyber-nationalism' and examines the roots of what has become a global Tamil 'ethnoscape'. It suggests that the 'Tamil national question' in Sri Lanka, during the Liberation Tigers of Tamil Eelam's (LTTE) search for independence, reconfigured and boosted the diasporic identities and the activism of groups of descendants of indentured South Indian migrant communities, some of whom have become part of a disadvantaged and discontented emergent global 'precariat'.[20] The chapter points to the development

---

[20]  Standing (2011).

of new spaces of political and economic agency among migrant and refugee communities that transcend national boundaries and outlines the way in which new migrants may create new languages of cultural and political agency, activism and empowerment for the descendants of old indentured migrant communities. Most interestingly of all, these new communities, as observed in previous research,[21] are often pan-South Asian. They pay little regard to former ethnic, caste and religious divisions amongst migrants, both old and new – a perhaps optimistic and positive development to anticipate in the future.

## Bibliography

Amrith, Sunil. 2013. *Crossing the Bay of Bengal: The Furies of Nature and Fortunes of Migrants*. Cambridge, MA: Harvard University Press.

Anderson, Claire (ed.). 2018. *A Global History of Convicts and Penal Colonies*. London: Bloomsbury Publishing.

———. 2022. *Convicts: A Global History*. Cambridge, UK: Cambridge University Press.

Ahuja, Ravi. 2006. 'Mobility and Containment: The Voyages of South Asian Seamen, c.1900–1960'. *International Review of Social History* 51 (special issue): 111–141.

Balachandran, Gopalan. 2012. *Globalizing Labour? Indian Seafarers and World Shipping, c.1870–1945*. New Delhi: Oxford University Press.

Bates, Crispin (ed.). 2001. *Community, Empire and Migration: South Asians in Diaspora*. London: Palgrave Macmillan.

———. 2017. 'Some Thoughts on the Representation and Misrepresentation of the Colonial South Asian Labour Diaspora'. *South Asian Studies* 33(1): 7–22.

Bates, Crispin, and Marina Carter. 2017. 'Sirdars as Intermediaries in Nineteenth-Century Indian Ocean Indentured Labour Migration'. *Modern Asian Studies* 51(2): 462–484.

———. 2021. 'Remigration of Indian Subalterns in the Colonial Indian Ocean'. *Journal of Colonialism and Colonial History* 22(1). DOI: 10.1353/cch.2021.0010.

Basu, Shrabani. 2011. *Victoria & Abdul: The True Story of the Queen's Closest Confidant*. London: The History Press.

Bahadur, Gaiutra. 2014. *Coolie Woman: The Odyssey of Indenture*. Chicago: University of Chicago Press.

Bose, Neilesh (ed.). 2021. *South Asian Migrations in Global History: Labour, Law, and Wayward Lives*. London: Bloomsbury.

Bose, Sugata. 2006. *A Hundred Horizons: The Indian Ocean in the Age of Global Empire*. Cambridge, MA.: Harvard University Press.

---

[21]  Bates (2001).

Carter, Marina. 1994. *Lakshmi's Legacy: The Testimonies of Indian Women in 19th Century Mauritius*. Stanley, Rose Hill, Mauritius: Editions de l'Océan Indien.

———. 1995. *Servants, Sirdars and Settlers: Indians in Mauritius, 1834–1874*. New Delhi: Oxford University Press.

———. 1996. *Voices from Indenture: Experiences of Indian Migrants in the British Empire*. London and New York: Leicester University Press.

Datta, Arunima. 2020. *Fleeting Agencies: A Social History of Indian Coolie Women in British Malaya*. Cambridge, UK: Cambridge University Press.

———. 2021. 'Responses to Travelling Indian Ayahs in Nineteenth and Early Twentieth Century Britain'. *Journal of Historical Geography* 71 (January): 94–103.

Desai, Ashwin, and Goolam Vahed. 2008. *Inside Indenture: A South African Story, 1860–1914*. Durban: Madiba Publishers.

Durgahee, Reshaad. 2021. *The Indentured Archipelago: Experiences of Indian Labour in Mauritius and Fiji, 1871–1916*. Cambridge, UK: Cambridge University Press.

Dhupelia-Mesthrie, Uma. 2009. 'The Passenger Indian as Worker: Indian Immigrants in Cape Town in the Early Twentieth Century'. *African Studies* 68(1): 111–134.

Emmer, P. C. 1986. 'The Great Escape: The Migration of Female Indentured Servants from British India to Surinam, 1873-1916'. In *Abolition and Its Aftermath: The Historical Context 1790-1916*, edited by D. Richardson, pp. 245–266. London: Taylor & Francis.

Fisher, Michael. 2004. *Counterflows to Colonialism: Indian Travellers and Settlers in Britain, 1600–1857*. New Delhi: Permanent Black.

———. 2006. 'Working across the Seas: Indian Maritime Labourers in India, Britain, and in between, 1600–1857'. *International Review of Social History* 51 (supplement 14): 21–45.

Gupta, Charu. 2015. '"Innocent" Victims/"Guilty" Migrants: Hindi Public Sphere, Caste and Indentured Women in Colonial North India'. *Modern Asian Studies* 49(5): 1345–1377.

Lal, Brij V. 1983. *Girmitiyas: The Origin of the Fiji Indians*. Canberra: Journal of Pacific History.

Lees, Lynn Hollen. 2017. *Planting Empire, Cultivating Subjects: British Malaya, 1786–1941*. Cambridge, UK: Cambridge University Press.

Hurgobin, Yoshina, and Subho Basu. 2015. '"Oceans without Borders": Dialectics of Transcolonial Labor Migration from the Indian Ocean World to the Atlantic Ocean World'. *International Labor and Working-Class History* 87 (Spring): 7–26.

Kerr, Ian. 1995. *Building the Railways of the Raj, 1850–1900*. Oxford: Oxford University Press.

Kumar, Ashutosh. 2017. *Coolies of the Empire: Indentured Indians in the Sugar Colonies, 1830–1920*. Cambridge, UK: Cambridge University Press.

McKeown, Adam. 2004. 'Global Migration 1846–1940'. *Journal of World History* 15(2): 155–189.

Metcalf, Thomas R. 2007. *Imperial Connections*. Berkeley: University of California Press.

Mongia, Radhika. 2018. *Indian Migration and Empire: A Colonial Genealogy of Modern State*. Durham, NC: Duke University Press.

Pande, Amba (ed.). 2018. *Women in the Indian Diaspora: Historical Narratives and Contemporary Challenges*. Gateway East, Singapore: Springer Nature.

Peebles, Patrick. 2001. *The Plantation Tamils of Ceylon*. London: Leicester University Press.

———. 2021. *The Plantation Tamils of Ceylon*. London: Leicester University Press.

Sen, Indrani. 2009. 'Colonial Domesticities, Contentious Interactions: Ayahs, Wet-Nurses and Memsahibs in Colonial India'. *Indian Journal of Gender Studies* 16(3): 299–328.

Singha, Radhika. 2019. *The Coolie's Great War: Indian Labour in a Global Conflict, 1914–1921*. London: Hurst & Co.

Sturman, Rachel. 2014. 'Indian Indentured Labor and the History of International Rights Regimes'. *American Historical Review* 119(5): 1439–1465.

Standing, Guy. 2011. *The Precariat: The New Dangerous Class*. London: Bloomsbury Academic.

Tinker, Hugh. 1974. *A New System of Slavery: The Export of Indian Labour Overseas 1830–1920*. London: Oxford University Press.

Vahed, Goolam. 2016. 'Family, Gender, and Mobility among Passenger Migrants into Colonial Natal: The Story of Moosa Hajee Cassim (c.1840s–1921)'. *Journal of Southern African Studies* 42(3): 505–522.

Yang, Anand. 2021. *Empire of Convicts: Indian Penal Labour in Colonial Southeast Asia*. Berkeley: University of California Press.

# Part I

# Agency and Resistance

# 1

# Negotiating Power in Colonial Natal

## Indentured Migrants in Natal, 1860–1911

*Goolam Vahed*

The Power of a Man is his present means to obtain some future apparent Good.
—Thomas Hobbes[1]

Where there is power, there is resistance and yet, or rather consequently, this resistance is never in a position of exteriority in relation to power.
—Michel Foucault[2]

Men make history, but they do not make it just as they please.
—Karl Marx[3]

The British colony of Natal imported just over 152,000 indentured migrants between 1860 and 1911 to work on its railways, municipalities, coal mines and sugar plantations. The indigenous Zulu population had access to land at mission stations at reserves and through private companies, and resisted absorption into the racist capitalist economy for as long as they could.[4] Therefore, despite the large indigenous Zulu population, white settlers turned to Indian labour. The indentured migrated for a variety of reasons. These ran the gamut from demographic and economic dislocation resulting from British colonialism to being a widow or outcast or perhaps simply possessing a desire to travel. Notwithstanding claims of duping and false representation, the many examples of return migration, (re)migration to different colonies and chain migration suggest that at least some of the indentured were consciously undertaking the journey and had a reasonable idea of what they were getting into.

---

[1] Hobbes (1660), ch. x.

[2] Foucault (1978), pp. 95–96.

[3] Marx quoted in Feuer (1969), p. 360.

[4] See Marks (1990).

Colonial societies and their plantations specifically were structured around power. Hobbes is cited in the epigraph because of his emphasis on the centrality of absolute power in human relations, while Marx's domination–repression conception of power sees power as residing in the bourgeoisie and a process of constant struggle between the bourgeoisie and the proletariat. The concept of power is highly contested in the social sciences. Broadly speaking, however, there is a difference between those who see power as an 'exercise of power-over' and those who define it as a 'power-to-do'.[5] Max Weber, for example, defines power as 'the probability that one actor within a social relationship will be in a position to carry out his own will despite resistance'.[6] Foucault has a similar perspective: 'if we speak of the structures or the mechanisms of power, it is only insofar as we suppose that certain persons exercise power over others'.[7] The power-to-do conception, as Hanna Pitkin explains, means that 'power is a something' – anything – which makes or renders somebody able to do, capable of doing something.[8] Power is capacity, potential, ability or wherewithal. In other words, power is a 'potentiality, not an actuality – indeed a potentiality that may never be actualized'.[9]

Foucault also made the crucial point that power is diffuse and operates within society rather than above it and asks that we examine micro-level techniques and tactics of power, which include such things as surveillance, control, encouragement, discouragement, suggestion, and so on. Employers, managers, overseers and *sirdars* (foremen) were able to keep workers in check through formal controls such as the battery of laws that were heavily weighted against workers.[10] It was at this micro level that power was most acute and sought to directly control and mould the indentured population. Workers had few protections even though a 'protector' of Indian immigrants was appointed on the recommendation of the 1872 Coolie Commission, to ensure that contracts were respected by employers. The secretary of state for the colonies appointed the Sanderson Committee which reported in April 1910 that protectors and magistrates were generally biased against workers as they usually belonged to the planter class. In Natal, J. A. Polkinghorn was a rare exception amongst protectors because of his willingness to challenge planters. He was frustrated at his inability to take action against a recalcitrant employer and wrote to the colonial secretary in 1906 that it was an

---

[5]  Allen (2016).

[6]  Weber (1978), p. 53.

[7]  Foucault (1983), p. 217; Allen (2016).

[8]  Pitkin (1972), p. 276.

[9]  Allen (2016).

[10]  See Tayal (1977); Henning (1993); and Desai and Vahed (2007); amongst others.

'injustice' that he was required to assign workers to such employers.[11] Mohandas K. Gandhi, who spent the years between 1893 and 1914 in South Africa, appeared to have little confidence in the protector, writing in an editorial in the *Indian Opinion* that the 'so-called "Protector" of indentured labourers' had 'assumed the role of "Exploiter". When we thus find that the sea has caught fire, where shall we get the water to quench it?'[12]

Studies of Indian indentured migration have proliferated in recent decades due to the rise of India as a global power and the efforts of the Indian state to offer limited citizenship to Indians in the diaspora. This has increased interest among academics and many ordinary Indians in the diasporic Indian population. There are many studies on the mechanics of the Indian indenture system – how it was put into place, the processes of recruitment, the journey to the colonies, the arduous working conditions, and so on – but the role of those migrants who resisted power structures or took the opportunity to make new lives in the colonies has been relatively understudied. This is not to underplay the repressiveness of the system. Hugh Tinker, drawing on British politician John Russell's 1840 description of the system of indenture, titled his study *A New System of Slavery*[13]; Gandhi wrote in 1907 that the system of indenture was an 'evil thing' because it essentially comprised unfree labour[14] while Amit Mishra concludes that 'the indenture labour regime was a form of servitude, though not essentially a new system of slavery, as the labour was denied of its economic freedom and occupational and territorial mobility in the indenture system'.[15]

While acknowledging the brutal conditions of indenture, the perspective taken by this study is that the indentured did not passively oblige with the dictates of colonial authorities and/or accept the ubiquitous power of their employers. That they continued to migrate to the colonies in large numbers, and many even returned to the colonies for a second term of indenture or to settle permanently, calls for an understanding of the indentured experience that goes beyond the indenture-as-slavery thesis.

Workers registered their grievances in different ways. Resistance was mostly individualistic in Natal, including slowing down the work pace through feigning illness or breaking tools, deserting employers, occasionally engaging in violence against authority figures and suicide. There were group protests as well, with one

---

[11] Natal Archives Repository (NAB), CSO 2854/1906.

[12] *Indian Opinion*, 27 August 1910. See Vahed (2018) for a reappraisal of the role of protectors.

[13] Tinker (1974).

[14] *Indian Opinion*, 15 June 1907.

[15] Mishra (2010), p. 229.

major violent confrontation, the Gandhi-led strike of 1913, capturing international attention.[16] Resistance, as understood here, went beyond 'working class heroism' to include agency and invention. Beyond defying or confronting their masters and the conditions of employment, many of the indentured showed great initiative and enterprise, imagination and courage in rebuilding their lives in Natal in the face of adverse social, political and economic conditions.

This study draws heavily on the records of the protector, who made notes on his visits to plantations while his office recorded the various complaints made by indentured workers about their working and living conditions. There are 196 boxes of records in the Natal Archives Repository. It is acknowledged that the archives are biased in capturing the voices of those in power. This was compounded by the fact that the workers' voices were captured through translators. Nevertheless, these records can be read 'against the grain' to give voice to the silenced.

## Resistance and Agency

As the Foucauldian injunction in the epigraph implies, power and resistance are not binaries but intertwined, rendering the concept of resistance ambiguous. Sherry Ortner argues that the aim of individuals in resisting power is not at all clear, nor are the workings of power itself – hence, the difficulty in characterising resistance.[17] In thinking of slaves or indentured workers' resistance, images of workers engaging in violent protests against employers likely come to mind. The liberation of enslaved people in Haiti under Toussaint L'Overture in 1804 and the freeing of the Amistad Africans a few decades later through 'lawfare' have been captured in film by Hollywood and served as exemplars of resistance.[18] Yet while violence lurked on many plantations, there were few instances of open physical resistance. This could have been because employers and the state monopolised power, monitored the movements of the indentured through a series of laws and controlled their freedom of association, and there were few opportunities to work and live in the colony outside of the ambit of the employer.[19]

Resistance, James C. Scott argues, does not have to aim to overthrow an established order to count as 'resistance'. Scott speaks of ways in which ordinary people attempt to exert control over their lives as 'everyday forms of peasant resistance', which 'stops well short of outright collective defiance'.

---

[16]  See Swan (1985).

[17]  Ortner (1995), p. 175.

[18]  See the films *Toussaint L'Ouverture* (2012) and *Amistad* (1997).

[19]  Desai and Vahed (2007), pp. 145–166.

Such actions require 'little or no coordination or planning' and 'typically avoid any direct, symbolic confrontation with authority'.[20] We know from the work of Raymond Williams and Stuart Hall, drawing on Antonio Gramsci, that culture is a dynamic process 'produced, reproduced, and transformed through human agency'.[21] Culture can manufacture consent and exercise control without violence, as people may 'consent to rule when they accept as given (or at least desirable relative to perceived alternatives) the values, norms, and versions of justice' prevailing at a given time. The relations between 'between and among consent, domination and resistance' are thus tenuous at best.[22] However, Scott dismissed the notion that the absence of violent collective resistance on the part of subaltern groups was due to the ideological hegemony of the ruling class. While accepting Scott's argument about everyday resistance, we need to be careful not to categorise every action as 'resistance' to the point that the concept becomes meaningless and also be aware that people may act in ways without being cognisant of the larger consequences of their actions.[23]

One of the ways in which the indentured sought to affirm their self-worth was by opposing the labels assigned to them. While the employers and authorities termed them 'coolies', the migrants themselves opposed the use of the term. In the Tamil language, *kuli* referred to payment for menial work for persons without customary rights. The 1872 Coolie Commission, which had been established to investigate the conditions on plantations, reported that the word 'coolie' was used in India to apply

> to the lowest classes only, and it is regarded as a term of reproach in the nature of abuse. On many estates this term was mentioned to us, in our conversations with the coolies, as one of their objections to the colony.... There is no doubt that the term is galling, and a source of annoyance.[24]

---

[20] Scott (1985), p. xvi.

[21] Ringrose et al. (2009), p. 5. 'Much of the current analyses continue to draw and build on theorizing that emerged out of the UK Gramscian tradition of Raymond Williams and Stuart Hall. In this view ... culture is understood through what people do, not, as more structural approaches would have it, through the symbolic or economic calculations assigned to them. The emphasis is on how the structure is produced, reproduced and transformed through human agency.'

[22] Ringrose et al. (2009), p. 5.

[23] Chandra (2015), p. 565.

[24] Coolie Commission (1872), p. 13.

While the proposed 'Coolie Agent' had his (it was always a he) title changed to that of protector of Indian immigrants, whites continued to refer to Indians, both free and indentured, pejoratively as 'coolies'. However, this is an indication that the indentured asserted their selfhood from their formative days in the colony.

The indentured and their descendants lacked the political clout to influence legislators in South Africa. This is not to say that they were powerless. Kevin O'Brien and Lianjiang Li speak of 'rightful resisters'.[25] This, Uday Chandra points out, refers to individuals and groups 'being aware of the structures of power pre-dominating in a particular society and within those structures to articulate their claims, exploiting crevices and cracks in social arrangements to push forward subaltern political agendas'.[26] In the context of indenture in Natal, for example, workers used the office of the protector of Indian immigrants and local magistrates, notwithstanding their limitations, to complain about the everyday conduct of employers in the hope that these authority figures would intervene on their behalf.[27]

Saba Mahmood's writings on agency and resistance from a feminist perspective have been criticised in certain quarters, but I found them helpful for this chapter. Mahmood is critical of academics who hold that only actions that 'impose a teleology of progressive politics' qualify as resistance. She regards it as fallacious to assume that there is a universal desire on the part of people to be free from relations of subservience.[28] Thus, we should not take for granted that the indentured naturally wanted to destroy relations of capitalist domination in Natal. Mahmood accuses those who assign some preconceived agency to the subalterns as being analytically and politically prescriptive, for underlying this thinking is the notion that workers must act towards self-determined goals and interests. Mahmood insists that 'the meaning and sense of agency cannot be fixed in advance'.[29] What 'progressive' academics and critics may see in the actions of certain peoples as

> a case of deplorable passivity and docility, may actually be a form of agency – but one that can be understood only from within the discourses and structures of subordination that create the conditions of its enactment. In this sense, agential

---

[25] O'Brien and Li (2006).

[26] Chandra (2015), p. 566.

[27] Vahed (2018).

[28] Mahmood (2005), pp. 9–10.

[29] Mahmood (2005), pp. 14–15.

capacity is entailed not only in those acts that resist norms but also in the multiple ways in which one inhabits norms.[30]

Individuals recognise when they are vulnerable and may purposely act according to certain norms and expectations to further their interests or for survival, and not because this behaviour is natural to them. Conversely, some Indians, such as *sirdars*, for example, benefitted from the system. They were known to exploit workers by borrowing money without repayment, running stores on plantations and even sexually abusing women. While they faced restrictions as part of the subordinate indentured group, they were key to enforcing employers' domination. Lyons therefore warns 'that subordinate deference is not always an inauthentic expression of feelings and emotions toward the dominant or powerful'.[31] Some individuals may be benefitting from the system and act accordingly.

The English social historian E. P. Thompson was passionate about excavating the 'agency' of the working classes in England. He uses the word 'making' in the title of his 1963 study, *The Making of the English Working Class*, to emphasise his point that the subalterns forged their own identities, organisations, leaders, ideas, ambitions, and religious, cultural and social activities. The working classes, in Thompson's estimation, did not idly accept their circumstances but contested them vigorously. Thompson makes this point powerfully in the Preface to the book:

> This book has a clumsy title, but it is one which meets its purpose. *Making*, because it is a study in an active process, which owes as much to agency as to conditioning. The working class did not rise like the sun at an appointed time. It was present at its own making.[32]

While Thompson's work has been subject to criticism from various quarters on the right and the left, its great strength, and a feature of the book that I found particularly appealing, is that he focuses on ordinary people and their role in shaping their lives and destinies, and more generally the historical process, often in the face of very great odds.

## 'Everyday Resistance'

Tinker observed that in resisting, the indentured mostly thought 'in terms of immediate objectives'.[33] They protested through such acts as absenteeism,

---

[30] Mahmood (2005), pp. 14–15.

[31] Lyons (2005), p. 108.

[32] Thompson (1966), p. 9.

[33] Tinker (1974), p. 226.

insubordination, theft, desertion, destruction of property and neglect of duty. Examples of what Scott calls 'everyday resistance' abound in the files of the protector, though the indentured themselves may not have seen their acts as 'resistance'. The story of Devasagayan Madan serves as a good example of the kind of everyday behaviour that sought to undermine the system by attempting to regulate the amount and intensity of work. Madan was assigned to the Blackburn Estate on 29 April 1884, and between then and October 1884, he was found guilty of stealing poultry, feigning illness, being absent without reason and having deserted once. Between May and September 1884, he was absent for 47 days and imprisoned for 10 days for theft. He deserted on the day of his release on 19 September 1884.[34] Many employers faced such problems. The proprietor of the Mount Edgecombe Estate, Marshall Campbell, related to the protector in 1885 that about a hundred workers had been absent each month, and an average of 30 were in the estate hospital each day. He established that workers would collect their rations and go and live in the surrounding bush until the next ration day. In contravention of the legal contract, he instituted daily rations for workers who reported to work. This curtailed the practice of absenteeism and desertion.[35]

Sabotage was another means to frustrate employers. Acts like malingering, breaking tools and petty theft were forms of retaliation against workers' immediate conditions and served the purpose of frustrating employers. For example, John Arnold's son, Alexander, was murdered by his employees on their farm in Pietermaritzburg in 1905. He related in court that during the month of June 1905, he was pressing hay on his farm in Pietermaritzburg and discovered that the machine's cover was missing. He obtained a replacement and made the employees pay for it because sabotage was common on his farm. His spanners and other small tools had been thrown away on two or three occasions, and he recovered the costs from the workers. This loss of income angered the workers, who got revenge by killing his son, who had been 'severe' with the workers.[36]

One of the most common forms of overt resistance was flight. For the most part, the indentured did not speak English or Zulu and were unfamiliar with the geographic terrain of Natal. Despite these problems, their attempts to escape indenture are a testament to their rejection of the system. The number of workers convicted for desertion increased by 150 per cent, between 1902 and 1907, from 450 to 1100.[37] Henry Polak, a trained lawyer who worked closely with Gandhi

---

[34] Smith Batten, estate manager, to Protector, 28 October 1884, NAB, II, I/22, I455/84.

[35] NAB, II, I/30, I313/85, 16 October 1885.

[36] Desai and Vahed (2007), pp. 22–24.

[37] Henning (1993), p. 111.

in advocating for Indian rights in South Africa, observed that 'ill-treatment' or 'abuse' by employers was the deserters' primary defence.[38] Desertions rose from the mid-1880s with the establishment of mining towns such as Kimberly in the Cape and Johannesburg in the Transvaal, which increased economic opportunities for Indians.

Employers were inconvenienced by desertion. Coopa Mutha and Mangalam worked for Sinclair in the Natal Midlands. They were imprisoned for several days on eight occasions for desertions: 26 September 1885, 16 October 1885, 5 November 1885, 25 November 1885, 9 December 1885, 28 December 1885, 11 January 1886 and 26 January 1886. They refused to return to their employer because of mistreatment. Durban resident magistrate Robert Finnemore instructed the superintendent of the Durban Prison on 27 January 1886 to send the prisoners back 'under a strong escort and by force. I insist on their going on foot, which has proved satisfactory hitherto'. The protector informed the colonial secretary on 3 February 1886 that the deserters would be sent as suggested by Finnemore, 'handcuffed, carried to the Durban railway station in a hand cart, forced onto the train and with great difficulty conveyed to Estcourt'. The protector feared that if the deserters were not forcibly returned to Sinclair, it would encourage other workers 'who desired a change of employment or locality to similarly rebel against authority'. Attorney-general Michael Henry Gallwey gave his consent on 15 February 1886.[39]

This progression of events points to the anxiety that desertion caused among employers and the desperate measures they undertook to curb this practice. Law 2 of 1870 punished those who harboured resisters, financially rewarded those who apprehended deserters and forced deserters to make up double the time at the end of their indentures.[40] These measures failed to stop desertion.

These types of protest are 'conventional' in that they were found in most sites where the indentured or other subalterns worked, including industrial establishments. Such actions did not challenge state power or even overthrow authority at the workplace but did allow the indentured to gain a sense of self-worth and perhaps helped to mitigate the worst effects of indenture. There were other actions that one would not typically associate with 'passive victims' of an oppressive labour system, and which may fall under the broad ambit of 'agency' and 'invention' and which were an equally powerful feature of indentured labour.

---

[38] Polak (1909), p. 413.

[39] NAB, II, I/32, I1121/86.

[40] NAB, II, I/96, I459/ 1900.

## Confronting the System

Some of the indentured did not shirk physical confrontation, even though the outcome was primarily tragic. The court records contain examples of homicide by the indentured. Sheik Ramthumiah arrived in the colony on 25 October 1905 and was assigned to Elizabeth Macdonald of Pietermaritzburg. He was 21 years old, of medium height, clean-shaven and had light complexion.[41] Ramthumiah wrote to his parents in Madras that he was experiencing problems with his employer. In reply to Ramthumiah's letter, dated 4 March 1907, his father, Sheik Allie, wrote that he was 'sorry to hear that there had been a quarrel between yourself and your mistress'[42] and asked what the problem was. That was the last Allie heard from Ramthumiah, who murdered Elizabeth Macdonald in May 1907.

Jessie Francis, who also worked for the Macdonalds, testified in court that she was cooking porridge in the kitchen while Ramthumiah was cleaning the knives. He suddenly stabbed her on the left shoulder with a butcher knife, and when Elizabeth Macdonald entered the kitchen, he stabbed her several times. She fell on the floor and bled to death before medical assistance arrived. Ramthumiah's attorney argued in court that Ramthumiah was troubled that his employer was turning against him because of the lies that Francis was feeding her. His behaviour was to be explained as 'temporary insanity'. However, in racist Natal, 'extenuating circumstances' did not apply because of the prejudices against Indians. For example, Ward, the district surgeon, was of the view that Indians were 'more excitable and [had] less power of self-control than Europeans'. S. Wynne Cole, a police officer, told the court that Indians suffered from what was known as 'run amok'. When Indians get this feeling, they behave like 'a wild animal' and 'generally assault anybody who comes in his path'. Given these prejudices, it is not surprising that Ramthumiah was sentenced to death.[43] We can dismiss the racist stereotypes about Indians. Homicide can result from various factors. These avenging actions may be interpreted as the behaviour of someone suffering loneliness, depression and anomie or as revenge against the employer class.

Violence and group protest dated to the earliest days of indenture and was not due to the influence of Gandhi in 1913, when thousands of the indentured joined his now famous strike. On 5 October 1909, for example, the acting protector reported that 91 men, who were against the terms of the indentured contract, from the Reunion Estate in Isipingo, south of Durban, had gone to his office as a group.

---

[41] Sergeant to Protector, NAB, II, I/151, I1157/ 1907.

[42] Sergeant to Protector, NAB, II, I/151, I1157/ 1907.

[43] Badassy (2005), pp. 40–46.

They were upset that Reuben Swales, the estate manager, had assaulted two of their co-workers, Mallan (81794) and Lakshmanan (131000),[44] who refused to do the assigned taskwork. Detective F. H. Pegge, who investigated the matter, reported an argument on 24 September 1909 between *sirdar* Murugan and Mallan over taskwork. Swales arrived on horseback and aggressively caught Mallan. This angered Mallan's fellow workers, who assaulted the manager with sugar-cane sticks. Swales escaped by 'firing his revolver'. According to Pegge, relations had been acrimonious on the estate because the workers believed that they were forced to do more work than was legally required and were inclined to gain revenge on Swales. Under the circumstances, Pegge felt that Swales's actions were 'indiscreet'.

Pegge concluded that the assault was planned and calculated since there was no cane around the area where Swales was assaulted, which suggested that the assailants had brought the cane to attack him. Swales submitted a deposition to magistrate W. R. Saunders of Umlazi on 25 September, stating that he managed 300 workers. On the day of the assault, Mallan declined to carry out *sirdar* Murugan's instructions. He intervened to get Mallan to comply, but the latter became impertinent and tried to hit him with a cane knife. It appeared to Swales that Mallan's attack was a pointer for the entire gang of 150 men to attack him. They were screaming 'Vetoo, vetoo', meaning 'Cut him, cut him'. Swales had no option but to fire his gun, which stopped the attack.

The police and estate authorities identified the following workers as so-called ringleaders – Lakshmann, Mallan, Vella Mundin, Natha and B. Venkulloo – and transferred them to other estates. The acting protector, Mason, found that managers at the estate carried revolvers in executing their duties to instil fear in the workforce and protect themselves. Swales, he reported, had a history of assaulting Indians and threatening them with his gun. Swales was fined by the magistrate but retained his managerial position because his bosses felt that 'good men' like him were hard to come by.[45] As this example, and others in the archives, show, there was a long history of resistance which dated to the earliest days of indenture.

## Being Inventive

The story of Kanniah Appavu is remarkable in showing how 'worldly' some of the migrants were. Kanniah arrived in January 1902 on the *Umkuzi* as a special servant and was allotted as a domestic worker to G. L. Graham. Within months of his arrival, Kanniah began to lodge complaints with the protector about

---

[44] The numbers in parentheses are the identification numbers of the migrants.

[45] Desai and Vahed (2007), pp. 149–151.

his working conditions. He complained in May 1902 of being made to work on Sundays,[46] and in December 1902, he protested that he was made to do 'bedroom work', did not receive all the rations due to him and was beaten by his master.[47] We see notions of masculinity in these complaints. In 1903, he again complained that he was hit by Graham and was made to empty night soil buckets and chambers. Such work was not appropriate for people of his caste in Madras.[48] The protector's office did not give Kanniah the redress that he sought. In 1904, he mailed two letters to his sister, Kanniammal, in India and asked her to hand them over to the emigration office. One letter was from him outlining his complaints, and the second was a letter he wrote for his sister to copy in her handwriting and hand over to the authorities. Kaniammal's letter stated that her brother was ill-treated by Graham and made to do work that transgressed caste rules. It further stated that three complaints to the protector had been in vain; unless Kanniah's request for a transfer was granted, he would commit suicide.

Kanniammal was coached on how to hand over the letters. Her brother told her to go at 11 in the morning, 'weeping bitterly and beating your breast'.[49] The request was not immediately granted, but the protector eventually relented in 1905.[50] The archives have no record of what happened to Kanniah. His narrative shows his imagination and persistence in getting redress and also underscores that amongst the indentured were well-educated individuals perhaps seeking a new start in life.

Twenty-year-old Chhaju Zaharia arrived in 1907 and was assigned to indenture with the Dundee Coal Company in northern Natal. Chhaju mentioned his caste as Jat, a north Indian agricultural caste, even though he was a Brahmin, since Brahmins were not welcomed as indentured migrants as the authorities believed they were not suitable for manual labour. Chhaju's father, Zaharia Brahmin, wrote to the emigration office in Calcutta (present-day Kolkata) in 1911 to establish the whereabouts and well-being of his son. He stated that Chhaju was married and had a wife to support, that Brahmins were 'delicate' and not accustomed to manual labour and that his wife and himself could no longer work and needed their son's support. The Calcutta office contacted the protector in Natal.

The protector replied that while Chhaju's indenture could not be terminated, he could buy out the contract for 17 pounds. With the assistance of villagers,

---

[46] NAB, II, I/107, I577/1902.

[47] NAB, II, I/112, I2136/1902.

[48] NAB, II, I/116, I/276, 1903.

[49] NAB, II, I/127, I1232/1904; see also Badassy (2005), p. 52–53.

[50] NAB, I/154, I2149/1907.

Zaharia raised the money and deposited it with the Calcutta office. However, to Zaharia's dismay, Chhaju informed officials that he was happy with his work situation in Natal and intended re-indenturing when his term expired in May 1912. Chaaju added that he 'liked South Africa better than India' and had no intention of returning to his motherland.[51] Not all migrants regarded indenture as 'a new system of slavery'.

## The Transformative Power of Indenture

Some indentured migrants used the system to transform their lives. Their resourcefulness certainly belies the notion of 'passive victims'. Many were enterprising and resourceful as they carved new lives for themselves. Natal's economy was diverse, and the ex-indentured had various economic choices. While most survived through hawking, market gardening and small retail trade, some accumulated great wealth.

The story of *sirdar* Sheosaran (10117) is remarkable. He was the son of Ram Charan Kahar of Nahinagar in north-west India and migrated to Natal in November 1874. Aged 24 years, he met and married Suhodree Kaharin (10114) on the journey to Natal. The couple were allotted to the Durban municipality and spent almost 14 years in Natal. Eyebrows were raised when they returned to their home village in April 1888. On 2 May 1889, about a year later, the police inspector in Aurangabad, Womesh Chunder Sen, wrote to Robert Mitchell, the emigration agent in Calcutta, that Sheosaran had become the talk of the village when he offered a diamond for sale in March 1889. It was valued at 3,000 rupees. There were rumours that he owned many other valuables. In light of local gossip, inspector Jhoomak Lal of Nahinagar arranged a search of the house and discovered another large diamond, some silk skirts and sheets, a watch, gold necklaces, bangles, rings and a medal from the Anglo-Zulu War of 1879. The officials suspected foul play as they were certain that Sheosaran could not have acquired these valuable items on his salary.

In his defence, Sheosaran stated that after completing his indenture with the municipality, he found work as a *sirdar* constable in the police department under superintendent Richard Alexander. He provided a detailed inventory of where and how each item was purchased and stated that the protector in Natal, Louis Mason, and his staff could corroborate his statement. The police in Calcutta queried the protector's office in Natal. The protector investigated the matter and reported to the colonial secretary on 26 June 1890 that several witnesses

---

[51] Desai and Vahed (2007), p. 54.

confirmed Sheosharan's story. The protector in Natal wrote to Robert Mitchell in Calcutta that there was nothing 'on the list to take exception to'. Sheosaran's astounding economic success underscores that there were indentured migrants who made the most of spaces in the system.[52]

For almost seven decades, from the early twentieth century to the 1970s, Sam China was a household name among Indian soccer lovers in South Africa. The six-year-old arrived in Natal in 1863 as an indentured migrant from the French colony of Pondicherry (present-day Puducherry) with his parents, Seeneevassen Maurimutoo and Anundoyee. When he was a teenager, Sam China, as Camatchee Seeneevassen came to be known, worked for the Overport Sugar and Coffee Estate. He gave up his right to a free return passage to India and instead left Natal in 1875 for the emerging diamond mining town of Kimberley. Along with five friends, he travelled on foot, a gruelling journey that took 21 days.[53]

A small number of ex-indentured Indians moved to Kimberley in the 1870s. Diamonds had been discovered in Kimberley in the late 1860s, and Sam China worked for the diamond company Rogers Bros. before opening a fruit business in the mid-1880s. The mining magnate Cecil John Rhodes was among those who knew Sam China personally. Sam China had two daughters. Patty married Natal boxing promoter Nat Moodley, while Valliamah married Leo Gopaul, the first Indian woman councillor in the Cape.[54]

Sam China was a keen sportsman and donated a trophy for which teams from Natal, the Cape and the Transvaal competed. The Sam China Cup, as it came to be known, was specially designed for Sam China by the London company Lezard and Robins. The tournament was held every two years under the auspices of the South African Indian Football Association (SAIFA) until 1973.[55] Sam China died in Kimberley on 9 September 1930 while attending one of the national tournaments. In what was a fitting farewell, the captains of each provincial team acted as pallbearers while the players wore black arm bands.

Variously described as a porter, supervisor, waiter, farmer, small businessman and philanthropist, Mulukmahomed Lappa Sultan left an indelible legacy in Natal. Eighteen-year-old Sultan arrived in Natal as an indentured migrant in July 1890. He had intended to go to Ceylon (present-day Sri Lanka), but the ship's engine failed, and he ended up in Natal instead. Sultan was allotted to work for the Natal Government Railways (NGR) in Durban, starting as a railway porter

---

[52] Desai and Vahed (2007), pp. 112–114.
[53] Desai and Vahed (2007), p. 291.
[54] Vahed, Desai and Waetjen (2010), pp. 155–156.
[55] Vahed, Desai and Waetjen (2010), pp. 155–156.

and progressing to supervisor. In 1895, Sultan left the colony of Natal and went to Johannesburg in the then Transvaal. The discovery of gold made Johannesburg the fastest-growing city in South Africa. Sultan worked as a waiter in one of the city's hotels for three years. He returned to Durban shortly before the outbreak of the South African War (1899–1902). He took up farming and, with his savings, opened the wholesale firm, M. L. Sultan and Sons (Pty) Ltd, on Victoria Street.

Sultan married Mariam Bee, a granddaughter of indentured migrants, on 20 October 1922. Mariam died at a young age, and in her memory Sultan established the M. L. Sultan Charitable and Educational Trust in 1949 for the upliftment of Indians 'irrespective of creed, caste or religion'.[56] His greatest legacy, arguably, is the M. L. Sultan Technikon, which was a direct result of the funds he contributed. Thousands of students have acquired technical skills as a result of this institution. In the post-apartheid period, when the M. L. Sultan Technikon merged with the whites-only Durban Technikon to form a non-racial Durban University of Technology, the site of the old campus retained the name M. L. Sultan. Running outside the *technikon* is a road renamed the M. L. Sultan Road.

The post-apartheid period is witness to a desire to search for 'roots', and many Indians in the diaspora have visited the villages and cities of India in search of family. Sultan's descendants have seemingly turned the family tree full circle by searching for their relatives in India. After several decades of investigation, an exchange of letters in April 2016 brought the Sultan family, which is now based in South Africa, England and Australia, in contact with relatives in India. A. H. Sultan, the grandson of M. L. Sultan, explained that the South African branch of the family lost touch with the family in India in the early 1970s. A friend in the village of Collam, Kerala, had been asked to look out for relatives, and, eventually, he located one Mulukmahomed Shamshudeen. Shamshudeen had in his possession a letter exchanged between his father and the father of another of M. L. Sultan's grandsons in Natal, Yunus Sultan. He also had in his possession an obituary that appeared in a local newspaper when M. L. Sultan died in 1953. It was sent to India by Yunus's father, M. E. Sultan.[57] According to Shamshudeen, he kept the dream alive that 'one day, my uncle's children will come looking for their roots'. And he hung on to every heirloom, letter, piece of paper, newspaper clipping and just about anything associated with M. L. Sultan, who left Kollam in 1890. When contact was made with him, he declared, 'I knew that you would come and I have kept everything

---

56 Desai and Vahed (2019), pp. 242–243.

57 *Post Natal*, 24–28 February 2016.

and I resisted my children's demand that I throw away the bundle of documents because it was taking too much space in our small house.'[58]

A. H. Sultan, who now lives in England, explained that they were convinced that given the enormous contribution that M. L. Sultan had made to his adopted land, 'surely he must have had family in India. But there was no link. Our previous two generations seem to have lost all contact'.[59] He found M. L. Sultan's diary and discovered that the latter had written letters to relatives, care of the Mohamedan School in the village of Kollam in Kerala. A. H. Sultan moved to England, but the desire to make contact with relatives was strong among members of his generation. He visited India several times without success. There was a breakthrough when a Bini Ajay joined the hospital in England where he worked. He discovered that she and her husband were from Kollam. They contacted a lawyer friend in Kollam, Joycutty, who, in turn, hired a resourceful local man, Feroz Khan, to search for the family. By chance, one afternoon, Khan asked an elderly man in the Malayalam language whether he had family in South Africa and was shocked when the reply came: 'I am Mulukmahomed Shamshudeen, my father is the nephew of M. L. Sultan.'[60] Khan called Joycutty, who, after verifying the story, contacted the doctor in England, and they passed on the news to A. H. Sultan.

A. H. Sultan contacted relatives in South Africa and Australia, and in April 2016 he and a delegation of seven – five surviving members of the fourth generation and two of the fifth – visited Kollam to meet with Shamshudeen, which they did in the company of Joycutty and Khan. At the end of the four-day trip, they discovered 168 cousins in Kollam, examined old documents, including letters written by the Sultan family in South Africa to family in India (the oldest letter found was dated 18 December 1897), and visited the mosque where their forefathers prayed and the cemetery where family members are buried.[61] In August 2016, the family arranged a reunion at the Al-Aansar Hall in West Road, Overport, with hope for the English, Australian and Indian members of the family joining then in South Africa. Unfortunately, due to visa delays, the Indian members were not able to travel to South Africa. With the benefit of technology, the remainder of the family met and connected with the Indian relatives.[62] This was only the start of what the family hoped would be an ongoing endeavour to keep the family connected across four continents.

---

[58]  *Post Natal*, 17–21 August 2016.

[59]  *Post Natal*, 24–28 February 2016.

[60]  *Post Natal*, 17–21 August 2016.

[61]  *Post Natal*, 17–21 August 2016.

[62]  *Post Natal*, 17–21 August 2016.

## Indenture: An Assessment

The indenture system in Natal functioned efficiently from an employer's perspective; there was a regular and constant supply of labour and little protest that appeared to threaten, jeopardise or impede the system's functioning. In response to negative publicity that threatened to stop indenture, the authorities usually instituted a commission[63] that made a few recommendations on the basis of which the system was allowed to continue. The absence of large-scale organised protest does not mean that Indian workers were docile or compliant. There are many examples of what we may term 'everyday resistance' on the part of workers to their immediate injustices. Such resistance did not aim to overturn the political or economic order but was often related to day-to-day grievances and included sabotage, desertion and feigning illness. It helped to deflect the abuse of *sirdars* and overseers, give workers a degree of autonomy and regulate the volume and intensity of the work they were compelled to do.

Collective resistance was rare because settlers monopolised armed violence. In addition, there were restrictions on the movement of the indentured and their freedom of association and an absence of strong leadership until the formation of the Natal Indian Congress (which largely represented middle-class interests). Collective action was also frustrated by the dispersal of workers across the colony, the constant turnover of labourers and differences of caste, region and ethnicity among the indentured. The violent protest against the three-pound tax in 1913,[64] which Gandhi led, did overturn the status quo in a limited way. While Indians were not given political rights, the removal of the tax allowed many to remain in Natal who otherwise may have been forced to return to India. Such protests helped to 'make one's life more bearable or ameliorate the material conditions of one's subordination', but we cannot infer that this was necessarily 'revolutionary or the harbinger of future revolution'.[65] Most of the migrants served out their contracts. They did more than survive; they rebuilt their lives and communities through marriage, religious institutions, leisure-time activities and institutions of education. Indenture was thus a complex system and cannot be painted as simply one in which the indentured, lacking all agency, were passive victims.

---

[63] There were these three major commissions: the Coolie Commission (1872), the Wragg Commission (1887) and the Indian Immigrants Commission (1909). See Meer (1980) for the reports of these commissions.

[64] This was a tax that the state imposed on Indians who had completed their indenture and chose not to re-indenture. It was an exorbitant amount, and many Indians became frustrated because they were forced to re-indenture.

[65] Chandra (2015), p. 566.

## Bibliography

Allen, Amy. 2016. 'Feminist Perspectives on Power'. In *The Stanford Encyclopedia of Philosophy*, edited by Edward N. Zalta. *Redwood City, CA: Stanford University Press*.

Badassy, P. 2005. '"... And My Blood Became Hot!" Crimes of Passion, Crimes of Reason: An Analysis of the Crimes against Masters and Mistresses by Their Indian Domestic Servants, Natal 1880–1920'. MA thesis, University of KwaZulu-Natal, Durban.

Chandra, Uday. 2015. 'Rethinking Subaltern Resistance'. *Journal of Contemporary Asia* 45(4): 563–573.

Coolie Commission. 1872. *Report of the Coolie Commission*. Colony of Natal, 11 September. South Africa: P. Davis.

Desai, Aswhin, and Goolam Vahed. 2007. *Inside Indenture: A South African Story 1860–1914*. Durban: Madiba Publishers.

———. 2019. *A History of the Present: A Biography of Indian South Africans, 1994–2019*. New Delhi: Oxford University Press.

Feuer, Lewis S. (ed.). 1969. *Marx and Engels: Basic Writings on Politics and Philosophy*. Glasgow: Fontana Books.

Foucault, Michel. 1978. *The History of Sexuality*, vol. 1. New York: Random House.

———. 1983 (1982). 'Afterword: The Subject and Power'. In *Michel Foucault: Beyond Structuralism and Hermeneutics*, edited by Hubert L. Dreyfus and Paul Rabinow, pp. 208–226. Chicago: University of Chicago Press.

Hall, Stuart. 1980. 'Cultural Studies: Two Paradigms'. *Media, Culture and Society* 2(1): 57–72.

Henning, C. G. 1993. *The Indentured Indian in Natal*. New Delhi: Promilla & Company.

Hobbes, Thomas. 1660. *Of Man, Being the First Part of The Leviathan*. https://web.archive.org/web/20030218000757/http://oregonstate.edu/instruct/phl302/texts/hobbes/leviathan-contents.html. Accessed on 12 December 2017.

Lyons, Barry J. 2005. 'Discipline and the Arts of Domination: Rituals of Respect in Chimborazo, Ecuador'. *Cultural Anthropology* 20(1): 97–127.

Mahmood, S. 2005. *Politics of Piety: The Islamic Revival and the Feminist Subject*. Princeton, NJ: Princeton University Press.

Marks, S. 1990. *The Ambiguities of Dependence in South Africa*. Baltimore: Johns Hopkins University Press.

Meer, Y. S. 1980. *Documents of Indentured Labour in Natal, 1851–1917*. Durban: Institute for Black Research.

Mishra, Amit. 2010. 'Indian Indentured Labourers in Mauritius Reassessing the "New System of Slavery" vs Free Labour Debate'. *Studies in History* 25(2): 229–251.

O'Brien, Kevin J., and Lianjiang Li. 2006. *Rightful Resistance in Rural China*. New York: Cambridge University Press.

Ortner, Sherry. 1995. 'Resistance and the Problem of Ethnographic Refusal'. *Comparative Studies in Society and History* 37(1): 173–193.

Pitkin, Hanna Fenichel. 1972. *Wittgenstein and Justice: On the Significance of Ludwig Wittgenstein for Social and Political Thought*. Berkeley: University of California Press.

Polak, H. S. L. 1909. *The Indians of South Africa: Helots within the Empire and How They Are Treated*. Madras: G. A. Natesan & Co.

Ringrose, Jessica, Marina Gonick, Emma Renold and Lisa Weems. 2009. 'Rethinking Agency and Resistance What Comes After Girl Power?'. *Girlhood Studies* 2(2): 1–9. DOI: 10.3167/ghs.2009.020202.

Sanderson Committee. 1910. *Report of the Committee on Emigration from India to the Crown Colonies and Protectorates*. London: H. M. Stationery Office.

Scott, J. 1985. *Weapons of the Weak*. New Haven, CT: Yale University Press.

Swan, M. 1985. *Gandhi: The South African Experience*. Johannesburg: Ravan Press.

Tayal, Maureen. 1977. 'Indian Indentured Labour in Natal, 1860–1911'. *Indian Economic and Social History Review* 14(4): 519–549.

Thompson, E. P. 1966. *The Making of the English Working Class*. New York: Vintage Books.

Tinker, Hugh. 1974. *A New System of Slavery: The Export of Indian Labour Overseas 1830–1920*. Oxford: Oxford University Press.

Vahed, Goolam. 2018. 'The Protector, Plantocracy, and Indentured Labour in Natal'. *Pacific Historical Review* 87(1): 101–127.

Vahed, Goolam, Ashwin Desai and Thembisa Waetjen. 2010. *Many Lives: 150 Years of Being Indian in South Africa*. Pietermaritzburg: Shuter and Shooter.

Weber, Max. 1978. *Economy and Society: An Outline of Interpretive Sociology*, edited by Guenther Roth and Claus Wittich and translated by Ephraim Fischoff. Berkeley: University of California Press.

Williams, Raymond. 1963 (1958). *Culture and Society*. New York: Columbia University Press.

# 2

# Stewed Plums, Baked Porridge and Flavoured Tea

## Poisoning by Indian Domestic Servants in Colonial Natal

*Prinisha Badassy*

This teapot, whose rage is writ too large to be cooped
within one pygmy chanticleer, surveyed amazed
by gulls and gannets, trumpets his fractious challenged.
Tempting to dub the din thanksgiving; or more; life
triumphs even on no longer trusted planets.

—Douglas Livingstone, 'Scourings at Station 19' (1991)

Poisoning occupies a special place in the history of crime. It requires a considerable degree of premeditation, and because it often produces very little incriminating evidence and until comparatively recently was virtually undetectable, it was an attractive and favoured method of killing during the late nineteenth and early twentieth centuries. Between 1880 and 1920, 18 high-profile cases of poisoning by Indian domestic servants in Natal were tried before the circuit, district and supreme courts. Due to the clandestine nature of poisoning, the difficulty of detection and the knowledge required for its successful execution, it is likely that this only represents a small proportion of the actual number of attempted poisonings – such is the predilection of historicity and nature of archival sources.

Under the Indian indenture system, approximately 152,184 indentureds voyaged to colonial Natal in the period between 1860 and 1911. Conventional and linear histories of these years have tended to present a static categorisation of Indians in Natal as those who toiled on the sugar plantations along the coastal belt of Natal and non-contracted traders commonly referred to as 'passenger Indians'. For the most part, indentured Indians were considered by the state and employers to be dispensable components of a capitalist bonded labour system. On the periphery of this indenture–trader dichotomy, Indians also took up positions as railway workers, constables, court messengers, miners, fishermen, fruit and vegetable hawkers, tea pickers, teachers, interpreters and, in this case, domestic servants. The private and personal spaces of colonial society within which domestic servants lived and worked – the settler homes – bore witness to entangling relationships between master and servant that were at times both volatile and tender. This chapter focuses on the crime of 'administering poison with intent to murder' and argues that the very act of poisoning manifests as a mode of agency, revenge and resistance by domestic servants against their masters and mistresses. The crime of poisoning in a settler community is rather revealing of the deep levels of anxiety and paranoia that proliferated in Natal's white community. The real or imagined threat posed by the familiarity and immediacy of domestic servants in the home fervently fuelled colonial imagination and fears about vengeful and ungrateful indentured labourers. In this context, crimes committed by domestic servants – murder, physical assault, rape, theft, arson, desertion and poisoning – have to be read as a discourse of subalternity in which individuals were responding to the unforgiving control of their masters rather than as an attempt at perturbing the colonial state and dismantling the system of indenture.

The intimacy of food preparation and its centrality to everyday life presented domestic servants with ample opportunity for employing this method of murder. The delegation of responsibility for the preparation and cooking of food to these servants frequently placed employers in a vulnerable position. Similar trends have also been observed in Victorian England, British India as well as antebellum America. In *Roll, Jordan, Roll*, Eugene Genovese argues:

> When well-bred house servants murdered their masters and mistresses, they chose the more genteel device of poison, which had the great advantage, apart from its propriety, of sometimes escaping detection. Cases of poisoning and suspected poisoning, however infrequent, kept the slaveholders nervous, especially since any undiagnosed or strange death could raise suspicion of foul play.[1]

Genovese adds that poison occupied a very prominent place in the 'arsenal of slave weapons' throughout much of the Americas and that many slaveholders lived in fear of being the victims of poisoning by their slaves.[2] He also argues that as soon as their journey to the plantations began, slaves resorted to poisoning their masters.[3]

In her thesis on slave healers, Sarah Cotton asserts that many slaves were found guilty of poisoning in the context of healing, as opposed to the preparing

---

[1] Genovese (1976), p. 362.
[2] Genovese (1976), p. 616.
[3] Genovese (1976), p. 616.

and serving of food. She contends that many slaves did not receive fair trials, and proving a case of poisoning was very difficult during the slave period.[4] By the early nineteenth century, with the advancements made in western medical and scientific knowledge, there were five accepted ways of testing for poison. These were dependent on the victim's symptoms, most often taking the form of stomach cramps and dizziness, chemical analysis of the substances which supposedly contained the poison, the victim's description of the taste, smell and experience of the poison, moral evidence such as the behaviour of the accused, and, most importantly, the identification of a substantial motive.

Fictional accounts about poison have not only been responsible for creating stereotypes about the 'poisoner' and the 'poisoned' but also for the perpetuation of these stereotypes. For instance, since women have generally been considered to be in charge of the kitchen and the preparation of food, most often the average 'poisoner' was described as female and their victims often children and adultering, abusive or forlorn husbands. While this may be true to a certain extent, as Katherine Watson shows in her true-crime book, *Poisoned Lives*, vis-à-vis the likes of Mary Cotton, Belle Sorenson Gunness, Nannie Doss, Florence Maybrick, Madeline Smith and, closer to home, Daisy de Melker, the scenario was quite the opposite in Natal.[5]

This chapter is made up of the contextualisation and analysis of a series of narratives, mainly found in the Natal state court records, of individuals whose lives came to be characterised by conflict with their masters and mistresses, in particular by the crime of 'administering poison with intent to murder or to cause grievous bodily harm'. The specific cases of Latchigadu and Murugen (1906), Dilsir Khan (1907), Ramsamy (1907), Mutumah (1907) and Ramanah (1908) are explored here as a litmus test for discerning whether the proximity and intimacy of the colonial household did indeed give rise to 'everyday acts of resistance', where individuals found ways of subverting a system of exploitation, repression and degradation.[6] The existing scholarly focus on collective, large-scale resistance and mobilisation against iniquitous labour control in the early years of the twentieth century by indentured Indians in Natal (primarily under the banner of Gandhi and the Natal and Transvaal Indian Congresses) has led to the muting of individual expressions of frustration and despair. This chapter pushes against this established literature by accounting for individual action where agency and resistance need to be seen not necessarily as a rejection

---

[4]  Cotton (1997).

[5]  See Bell (2001); Marriner (1991); and Watson (2004).

[6]  Borrowed from Scott (1985).

of labour but as a response to the conditions under which the indentured were forced to work and live.[7]

## Dilsir Khan, the 'Milkboy'

Dilsir Khan was indicted for the crime of administering poison with intent to kill on 6 May 1907. The state accused Khan of attempting to kill Emma English (who had since deceased at the time of the trial) together with Amelia Jane Dix, Daniel Alfred English, Geoffrey Dix English, Claude English and Frank Quinton Stubbings, but, owing to many inconsistencies in the case, the assistant magistrate found it very difficult to reach a decision regarding the prisoner's committal.[8] Collusion in cases such as this was very common, and despite being accused of dreaming up the murder, Khan, who was a 'milkboy' and responsible for chopping wood, had apparently also instructed a fellow female servant, Topi, to breathe life into his plan.[9] What was even more surprising was that Khan's alleged accomplice was merely 13 years of age.

According to Topi's testimony, she was instructed by Khan to lace the plums and tea, which she served the English household, with a substance that she later said was procured by Khan. In a letter to the chief magistrate of Pietermaritzburg, the assistant magistrate, L. Moe, stated that he believed the evidence adduced by the Crown was insufficient to justify a committal against Khan. According to Topi, she was asked by Khan to mix the poison with the fruit and tea and told that it was *tshevu* (poison), but she did not, in fact, know what *tshevu* was.[10] The assistant magistrate found this highly suspicious in view of the age of the girl and the fact that when she had first made a deposition, she had denied all knowledge as to how the poison was administered to the tea and plums.

The type of poison that was used appeared to have been cyanide of potassium, according to Herbert Rochefort Brown, the assistant government analyst; when swallowed, it produced its effects very rapidly. As a rule, the first symptom experienced would be a sense of constriction at the back of the throat and a slight

---

[7]  See also Vahed (2014), pp. 95–120.

[8]  Geoffrey and Claude English were the sons of Emma and Daniel English.

[9]  Pietermaritzburg Archives Repository (PAR), Registrar, Supreme Court (RSC), 1/1/95/12/1907, Supreme Court Criminal Cases, *Rex v. Dilsir Khan*, charged with administering poison with intent to commit murder, 1907; PAR, AGO, I/1/315/42/1907, Supreme Court Criminal Cases, *Rex v. Dilsir Khan*, charged with administering poison with intent to commit murder, 1907.

[10]  PAR, Attorney General's Office (AGO), I/1/315/42/1907, Supreme Court Criminal Cases, *Rex v. Dilsir Khan*, charged with administering poison with intent to commit murder, 1907.

burning sensation on the tongue. Almost immediately after this, convulsions may occur, which may be severe enough to cause the individual to fall to the ground. The patient may also vomit excessively, and if the quantity taken is sufficiently large, consciousness may be lost immediately. A 'great depression of the vital functions may also be experienced, and as result death ensues an hour or so after the consumption of the poison'.[11] On his analysis of samples of both the stewed plums and tea, Brown confirmed that since the acidity of the samples was very high, a considerable amount of cyanide had been put in, such that through fermentation the cyanide of potassium had converted to prussic acid.[12]

According to Amelia Jane Dix, who lived with her daughter, Emma, and her husband, Daniel Alfred English, on the morning of Saturday, 19 January 1907, she was in the kitchen with Topi, making tea. There were no other servants present at the time except for one of the other Indian servants, Ranee (whose assumed name was 'Mary'[13]), who was busy in the dining room. Mrs Dix had poured four cups of tea and left them on the dresser in the pantry. She had then gone into the dining room to get some spoons. When she returned to the pantry she noticed that the cups of tea were not full enough, and so she poured a little more into them. She then placed a cup of tea on the dining table for a certain Stubbings, who worked as a nurseryman and boarded with Mrs Dix and her husband, and then Mrs Dix took two cups of tea to Emma and Daniel's bedroom. When she finally tasted her own cup of tea, which she had left in the pantry, it was cold and did not look 'very nice'. She poured in some more tea, and when she drank it, she immediately felt 'helpless and powerless and fit to die'. At the presiding trial, when asked by W. S. Bigby, attorney for the Crown, what her throat felt like, Mrs Dix replied:

> I had a choking sensation. I vomited very much, nothing but white froth. I had to hold on to everything to get myself to the bedroom. I fancy it might have been a dying feeling. I do not know how I managed to get from door to door into my bedroom. I vomited in my bedroom and then lay upon the bed. I felt helpless – dying.[14]

---

[11] PAR, AGO, I/1/315/42/1907, Supreme Court Criminal Cases, *Rex v. Dilsir Khan*, charged with administering poison with intent to commit murder, 1907.

[12] Prussic acid is an alternate term for hydrogen cyanide, which is a highly volatile and dangerous poison and can be synthesised by thermal decomposition.

[13] For more on the ubiquitous use of 'Sammy' and 'Mary' as derogatory shorthand names of indentureds in Natal, see Badassy (2018).

[14] PAR, RSC, 1/1/95/12/1907, Supreme Court Criminal Cases, *Rex v. Dilsir Khan*, charged with administering poison with intent to commit murder, testimony of Mrs Dix, 1907.

After being prescribed a swig of brandy by Doctor Campbell Watt, Mrs Dix said she felt a little relieved and thought that it would be best if she 'took a little dinner' that evening.[15] When she proceeded to taste the plums, her husband immediately pulled them away from her as he noticed a discolouration of the plums. In her closing statement, unsurprisingly, Mrs Dix said she believed that 'the girl Topi was very saucy and impertinent', while she found the 'boy', Dilsir, to be 'very tiresome, and lazy and not at all straightforward and honest'.[16] These were sentiments not uncommon in the Natal settler society or the empire at large.

Topi represented a very unusual individual for the period in question. First, she would have formed part of the 3 per cent of African women who were employed as domestic servants in the entire colony, and she was only 13 years old.[17] On 31 January 1907, she was subpoenaed by the city magistrate for an examination. In her deposition, she stated:

> I work for Mr DA English and I live on this farm at Hilton Road, near Town Bush Valley. On Wednesday the 16th inst. I had a conversation with Dilsir Khan who complained that my master ill-treated him and wouldn't give him time to eat his meals. The accused gave me the 'muti'[18] and told me to put it into the food of the white man and requested me not to say that he had given the 'muti' to me. He gave me two lumps of it and he told me also to put some of it in the plums; the other he said I should put in the tea. This was on a Friday some time ago. I did what accused told me and put the 'muti' into the tea and the plums; that was on the next day, Saturday. [I did not know when accused gave me the 'muti' – he gave me two pieces of it – that it was poison. I heard that from an Indian in the employ of my master after I had put it into the tea and plums.] Accused did not tell me what effects it would have. It did not strike me that the accused might have a spite against my employer. When [accused] told me [my master] was giving me too much work to do, I did not think he meant to injure him. I noticed Mrs Dix was very sick after I had put the 'muti' into the tea. I did not disclose then that I had put the 'muti' into the plums, which I had then already done. I first told a native detective of what I had done. I did not tell accused that the master and his family were sick as a result of eating the 'muti.' After the accused returned that morning from delivering milk, he did not ask me whether I had put that 'muti' into the food. I did not speak to him again

---

15   PAR, RSC, 1/1/95/12/1907, Supreme Court Criminal Cases, *Rex v. Dilsir Khan*, charged with administering poison with intent to commit murder, testimony of Mrs Dix, 1907.

16   PAR, RSC, 1/1/95/12/1907, Supreme Court Criminal Cases, *Rex v. Dilsir Khan*, charged with administering poison with intent to commit murder, testimony of Mrs Dix, 1907.

17   *Census Report of the Colony of Natal 17th April 1904* (1905).

18   This is a Zulu term which refers to indigenous medicine, in the form of herbs, parts of plants and animals, as well as chemicals.

on the subject. I was not afraid after I had put the 'muti' into the food as to what would happen. When I saw Mrs Dix was ill, I thought she had been made ill by the 'muti'.[19]

Reading through the trial transcript, it appears that Khan was able to exploit the vulnerability of Topi, but his testimony implicated others besides her. He pleaded not guilty to all charges, and according to his sworn testimony, he described how on Thursday while working, a fellow servant, Lala, had expressed his anger at Mr English for threatening his mother, Ranee, with imprisonment for supposedly bringing poison into the kitchen. Lala apparently went on to say, 'I would never allow my mother to go to prison. I would not care how much money I spent. I would keep her out of prison.'[20] According to Lala, Mr English had also warned him by saying that 'if he found poison again in the kitchen, he would punish the person who brought it'.[21] Khan then described how that Monday evening he was told of Ranee's imprisonment by another Indian. However, that was not all Khan was to hear of Ranee that evening, for that night he was visited by Ra, Narain, Beelwa and Ramu, all of whom worked for Mr English. According to Khan, they all declared that the police had taken Ranee 'away for nothing', and that 'it had all been done at the instigation of' Mr English, 'who was not a good man'.[22] He also said that all three admitted that they did not care to work for Mr English any longer and would be leaving after that month.

Khan swore that he understood the charge against him but emphatically denied poisoning his master. If anything, Khan was extremely well informed of Mr English's nature for he spoke yet again of another servant, Berber, who had said to him that 'my master was very cruel, and deserved to be killed'.[23] Berber apparently went on to say that Khan should be very careful so as not to be implicated. This case points yet again to collusion, since that Monday, after Mr English had gotten sick, a policeman questioned Khan about whether he knew who had put poison in the food, and Berber, Ra, Narain, Gothal and Ramu

---

[19] PAR, RSC, 1/1/95/12/1907, Supreme Court Criminal Cases, *Rex v. Dilsir Khan*, charged with administering poison with intent to commit murder, testimony of Topi, 1907.

[20] PAR, RSC, 1/1/95/12/1907, Supreme Court Criminal Cases, *Rex v. Dilsir Khan*, charged with administering poison with intent to commit murder, 1907.

[21] PAR, RSC, 1/1/95/12/1907, Supreme Court Criminal Cases, *Rex v. Dilsir Khan*, charged with administering poison with intent to commit murder, testimony of Dilsir Khan, 1907.

[22] PAR, RSC, 1/1/95/12/1907, Supreme Court Criminal Cases, *Rex v. Dilsir Khan*, charged with administering poison with intent to commit murder, testimony of Dilsir Khan, 1907.

[23] PAR, RSC, 1/1/95/12/1907, Supreme Court Criminal Cases, *Rex v. Dilsir Khan*, charged with administering poison with intent to commit murder, testimony of Dilsir Khan, 1907.

had apparently all promised to give Khan one pound each if he went to court and denied all knowledge of the poisoning, which he refuted.

However, what emerges from the cross-examination of Khan by Bigby in court was that Khan had worked in the garden before becoming a 'milkboy' for the English family and was aware of the fact that the English used cyanide to fumigate the trees. He even knew that Mr English kept the cyanide under lock and key in the storeroom. However, in his testimony, Khan argued that he fervently believed that the other servants were implicating him. He informed the court that the reason he believed Topi was responsible for administering poison was as a result of an assault incident that had occurred sometime before the poisoning. Khan said that about six months earlier, Topi had been busy washing dishes, and when she 'threw dirty water' on him, he got so annoyed that he slapped her. Khan said that the only way Topi could have gotten the poison was through Lala. In his reasoning for Lala's involvement, Khan said:

> Because I had an altercation with him [Lala] on one occasion, and I gave him two slaps, and my master also beat him on that occasion; on another occasion, when my master went to strike him, he ran away. Lala was very much enraged on that occasion he came to me and said if my master strikes me in this way I will run away and leave my work, or do some sort of harm.[24]

When asked about the other Indians working for Mr English, Khan stated:

> All three of them who are working there said to me that my master is very bad and we ought to thrash him, and he ill-treated them and they could not stand it. We who are working under indenture considered him as our father and master, but it was the free men who talked in that way.[25]

At the conclusion of the trial, Khan was found guilty by the jury, and he received a 10-year prison sentence for the crime. In most successful convictions of poisoning, prisoners were subjected to an imprisonment of three to ten years with hard labour. While this particular case highlights the problems of complicity, collusion and the difficulty for the courts to establish a motive as evidence, it also points to the degree to which animosity between free and indentured Indians in the colony may have further complicated the master–servant relationship. Levels of hierarchy that operated on and off the plantation between free and

---

[24] PAR, RSC, 1/1/95/12/1907, Supreme Court Criminal Cases, *Rex v. Dilsir Khan*, charged with administering poison with intent to commit murder, testimony of Dilsir Khan, 1907.

[25] PAR, RSC, 1/1/95/12/1907, Supreme Court Criminal Cases, *Rex v. Dilsir Khan*, charged with administering poison with intent to commit murder, testimony of Dilsir Khan, 1907.

unfree field labourers and domestic servants did little to assuage already fractured egos and masculinities. Individuals who were considered to be allies of their masters and supposedly enjoyed much leniency and privilege were thus viewed by other Indians with much cynicism and betrayal. By the end of the court case, there was some uncertainty as to whether Khan was acting on his own conviction or whether he was, in fact, implicated by the other servants. In both instances, however, mitigation rests quite heavily on the levels of ill-treatment meted out to these servants by Mr English.

## The Adams Family: Part One

George Roberts Adams and Sarah Austin Adams lived and worked on the Blackburn Estate, Inanda Division, with their son, Cyril Adams, and two stepchildren, Francis Margaret Dales Preston and George Preston (ages unknown). On 21 September 1906, at the Durban and Coast District Circuit Court trial, Murugen, who served as the Adams family's 'kitchen boy', and Latchigadu, a general servant, were called before the attorney general on charges of poisoning by arsenic. On 4 July 1906, the Adams family sat down to afternoon tea. Mr Adams rang the bell to get the attention of Latchigadu, but when he did not respond, he sent one of his children, George, to the kitchen to look for their 'kitchen boy'. When he did finally answer Mr Adams's call, Latchigadu was asked to bring through a jug of water. Latchigadu returned to the kitchen, and George apparently looked through the crack of the door and saw him place something in the jug. He immediately informed his mother, who refused to use the water, but her husband and daughter both brewed their cups of tea with it. For dinner, they were served soup, and Mrs Adams remarked that it tasted peculiar and gave her bowl to their dog. Mr Adams and Francis, however, drank all of their soup. Half an hour later, though, they experienced 'tremendous pains' in their stomachs, and their dog began frothing at the mouth.[26]

The next morning, Mr Adams and Francis, both of whom felt a little better, were served cocoa by Latchigadu, but they again experienced an excruciating pain similar to the one they had the previous night. That same morning, Latchigadu also asked if he could prepare the porridge that was always cooked by Francis, and even though his request was refused, he nonetheless helped Francis and brought her water. Francis noticed that the water contained white sediment, and when she showed it to her stepmother, Mrs Adams ordered her to leave it in

---

[26]  PAR, AGO, I/1/306/108/1906, Durban and Coast District Circuit Court, *Rex v. Latchigadu and Murugen*, charged with administering poison with intent to commit murder, 1906.

the sewing room and keep it well out of reach of the servants.[27] Mrs Adams then transferred some of the water into pickle bottles and took it to Doctor J. F. Elliott, the family's medical attendant.

According to various testimonies presented to the attorney general, Murugen had, in fact, been responsible for giving Latchigadu the arsenic to be administered. In her deposition, Mrs Adams claimed that a month prior to this incident, she had reprimanded Murugen, and in response he had muttered, 'Latay vatty poodum', which, according to Mrs Adams's understanding of Tamil, translated to 'I shall cut your head'.[28] Latchigadu's deposition offers some insights into the matter:

> I work in the garden of Mr Adams. I also, when called, help the kitchen boy. [H]is name is Murugen. Last [M]onday, during teatime, my mistress asked for hot water. I poured some into a jug. [A]s I was about to take it to the dining room, Murugen said I had better put some kind of stuff, which he handed me, in the water. [H]e said that it would clean the water. I did as Murugen ordered me. Murugen said that he always put stuff in the water that is wanted by the master and that I must always put it in the food or water when required by the family. It is a greyish powder. Murugen threatened to beat me when I confessed to the mistress. He said he would break all my bones. I believe I can produce some of the powder in court. My mistress told me not to throw away the water three times, but Murugen ordered me to throw it away. [A]nd being afraid of him, I did so. Murugen had been trying to kill my master because he refused to let him off work when sick. I asked to be allowed to mix the porridge because Murugen said I was to do so and place some powder in it. The powder was kept on the shelf where nobody would suspect it to be unless you knew of it being there. I think it is still there.[29]

At the closure of the court case, both Latchigadu and Murugen were found unanimously guilty, and perhaps owing to his young age or his apparent coerced complicity, there was a 'recommendation to the mercy of Latchigadu'. As a result, Latchigadu was sentenced to 20 strokes with the birch, while Murugen received 10 years of imprisonment with hard labour and 15 lashes. In most studies on poisoning, arsenic appears to have been the most popular choice for

27  PAR, AGO, I/1/306/108/1906, Durban and Coast District Circuit Court, *Rex v. Latchigadu and Murugen*, charged with administering poison with intent to commit murder, 1906.

28  PAR, AGO, I/1/306/108/1906, Durban and Coast District Circuit Court, *Rex v. Latchigadu and Murugen*, charged with administering poison with intent to commit murder, 1906.

29  PAR, AGO, I/1/306/108/1906, Durban and Coast District Circuit Court, *Rex v. Latchigadu and Murugen*, charged with administering poison with intent to commit murder, deposition of Latchigadu, 1906.

would-be murderers as well as those contemplating suicide.[30] In her *Memoir of Family Secrets*, Gail Bell calls arsenic 'the queen of poisons'.[31] For years, arsenic was the most popular of all poisons because it was relatively cheap and widely available, and its white-powder form made it easy to camouflage it with other food substances as well as mimic the effects of food poisoning or cholera. According to Watson, arsenic victims would often experience excruciating pain in their stomach, vomiting, diarrhoea and a thirst that was impossible to quench.[32] In India, David Arnold confirms, arsenic was not only easily available, sold in local bazaars and a common household item, but it was also frequently cited as the cause of death or illness in cases of intimate domestic poisoning by husbands, wives or servants.[33] In Natal, arsenic was relatively easy to obtain from the local chemist as an exterminating agent for rats or as a skin whitener. The toxic substance could easily be purchased at the Reed and Champion Chemist and Druggist for three shillings per pound.[34] Access to drugs and patent medicines of these kinds by the general public was granted by the passing of the 1905 amendment to the Medical, Dental and Pharmacy Act that now allowed industrial and agricultural products containing poisons to be sold by general dealers with a licence.

## The Adams Family: Part Two

Six months later, on 30 January 1907, the Adams family were again the victims of poisoning – this time by the seeds of the *Datura stramonium* plant and by their new 'kitchen boy', Ramsamy, whom the family engaged as Murugen's replacement. In his deposition, Kayrathrie, the 'house boy', stated:

> I am the adopted son of Bugwansing and work for Mr Adams of Blackburn Estate as a house servant. The day before yesterday I saw Ramsamy, my master's cook, put some stramonium seed into a dish of cooked tomato stew and serve it on the table. When he placed that dish on the dining table no one was present. I made the report to my mistress when she came home. This was the first time I saw him put the seed in the food.[35]

---

[30] See, for instance, Bell (2001); Marriner (1991); Bartrip (1994, pp. 891–913); and Couzens (2005).

[31] Bell (2001), p. 135.

[32] Watson (2004).

[33] Arnold (2016), pp. 118–127.

[34] PAR, Indian Immigration Department (IID), 1/54/I358/1890, tenders, drugs etc. for the year ending 14 April 1891, 1890. I would like to thank Julie Parle for the very useful catalogue of drugs and chemicals that were available in the colony.

[35] PAR, AGO, I/1/318/55/1907, Durban and Coast District Circuit Court, *Rex v. Ramsamy*, charged with administering poison with intent to commit murder, 1907.

The following morning, on Wednesday, the Adamses ate porridge for breakfast that had been prepared by Ramsamy. The porridge had a bitter taste and Mr Adams, Mrs Adams, Francis, George and Cyril experienced a stinging sensation in their throats. Later that morning, Mrs Adams noticed that Cyril, her two-year-old son, was drowsy and struggled as he walked. By lunchtime, he had recovered slightly, but after eating what she called the 'tomato chutney with rice, ... he kept falling down and subsequently vomited'.[36] Mrs Adams then offered some of the chutney and rice to Kayrathrie but later found that he had not eaten it. When she questioned him, he cried and said, 'O kana hum nai kaija', which, according to her, translated as 'I shall not eat the food.'[37] On hearing this and judging from his demeanour, Mrs Adams became suspicious and asked him why he cried and refused to eat the food. Kayrathrie said that he refused to eat because Ramsamy had warned him not to eat any of the chutney and on that morning had given him some powder and instructed him to place it in the pot that contained the chutney. The following day, the Adamses acquired the assistance of Detective M. Walker of the Criminal Investigating Department,[38] and after several depositions, it was alleged that Manupa, who was the 'stable *sirdar*' and a very good friend of Murugen, had, in fact, shown Ramsamy where the *Datura stramonium* plants grew behind the stables and incited Ramsamy to administer the poison, as Manupa believed that both his mistress and master 'were bad people'.[39] No concrete evidence against Manupa could be obtained, but on 22 May, Ramsamy, with scant incriminating evidence, was found guilty of the crime and sentenced to four years of imprisonment with hard labour.

The medicinal and chemical properties of the *Datura stramonium* plant were well-known by the colonial authorities as well as the white settler community and Indian immigrants.[40] *Datura stramonium*, or jimsonweed as it is commonly known, was believed to have originated in India. As Arnold illustrates in *Toxic*

---

[36] PAR, AGO, I/1/318/55/1907, Durban and Coast District Circuit Court, *Rex v. Ramsamy*, charged with administering poison with intent to commit murder, 1907.

[37] PAR, AGO, I/1/318/55/1907, Durban and Coast District Circuit Court, *Rex v. Ramsamy*, charged with administering poison with intent to commit murder, 1907.

[38] 'Durban Criminal Court, Opening of Criminal Sessions: Alleged Poisoning', *Natal Mercury*, 22 May 1907; 'Durban Criminal Court, Opening of Criminal Sessions: The Poisoning Case', *Natal Mercury*, 24 May 1907.

[39] PAR, AGO, I/1/318/55/1907, Durban and Coast District Circuit Court, *Rex v. Ramsamy*, charged with administering poison with intent to commit murder, 1907.

[40] In 1895, as a result of the occurrence of many cases of poisoning by eating wild fruits or seeds that had been reported in the colony, John Medley Wood, the director of the Natal Herbarium, was asked to publish a list of such poisonous plants. See Wood (1895).

*Histories*, by the nineteenth century in India, *Datura stramonium* was commonly grown in 'gardens, along roadsides and on waste ground' and had come to be branded as a 'pernicious drug and an intoxicating poison'.[41] The dangers of *Datura stramonium* featured prominently in discourses around poisoning panics and criminality in the subcontinent well into the 1920s and the 1930s. It is evident, from Clare Anderson's *Convicts in the Indian Ocean*, that knowledge and awareness about the plant travelled mercilessly through the Indian Ocean to port colonies in Mauritius and Natal alike. In Mauritius, Anderson shows, how *Datura stramonium* – along with other poisonous botanicals – was often used by robbers to stupefy and render their victims helpless.[42]

The whole plant is classified as a narcotic, but the seeds of *Datura stramonium* are considered to have a very strong aphrodisiac effect. The seeds are also used medically to treat skin disorders, ulcers, bronchitis and asthma.[43] Moreover, the seeds could easily be mistaken for capsicum or chilli seeds. In large doses, the effects of *Datura stramonium* on the individual are dryness of the throat, thirst, nausea, giddiness, nervous agitation, dilatation of the pupil, obscurity of vision, headache and, in some cases, perspiration.[44] As Karen Flint has shown in her research on African healers in south-eastern Africa, African and Indian labourers often shared remedies and knowledge about local plants as well as Ayurvedic herbs.[45] Being in such close proximity to each other, Indian and African labourers would have no doubt shared experiences of the effects of plants such as this.[46] From Aboobakker Amod's account in the *Report of the Indian Immigrants Commission* of 1885–1887, it is evident that the plant was popular among Indian immigrants.

> The cause of so many suicides taking place among Indians here are, firstly, adultery; secondly, drink; thirdly, the breaking of marriage contracts as regards the children. I do not think that suicide is committed owing to the nature of the work a man has to do. Fourthly, the use of ganga and the juice of datura drives them frantic, and they commit suicide and sometimes homicide. I think that Government should take these matters of drinking and smoking noxious drugs, in hand, and should pass stringent laws concerning them.[47]

---

[41]  Arnold (2016), pp. 63–64.

[42]  Anderson (2000), pp. 75–80.

[43]  Steenkamp et al. (2004).

[44]  Helwig (1999), p. 1384; Krenzelok, Jacobsen and Aronis (1995); Flanagin (1989).

[45]  Flint (2001).

[46]  For a broader history of Indian–African relations on the south-east coast of Africa, see Marks (1987); Parle (2007); and Hughes (2007).

[47]  *Report of the Indian Immigrants Commission, 1885–1887*, reprinted in Meer (1980), p. 390.

That the Adams family had fallen victim to two incidents of poisoning in the space of six months not only starkly points to the inherent ambivalence in relations between labourers and settlers, but also conveys the deep sense of paranoia and suspicion expressed on the part of white settlers towards their servants. In addition, it indicates a wider moral panic that seems to have gripped Natal settler society between 1906 and 1908.[48] It may be true to a rather large extent that the poison panics that gripped European settler communities in British India in the late nineteenth century were readily transposed to Natal. Many of the cases examined and discussed in this chapter were brought before the courts during these two years. This increase in the number of convictions perhaps suggests that perceived threats of poisoning by servants were part of a larger settler anxiety that precipitated in the post-South African War years and was compounded by a better-developed legal, penal and forensic system, an increase in the population of the colony and widespread economic depression. Regardless, what is evident here is that even though the case against Latchigadu and Murugen was concluded on the grounds that arsenic was used as the poison (despite the widely prevalent use of arsenic in everyday living), the verdict against Ramsamy was reached on hearsay. All three were found guilty. It is well documented that courts in Natal, as is in other settler societies, were favourable and lenient towards white colonialists. Indentured and free Indians and Africans in the colony who found themselves arraigned often came under the harsh gavel of prejudice and racially biased juries.

## Mutumah and Morning Tea

About two months after Ramsamy's trial had concluded, on 4 July 1907, another case of poisoning was called to the Supreme Court. This time, however, the accused was an Indian woman. Mutumah lived with her husband, Yellappa, on the premises of Patricia and Frederick William Larkin, who was a gardener and manager of a nursery in Town Bush Valley, Pietermaritzburg. Mutumah (or Mary as she was called by the Larkins) used to help Mrs Larkin around the house in exchange for jewellery and was never formally employed by the Larkins. Mutumah, like Dilsir Khan, was accused of administering cyanide of potassium to the drinking water and a pot of tea that was prepared for Mr and Mrs Larkin. On the morning of 2 February, Mr Larkin had noticed that the breakfast tea had a very peculiar taste, and when he examined the zinc bath from where the water was obtained, out on the veranda, he noticed that the inside of the bath felt 'very slimy'. Again, on the evening of 15 February, Mrs Larkin noticed that the tea

---

[48] For an interesting comparative analysis, see Arnold (2017).

had a very bitter taste.[49] Despite not knowing what cyanide of potassium tasted like, on tasting the tea that morning, both Mr and Mrs Larkin assumed that it tasted like cyanide because of the incident that had occurred with the English family. After putting the teapot under lock and key, Mr Larkin went to the English household to consult with Mr English about his findings concerning their incident with Dilsir Khan and to 'ring up the police'.[50]

According to Mrs Larkin:

> Mutumah used to work for me voluntarily and for the services rendered, I gave her a present at Christmas 1906. On two occasions prior to New Year 1907, we had noticed that our tea had a peculiar taste. On the 2nd occasion, I took some of the tea and asked Mary if she would taste it; she declined to take it saying that she only drank coffee. I threw the tea away and made fresh tea. I used to miss articles, tea, soap, sugar, etc., and I suspected that and I used to tax her with it. She was also rather inquisitive. On leaving the house I would put paper on the contents of my box, and on returning I would find the paper turned over and the clothes disarranged. Mary was the only one who had access to my room and box, and I used to leave my keys with her when going down into the garden. For these reasons I scolded her on several occasions and eventually told her I did not wish her to work for me any longer and forbade her to come anywhere near the house. The cyanide is kept in the fumigating house in a safe. Both the house and safe are kept locked. The boys who had to do work in connection with fumigation were before given cyanide but now this practice has ceased. Mary might have obtained the cyanide from them. Her husband is the man with whom she was living was friendly with the boys who worked in connection with fumigation. Mary was originally brought out from Durban, but Yellappa did not obtain our permission to bring her out as he should have done. The Indians working for Mr English are often in the habit of coming over and visiting our Indians.[51]

Yellappa had apparently paid a fellow servant, Gopal, four pounds to collect Mutumah from Durban. Gopal was subsequently appointed by Detective Brandon of the Criminal Investigating Department to assist him with the examination of

---

[49] PAR, RSC, 1/1/98/24/1907, Supreme Court Criminal Cases, *Rex v. Mutumah*, charged with administering poison with intent to murder, 1907; PAR, AGO, I/1/322/66/1907, Supreme Court Criminal Cases, *Rex v. Mutumah*, charged with administering poison with intent to murder, 1907.

[50] PAR, RSC, 1/1/98/24/1907, Supreme Court Criminal Cases, *Rex v. Mutumah*, charged with administering poison with intent to murder, 1907.

[51] PAR, AGO, I/1/322/66/1907, Supreme Court Criminal Cases, *Rex v. Mutumah*, charged with administering poison with intent to murder, deposition of Patricia Larkin, 1907.

witnesses and interpretation. The city clerk of the peace had reason to believe that it was Gopal who had, in fact, given Mutumah the cyanide to administer to the food and water of the Larkins since he was in possession of a key to the chest in which the cyanide was kept. Apparently, sometime earlier, he had made 'improper overtures' towards Mutumah and asked her not to tell her husband.[52] Besides asking her to prepare his food, he had also said to her, 'If you come again with those words to me, I will give you slippers.'[53] However, at the trial, Gopal claimed that Mutumah had admitted to administering the poison. According to Gopal, Mutumah had told him that 'Mrs Larkin was a bad lady and whenever the Indians talk about her she is generally annoyed with them and tries to threaten to strike them'. Gopal then went on to say:

> She [Mutumah] said, 'I was working in the kitchen, and she very often was annoyed with me, and you must be very careful.' Then she asked me to go into her room. I did so, and I took my seat near the door, and she sat at another place in the room. Then she asked me if I did not repeat what she had to say she would relate things. Then she told me that she had put some medicine in a kettle. It was a white medicine, she said. I asked her 'when you put this medicine in, did she take it?' Then she replied that when Mr Larkin partook of the tea, he tasted it and felt bad, and then Mrs Larkin partook of the same tea, and then she tasted it, and she felt bad. It was not a nice taste. Then she said that Mrs Larkin called to the accused 'Buya lapa'. She went there. Then she said, 'Mary, puza lo tea' (Mary, drink the tea). Then she replied that she does not take tea, but she takes coffee. Then I also said, 'What else did you do?' She said, 'I put some medicine in a bath outside. Then Mr Larkin took a cup of water from this bath, and drank, but he did not like the taste of the water, and he threw the water away.' She also said that she had put on two occasions some medicine in a paraffine [sic] tin of water. She said she found the medicine on Mr Larkin's ground.[54]

When the government analyst, Doctor W. Watkins-Pitchford, returned his findings after analysing the tea leaves and water, he asserted that the bottles of 2 February only contained in the region of 0.08 and 0.17 grains of cyanide of potassium. The water bottled from the night of 15 February did not have any traceable

---

[52] PAR, RSC, 1/1/98/24/1907, Supreme Court Criminal Cases, *Rex v. Mutumah*, charged with administering poison with intent to murder, 1907.

[53] PAR, RSC, 1/1/98/24/1907, Supreme Court Criminal Cases, *Rex v. Mutumah*, charged with administering poison with intent to murder, 1907.

[54] PAR, RSC, 1/1/98/24/1907, Supreme Court Criminal Cases, *Rex v. Mutumah*, charged with administering poison with intent to murder, 1907.

grains of cyanide and had 'an offensive, urinous odour and [was] very turbid'.[55] Taking this into account and the fact that for a very brief period of two weeks at the beginning of February, the Larkins had engaged Ramsamy as a 'kitchen boy', the city clerk of the peace found Gopal's evidence very suspect and problematic and argued that in implicating Mutumah he might have had been merely hiding his guilt since it was well known that he had a key to the safe in which the cyanide was kept. He also made a point of the fact that owing to the recent poisoning at the English household, Mr and Mrs Larkin were acting on intense fears and suspicions. He also added that during this time there were close to 10 other Indians living on the property and it was possible that any one of them could have attempted the poisoning. Mutumah was eventually unanimously found not guilty, but this case is significant in hinting at the overestimation of the threat of poisoning prevalent amongst white settler families during this period.

## Ramanah and the Biscuit Tin

Ramanah had been working in the colony for the Marsden family for three years when, on 6 January 1908, he was charged with attempted murder and administering poison with intent 'to do some grievous bodily harm'.[56] Apparently, Ramanah was the only house servant that had access to the bedroom of Nora Lydia Marsden, the daughter of Sarah Ann and Herbert Marsden, a tailor in Mountain Rise, Pietermaritzburg. Ramanah was accused of depositing hydrochloric acid in the water bottles, on the soap, bedclothes, tablecloth, sponge and tooth powder that belonged in the bedroom of the daughter. Doctor Robert A. Buntine was responsible for analysing the samples forwarded to him and confirmed that the water bottle containing 13 fluid drachms of clear water had only 0.33 per cent hydrochloric acid (HCl) added to it and that the HCl was in the form of the commercial spirit of salt. He also added that the water containing the strongest solution of HCl, in relation to the other items that were tested, could not reasonably be termed 'poisonous', and that about half a pint

---

[55]  PAR, RSC, 1/1/98/24/1907, Supreme Court Criminal Cases, *Rex v. Mutumah*, charged with administering poison with intent to murder, report of government bacteriologist, W. Watkins Pitchford, 1907.

[56]  PAR, AGO, I/1/330/1/1908, Supreme Court Criminal Cases, *Rex v. Ramanah*, charged with attempting to administer poison with intent to murder, or otherwise attempting to administer poison with intent to do some grievous bodily harm, 1908.

would, in fact, form a medicinal dose and about six pints would be required to produce a fatal effect.[57]

The trial was initially scheduled for 8 January, but owing to the absence of material witnesses, Vaughan Williams, who represented the state, requested that it be adjourned to March. Between January and March, Ramanah remained in the custody of the state until 8 March, when he pleaded not guilty and attempted to represent himself in opposition to G. E. Robinson, who was the new state prosecutor. The evidence brought forward in the court case showed that besides being the only servant of three employed by the Marsdens to service the home, a bottle containing some HCl was found in a biscuit tin under Ramanah's bed, in the room he shared with Sukhai, the 'garden boy'.[58] Sukhai's deposition stated:

> I am indentured to Mr Marsden and accused is a fellow servant. I remember the police coming and searching the premises. I saw the drugs found in accused's box. I do not work in the house of my master, but only in the garden. I know nothing about the poison that has been put in my master's bottles. I occupy the same room as accused. I do not know to whom the drugs found in accused's box belong. The native has a room of his own; he does not come into our room. I did not put the poison into my master's water bottles. I have been with the accused in the same room about 10 months. I saw the drugs for the first time when the detectives found them. We used not to keep our room locked, but since the searching of the room, I have provided myself with a lock. Whenever we were intending to be absent from our room for any time we used to secure our door with a string. The productions now on the table are the drugs which I have referred to. I have never seen the accused use the contents of the bottle. The native servant Gwebu used not to come to our quarters, and he used not to ask me for rice and other articles. Neither did he threaten to beat me at any time. I have never at any time heard the native Gwebu ask accused for rice or other article, nor have I ever heard him threaten accused.[59]

---

[57] PAR, RSC, 1/1/99/3/1908, Supreme Court Criminal Cases, *Rex v. Romanah*, charged with attempting to administer poison with intent to murder, or otherwise attempting to administer poison with intent to do some grievous bodily harm, 1908. The spelling of Ramanah's name in the records of the Supreme Court is slightly different with an 'o' taking the place of an 'a'.

[58] PAR, RSC, 1/1/99/3/1908, Supreme Court Criminal Cases, *Rex v. Romanah*, charged with attempting to administer poison with intent to murder, or otherwise attempting to administer poison with intent to do some grievous bodily harm, 1908.

[59] PAR, AGO, I/1/330/1/1908, Supreme Court Criminal Cases, *Rex v. Ramanah*, charged with attempting to administer poison with intent to murder, or otherwise attempting to administer poison with intent to do some grievous bodily harm, deposition of Sukhai, 1908.

According to Nora, she first noticed that her water bottle had been tampered with on 12 October. She then decided to check the other bedrooms and found that the water bottle in her mother's bedroom had also been interfered with. She poured out most of the water from her water bottle but realised that she should keep some of the water. She knew that neither her mother nor her other sisters had put anything into the bottles and decided that she would observe Ramanah over the next couple of days to ascertain whether it was him or not. The very next day, after Ramanah had filled the bottles, Nora and her mother examined the water, and upon tasting it, they found that the water had a 'pungent, acrid, and bitter' taste and left a drying sensation in their mouths.[60] They decided to keep those bottles of water so that they could be sent to the government bacteriologist for analysing. Later that day, Nora detected a 'stinging smell' in the bedroom of her sister, and when she and her mother went to inspect, they found that the quilt had huge yellow stains.

When asked about their relationships with their servants, and if there was any animosity between them that could have caused Ramanah to behave in this manner, neither Herbert and Sarah nor Nora could think of any reason. There was only one occasion when Herbert had any trouble with him, and this did not appear to be the result of ill feelings between master and servant. According to Herbert:

> About two or three months ago, he came in the first thing in the morning, and he seemed to be demented and as laying his head on the tiles of the kitchen floor caught hold of a carving knife and made a pass at his throat. I took the knife from him and it was practically a day before he really recovered himself. He must have been taking some drug or the other.[61]

This incident, which supposedly indicated that Ramanah was suicidal and discontent with his situation, was used as evidence by the state in its attempt to establish a motive for the crime. Gwebu, the 'native servant', however, further elaborated on the story and stated in court that, on this very day, Ramanah had said that 'the whole lot of them were nasty'. Gwebu also stated that since he could understand a little of Ramanah's language, he had often heard him say that his

---

[60] PAR, AGO, I/1/330/1/1908, Supreme Court Criminal Cases, *Rex v. Ramanah*, charged with attempting to administer poison with intent to murder, or otherwise attempting to administer poison with intent to do some grievous bodily harm, deposition of Sukhai, 1908.

[61] PAR, RSC, 1/1/99/3/1908, Supreme Court Criminal Cases, *Rex v. Romanah*, charged with attempting to administer poison with intent to murder, or otherwise attempting to administer poison with intent to do some grievous bodily harm, 1908.

master 'was not a nice one'.[62] Ramanah, on the other hand, remained insistent that he did not feel any bitterness towards his master. In his closing statement, Ramanah stated:

> I came to this country to work. I have worked well. I have no complaint against my master or my mistress; neither have they with me. I have worked five years and three months. I do not know anything about the medicine; my master's children are always at home. When I go inside they always follow me into the rooms, and they could have seen me if I had done anything wrong. The biscuit tin was under my bed. I admit the tin was there. I do not know who placed the stuff in that tin. When the native servant comes into the kitchen, he wants me to give him sugar and other articles belonging [to] my master, but I have refused to do so. One day he said, 'I will see you one day', which I took to be a threat; he spoke in an angry tone. My door is always left open. When I go for a walk I generally tie up the door. I always had a good name for my employer. I have no complaint against him.[63]

Ramanah was found guilty and sentenced to three years of imprisonment because there appeared to be no direct motive in the form of revenge against assaults and ill-treatment, as had been the case for the other poisoning incidents. The jury was apparently convinced by Wilfred Pitchford's argument that the acid, in the form that it was found, would have been very difficult to acquire and therefore suggested that in all probability Ramanah has gone to some lengths to acquire it. Pitchford stated that despite the fact that diluted HCl was used as a medical tonic, it could not be bought without a doctor's prescription or for commercial purposes, as it appeared on a chemist's schedule of poisons. In this colony, it would have been bought on a small scale by plumbers and tinsmiths who used it to dissolve zinc in order to make what was called 'killed spirits of salts' for soldering purposes.[64] Pitchford concluded that from his knowledge, there was no apparent reason why Ramanah would be in the possession of the acid except

---

[62] PAR, RSC, 1/1/99/3/1908, Supreme Court Criminal Cases, *Rex v. Romanah*, charged with attempting to administer poison with intent to murder, or otherwise attempting to administer poison with intent to do some grievous bodily harm, 1908.

[63] PAR, RSC, 1/1/99/3/1908, Supreme Court Criminal Cases, *Rex v. Romanah*, charged with attempting to administer poison with intent to murder, or otherwise attempting to administer poison with intent to do some grievous bodily harm, 1908; PAR, AGO, I/1/330/1/1908, Supreme Court Criminal Cases, *Rex v. Ramanah*, charged with attempting to administer poison with intent to murder, or otherwise attempting to administer poison with intent to do some grievous bodily harm, deposition of Sukhai, 1908.

[64] PAR, RSC, 1/1/99/3/1908, Supreme Court Criminal Cases, *Rex v. Romanah*, charged with attempting to administer poison with intent to murder, or otherwise attempting to administer poison with intent to do some grievous bodily harm, 1908.

for soldering purposes and that if he had bought it from one of the druggists or chemists in the colony, such as Reed and Champion, there would be some record of it.[65] The fact that very little concentrated HCl was found on the articles from Nora's bedroom and that he had placed it on the soap, bed linen, towels, sponge and tooth powder accounted for very little, since Mr Robinson made it a point to prove that this was as a result of Ramanah's inadequate knowledge of the poison and desperate attempt to injure or cause the death of his masters and mistresses.

## Conclusion

Many authors have shown us that while middle-class households in the metropoles and white settler homes in India and parts of Africa were desperately dependent on domestic servants, they were also regarded as a threat and as strangers who intruded on the private and intimate aspects of a household. This has been illustrated in the case of Mrs Larkin with her box, who as a rule did not allow any of her servants into the dining room, and the Marsden family, who allowed only one of their servants to enter their bedrooms. In their roles as caretakers of the family, it was generally expected that house servants would be loyal and submissive. However, in the cases of Khan, Murugen, Ramsamy and Ramanah, the servants were not obedient but instead purportedly plotted to poison their masters and mistresses. Just as Genovese has argued, poisoning was one of the few means through which house slaves could avenge their frustrations.

In his book, *The Power of Poison*, John Glaister describes the nature of poisoning in relation to other forms of crime. He argues 'the innate character of the crime of homicidal poisoning demands subterfuge, cunning and, what is equally important, usually a period of careful planning, and also not infrequently the repetition of the act of administering poison'.[66] It is for this reason alone – that poisoning is based on premeditation and the fact that potential poisoners could commit the crime at any moment – that suspicions of these domestic servants were aroused and heightened and caused masters and mistresses to distrust their servants. Mr Larkin is an apt example of this in that despite assuming that the unusual taste of the water was cyanide, it was only as a result of the poisoning incident that occurred at the English household that he believed Mutumah had been responsible for administering the poison. The fact that she was found not guilty and that in all probability it could have been any one of the

---

[65]  PAR, II, 1/54/I358/1890, tenders, drugs etc. for the year ending 14 April 1891, 1890.

[66]  Glaister (1954), cited in Couzens (2005), p. 379.

ten Indians living on the estate suggests that white settler anxieties about the threat posed by domestic servants (both African and Indian) were predominant and hints at the larger fears about the unravelling of the hegemony represented by the master–servant relationship.

Because of the particularly calculated elements that poisoning entailed, the crime reveals a great deal about the feelings and circumstances of those who committed them. In her work on eighteenth-century Mauritius, Meghan Vaughn asserts that poisoning was the 'colonial crime par excellence', 'a crime of stealth' and 'a crime of the powerless'.[67] What is important is that the number of these crimes recorded in the Natal court indexes points to the more ubiquitous feelings of inequity and ill-treatment as experienced by Indian domestic servants at the hands of their white masters and mistresses. Consequentially, the trials of the court cases discussed in this chapter worked to establish whether aggrieved servants were resentful and acting out in defiance against the subjugation of indenture. In all cases examined here, state prosecutors worked tirelessly to establish reasonable malice aforethought. In cases of capital crimes, lawyers were obliged to establish or prove intent – alternatively *mens rea*, or guilty mind – rather than motive. In other words, the question of whether the accused intended to commit the crime, implying forethought vis-à-vis the reasons why they might have committed the crime, was of the highest importance in these court cases. To proffer a conviction, it was only necessary to prove intent, but establishing a motive was essential when sentencing was decided upon.

If read on a spectrum of resistance, poisoning is violent, subdued and clandestine. The crime of poisoning as seen by white colonials as an insidious and subversive act replicated and reinforced the rhetoric of settler panic and paranoia. However, poisoning also allowed domestic servants the agency to portray an outward acquiescence while exercising a way of subverting the system. In the face of daily repressions – assault, food deprivations, abusive language and insults, refusal of medical care, disallowance of pass permits and controls over leisure time – poisoning as a form of resistance for domestic servants carried with it the impetus to restore any semblance of dignity and autonomy that these indentured Indians held on to. This does not suggest that other crimes of physical and indecent assault, rape, theft, arson, and so on, were not also acts of resistance and agency, but rather that these crimes were situated at varying points on a continuum of violent interactions between masters, mistresses and servants and that each possessed its own performative terrain.

---

[67] Vaughan (2005), p. 98.

## Bibliography

Anderson, Clare. 2000. *Convicts in the Indian Ocean: Transportation from South Asia to Mauritius, 1815–53*. London: Palgrave Macmillan.

Arnold, David. 2016. *Toxic Histories: Poison and Pollution in Modern India*. Cambridge, UK: Cambridge University Press.

———. 2017. 'The Poison Panics of British India'. In *Anxieties, Fear and Panic in Colonial Settings: Empires on the Verge of a Nervous Breakdown*, edited by Harald Fischer-Tiné, pp. 49–72. Switzerland: Springer Nature.

Badassy, Prinisha. 2018. '"Is Lying a Coolie's Religion?" The Household Sammys and Marys of Colonial Natal, 1880–1920'. *African Studies* 77(4): 481–503.

Bartrip, P. W. J. 1994. 'How Green Was My Valance? Environmental Arsenic Poisoning and the Victorian Domestic Ideal'. *English Historical Review* 109(433): 891–913.

Bell, Gail. 2001. *The Poison Principle: A Memoir of Family Secrets and Literary Poisonings*. London: Macmillan Publishers.

*Census Report of the Colony of Natal 17th April 1904*. 1905. Presented to His Excellency the Governor of Natal, June. Pietermaritzburg: P. Davis & Sons, Government Printers.

Cotton, Sarah Mitchell. 1997. 'Bodies of Knowledge: The Influence of Slaves on the Antebellum Medical Community'. MA thesis, Virginia Polytechnic Institute and State University, Blacksburg, VA.

Couzens, Tim. 2005. *Murder at Morija: Faith, Mystery and Tragedy on an African Mission*. Charlottesville: University of Virginia Press.

Flanagin, Annette. 1989. 'Stramonium Poisoning'. *JAMA: Journal of the American Medical Association* 262(5): 687–691.

Flint, Karen. 2001. 'Negotiating a Hybrid Medical Culture: African Healers in Southeastern Africa from the 1820s to 1940s'. PhD thesis, University of California.

Genovese, Eugene. 1976. *Roll, Jordan, Roll: The World That Slaves Made*. New York: Vintage Books.

Glaister, John. 1954. *The Power of Poison*. London: Christopher Johnson.

Helwig, David. 1999. 'Ontario Police Warn of Jimson Weed Dangers'. *Canadian Medical Association Journal* 161(11): 1384.

Hughes, Heather. 2007. '"The Coolies Will Elbow Us Out of the Country": African Reactions to Indian Immigration in the Colony of Natal, South Africa'. *Labour History Review* 72(2): 155–168.

Krenzelok, E. P., T. D. Jacobsen and J. M. Aronis. 1995. 'Jimsonweed (*Datura Stramonium*) Poisoning and Abuse: An Analysis of 1,458 Cases'. *Journal of Toxicology: Clinical Toxicology* 33(5): 500–501.

Livingstone, Douglas. 1991. 'Scourings at Station 19'. In *A Littoral Zone*, p. 47. Cape Town: Carrefour.

Marks, Shula. 1987. *Not Either an Experimental Doll: The Separate Worlds of Three South African Women*. Bloomington: Indiana University Press.

Marriner, Brian. 1991. *Forensic Clues to Murder: Forensic Science in the Art of Crime Detection*. London: Arrow Books Limited.

Meer, Y. S. (ed.). 1980. *Documents of Indentured Labourers, 1852–1917*. Durban: Institute of Black Research.

Parle, Julie. 2007. *States of Mind: Searching for Mental Health in Natal and Zululand, 1868–1918*. Pietermaritzburg: University of KwaZulu-Natal Press.

Scott, James. 1985. *Weapons of the Weak: Everyday Forms of Peasant Resistance*. New Haven, CT: Yale University Press.

Steenkamp, P. A., N. M. Harding, F. R. van Heerden and B-E van Wyk. 2004. 'Fatal Datura Poisoning: Identification of Atropine and Scopolamine by High Performance Liquid Chromatography/Photodiode Array/Mass Spectrometry'. *Forensic Science International* 145(1): 31–40.

Vahed, Goolam. 2014. 'Power and Resistance: Indentured Labour in Colonial Natal, 1860–1911'. In *Resistance and Indian Indenture Experience: Comparative Perspectives*, edited by Maurits S. Hassankhan, Brij V. Lal and D. Munro, pp. 95–120. New Delhi: Manohar.

Vaughan, Megan. 2005. *Creating the Creole Island: Slavery in Eighteenth-Century Mauritius*. Durham, NC: Duke University Press.

Watson, Katherine. 2004. *Poisoned Lives: English Poisoners and their Victims*. London: Hambledon and London Limited.

Wood, John Medley. 1895. 'Poisonous Plants of Natal'. In *The Natal Almanac, Directory and Yearly Register*. Pietermaritzburg: P. Davis & Sons.

# 3

# Labour Resistance in Indenture Plantations in the Assam Valley

*Rana Pratap Behal*

## The Growth of the Tea Industry

The tea industry was the earliest commercial enterprise established by private British capital in the Assam Valley in the 1840s. It grew spectacularly during the last quarter of the nineteenth century and continued to expand in the first half of the twentieth century. Tea production increased from 6,000,000 pounds in 1872 to 75,000,000 pounds in 1900, and the area under tea cultivation expanded from 27,000 acres to 204,000 acres.[1] From the mid-1860s, labour for the Assam Valley plantations was mobilised under the indenture system. Employment in the Assam Valley tea plantations increased from 107,847 employees in 1885 to 247,760 in 1900.[2] At the end of colonial rule, the Assam Valley tea plantations employed nearly half a million labourers out of a total labour population of over three quarters of a million, more than 300,000 acres were under tea cultivation (with a million acres under the control of the tea companies) and 397 million pounds of tea were being produced.[3] The important features of this plantation enterprise were the monopolitic control of private British capital, production for a global market and the employment of a migrant labour force recruited and transported under indenture contracts from different parts of British India.

## The Indentured Labour Regime

Having failed to 'persuade' the indigenous communities of Assam to work in the plantations, the planters brought labour from other parts of the Indian subcontinent. Recruitment was arranged by British managing agencies based in Calcutta through a hierarchy of local intermediaries known, for example,

---

[1] Appendices in Behal (2014).

[2] *Report of the Assam Labour Enquiry Committee* (1906).

[3] Behal (2014).

as *arkattis* and *sirdars*. This mobilisation was described at the time as the 'coolie trade'. Through a process of recruitment, transportation and employment, the colonial plantation regimes transformed Indian agrarian communities into labouring 'coolies'. During the course of this transformation, their castes and their religious, regional, social and cultural diversities were homogenised under the disparaging term 'coolie', which was universally used by planters in plantations around the globe and the colonial bureaucracy. Individuality was subsumed within anonymous 'gangs' and 'muster rolls' and only survived in the plantation 'coolie lines' for the duration of their working lives. Labourers were converted into what James Duncan has described as 'abstract bodies ... that are made docile, useful, disciplined, rationalised, and controlled sexually'.[4]

Another common and significant feature of plantation life under the indenture regime was the immobilisation of the labour force upon arrival. Their freedom of contact with the outside world was severely curbed. The nature of the work and the frenetic pace of expansion within the tea industry during the second half of the nineteenth and the early decades of the twentieth centuries made a residential labour force compulsory. When faced with the challenge of 'absconding' and 'deserting' labourers, the planters used legal, extra-legal and economic coercion as a means to control and retain their workers. The penal contract and right of private arrest given to the planters under the indenture system became instruments of immobilisation. These strategies of control were enforced through a hierarchical power structure centred around the managerial authority of European planters and their native assistants.[5]

A further characteristic of British capitalist plantations was the extraction of hard labour at low wages. Most British capitalist Assam plantation enterprises remained solvent and highly profitable despite regular fluctuations in the price of tea in the global markets throughout the nineteenth and twentieth centuries. This was achieved through the strategy of over-tasking work at low wages, very often lower than the statutory minimum under the contract. Working hours and task specifications were at the discretion of the planters, and despite the provisions of the labour laws, they extracted excess labour by giving extra tasks and prolonging the working day. The consequences of overwork and poor wages were malnutrition and high rates of sickness and mortality among the migrant Indian labour force.[6]

---

[4] Duncan (2002).

[5] Behal (2007).

[6] Behal (2014), ch. 5.

The dominant image of the European capitalist plantation as an authoritarian institution is universally acknowledged. The use of brutal physical punitive devices such as flogging to tame and control workers was well known among contemporary critics and supporters of indenture plantation regimes in European metropolises and colonial power centres. That indentured labourers were subjected to physical, economic and sexual coercion might have been overlooked or underplayed in these circles, but it was not denied. This was true even among the highest level of colonial official hierarchies. Some labelled it slavery and others perceived it as paternalism.[7] Revisionists may underplay but do not deny the use of extra-legal and coercive methods of labour extraction by the European planters. Furthermore, employed under penal contracts, the labourers were totally dependent on the employer for simple amenities and the necessities of everyday life, providing an opportunity for the planters to establish unquestioned control over them. This hierarchy based on coercion and extra-legal authority and aided and abetted by the colonial state was to dominate production relations in the Assam Valley tea plantations for over a century.

The colonial state overlooked the use of extra-legal methods by planters against their labour force and even reinforced their authority through legislative devices. The Assam Contract Act VI of 1865 introduced the penal indenture contract, which remained formally in force in the Assam Valley tea plantations until 1926, undergoing periodic modifications in 1870, 1873, 1882, 1901 and 1908. The penal contract stipulated a differential minimum monthly wage – 5 rupees for men, 4 rupees for women and 3 rupees for children – a five-year contract term, a nine-hour workday and the appointment of an inspector of labour empowered to cancel labour contracts on complaints of ill-treatment. The main provision of the Act lay in the sanctions for breach of contract by labourers: planters were given powers to arrest 'absconding' labourers without a warrant within the limits of the districts. Non-compliance with the terms of the contract by labourers was considered a criminal offence punishable by imprisonment. If convicted under this provision, the period of imprisonment was to be added to the term of the contract.[8] The indenture system was further modified and strengthened with the passing of the Labour Districts Emigration Act I of 1882, which was designed to serve the need of planters to regulate and control an expanding labour force.[9] The granting of such extraordinary powers and the introduction of penal clauses were justified on grounds of the 'exceptional' circumstances of Assam.

---

[7]  Behal (2010).

[8]  Das (1931).

[9]  Behal and Mohapatra (1992).

Stuart Bayley, the chief commissioner of Assam and later a member of the viceroy's council, put forward this argument: '[C]ircumstances of tea gardens are still so far exceptional as to require exceptional treatment and exceptional legislation to regulate the relations between the planter and his labour.'[10] The difficult conditions for planters included poor means of communication, geographical isolation from the administrative centres and the 'tardiness' and 'inefficiency' of the local police. The labourers, on the other hand, it was argued, were ensured a minimum wage, housing and medical facilities and subsidised rice.

The special official enquiries carried out in 1868, 1874, 1901 and 1906 and the annual reports on immigrant labour in Assam revealed that statutory minimum wages to indentured labour in Assam were not paid, recruitment abuses flourished and appalling transportation, living and working conditions continued to result in the high mortality of the labour force. The 'protective' provisions for labourers within Act I of 1882 often remained unimplemented. The office of the protectorate continued to be ineffective, using the excuse that many of them lacked knowledge, and the distant locations of the plantations were an impediment to their inspections.[11]

In the coming decades, physical and economic coercion, confinements, judicial discrimination, lack of freedom of mobility within and outside the gardens, low wages, malnutrition, disease, high mortality and non-reproduction (as a consequence of high death and low birth rate) were the characteristic features and harsh realities of life on the plantations. Wages below subsistence level, often supplemented by wages in kind, defined the wage structure in the Assam Valley tea plantations.[12] These and the aforementioned attributes were specific to a plantation structure that operated in contrast to a viable free labour market. How did the labouring communities of Assam Valley tea plantations respond to the process of transformation hoisted upon them by their employers? The characterisation of the plantation workers through the eyes of the planters is central to these questions: Were they truly an ignorant, unintelligent body of men and women who resisted change and were prone to violence and immune to economic incentives as alleged by their employers and the colonial bureaucracy? Did they allow themselves

---

[10] Government of India (GOI), Department of Revenue and Agriculture, Emigration A, Nos. 68–72, December 1880, National Archives (NA).

[11] *Report of the Commissioners Appointed to Enquire into the State and Prospects of Tea Cultivation in Assam, Cachar and Sylhet* (1868), pp. 68–72; *Report on the Tea Industry*, in *Reports on Tea and Tobacco Industries in India*, Parliamentary Papers (PP), House of Commons (HC), vol. 48, no. C.982 (1874), p. 24; *Annual Report on Labour Immigration into Assam* (1901).

[12] Behal (2003).

to be tamed, disciplined and controlled by their employers without resistance? We shall look for answers in the following discussions.

## Resistance

For any act of defiance and resistance by labourers, punitive measures such as flogging and confinement became a normal practice in the tea estates. The planters perceived the labouring tribal and semi-aboriginal communities as inherently inferior humans. This attitude was akin to that of the white masters towards their black slave labour in the antebellum era in southern America. The British tea planters established an omnipotent, super authority over their labour force within what has been termed as a 'paternalistic' framework.[13] They considered intervention in the social and personal lives of labourers as part of their 'paternalist' obligation.[14]

Within the boundaries erected by the plantation regime to tame and discipline them, the labourers expressed their protests in varied forms over time. During the indenture period, acts of resistance included desertions and what the official reports termed riots, assaults, intimidations and unlawful assemblies. There were also cases of strikes, but these were not recognised as such in official reporting. These acts of resistance were both individual and collective and often led to violence being committed by workers in retaliation against extreme forms of physical and economic coercion and other indignities. Economic grievances were important factors provoking workers' actions; yet demands for social and cultural rights were equally significant. Protests against the sexual exploitation of women were a regular occurrence.

## Desertion

The earliest reference to resistance was to the actions of the Cacharee labourers in the Assam Company's garden in 1859. They struck work, demanding a raise in their wages.[15] Rejecting the rhythm of plantation life, most commonly by running away, was one of the most important forms of resistance by the migrant workers, and under the labour laws it was a criminal offence. Desertion symbolised the repudiation of the relationship of servitude that the emigrants had been coerced into under the indenture regime. It could be both an individual and a collective act

---

[13]  Behal (2010).

[14]  Griffiths (1967), p. 376.

[15]  Antrobus (1957), pp. 97–98.

and is comparable to what Peter Wood described in relation to slaves in eighteenth-century South Carolina as the act of 'stealing themselves'.[16] The effort, courage and risk involved in this act reflected the intense desire of the runaways to reject a life of subordination. Prior to 1865, a deserter from the tea gardens, if caught, was punished under Section 492 of the Indian Penal Code and sentenced to one month's imprisonment.[17] In addition, there was an elaborate and cruel system of deterrent punishment. Once caught, many deserters were tied up and flogged by the planters, and the reward paid to their captors was deducted from their future earnings.[18] Yet severe flogging could mean no future earnings at all: 'often runaways, enfeebled by their sufferings in the jungles, died under or from the effect of the floggings they received when caught'.[19]

The act of desertion was not easy in itself. Serious efforts were made to prevent desertions, and it was extremely difficult to succeed in running away. Chowkidars, or watchmen, kept close surveillance over the labourers' living quarters, and it was reported that hill men were specially employed to track down 'absconders' with a promise of a reward of 5 rupees per head. Dogs also seemed to have been specially trained for this purpose in practices reminiscent of the slaves tracked down by dogs in the British-owned plantations of Jamaica during the seventeenth century.[20] In the tradition of the slave owners of South Carolina, the Assam tea planters had an organised system of recovering deserters through advertisements in market town posters and newspapers.[21] However, the severity of the hardships undergone and the potential punishments did not substantially deter deserters, and the scale of desertions did not diminish, as is clear from the official reports.

Those who could not 'steal themselves away' did adopt strategies to resist day-to-day work under coercion. These included shirking and sabotaging the work process and schedule. George Barker, a planter in Assam, recalled his recipe for dealing with 'shirking' labourers in his garden during the 1880s:

> Various forms of punishment – from a good thrashing to making him do two or three times the amount [of work] over again – are inflicted, but always with the same after-result, that if an opportunity presents itself he will invariably adopt all the

---

[16] Wood (1974), p. 239.

[17] *Report of the Commissioners* (1868), p. 50; PP, HC, vol. 48, no. C.982 (1874); Akhtar (1939), p. 42.

[18] PP, HC, vol. 48, no. C.982 (1874), p. xxi.

[19] PP, HC, vol. 48, no. C.982 (1874), p. xxi.

[20] Dunn (1972), p. 248.

[21] Wood (1974), pp. 239–242.

devices of which he is master (and they are many) to shirk his work; a result, I regret to say, that is not entirely confined to the black labourer.[22]

Reminiscing on his days in the plantations, another planter, W. M. Fraser, recollected his experiences during the 1890s as a senior manager chastising women labourers for faulty leaf plucking: 'The ground become strewn with bad leaf, while from one woman to the other went the admonishing Thomson, his tongue and hands fully employed.'[23] In another case, F. A. Hetherington, a young assistant manager, recorded the punishment he had inflicted on women labourers for plucking bad leaf on 1 August 1901: 'Went round the new lines plucking and nearly caused a riot by clouting three women.... They were plucking into *kapre*, which was strictly forbidden.'[24]

## Official Perception

Very often information on incidents of protest and resistance in the tea gardens was deliberately suppressed in official reporting in order to present a picture of well-being and harmony. Reports frequently invoked the low level of prosecution under the penal law as a sign of the good relations prevailing on the plantations. However, despite the efforts to project labour relations as harmonious, the growing number of episodes of rioting, mobbing, assaults and unlawful assembly displayed a different reality. In 1901, the chief commissioner observed that there was a considerable increase in general 'criminality' amongst tea-garden labourers.[25] In 1903, instances of serious conflict between European planters and the labour force were numerous enough to merit the attention of the governor-general, George Curzon, who wrote that 'the number of assault cases are steadily increasing in Assam and the relations between masters and coolies in many plantations are becoming a public danger'.[26] On Curzon's insistence, a detailed report on the question of relations between the employers and labour was prepared and submitted. The details given in this report provide us with a range of factors that provoked resistance from the labourers and dictated the nature and extent of the punishment meted out to them. From the report, it appears that acts of violence, both minor and serious, committed by labourers against managers and assistant

---

[22]  Barker (1884), p. 130.

[23]  Fraser (1935), p. 15.

[24]  Hetherington (1994), p. 24.

[25]  *Annual Report on Labour Immigration into Assam* (1901), p. 12.

[26]  GOI, Department of Revenue and Agriculture, Emigration A, No. 11, November 1903, NA.

managers were retaliatory in nature. The issues at the root of some cases were economic – for examples, low wages, deductions for short work, denial of rice as a part of wage in kind, extraction of excessive work, and so on. In other cases, the primary causes were anger against physical coercion, confinement and indignities such as public caning, flogging, beating (sometimes causing death) and insults. There were also instances of violence against managers and assistant managers in retaliation to the sexual harassment of women labourers and severe chastisement for drunkenness.[27]

## Awareness of Rights and Solidarity

Contrary to the stereotype of the 'ignorant' and 'helpless' labourer, the migrant workforce often showed a great deal of awareness of their rights. On many occasions, they tried – even if unsuccessfully – to go up to the offices of deputy commissioners en masse to register their complaints against maltreatment and the extraction of excess work by their managers, demanding redressal of their grievances and sometimes threatening action. As early as 1866, in relation to a case of flogging of labourers on the charge of desertion at Serajoolee tea garden in Darrang, Captain Lamb, the deputy commissioner, reported that the labourers were prevented from coming to his office to complain about ill-treatment at the hands of their manager and assistant manager.[28] In 1888, some female labourers were flogged in Mesaijan tea garden. As a result, a large body of them left the garden and came to the office of the deputy commissioner of Lakhimpur, H. W. Cole, to detail the abuses.[29] They persuaded him to order an enquiry, and the investigation, conducted by the district superintendent of police and Cole himself, found that the female labourers, Panu, Khumti and Sukhi, had been beaten and flogged for desertion and short work. They were tied to a post on the porch of the manager's house, with their clothes lifted up to their waists, and beaten on the bare buttocks with a stirrup leather by the orders of the assistant manager, Anding. In this instance, a rare occurrence, the labourers succeeded in getting Anding sentenced by the court to ten months of rigorous imprisonment and a fine of 450 rupees.[30]

---

27 Government of Assam (GOA), Revenue A, Nos. 77-17, August 1904, Assam State Archives (ASA).

28 *Papers Connected with the Coolie Trade in Assam or Elsewhere*, in PP, HC, vol. 50, no. 124 (1867), p. 2.

29 GOA, Revenue A, Nos. 77-17, August 1904, ASA, p. 12.

30 *Annual Report on Labour Immigration into Assam* (1888), p. 71.

In 1892, Cole reported that the 'tendency for coolies to come in numbers to complain in court appears to be increasing, and employers urge with justice that there should be a penalty for coolies leaving the garden when the procedure of section 134 has been complied with'.[31] This observation was recorded when the Rewa labourers of Khobang tea garden struck work and appeared at his office to complain about the extraction of excess work by the manager and lack of sufficient food. Many of them did not want to renew their contract either. He 'persuaded' them to go back instead of taking action against the manager and was soon informed of a 'riot' in the garden. In this case, the labourers not only assaulted the manager but also targeted the *hazira muhrriri* (supervisory field staffer) from the lower ranks of the plantation hierarchy, holding him responsible for payment of short wages. Eight labourers were sentenced to three months' rigorous imprisonment in this case.

Many among the district officials began to acknowledge the growing awareness of rights and familiarity with the provisions of the labour laws among the workforce in the tea plantations. The Labour Immigration Resolution of 1902–1903 observed:

> The coolies are aware that the conditions of their employment are regulated by rules, not by the bargaining of the market; the rules are unfavourable to them in some respects but favourable to them in others, and they resent any attempt to exact more labour than the rules warrant.[32]

P. J. Melitus, the commissioner of Assam Valley districts, however, did not think that labourers were knowledgeable about the rules. Yet he was aware that over the years and through experience 'round the rule certain local practices, or *dusturs*' had grown up in the tea gardens. The labour force had developed a sense of what was beyond the norms of these practices; any 'departure from *dusturs* in a direction unfavourable to them which they really resent'.[33] Cole also observed that over the past 10 years, there had been an increasing tendency among labourers towards 'unlawful assembly' and that the 'attitude of coolie towards his employer has deteriorated'. Among the various causes of this tendency among the labourers that he enumerated was 'a fair knowledge of the labour laws, gained by experience'. He further commented that 'the publicity and importance attaching to cases

---

[31] GOI, Department of Revenue and Agriculture, Emigration A, Nos. 8–13, December 1892, NA, p. 49.

[32] GOA, Revenue A, Nos. 77–17, August 1904, ASA, p. 12, p. 13.

[33] GOA, Revenue A, Nos. 77–17, August 1904, ASA, p. 12, p. 13.

between employers and employed, the frequent discussion in the press – European and Native – have not been without their result on the mind and attitude of the coolies'. Cole added a cautionary note, borne out of his stereotypical perception of the labourers, that while 'no one wishes to curtail a coolie's knowledge of the law under which he labours, nor his power to resist *bona-fide* oppression, but the danger lies in the coolie being an unthinking individual, easily led, especially in his cups, ready to resort to violence on insufficient provocation'.[34] D. H. Lees, the deputy commissioner of Darrang, also observed a deterioration of relations between the employers and their labourers. He attributed this to stricter discipline being enforced on many gardens and the extraction of excessive work 'in order to secure economy':

> Work on tea gardens has therefore become more irksome, and coolies, being now better acquainted with their rights, are more and more disinclined to endure the strict discipline under which they are kept. The growing dislike to work on tea gardens is shown by the increasing number of coolies who leave the gardens.[35]

Labourers did not always merely react to the planters' acts of violence; they also sometimes demanded certain social and cultural rights. At the Halimguri tea estate in Sibsagar district, it was reported that some Santhal labourers attacked the manager, James Begg, on the day of Kali Puja (the worship of the Hindu goddess Kali). They had demanded a holiday on that day, and the manager not only refused it but also tried to force them to work. Though the manager was not hurt, the court sentenced one labourer to six months' rigorous imprisonment, two to five months and seventeen to shorter terms.[36]

Labourers mainly acted in groups, rarely alone, and officials investigating cases of rioting, and so on, repeatedly pointed out that these often occurred owing to assaults by the European staff. Cole, the deputy commissioner of Lakhimpur, reported in 1900:

> Blows given by managers, or more commonly by assistant managers, to coolies, either for bad work or refusal to work, were the immediate cause of most of the rioting cases which occurred during the year.[37]

---

[34] GOA, Revenue A, Nos. 77–17, August 1904, ASA, p. 12, p. 13.

[35] GOA, Revenue A, Nos. 77–17, August 1904, ASA, p. 12, p. 13.

[36] *Annual Report on Labour Immigration into Assam* (1900), p. 23.

[37] *Annual Report on Labour Immigration into Assam* (1900), p. 22.

Referring to the reaction of the labourers, it was observed that in such cases the 'coolies have generally come up prepared to risk and sometimes go to the length of tempting the manager to strike them'.[38]

## Dignity

One of the most important issues around which the labourers were provoked to violent action was the indignity perpetrated on them by garden managers and their assistants. In 1890, a gang of 40 labourers at Silghat tea garden in Nowgong district assaulted the manager because he had beaten a woman labourer on the pretext of disobeying orders. While the manager was acquitted of the charge, 14 labourers were sentenced to nine months' rigorous imprisonment. In 1892, labourers assaulted the manager of Maduri tea garden, Sibsagar, because of the sexual harassment and ill-treatment of a labouring girl. In this case, the manager was convicted of wrongful restraint and simple assault and was sentenced to a week's imprisonment and a fine of 100 rupees. In 1893, the labourers of Boekl tea garden, Lakhimpur, attacked the manager and the assistant manager with sticks and bricks after a labourer was publicly caned. One labourer was sentenced to a rigorous imprisonment for six months and five others for five months.

The violent clash between coolies and the management of Rowmari garden in Lakhimpur district during 1903 was a typical example of overt conflict in the plantations. The ostensible cause of violence was the garden management confiscating the umbrellas that the coolies used while plucking tea leaves during the rains and forcing them instead to wear broad-rimmed hats (*jhampi*). The ferocity of the assault for an apparently trivial reason surprised the investigating official, and initially it was ascribed to their natural 'excitability' and to a few 'malcontents' who made the reversion from umbrella to a *jhampi* a matter of prestige. The next day, they all marched to the magistrate's court at Dibrugarh to complain about the management. It was a collective action seeking the redressal of their grievances, and they refused to work until the matter had been dealt with.[39] It must not be forgotten that such resistance was dealt with via extremely harsh punishments, ranging from long years of incarceration in prison to death sentences awarded to 'recalcitrant' workers by the judiciary. The urge to

---

[38]  *Annual Report on Labour Immigration into Assam* (1900), p. 22.

[39]  GOI, Department of Revenue and Agriculture, Emigration A, No. 11, November 1903, NA.

stand up against public indignities must therefore have had been an incredibly strong one.

## Cultural Traditions as Means of Resistance

The migrant labour communities kept memories of their social cultural traditions and practices alive to prevent them from being marginalised or erased. They grieved for their dead and deserted ones, celebrated their festivals and conducted their marriage and childbirth ceremonies in their traditional cultural and social forms. Dancing, drinking and music formed an integral part of these occasions. In keeping the memories of their experiences alive, these diverse labour communities helped themselves cope with the everyday life of grief and wretchedness. Both Barker and Crole (another planter), in their own cynical and convoluted ways, gave a graphic account of cultural celebrations among the labourers on the occasions of marriages and festivals. Barker described the three free days given to labourers in between the expiry of one contract and the signing of a new one, noting that the holiday was given to 'certain amount of debauchery'.[40] On every native holiday and on Sunday, when all work ceased, labourers went to make their weekly purchases at the *haat* (market). After the *haat* was over, the remainder of the day was given over to 'nautches and carousing' – a reference to traditional dances and singing. Referring to the festivals and marriage and birth celebrations, Barker commented:

> [T]he din is terrific, five or six tum-tums all along at once, mixed a varied assortment of discordant wails and the perpetual monotony of the curious droning noise, that forms the basis of all native minstrelsy. This *hullabaloo* (I know no other more appropriate term), kept up without a lull until two or three in the morning, forms a charming accompaniment to a restless night. Continual tum-tumming in the lines is at first, to the uninitiated, a source of maddening annoyance.[41]

While these dance forms, music and songs may have appeared exasperating, wild, weird and even sinister to the alien European planters, these forms of folk traditions carried and reflected the migrants' painful and deceitful experiences of recruitment and their harsh lives in the plantations. Some of the most popular songs – the Jhumur folk songs and dances – are still regularly performed. They are associated with Karam Puja (the most important agricultural festival

---

[40] Barker (1884), p. 175.
[41] Barker (1884), p. 176.

of tea-tribe communities of Assam) and occupy a very prominent place in the cultural life of the tea garden labourers of the Assam Valley. Karam Puja was, and still is, celebrated during the festive season of August–September and is followed by the festival of Vijaya (Dusherah) during November–December every year. Every Karam Puja is accompanied by a Jhumur folk dance.[42] Jhumur is a collective and composite piece and revolves around love songs based on the Radha and Krishna episode and is enjoyed by all ethnic groups of tea garden labourers.[43] According to Pashupati Prasad Mahato, the male and female dancers, accompanied by *dhol* and *mandal* (traditional folk musical instruments), generate a colourful social cohesiveness between the diverse social clusters of migrants. Recently put together and translated by Indian scholars, some of these Jhumur songs are self-explanatory in their contents. Within them, there is a description of the day-to-day life of exploitation, love, protest, and so on, among labouring communities in tea gardens. One of the famous Jhumur composers of Jharkhand, Uday Karmakar, from erstwhile Manbhum, composed a song in the last part of the nineteenth century that is still prevalent among the labour communities:

Paka Khatai lekhaeli nam

Re Lampatiya Shyam

Phanki diye bandu chalali Assam

Depughare maritari

Uthailele terrene kori

Hoogli sahare dekholi Akash

Mane kari Assam Jabo

Jora Pankha tanabo

Sahab dilo Kodaleri Kam

Dina Udaya bhane

Akale peter tane

Tipki tipki pareh gham

Our names were written in the permanent book. The recruiter, Shyam, deceived us and sent us to Assam. We were beaten in the depot-*ghar* (godowns where labourers were kept during transit). We first saw the sky in Hoogly town. We thought we would be engaged to draw fans in Assam, but the Sahibs gave us spades. We sweat while working.[44]

---

[42]  Sengupta and Sharma (1990).

[43]  Mahato (1990).

[44]  Mahato (1990), p. 140 (translation by Mahato).

The following Karma-Jhumur is still very popular in almost all the tea gardens:

Sardar bole kam kam

Babu bole dhari an

Saheb bole libo pither cham

Re Jaduram,

Phanki diye bandu pathali Assam

The Sardar asks for more work. The Babu abuses and the Sahib threatens to peel the skin of the back. Alas! Jahuram, you sent me to Assam by deceiving.[45]

It has been pointed out that the Jhumur songs and dances convey the aesthetic sense of the people. They communicate the life, joys and sorrows of the community. The authorship of the songs is not known as they are preserved by oral tradition. The language of the folk songs and folklore provide us with an insiders' view of life under indentured labour.[46]

## Protests during the 1920s

Labour resistance around the issues of wage levels and prices acquired new intensity during 1920–1922.[47] In these years, the numbers involved in plantation struggles surpassed all previous figures. Mass unwillingness to accept the indenture system became noticeable, and resistance took on an organised and distinctly political form. The intensity of the revolt was sufficiently alarming for the government to appoint an enquiry committee to investigate.[48] The qualitative difference between earlier labour unrest and the phenomena witnessed from 1920 was recognised indirectly in the language of the bureaucracy. With the termination of penal provisions within the labour legislation, the official terminology broadened to describe the collective actions of workers. Terms such as 'strike', 'disturbances' and 'exodus' were added to the older repertoire of 'unlawful assembly', 'intimidation', and so on. Between September 1920 and January 1922, a number of strikes, disturbances and riots were reported from all three districts (Lakhimpur, Sibsagar and Darrang) in the Assam Valley.[49] These events showed an increasing articulation by the

---

[45] Mahato (1990), p. 141 (translation by Mahato).

[46] Sengupta and Sharma (1990), p. 225.

[47] Behal (2003).

[48] *Report of the Assam Labour Enquiry Committee* (1921–1922), p. 1; *The Bengalee*, 29 June 1921.

[49] *Annual Report on Labour Immigration into Assam* (1920–1921).

labourers of their grievances and an identification of a hierarchy of exploiters. For example, in a number of cases, their targets of attack were not only the European but also the Indian staff. There were cases of the *keya* (Marwari) trader shops and weekly bazars being looted and property being attacked.[50]

The significant upsurge of labour unrest at this time needs to be explained. The planters and their spokesmen alleged that the ignorant and illiterate labourers were incited and influenced by outsiders who were part of the Gandhian non-cooperation movement. Colquhoun, the deputy commissioner of Lakhimpur, however, in discussing strikes in his district, stated, 'There is little or no evidence to show that the strikes were due to the influence of Congress agitators. In my opinion the strikes were mainly due to economic causes, i.e. the high cost of living.'[51] The the Assam Labour Enquiry Committee of 1920–1921 did not find any evidence of any direct link between the non-cooperation movement and the strikes of plantation labourers of the Assam Valley. Low wages and rising prices, combined with the extortions of shopkeepers and *babus* (clerical staff in the administrative office), pushed the labourers into direct action. The looting of *keya* shops and the attacks on the Indian staff by the labourers were a consequence of the exploitation and coercion practised by the former. The Enquiry Committee found evidence of doctor *babus*, shopkeepers and garden clerks extorting money from labourers in a number of gardens.[52]

## The Impact of Resistance

The labour revolts of 1920–1922, despite their intensity and extent, did not succeed in forcing the employers to accede to their demands. The main reason for this failure lay in the fact that these struggles remained isolated, and no linkages emerged between them. Although they coincided with a general mass movement in the province (in the form of the non-cooperation movement), these revolts were barely affected by it. As a result, no organised effort, either from inside or outside the labour struggles, could be constructed in order to pressurise the employers into considering the labourers' demands. In opposition, the planters were highly organised, influential and the most powerful commercial and industrial lobby in the province. The efficiency of their organisation was demonstrated when the state assisted them in the ruthless repression of the labourers' revolts.[53]

---

[50] *Report of the Assam Labour Enquiry Committee* (1921–1922), pp. 6–7.

[51] *Report of the Assam Labour Enquiry Committee* (1921–1922), p. 19.

[52] *Report of the Assam Labour Enquiry Committee* (1921–1922), pp. 9–16.

[53] GOA, Financial Department, Immigration Branch B, Nos. 20–112, March 1922, ASA, p. 221; *Annual Detailed Report of the General Committee of Indian Tea Association* (1920), p. 137.

The growing militancy among the labour force was not without its impact. The arbitrary power of private arrest had been subject to critical comments from Joseph Bampfylde Fuller, the governor of Assam, and Curzon expressed his unhappiness too.[54] Eventually, the government of Assam sought the complete withdrawal of its provision. These recommendations were reiterated by the Enquiry Committee, which led to the amendment of Act VI of 1901, called Amendment Act XI of 1908, that struck a blow at the penal contract system in Assam, dismantling the legal basis of the indenture system. However, the actual operations of the indenture system survived as labour continued to be engaged under Workmen's Breach of Contract Act XIII of 1859. It received its death blow only after the major labour upsurge of 1920–1922, which arguably led to its abolition in 1926.[55]

## The Post-Indenture Period until 1947

The official dismantling of the indenture regime allowed for larger and more organised protests to occur. However, the planters now proceeded to work out their own internal system designed to curb labour mobility within the tea districts. The planters' association adopted 'labour rules' and 'wage agreements' in order to prevent employers from engaging labour that had absconded from another garden without the permission of the previous employer.[56] Failure to observe this would result in the payment of compensation. That labour in the post-indenture era continued to be fettered, and denied mobility was recognised in Omeo Kumar Das' 1937 resolution, the Assam Tea Garden Labourers' Freedom of Movement Bill, which was tabled in the Assam legislative assembly:

> The freedom of movement of tea garden labourers is limited in a manner unheard of in any other industry. They are not allowed to go out of the estate whenever they want to do so. It is a common practice to engage night *chowkidars* to keep watch over the lines and prevent labourers from leaving the estates. The impression had been created in the minds of the labourers that they have no right to go out of the gardens of their own will. This constant restraint on their right of free movement has reduced them to a state of slavery![57]

---

[54] GOI, Department of Revenue and Agriculture, Emigration A, No. 11, November 1903, NA.

[55] Behal and Mohapatra (1992), pp. 167–168.

[56] *Royal Commission on Labour in India* (1931), vol. 6, part 1, p. 386.

[57] GOA, General and Judicial Department, Immigration Branch B, File No. 118, 1939, GIM, 49; *Assam Administrative Report* (1938–1939), p. ii; Guha (1977), p. 243.

## Exodus

The aforementioned tactics might have prevented the workers' struggle from crystallising into a unified and organised labour movement in the Assam Valley, but they adopted new strategies and forms of resistance. Riots, assaults and strikes continued to be reported, but the post-indenture period witnessed a new and novel form of labourers' resistance that was described in officialese as 'exodus'.[58] Exodus in the Assam Valley tea plantations referred to a large number of workers in one or more gardens leaving work and walking out of the plantations. Like desertion, exodus was a political act that consisted of the collective rejection of the imposed rhythm of life in the plantation regime. The shifts in the character of protest do not represent any ascending order or teleological sequence; they were often in response to the changing configuration of power and the historical context. While new and more organised forms of resistance were developing, older forms – such as desertion, 'unlawful assembly' and 'mobbing' – continued to persist into the 1920s. The newer forms of protest – for example, strikes and exodus – forced a broader recognition of all labour action in official reporting. The increasing intensity of labour militancy during the 1930s, in response to the sharp decline in wages due to the Great Depression of 1929–1930, paved the way for the emergence of trade unions in the Assam tea plantations. While in cases of desertion the workers defied the indenture regime that defined desertion as 'criminal' under the penal system, exodus represented a collective expression of utter rejection of the plantation regime.

## The Great Depression of 1929–1930

The Great Depression Depression of 1929–1930 caused a slump in the tea industry. A fall in demand led to a sharp decline in the export of tea, and the situation worsened when internal tea consumption also dropped. Stocks of tea piled up in both London and Calcutta, and prices fell. Consequently, profitability was adversely affected, and none of the companies declared dividends during 1930 and 1931. To combat this, the industry resorted to measures that sacrificed the earnings of labourers: direct wage cuts and control of production. The labourers reacted severely to the wage cuts. The district official for the Assam Valley tea gardens reported more than 20 strikes, specifically, over the issue of wages during the year 1931 alone. These strikes, which spread all over the Assam Valley

---

[58] *Annual Report on Labour Immigration into Assam* (1922–1923, 1923–1924, 1924–1925).

plantations, involved large numbers of labourers and lasted for periods longer than before.[59] The planters suppressed most of these strikes with state assistance.

## Organisational Activities

The formation of trade-union activities was a relatively slow process. Only in the late 1930s did trade unions emerge in their embryonic form in the Assam Valley tea plantations. The controller of emigrant labour reported in 1939 that there was 'an unusually large number of strikes, viz., 17 and much unrest'.[60] The number of strikes reported in another official report was much larger, namely 37, for that year.[61] A secret official document reported one Chota Nagpuri Association as early as April 1938. The central figure of this association was P. M. Sarwan, who was described as the moving spirit behind it. Its main objective was the amelioration of the welfare of tea garden labourers.[62] A few other labour unions were also formed during 1939 in the Assam Valley, although the available evidence tells us very little about their activities.[63] In most of the reported strikes in tea gardens during 1940, there is no reference to unions.[64]

## The Employers' Response

Regardless of the infrequency of unions, the intensity of the labour unrest alarmed the planters and the government. The government of Assam expressed its anxiety over the 'frequency of strikes and disturbances on the tea gardens in several parts of the province'.[65] The Indian Tea Association (ITA), the apex body of the tea industry in India, made anxious representations to the government, and the attention of the Labour Ministry was drawn to the need for urgent action in order to

---

[59]   Behal (2014); GOA, General and Judicial Department, Immigration Branch B, Nos. 1–15, 41–50, 108–124, June 1931, ASA; GOA, General and Judicial Department, Immigration Branch B, Nos. 71–64, September 1931, ASA; GOA, General and Judicial Department, Immigration Branch B, Nos. 16–26, December 1931, ASA; *Annual Report on Labour Immigration into Assam* (1931).

[60]   *Report on the Tea District Emigrant Labour Act* (1939), p. 386.

[61]   Rege (1946), p. 72.

[62]   'Fortnightly Report for Assam for the First Half of April', Home Political, 1938, File No. 18/4/1938, Poll, D.O. No. 260-C.B., NA, p. 1.

[63]   *Assam Legislative Assembly Proceedings* (1940), vol. I, ASA, p. 242.

[64]   Rege (1946), p. 72.

[65]   GOA, General and Judicial Department, Immigration Branch B, File No. 118, 1939, GIM, 49, p. 167.

maintain law and order.[66] The emergence of trade unions in the tea gardens, even in embryonic form, became a major concern for the ITA. The latter's initial response was the total rejection of the very idea of trade unions. It was argued that conditions in the gardens were fundamentally different from those in industrial areas: 'In most gardens the labour is simple and primitive, and if unions are started they would most probably be run by outsiders. In such cases the prevailing opinion is that they should be discouraged.'[67] However, by 1939, confronted with the new political situation of spreading nationalism and, more alarmingly, communist activities in labour politics, the ITA began to review and modify its strategies. Instead of total opposition, it was decided that a policy of conditional recognition of unions in the tea gardens would be followed. This policy remained on paper for the time being, as in September 1939 the colonial government imposed the Defense of India Rule at the onset of the Second World War. This suppressed the trade union movement in Assam for the time being.[68]

The early years of the 1940s were a setback for the labour struggles in the tea gardens and in Assam as a whole. The passing of the Defense of India Rule put a break on trade-union activities, restricting agitators in order to secure stable conditions for the war effort, and Dattaraya Varman Rege reported a definite reduction in the number of strikes after 1941.[69] However, worker discontent was still very much alive. As a consequence of the Second World War, there was a fantastic increase in prices that led to a sharp decline in real wages. Simultaneously, the tea industry's efforts to extract excessive work to meet higher production targets created a deep sense of resentment among the labourers. 'The economic conditions,' it was reported, 'are producing signs of discontent, both among regular labour forces and in Defense projects.'[70] Moreover, the labour struggle outside the plantations was moving towards the formation of a provincial-level labour organisation. The Assam branch of the All India Trade Union Congress AITUC was formed in 1943 and held its first conference at Dibrugarh on 28 November.[71] It became fairly active in the course of the next two years. The communist workers

---

[66]  *Indian Tea Association Report* (1939), p. 26.

[67]  *Indian Tea Association Report* (1937), p. 37.

[68]  *Assam Administrative Report* (1938–1939); Griffiths (1967), p. 384; Bhuyan and De (1978), p. 270.

[69]  Rege (1946), p. 72; Griffiths (1967), p. 384.

[70]  'Fortnightly Report for Assam for the First Half of April', Home Political, 1938, File No. 18/4/1938, Poll, D.O. No. 260-C.B., NA, p. 1

[71]  *All India Trade Union Congress Papers* (AITUC), 1942–1944, File No. 45, Nehru Memorial Museum and Library, New Delhi, p. 25

of the AITUC were also making efforts to establish contact with the tea garden labourers.[72]

The ITA, faced with these developments, adapted and adjusted its policies with regard to the emerging trade unions. It was forced to implement its earlier proposals on trade unions – recognising them but only under acceptable leaders who were willing to accept its terms and conditions. These terms and conditions dictated that the leaders were to have no affiliation to the Communist Party of India; the white-collar staff and labour were not to belong to common unions; and, finally, one-third of the garden labour force had to be paying members.[73] While remaining hostile to communist dominated unions, the ITA made an alliance with the newly formed Indian National Trade Union Congress (INTUC), a Congress party trade union that accepted its conditions.[74] The INTUC on its part assured the ITA that its activists would conform to 'legitimate' trade union activity and not upset the existing labour management relations.[75]

## Conclusion

From the 1860s onwards, the Assam Valley witnessed the growth of a plantation structure woven around the obnoxious indenture system. The planters wielded a kind of extra-legal authority over their labour force comparable to that of white masters over their black slaves in the antebellum era in southern America. Within this structure the workers were subjected to physical coercion and social control that severely restricted their mobility within and outside the plantations and isolated them from the outside world. Within the boundaries erected around vast, isolated spaces by the plantation regime to tame and discipline labour, workers' expressions of protest took different forms over time. During the indenture period, acts of resistance included desertions and what the officials termed riots, assaults, intimidations and unlawful assemblies. There were cases of strikes, but these were not recognised as such in official reporting. These acts of resistance were both individual and collective. While economic grievances were important provocations behind the workers' actions, there were other equally significant issues such as demands for social and cultural rights. One common and persistent feature was workers resorting to violence in retaliation to extreme forms of physical

---

[72]  GOA, 1943–1947, General and Judicial Department, File No. GIM 7, ASA; Behal (2007), pp. 153–154.

[73]  Griffiths (1967), p. 391; Guha (1977), p. 293.

[74]  Behal (2007), p. 154.

[75]  Guha (1977), p. 296.

and economic coercion, imposed indignities and the sexual harassment of female workers by planters. The labour communities sought to cope with their everyday lives of grief and wretchedness by preserving and practising their cultural and social traditions. Through the celebration of these, they resisted becoming tamed and disciplined 'coolies'.

The dismantling of the indenture system as a consequence of increasing labour militancy provided opportunities for more organised forms of protest. The years between 1920 and 1922 witnessed the increasing articulation of workers' grievances and more intense protests in the form of strikes. One immediate result of the 1920–1922 labour activism was the withdrawal of the final vestiges of the indenture system with the abolition of Workman's Breach of Contract Act of 1859 in 1926. Official withdrawal of the indenture system prompted employers to work out their own internal mechanisms in the form of 'labour rules' and 'wage agreements', which effectively curbed labour mobility within the tea plantations. While this might have prevented workers' struggles from crystallising into a unified labour movement in the Assam Valley, they still adopted novel forms of resistance, including exodus. Exodus, like desertion, represented a political act of mass rejection of the imposed rhythm of life in the plantation regime.

The shifts in the character of protests do not represent any ascending order or teleological sequence. They were often in response to the changing configuration of power and shifting historical contexts. While new forms of resistance were developing, older varieties continued to persist. Overlapping methods such as acts of desertion, 'unlawful assembly' and 'mobbing' persisted well up to 1920, when more highly planned protests in the form of strikes and exodus found recognition in official reporting. The increasing intensity of labour militancy during the 1930s, as a reaction to the sharp decline in wages during the Depression, paved the way for the emergence of trade unions in the Assam tea plantations. The imposition of the draconian Defense of India Rule by the colonial state at the onset of the Second World War might have initially constrained the activities of trade unions; however, more planned protests surfaced during the war years despite it. Once again the character of dissent was shifting – this time under the growing influence of communist activities. The impact of agricultural protest would now be felt in political decisions away from the plantation side, as planters, desperate to counter the looming presence of communism, forged alliances with the newly formed Congress trade union leadership under the backing of the Congress government.

# Bibliography

Akhtar, S. M. 1939. *Emigrant Labour for Assam Tea Gardens.* Lahore: Arafat Press.

*Annual Detailed Report of the General Committee of Indian Tea Association.* 1920. Jorhat: Tocklai Tea Research Centre.

———. 1939. Jorhat: Tocklai Tea Research Centre.

*Annual Report on Labour Immigration into Assam.* 1888. Shillong: Assam Secretariat Press.

———. 1900. Shillong: Assam Secretariat Press.

———. 1901. Shillong: Assam Secretariat Press.

———. 1921–1922. Shillong: Assam Secretariat Press.

———. 1922–1923. Shillong: Assam Secretariat Press.

———. 1923–1924. Shillong: Assam Secretariat Press.

———. 1924–1925. Shillong: Assam Secretariat Press.

———. 1931. Shillong: Assam Secretariat Press.

Antrobus, H. A. 1957. *A History of the Assam Company 1839–1953.* London: T. & A. Constable Ltd.

*Assam Administrative Report.* 1938–1939. Shillong: Assam Secretariat Press.

Barker, George. 1884. *Tea Planter's Life in Assam.* Calcutta: Thacker, Spinks & Co.

Behal, Rana P. 2003. 'Wage Structure and Labour: Assam Valley Tea Plantations, 1900–1947'. In *NLI Research Studies Series*, vol. 43. Noida: V.V. Giri National Labour Institute.

———. 2007. 'Power Structure, Discipline and Labour in Assam Tea Plantations under Colonial Rule'. In *India's Labouring Poor: Historical Studies c. 1600–2000*, edited by Marcel van der Linden and Rana P. Behal, 143–172. Delhi: Foundation Books.

———. 2010. 'Coolie Drivers or Benevolent Paternalists? British Tea Planters in Assam and Indenture Labour System'. *Modern Asian Studies* 44(1): 29–51.

———. 2014. *One Hundred Years of Servitude: Political Economy of Tea Plantations in Colonial Assam.* New Delhi: Tulika Books.

Behal, Rana P., and Prabhu P. Mohapatra. 1992. '"Tea and Money versus Human Life": The Rise and Fall of the Indenture System in the Assam Tea Plantations 1840–1908'. In *Plantations, Proletarians and Peasants in Colonial Asia*, edited by E. Valentine Daniel, Henry Bernstein and Tom Brass, 142–172. London: Frank Cass.

Bhuyan, Arun Chandra, and Sibopada De (eds.). 1978. *Political History of Assam, 1920–1939*, vol. 2. Gauhati: Government of Assam.

Das, Rajani Kanta. 1931. *Plantation Labour in India.* Calcutta: R. Chatterji.

Duncan, James S. 2002. 'Embodying Colonialism? Domination and Resistance in Nineteenth-Century Ceylonese Coffee Plantations'. *Journal of Historical Geography* 28(3): 317–338.

Dunn, Richard. 1972. *The Rise of the Planter Class in the English West Indies, 1624–1713*. Chapel Hill, NC: University of North Carolina Press.

Fraser, W. M. 1935. *The Recollections of a Tea Planter*. London: Tea and Rubber Mail.

Griffiths, Percival. 1967. *The History of the Indian Tea Industry*. London: Weidenfeld and Nicolson.

Guha, Amlendu. 1977. *Planter Raj to Swaraj: Freedom Struggle and Electoral Politics in Assam 1826–1947*. New Delhi: Indian Council of Historical Research.

Hetherington, F. A. 1994. *The Diary of a Tea Planter*. Sussex: The Book Guild Ltd.

*Indian Tea Association Report*. 1939. Jorhat: Tocklai Tea Research Centre.

Mahato, Pashupati Prasad. 1990. 'World View of the Assam Tea Garden Labourers from Jharkhand'. In *Tea Garden Labourers of North East India: A Multidimensional Study on the Adivasis of the Tea Gardens of North East India*, edited by B. Datta-Rayand Sebastian Karotemprel, 131–142. Shillong: Vendrame Institute.

*Proceedings of the Annual Meeting of General Committee of Assam Branch of India Tea Association*. 1920. Jorhat: Tocklai Tea Research Centre.

Rege, Dattaraya Varman. 1946. *Report on an Enquiry into the Conditions on Labour in Plantations in India*. Delhi: Manager of Publiations.

*Report of the Assam Labour Enquiry Committee*. 1906. Shillong: Assam Secretariat Press.

———. 1921–1922. Shillong: Assam Secretariat Press.

*Report on the Tea District Emigrant Labour Act*. 1939. Shillong: Assam Secretariat Press.

*Report of the Commissioners Appointed to Enquire into the State and Prospects of Tea Cultivation in Assam, Cachar and Sylhet*. 1868. Calcutta: Government of India.

*Royal Commission on Labour in India*. 1931. Calcutta: Government of India.

Sengupta, Sarthak, and J. L. Sharma. 1990. 'Jhumar: Folksongs and Dances of Tea Garden Labourers of Assam'. In *Tea Garden Labourers of North East India: A Multidimensional Study on the Adivasis of the Tea Gardens of North East India*, edited by B. Datta-Ray and Sebastian Karotemprel, 214–226. Shillong: Vendrame Institute.

Wood, Peter H. 1974. *Black Majority: Negroes in Colonial South Carolina from 1670 through the Stono Rebellion*. New York: W. W Norton & Company.

# 4

# A Forgotten Narrative of the Satyagraha Campaign

## The Treatment of Prisoners between 1907 and 1914*

*Kalpana Hiralal*

Under the leadership of Mohandas K. Gandhi, the Indian community staged the first non-violent mass movement in South Africa. This involved defiance of unjust laws, courting of imprisonment, boycotts, marches and strikes. In the Transvaal, then under British rule, 3,000 Indians, including more than one-third of adult males and even some children, went to prison and suffered privations between 1908 and 1911. Over a hundred were deported to Bombay and Colombo, often leaving their families behind without support. In 1913, the struggle extended beyond the Transvaal when nearly 40,000 workers, equivalent to over half of the adult Indian population of Natal, struck work. Almost 10,000 were imprisoned, some in mining compounds. Some workers were killed and many injured. Yet in the vast corpus of literature on the Satyagraha campaigns, the treatment of Indian prisoners, both men and women, has not been examined or documented fully.

Existing studies have focused mainly on the leadership of Gandhi and the socio-economic background of the Indian resistance in South Africa.[1] Gendered aspects of the struggle have mainly been documented through a feminist lens seeking to debunk the myth of docile Indian women in the diaspora.[2] Surendra Bhana and Neelima Shukla-Bhatt published poems written in Gujarati, English and Hindi during the movement and produced an interesting literary study of the struggle.[3]

---

* Certain parts of this chapter were originally published in and have been extracted, in a revised form, from Enuga Reddy and Kalpana Hiralal's *Pioneers of Satyagraha: Indian South Africans Defy Racist Laws, 1907–1914*, published by Navajivan Publishing House, Ahmedabad, in 2017. All rights reserved. Reproduced with the permission of the copyright holders and the publisher, Navajivan Publishing House.

[1] Bhana and Dhupelia-Mesthrie (1981); Beall and North-Coombes (1983); Swan (1984); and Guha (2013).

[2] Mongia (2006); Hiralal (2010); and Hiralal (2009).

[3] Bhana and Shukla-Bhatt (2011).

In addition, numerous biographies of Gandhi deal with the Satyagraha campaigns, but they are focused on Gandhi, his leadership and spiritual development.[4] However, none of the aforementioned studies has examined, in-depth, the prison conditions and treatment of *satyagrahi*s.[5]

Gandhi's *Collected Works* and the *Indian Opinion* are perhaps the only first-hand insights on the prison conditions of both men and women incarcerated in Durban and Johannesburg during the Satyagraha campaigns between 1907 and 1914. This chapter documents the treatment and impact of prison conditions on *satyagrahi*s between 1907 and 1914. For many resisters, the prison became a site of struggle; it did little to deter or diminish their resilient spirit. They became more defiant amidst the plethora of discriminatory laws and repeated imprisonment. In exploring the incarceration of Satyagraha prisoners, this chapter shifts the focus from the coloniser to the colonised, to the marginalised and subaltern groups, 'viewing them as important historical actors in their own right'.[6] Clare Anderson, in her study on the 1857–1858 Indian uprising, shares a similar trajectory revealing how prisons became 'sites of Indian resistance'.[7] Taylor Sherman provides insightful analysis by locating his study within the broader framework of state violence and punishment. Sherman alludes to the 'coercive network' of state practices, which consisted of fines, detention without trial and physical force, and how they functioned 'in tandem with prison' to 'maintain law and order'.[8] This chapter adds to the aforementioned discourses by providing insights into the state response and use of its 'coercive' powers in the context of the Satyagraha prisoners during the campaigns of 1907 and 1914.

## Historical Context

In the mid-nineteenth century, the demand for cheap, sustainable and steady labour to serve the capitalist needs of the colonial plantations led to the import of indentured workers to Natal. After the completion of their five- or ten-year contracts, some either returned to India, whilst others settled in the colony. Many moved inland to the Transvaal, whilst others moved further south-west to the Cape. However, together with the 'passenger Indians' – those who arrived unencumbered by labour contracts – they threatened the economic interests

---

[4] Reddy and Hiralal (2017), p. 5.

[5] *Satyagrahi*s, or resisters, refer to those who participated in the Satyagraha campaign.

[6] Anderson (2007), p. 12.

[7] Anderson (2007), p. 14.

[8] Sherman (2010), pp. 4–5.

of the colonialists.[9] This led to a series of discriminatory legislations against the Indian community in Natal, the Cape and the Transvaal.[10] Frustrated, particularly by the efforts of the Transvaal government to curtail their economic and social mobility, Indians in the Transvaal, under the leadership of Gandhi, embarked on their first Satyagraha campaign in 1907. It was initially directed against the Asiatic Law Amendment Ordinance (commonly known as the Asiatic Registration Act), 1906, and the discriminatory provisions of the Immigration Restriction Act, 1907, which restricted the immigration of even former residents of the colony who had left during the Anglo-Boer War (1899–1902). The campaign resumed in 1913 when the courts declared non-Christian Indian marriages invalid, and the government failed to fulfil its promise to abolish the three-pound tax on former indentured workers, their wives and children. The struggle went through three phases: (*a*) Indians' decision to defy the Asiatic Ordinance made at a mass meeting on 11 September 1906 to the provisional agreement with general Jan Christian Smuts on 30 January 1908; (*b*) the renewal of resistance in July 1908 until the provisional settlement with Smuts in May 1911; and (*c*) from September 1913 to the passage of the Indians' Relief Act in June 1914. The first two phases took place in the Transvaal and the last in Natal and the Cape.[11]

In 1906, the Transvaal government published a draft Asiatic Ordinance requiring the Asiatics (mainly Indians and about a thousand Chinese) to register again, obliging them to provide 10 fingerprints and show the registration certificates to police officers on demand. This Ordinance was replaced by an Act of the Transvaal Parliament when the colony became self-governing in 1907. Community organisations, the Hamidia Islamic Society and the British Indian Association (BIA) organised a huge mass meeting on 11 September 1906 to protest against the Ordinance. At this meeting, the community took an oath to not register and even engage in protest action until the law was repealed. Soon after, the Immigration Restriction Act of 1907 was introduced, making it almost impossible for former Asiatic residents of the Transvaal to enter the colony.[12] The trading class in the Transvaal were seriously affected by this legislation; licences were refused to traders and hawkers unless they produced registration certificates. A settlement was reached between colonial secretary-general Smuts

---

[9] It was the 'passenger Indians' who were mainly a key economic threat, particularly in the retail trade.

[10] Natal, the Cape and the Transvaal were the main areas of Indian settlement. Indians were barred from the Orange Free State (OFS).

[11] Reddy and Hiralal (2017), p. 6.

[12] *Indian Opinion*, 31 August 1907.

and Gandhi in 1908, which stipulated that Indians would register voluntarily and would not be harassed by the police. However, the government did not repeal the Immigration Restriction Act, and the Indian community resumed resistance on 16 August 1908 and registration certificates and licences were burnt at a mass meeting. By late 1909, the number of *satyagrahi*s had dropped to less than 100. However, the government of the Union of South Africa still came under severe criticism from India and Britain.[13] Subsequently, a provincial settlement was reached in May 1911. Passive resistance was suspended, and the resisters were released from prison.

Satyagraha was resumed in 1913. Two significant issues arose during this period. First, the marriage issue developed when the courts declared in 1913 that marriages under religions that recognised polygamy – predominantly Hindu and Muslim marriages – were invalid in South Africa. Second, there was the failure to repeal the exorbitant three-pound tax on former indentured labourers and their wives and children in Natal. Given the seriousness of the grievances, the Satyagraha campaign in 1913 by the Indian community was on a much larger scale.[14]

Well over 20,000 men, women and children went on strike. In the Natal midlands, the strike commenced in the district of Newcastle in November 1913 and spread to several mines. Approximately 2,500 men left their work, and the majority headed for the Transvaal to defy the immigration laws. Indentured women in the mines, too, resisted and participated in the march to the Transvaal. The strike, by the first week in November, also spread to the coastal districts of Natal. On the north coast, it lasted for approximately four weeks; in the south, it was 'only a few days', whilst in one part of Zululand (Amatikulu), it lasted for a week.[15] There were no complaints or grievances against mine employers or the plantation estates; the main issue was the three-pound tax, which seriously affected former indentured workers. The strike affected between 17,000 and 19,000 indentured labourers and had severe financial implications, both for the economy and the personal well-being of the workers. It led to the loss of wages, exceeding 30,000 pounds. Monies were also withdrawn from the government savings bank and from employers, with whom many Indians deposited for safekeeping or investment. Many women who took part in the procession to the Transvaal sold their jewellery.

---

[13] In 1910, the four provinces – the Natal, the Transvaal, the Cape and the OFS – were incorporated in the Union of South Africa. South Africa became a self-governing dominion of the British Empire, and political power was transferred to a small white minority group.

[14] Reddy and Hiralal (2017), p. 8.

[15] Gandhi Luthuli Documentation Centre (GLDC), protector of Indian immigrants for the year ended 31 December 1913, 1107/463.

And, according to the protector of Indian immigrants, 'one couple spent as much as £20 in this way'.[16] Eventually, the government agreed to set up a Commission of Inquiry to investigate the grievances of the Indians, and most returned to work by the end of January 1914.[17]

## Prison Diet, Labour and Violence

The governments of the Transvaal and later the Union of South Africa resorted to severe penal measures to curtail Indian resistance during the Satyagraha campaigns between 1907 and 1914. The courts routinely sentenced the Indians to imprisonment with hard labour or imposed heavy fines. The majority chose the former. Durban and Pietermaritzburg were the key places of detention. Many Indians were willing to fight until the struggle was over and to continue to suffer imprisonment.[18]

One of the chief complaints from prisoners was the quality of food. They were served with mealie meal, pap and fat, which they found inedible, and they were subsequently 'left in a condition of semi-starvation'.[19] In September 1908, the resisters Ismail Juma, Valabhdas Patel and Moosa Ismail Adia complained to the chief warder that they were leaving the prison in a 'half-starved condition'.[20] U. M. Shelat, who served a six-month sentence from June to December 1909, was confined to a solitary cell and put on a spare diet of rice and water twice a day for refusing to carry slop pails. His weight plummeted from 139 pounds to just 110, becoming weak and worn.[21]

Many Indians requested ghee (clarified butter) – a staple Indian food – to be included in their prison diet, but their request was refused. They also complained about the discrepancy and unfairness of the food allocated in some prisons. Copies of diet scales were posted on walls, allowing all prisoners to see what rations they were entitled to. These diet scales varied from one prison to another in the Transvaal. The result was that whereas in some prisons ghee and rice were provided for, in others it was compulsory to eat crushed mealies with fat. In addition, there

---

[16] GLDC, Protector of Indian Immigrants for the year ended 31 December 1913.

[17] GLDC, Protector of Indian Immigrants for the year ended 31 December 1913.

[18] *Indian Opinion*, 10 October 1908.

[19] *Indian Opinion*, 17 October 1908.

[20] *Indian Opinion*, 3 October 1908.

[21] *Indian Opinion*, 1 January 1910. Shelat claimed that as a Brahmin he could not carry slop pails. He was subsequently penalised and placed in solitary confinement.

were also serious concerns raised by Indian prisoners – who were vegetarians – that the mealie meal that was given to them was mixed with animal fat.[22]

The chairman of the BIA, A. M. Cachalia, alerted the government to the aforementioned hardships. He argued that whilst mealie and pap were nutritious meals, they did not conform to the dietary habits of the Indians imprisoned: 'Mielie pap is not the national diet of Indians.'[23] Moreover, the consumption of fat was a slight to Indian cultural practices. Orthodox Indians, and in particular Hindus, were not allowed to consume animal fat, whilst Muslims could only eat from an animal that had been ritually slaughtered.[24] Cachalia also differentiated the *satyagrahi*s from the standard prisoners and said that 'these Indians are not strictly speaking criminals and belong in the opinion of the Association to the highest class among the Indian community in South Africa'.[25] Cachalia urged the government to change the prisoners' diet to include bread, rice, ghee and vegetables.[26]

It had become evident to the Indian community that the government was doing its utmost to make the lives of the resisters miserable, to 'starve Indians into submission by compelling them to accept a diet totally unsuited to their habits of life'.[27] The attitude and response of the government confirmed these suspicions. They remained steadfast, unsympathetic and unbending and issued an ultimatum: accept the current conditions or pay the hefty fines. Moreover, the director of prisons, A. Hanrette, argued that any changes to the prisoners' diet required government sanction.[28] Local newspapers were sympathetic and castigated the authorities for their defiant attitude. The *Indian Opinion* noted, 'There was no uniform policy regarding the prison diet. In Natal, in some prisons, Indians were given their national food; in another they have to eat or to reject mealie pap and fat.'[29] The *Rand Daily Mail* concurred, 'The complaint made seems to us to carry a good deal of weight.'[30] They reprimanded the government for their bias and prejudicial attitudes towards Indian prisoners:

---

[22] *Indian Opinion*, 17 October 1908.

[23] *Indian Opinion*, 17 October 1908.

[24] *Indian Opinion*, 17 October 1908.

[25] *Indian Opinion*, 17 October 1908.

[26] *Indian Opinion*, 17 October 1908.

[27] *Indian Opinion*, 3 October 1908.

[28] *Indian Opinion*, 3 October 1908.

[29] *Indian Opinion*, 31 October 1908.

[30] *Indian Opinion*, 31 October 1908.

[A] strict Hindu animal fat might be so objectionable that he would die rather than touch it.... There would be a great outcry if a European vegetarian in prison was forced to eat beefsteak or starve, or if a Hebrew was compelled to take pork or go without anything, or if a teetotaler was made to drink whisky and soda or else die of thirst.... The Indians might well be allowed their rice and ghee, whatever prison they may happen to be in.[31]

Forced hard labour was another serious complaint by the prisoners. This consisted of working long hours in the quarries and roads under dreadful weather conditions. This type of 'back-breaking' labour was a common penal measure sanctioned by the authorities to break the spirit of the *satyagrahis*. For example, Jhinabhai Desai fainted from hard labour in Volksrust prison in 1908.[32] Syed Ali, a trader, was sentenced in August 1908 to seven days in Boksburg prison with hard labour for trading without a licence. He recalls his experience:

On the 20th August the work given me was that of carrying and emptying closet buckets. I complained to the gaoler about this work, and I received a kick and slaps. I still persisted in my complaint, and told him that I would be glad to break stones but would like to be relieved from the work of carrying and emptying these buckets. I was then kicked again. I became helpless and I had to carry those buckets.[33]

However, it was the death of a young, 18-year-old resister, Nagappan, that inflamed public opinion. He was sentenced in June 1908 to 10 days of hard labour for hawking without a licence. Affidavits submitted by two resisters, Veeramuthu and I. A. A. Moodaly – who shared a prison cell with Nagappan – reveal the abusive treatment meted out to him. Their testimonies reveal that on 22 June, 10 prisoners were taken from the Johannesburg Fort Prison to a road camp, where their diet consisted of only mealie pap. Amidst the cold Transvaal winter, they were allowed only one blanket and a mat to sleep on. They were not permitted water for washing or cleaning their teeth. Nagappan became very ill on 26 June. He was also physically assaulted with a *sjambok* (a long, stiff whip made of leather) by one of the warders, and his health subsequently deteriorated. Veeramuthu, subsequently, sought the assistance of the chief warder, who ignored his plea to assist Nagappan and exclaimed, 'Let him die like the other b...'[34] In his emaciated

---

[31]  *Indian Opinion*, 31 October 1908.
[32]  *Indian Opinion*, 17 October 1908.
[33]  *Indian Opinion*, 26 September 1908.
[34]  *Indian Opinion*, 10 July 1909.

state, Nagappan was ordered by the chief warder to work on the roads. However, in a few days Nagappan died.

A state autopsy on Nagappan concluded that the cause of death was acute double pneumonia and heart failure. Still, the attending doctor, W. Godfrey, was not convinced that alone was a factor.[35] He requested that the registrar of deaths hold 'some sort of an inquest' and that the attorney-general be informed of the treatment meted out to sick prisoners at different prison compounds as '[i]n my opinion, the boy's death has been accelerated by the conduct of the gaol officials, if all is true'.[36] Gandhi reflected on the bravery of Nagappan:

> Winter in the Transvaal is very severe; the cold is so bitter, that one's hands are almost frozen while working in the morning. Winter therefore was a hard time for the prisoners, some of whom were kept in a road camp where no one could even go and see them. One of these prisoners was a young Satyagrahi eighteen years old of the name of Swami Nagappan, who observed the jail rules and did the task entrusted to him. Early in the morning he was taken to work on the roads where he contracted double pneumonia of which he died after he was released (7 July 1909). Nagappan's companions say that he thought of the struggle and struggle alone till he breathed his last. He never repented of going to jail and embraced death for his country's sake as he would embrace a friend.[37]

The Indian community was outraged upon the death of Nagappan and tabled a resolution at a mass meeting at the Hamidia Mosque in Johannesburg on 11 July 1909, calling upon the government to make an 'urgent thorough and open investigation' into the circumstances surrounding Nagappan's death.[38] These events merely fueled *satyagrahi* anger and mobilised resistance.

Resisters also complained of physical assaults and verbal abuse. Syed Ali described how he was forced 'to strip naked'; warders used 'abusive language' and threatened with a *sjambok* for defying orders and retorts as well 'kicked'.[39] His health deteriorated, and he suffered a chest infection and was 'discharging blood'.[40] The resisters E. S. Asvat and N. S. Pillay complained of overcrowded prisons and verbal abuse, besides physical torture. At times authorities even

---

[35] *Indian Opinion*, 10 July 1909.

[36] *Indian Opinion*, 10 July 1909.

[37] Gandhi (1961), p. 224.

[38] *Indian Opinion*, 17 July 1909.

[39] *Indian Opinion*, 26 September 1908.

[40] *Indian Opinion*, 26 September 1908.

considered erecting marquees and tents to accommodate the overflow.[41] One hundred and fifteen prisoners were huddled in a cell with a maximum capacity of 50; there were 40 prisoners in another cell that could only hold 25.[42] However, this was a deliberate act by the government because it sought to segregate the prisoners according to race. The director of prisons, Hanrette, noted that it was necessary, as 'it was not deemed correct to mix Indians with Native prisoners. The overcrowding was not, however, to an extent which might be regarded as a menace to health'.[43] He further added that there was no evidence of assaults and that no offence 'was intended' by the word 'coolie'.[44] He also cautioned the BIA to encourage prisoners to submit legitimate grievances during detention as it is 'somewhat more difficult for the Department to test the truth of the statements when the complainants are not available'.[45] However, the treatment of Indian prisoners continued to draw sharp criticism from the BIA, who were not asking for 'favoured' or preferential treatment but insisted that the authorities show compassion, humanity and respect towards those incarcerated.[46]

The treatment of Indian resisters worsened during the Satyagraha campaign of 1913. The failure of the government to validate Indian customary marriages and the removal of the three-pound tax led to a resumption of the struggle. In 1913, the struggle was on a larger scale involving former passive resisters, women, youths, and mine, railway and plantation workers. Many were arrested and sentenced to three months of imprisonment with hard labour. Men and women, as well as some children, served their sentences in Pietermaritzburg and Durban or makeshift prison compounds next to mines. Conditions were deplorable. Many of the complaints that plagued resisters during the 1907–1911 Satyagraha campaign resurfaced: overcrowding of prisons, physical and verbal abuse and a poor diet. During the 1913 struggle, resisters adopted hunger strike as a mode of protest against inferior food and unfair treatment in prisons. In the Pietermaritzburg prison, 60 men, including Parsee Rustomjee, Manilal Gandhi and Ramlal Gandhi, went on a hunger strike against the inferior quality of food and ill-treatment of prisoners.[47] Only after the government agreed to the prisoners' demands did the hunger strike end, and the 60 prisoners were moved to the prison in Durban where the conditions were no better.

---

[41] *Indian Opinion*, 10 October 1908.

[42] *Indian Opinion*, 19 December 1908.

[43] *Indian Opinion*, 19 December 1908.

[44] *Indian Opinion*, 19 December 1908.

[45] *Indian Opinion*, 19 December 1908.

[46] *Indian Opinion*, 19 December 1908.

[47] *Indian Opinion*, 10 December 1913.

The government carried out an internal investigation in the wake of the hunger strikes and found evidence of ill-treatment, but officials concerned sought to deny or undermine the complaints.[48] However, the superintendent of the prison acquiesced that ghee was of inferior quality and 'uneatable'.[49] Regarding prison clothing, second-hand or 'worn' clothing given to prisoners was 'unavoidable owing to the large influx of prisoners, and unfavourable weather for drying purposes', and insufficient allocation of blankets was due to 'climatic conditions and health reasons'.[50] The district surgeon, W. H. Addison, also concurred with the superintendent regarding the poor quality of food fed to the prisoners:

> The Indian ration consisting of brown bread, white bread, and thin porridge was good, fresh and wholesome food. The brown rice ration was good and wholesome food, but in my opinion might have been prepared a little better, as I found a few weevils in some of the tins. The ghee, as far as I could judge, without tasting it was good, but I disliked the way it was served up, wrapped in old South African Railway condemned papers.[51]

Women, too, did not escape the horrors of imprisonment. They formed an integral part of the Satyagraha campaigns, particularly in 1913. They were prevented from participating in 1907, primarily because of the conservative attitudes governing women's traditional roles. Gandhi alluded to the eagerness of women and the patriarchal attitudes that permeated Indian society: 'Some brave women had already offered to participate, and when Satyagrahis went to jail for hawking without a licence, their wives had expressed a desire to follow suit. But we did not think it proper to send women to jail in a foreign land.'[52] However, whilst they were not allowed to join the struggle, they protested in other ways. In July 1909, a meeting of Indian women was held in Pretoria (a predominantly Indian residential area) to protest against the arrest of approximately 70 passive

---

[48]  British Library (BL), Despatches on Indians in South Africa, Telegram, Prisons, Pretoria, to Superintendent, Durban, 2 December 1913, BP2/2 (20).

[49]  BL, Despatches on Indians in South Africa, the Governor-General to the Secretary of State, 31 December 1913, Report by the District Surgeon, Dr. W. H. Addison, Durban, 2 December 1913, p. 4.

[50]  BL, Despatches on Indians in South Africa, the Governor-General to the Secretary of State, 31 December 1913, Report by the District Surgeon, Dr. W. H. Addison, Durban, 2 December 1913, p. 4.

[51]  BL, Despatches on Indians in South Africa, the Governor-General to the Secretary of State, 31 December 1913, Report by the District Surgeon, Dr. W. H. Addison, Durban, 2 December 1913, p. 4.

[52]  Reddy and Hiralal (2017), p. 142.

resisters from the area. At the meeting, the women lamented the imprisonment of their husbands and sons – who were the primary breadwinners of their homes – and challenged the government to 'arrest them too'.[53] Their courageous efforts drew admiration from Europeans. Harriott S. Polkinghorne, a local white woman, described Indian women as 'brave' in their fight 'for liberty and just treatment in the Transvaal ... their splendid pluck and endurance, and bid them be of good courage, for in the end righteousness must prevail'.[54]

In 1913, the scenario was different, with many women going to jail. The three-pound tax and the non-recognition of Indian customary marriages made it impossible to isolate women from the struggle. These two grievous issues struck at the heart of Indian womanhood. They courted imprisonment by crossing the Transvaal border, hawking without licences and inciting labourers in the mines and railways to strike.[55] Many opted for imprisonment rather than paying the fine and were incarcerated in Durban and Pietermaritzburg. Bhawani Dayal and his wife, Jagrani, both resisters, were imprisoned in Pietermaritzburg. Bhawani recorded his experiences and those of many men and women detained in 1913:

Prison cells were dark and damp. Many cells were infested with 'blood-sucking bugs' which hardly allowed the prisoners to sleep in comfort. Prisoners were awoken at 3 a.m. in the morning to enter the latrines, followed by a bath. At 5 a.m. they were taken for breakfast. Breakfast consisted of black tea and mealie meal porridge. Their working hours were between 7 a.m. and 5 p.m. Lunch consisted of rice and beans or rice and curry. During supper they were given curry, hand-made bread and coffee. Only on Sundays non-vegetarians were given a small portion of meat. All prisoners were given two thin blankets, one to sleep on and the other to cover their bodies. Men were subjected to hard labour – breaking stones. They had to work under the supervision of prison warders who, at times were verbally abusive. If passive resisters slackened in their chores they were called 'coolies' and often whipped.

Jagrani, together with her one and a half-year-old son, Ramdutt, Valliamma Munuswami and Kasturba Gandhi, were all imprisoned in Pietermaritzburg. Women prisoners were treated very harshly. Often uncomplimentary language was hurled at the women inmates. They worked in the prison gardens planting carrots and other vegetables, which were used to prepare prison meals. The women prisoners used to wash their own clothes. Jagrani would often wash Kasturba's clothes while she attended to Jagrani's six month old son, Ramdutt.[56]

---

53  *Indian Opinion*, 10 July 1909.
54  *Indian Opinion*, 19 March 1910.
55  Hiralal (2009).
56  Reddy and Hiralal (2017), p. 169.

Imprisonment affected the health of many women, whilst other stories were more tragic. Some women found the mealie meal 'uneatable' and refused to eat. Kasturba Gandhi found prison a severe challenge and was not allowed to receive food from outside the prison. When she was released, she was physically weak and in poor health. Valliamma, a teenage resister, refused early release, despite her failing health. She died soon after release.[57] Prison conditions also affected the health of Bai Fatima and her mother, Bai Hanifa. Bai Fatima died at an early age.[58]

## Deportations from the Transvaal

Another form of punishment the government resorted to was deportations of 'illegal' immigrants. Initially, passive resisters were ordered by the courts to leave the Transvaal (if they did not possess the Asiatic Registration Certificate or permits) and were deported to Natal.[59] But almost all defied the orders or returned from Natal and were sentenced to hard labour, usually for three or six months. However, from October 1908, the Transvaal government began to detain and later deport resisters outside the country. Systematic deportations to India started in earnest in 1909 in collusion with the Portuguese authorities. 'Illegal' immigrants, even those with residence rights in Natal, were sent to Delagoa Bay and held there by the Portuguese authorities until they were deported to Bombay or Colombo.[60] These deportations were arbitrary and illegal, as individuals had no recourse before the courts. The cases were tried administratively in semi-secrecy, and there was no appeal to the Supreme Court. In January 1909, 11 Indians were deported from Krugersdorp to the Portuguese territory of Ressano Garcia. Amongst them were Ebrahim Moosa Dahya, Ebrahim Adam, Suliman Ismail, Ismail Acooji, Ranchodji Gopalji, Hoosen Nizam Mahomed Essack, Govind Dayal, Goolab Prag, Soma Mitha and Bhikha Keshav. Several of them had educational qualifications, were traders, hawkers, long-standing residents of Natal and the Transvaal, some as long as 14 years, and were forced to leave behind their families and dependents.[61] As alluded to earlier, these systematic deportations to India and the Portuguese territories were unconstitutional. They had a detrimental impact

---

[57]  Reddy and Hiralal (2017), p. 317.

[58]  Reddy and Hiralal (2017), p. 155.

[59]  Many of these resisters were from Natal who were defying immigration laws and were not in possession of the Asiatic Registration Certificate or permits to enter the Transvaal.

[60]  *Indian Opinion*, 26 March 1910.

[61]  *Indian Opinion*, 26 March 1910.

on individuals and their families and elicited hostile reactions from the Indian community. The *Indian Opinion* noted:

> Indians who are born in South Africa are being deported to India. Sons are torn from their parents, fathers from their sons and husbands from wives. Wage earners are picked up and sent away to India, leaving their dependents to God's mercy. Men who have been for twenty years in the Transvaal are being deported. Such cases are probably without parallel in the world.[62]

Deportations were a state reaction to continued defiance by Indians during the first Satyagraha campaign. The government was keen to quell any form of resistance and did not shy away from ruthless action. The *Indian Opinion* described these deportations as a process of 'hunting Asiatics out of the Colony', the resisters' only 'offence is that they value their freedom and conscience above everything'.[63] Moreover, the Indian community became increasingly frustrated with the British and Indian governments, describing their silence and inaction as 'callous' to the 'sufferings' of the Indian people.[64]

## Conclusion

The Satyagraha campaign between 1907 and 1914 was one of the significant resistance movements undertaken by a minority group in South Africa at the turn of the century. Challenging the might of the British Empire was no easy task, and the narratives in this chapter have highlighted how oppressed communities reacted to colonialism in Africa. Several key issues can be discerned from the narratives. First, prisons became another site for political resistance. Thousands were imprisoned, with the vast majority opting for prison life rather than the payment of fines. Prison conditions were undoubtedly harsh, but this did little to hinder the struggle. On the contrary, it was a small price to pay to reinstate the honour and dignity of the Indian community and the 'motherland', India. Second, resistance did, to some extent, forge a sense of collective 'sisterhood', albeit a limited one, amongst Indian women, who were diverse in terms of their migration status (indentured versus 'passenger'), origin, class, language, caste and religion.[65] These differences did, to some extent, polarise women; 'passenger Indians' were sometimes criticised for being an endogamous group, who married

---

[62] *Indian Opinion*, 19 March 1910.

[63] *Indian Opinion*, 19 March 1910.

[64] *Indian Opinion*, 19 March 1910.

[65] Hiralal (2010, 2009).

within their ethnic and caste groups and rarely socialised with those of the indentured class. Whilst the first Satyagraha campaign between 1907 and 1911 was confined mainly to the Transvaal and involved mainly traders and merchants, the movement of 1913 was on a larger scale, a collective effort consisting of men, women and children from various backgrounds: petty traders, hawkers, merchants, housewives, labourers, domestic servants, waiters, priests and teachers. In 1913, both the marriage issue and the three-pound tax, which affected 'passenger' Indians and ex-indentured women, respectively, cemented collective unity and resistance. Women joined the struggle, irrespective of their backgrounds, because both issues were an onslaught on their womanhood, violating their status as wife and mother. Women therefore identified as women and not as separate ethnic entities. This camaraderie endured during incarceration, but sadly not beyond; after 1913, class and ethnic prejudices prevailed and became firmly entrenched. Third, the Satyagraha campaigns between 1907 and 1913 did, to a degree, forge a sense of collective identity amongst the Indian community. Class and ethnic barriers temporarily dissipated, as alluded to earlier, as the Indian community fought as a collective. In addition, the defiant attitude and actions of the resisters are also indicative of how they perceived their place within South African society and their ties to India. The vast majority of resisters were either born in India or descendants of indentured laborers. For resisters like Nagappan and Valliamma, who were prepared to die for the 'motherland' (India), upholding its value and 'dignity' catalysed resistance even if it emboldens imprisonment. Valliamma had no regrets regarding her imprisonment and added, 'Who would not love to die for one's motherland.'[66] For Francis Coomarasamy and Solomon Ernest, 'We are ... doing our duty for our country's sake and national honour.'[67] Bai Fatima Sheikh Mehtab called upon Indian women to be 'patriotic to ... mother India' and participate in the 1913 struggle.[68] Gandhi's return to India in 1915 did not diminish the Indian connection. During the Indian independence, local newspapers such as the *Indian Opinion* kept the Indian community abreast of the Indian freedom struggle and the 'sense of belonging to the "motherland" was heightened as the nationalist movement grew in stature'.[69]

Nevertheless, the reactions and experiences of passive resisters differed, and some emerged from the struggle with a different sense of who they were within South African society. This chapter, focusing on the treatment of *satyagrahi*

---

[66]  Gandhi (1961), pp. 283–284.

[67]  *Indian Opinion*, 5 March 1910.

[68]  *Indian Opinion*, 23 October 1913.

[69]  Chetty (1991), p. 5.

prisoners, addresses an untapped narrative in one of the most significant mass movements in South Africa at the turn of the century. It also shifts the focus to the colonial state and the subsequent union government, considering their attitude and response towards oppressed groups fighting for freedom and justice.

## Bibliography

Anderson, Clare. 2007. *The Indian Uprising of 1857–8: Prisons, Prisoners and Rebellion*. London: Anthem Press.

Beall, J. D., and M. D. North-Coombes. 1983. 'The 1913 Natal Indian Strike: The Social and Economic Background to Passive Resistance'. *Journal of Natal and Zulu History* 6(1): 48–81.

Bhana, Surendra, and Neelima Shukla-Bhatt. 2011. *A Fire That Blazed in the Ocean: Gandhi and the Poems of Satyagraha in South Africa, 1909–1911*. New Delhi: Promilla & Co.

Bhana, Surendra, and Uma Dhupelia-Mesthrie. 1981. 'Passive Resistance among Indian South Africans'. Unpublished paper presented at the conference of the South African Historical Association, University of Durban-Westville, July.

Chetty, D. 1991. '"Sammy" and "Mary" Go to Gaol: Indian Women and South African Politics in the 1940s'. Unpublished paper presented at the conference on Women and Gender in Southern Africa, 30 January–2 February 1991, University of Natal, Durban, 1–23.

Gandhi, Mohandas K. 1958–1994. *The Collected Works of Mahatma Gandhi*. New Delhi: Publications Division, Government of India.

———. 1961. *Satyagraha in South Africa*. Ahmedabad: Navajivan Publishing House.

Guha, Ramachandra. 2013. *Gandhi before India*. London and New Delhi: Penguin Books.

Hiralal, Kalpana. 2009. '"Our Plucky Sisters Who Have Dared to Fight": Indian Women and the Satyagraha Movement in South Africa'. *Oriental Anthropologist* 9(1): 1–22.

———. 2010. 'Rethinking Gender and Agency in the Satyagraha Movement of 1913'. *Journal of Social Sciences* 25(1–3): 71–80.

Mongia, Radhika. 2006. 'Gender and the Historiography of Gandhian Satyagraha in South Africa'. *Gender & History* 18(1): 130–149.

Patel, Raojibhai M. 1990. *The Making of the Mahatma, Based on 'Gandhijini Sadhana': Adaptation in English by Abid Shamsi*. Ahmedabad: Ravindra R. Patel.

Reddy, Enuga, and Kalpana Hiralal. 2017. *Pioneers of Satyagraha Indian South African Defy Racist Laws 1907-1914*. Ahmedabad: Navajivan Publishing House.

Sherman, Taylor C. 2010. *State Violence and Punishment in India*. London: Routledge.

Swan, Maureen. 1984. 'The 1913 Natal Indian Strike'. *Journal of Southern African Studies* 10(2): 239–258.

# 5

# Toilers across the Seas

## Racial Discrimination and Political Assertion among Sikhs in Canada*

*Chhanda Chatterjee*

New research on the workings of the 'web of empire' have revealed that the British Empire was not only sustained by raw materials from India but depended significantly on its manpower working as 'coolies', or indentured labourers, in distant plantations in Mauritius, Fiji, West Indies, East and South Africa, and the Straits Settlements. The white dominions of Canada, Australia and the United States (US) similarly depended on low-paid labourers from the East for much of their work of opening up and colonising the prairie wastes. Initially, the bulk of migrants from India in North America came from among the strong and hard-working Sikhs of the Punjab province of India, who found it lucrative to work in these places, lured by the comparatively higher wages than they could obtain at home. However, as the market for labour became saturated by the first decade of the twentieth century, these countries began to erect legal barriers to the free entry of these Indian migrants under pressure from domestic workers, unwilling to face competition from migrants. This came as a great shock to migrant Indians, who had until then been thinking of the empire as a vast field of 'shared opportunities'.

In 1908, Canada tried to exclude Indian migrant labour by legislation, which insisted on 'continuous passage' for entering into the ports of the country. This would automatically disable Sikh migrants, who had to change ships to reach Canada. Gurdit Singh's attempt to charter a Japanese ship, *Komagata Maru*, in June 1914 to ensure continuous passage for the Sikh migrants to Canada was a challenge to this legal barrier against the migrants. The turning back of this ship from Vancouver shattered the belief of the migrants

---

* A previous version of this chapter was originally published as an article titled 'Sikhs on the Cross-Roads: Flows between Punjab, Canada and Calcutta' in a special issue on the Ghadar Movement in the *Journal of Sikh and Punjab Studies*, vol. 26, nos. 1–2 (Spring–Fall) © Global Institute for Sikh Studies, New York, 2019. All rights reserved. Reproduced with the permission of the copyright holder and the publisher, Global Institute for Sikh Studies.

in an equal imperial citizenship, and it became incendiary material for the revolutionary nationalist propaganda of the Ghadr conspirators, based in San Francisco. Student radicals in Canada and America, such as Lala Har Dayal, Kartar Singh Sarabha, G. D. Kumar and Husain Rahim tried to contact radicals all over the world, in India House in the United Kingdom (UK), France, Egypt, Turkey and Switzerland, and tried to spread their message through journals, like the *Ghadr* and the *Hindustanee* from San Francisco and the *Al Kasas* from Egypt. They even linked their efforts with German imperialist conspirators to gain funding and guidance in their common mission against British imperialism. British intelligence in India caught a scent of these conspiracies, and the onset of the First World War added to their worries. There was the fear that these disgruntled men would fall prey to enemy conspiracies. The *Komagata Maru* was forbidden to disembark its passengers till it reached Budge Budge Ghat, where a special train had been kept ready for transporting the men directly to Punjab. The new Ingress into India Ordinance of 1914 made it possible for colonial police to restrict the movement of arrivals from outside the country. Resistance from the passengers led to an affray, resulting in some casualties. This incident knocked the bottom out of the myth of equality before imperial law and revealed the unholy nexus between the white dominions and the authorities at the imperial centre. The failed effort of Gurdit Singh became a symbol of the united effort of radicals to spread across several colonies in defiance of the 'black laws'. The nervous reaction of the British administration in Calcutta (present-day Kolkata) on the eve of the First World War conferred an aura of martyrdom on the migrants returning from Canada.

## Imperial Citizens Sharing in Opportunities

Long before the Sikhs became a mainstay of the British Indian Army following the rebellion of sepoys from the North-Western Provinces and Awadh region in 1857, their robust physique had drawn the admiring attention of the imperial authorities, suffused as they were with an ideology concerning 'martial races'. Military engagement with the Sikhs during the Anglo-Sikh wars from 1945–1946 to 1948–1949 drew accolades from army generals who fought against them.[1] Clare Anderson's macro study on the fate of a Sikh prisoner of the Second Sikh War in Multan has revealed how the honourable conduct of Sikhs created a favourable impression on the jailor in Moulmain (present-day Mawlamyine) in Burma (present-day Myanmar), and the prisoner Narain Sing was eventually promoted

---

[1]  Innes and Gough (1897).

to the position of a head constable in Burma long before the sepoy uprising.[2] The overbearing nature and supercilious behaviour of some Sikhs was even to their advantage in their employment in the police forces of distant British colonies.[3] Isabella Jackson's study of Shanghai has corroborated these findings.[4] Recruited in large numbers to bolster the imperial police and military, they were employed in defence of the British colonies. In the course of their sojourns around the globe, Sikhs became aware of the difference in wages offered in white British colonies – America, Australia and Canada – and those in their country of origin. Since they were obliged to proceed to any corner of the earth as servants of the British Empire, they considered it their right to be able to settle in any region ruled by the British crown. They were proud to be citizens of the British Empire and regarded it as a vast arena for 'shared opportunities'.[5]

## Impulses for Migration

Since the close of the nineteenth century, many Sikhs were finding it difficult to make their living in their home province of Punjab. The Central Punjab districts were overpopulated (the population density being 845 per square miles in Jullunder and 860 in Hoshiarpur according to the census of 1901) and were showing signs of underemployment in the over-exploited agricultural sector. The canal colonies had started bringing their cheaper canal-watered produce to the market, and the Central Punjab districts were unable to undercut their prices with their uneconomical products irrigated with well water at a much greater cost.[6] The canal colonies had their own woes in that they had to face a serious labour shortage after an outbreak of the bubonic plague ravaged the countryside between 1901 and 1911, with nearly 60,000 Punjabis dying from this disease every year. The destruction of the cotton crop, the mainstay of the canal colonies, by the bollworm in 1905–1906 drove the peasants to despair. Finally, the imposition of a tax for the use of canal water in 1906 in the Bari Doab colonies in the Central Punjab districts added insult to injury. A sense of disillusionment was rife among the Punjab Sikhs and caused many of them to turn towards the possibility of either making a quick return by selling their labour in the white dominions or relocating to them entirely with their families.

---

[2]  Anderson (2010).

[3]  Anderson (2010).

[4]  Jackson (2012).

[5]  Metcalf (2007), introduction.

[6]  Fox (1985), ch. 4.

## Opportunities in Canada

In the 1880s, Canada was being opened up and reclaimed from the wild, and Punjabis made their contributions to its settlement and colonisation. Between 1903 and 1907, Canada's economy boomed, and the federal government of Canada launched two new railway lines, the National Trans-Continent and the Grand Trans-Pacific lines, to run alongside the existing Canadian Pacific line. Railway workers were much in demand to lay down the tracks and maintain them. The railways also absorbed all the coal produced in British Columbia, Alberta and Northern Ontario and created a flourishing market for labour in the mining industries. In addition, Sikhs could put their experience of working in the sawmills of the forest-clad districts of Hoshiarpur to good use in the lumber industries of Vancouver, including in the saw and shingle mills of the lower Fraser Valley of the Vancouver region, Vancouver Island and in the interior of British Columbia.[7] Sikhs were also highly in demand as fruit-pickers in the orchards of the Sacramento Valley and as workers in cattle farms and salmon canneries.[8]

The case of the Sikh migrants in Canada and America was very similar, as reported in an enquiry conducted into the condition of Sikh migrants from India to the US. An official in the construction department of the South Pacific Railroad Company who spoke to Dady Burjor, a Parsee engaged by His Majesty's consul general in San Francisco on the request of W. C. Hopkinson of the India Office to collect information on the Indian immigrants, was full of praise for the Hindu labourers, finding them to be 'hard working, obedient and pliant'. The usual wages received by them per day were 1.60 dollars in American gold currency, which was equivalent to about 4 rupees and 10 *annas*. A Sikh with an asparagus farm near Antioch reported that in the season of picking and packing, some of his fellow countrymen earned as much as 3 and 4 dollars a day, equal to 9 to 12 rupees in Indian currency. It could even go up to 5 or 6 dollars in peak seasons, as in the case of picking beetroots near Chico, California. There, the work began at 6 a.m. and continued until midnight or 2 a.m. the next morning in order for the entire consignment to be packed into the railway freight cars within a certain time. One government official expressed his amazement at the Sikhs' physical powers of endurance and thought that they worked like 'animals'. These labourers were able to save up a large portion of their earnings as they had a very frugal lifestyle; they were able to survive on a meagre meal of 'dal' and 'chapatis', rice, vegetables and a little milk, which would not cost them beyond 12 dollars or 14 dollars per month.

---

[7] Juergensmeyer (1979).

[8] Johnston (1988).

Thus, in five to six years they were able to save between 3,000 to 5,000 dollars in American currency and bring the money home.[9] Lured by these prospects, the Sikhs aimed to enter these high-wage zones and competed directly with white working-class labourers.

## Local Resentment against Immigrant Sikh Labourers

The boom in the Canadian economy was short-lived, and from the turn of the century, the white labourers of Canada began to resent the unequal competition created by the influx of cheap workers, which forced them to work for lower wages. Unlike the Chinese, after settling in these places, the migrant Sikhs did not conform to the local culture but lived in isolated enclaves. A failure to assimilate with the local population made them stand out, and white inhabitants developed an antipathy towards them. Once the initial demand for hard-working, underpaid labour was exhausted, and the far-flung prairies of Canada and America had been colonised, resentment grew towards the large number of non-white migrants filling the dwindling labour market. White men soon formed their own unions to lobby their country's administration in opposition to these 'trespassers' from distant non-white colonies. The Canadian administration responded by bringing novel laws into force. These included the 'continuous voyage' clause of 1908, which dictated that migrants could not use multiple journeys to reach Canada, which was aimed to prevent large numbers of migrants arriving from India.

The federal government was pressed to bar the entry of non-white immigrants by workers' unions dominated by white Canadians. The presence of Indians was particularly disliked because of their distinct cultural practices, which some complained stood out against western cultural mores. While immigrants from China or Japan showed themselves to be much more amenable to the ways of the country where they had settled, Burjor reported that Indians continued to remain strongly attached to their religious and social practices and did not assimilate well into the prevalent culture of the country of their domicile:

> An Oriental as a rule cherishes an undying love for the land of his birth and nativity and devoutly religious and spiritual races like the Hindu never will be assimilated with or be absorbed by the vast white population of ninety million people of this country.... It is only a race of superior calibre and tenacity that refuses to be engulfed

---

[9]   Report of DS Dady Burjor, 24 California Street, San Francisco, 30 January 1914, on 'Indian Immigration into US', in NAI, Home Political B, Simla Records 1, Proceedings of November 1914, no. 77.

in the vortex of superior force.... They lay by all they can during their stay in the country and save it to be spent in their own native land.[10]

## Canadian Measures to Check Immigration from India

In 1911, the Ministerial Association of Vancouver set up a special committee to go into the question of 'Hindu' (a blanket term for all Indian immigrants) immigration. Henry Herbert Stevens, the member of parliament (MP) for Vancouver, played a leading part in this committee. A special reason for their anxiety was the attempt of the immigrants to bring their families. The concern was that this would create isolated enclaves of 'oriental' culture on Canadian land. The local Christian Association passed resolutions against the admission of Indian women, and the government exerted its utmost to prevent such a development.[11] Malcolm Reid, an agent and inspector with the Immigration Department, J. B. Larkin and William Charles Hopkinson from the Immigration Criminal Investigation Department (CID), and Stevens chalked out a plan to pack off the Sikhs to British Honduras (present-day Belize) in Central America. However, the Sikhs were unwilling to migrate to a zone with low wages where the early immigrants had been brought in as indentured labourers.

The introduction of discriminatory treatment attracted the attention of student radicals in Canada and America, such as Lala Hardayal, Kartar Singh Sarabha, G. D. Kumar and Husain Rahim. From their base in San Francisco, they tried to contact radicals all over the world, in India House in the UK, and in France, Egypt, Turkey and Switzerland. On the eve of the First World War, they even linked their efforts with German imperialist conspirators to gain funding and guidance in their common mission against British imperialism. The radicals edited journals, such as the *Ghadr* and the *Hindustanee* from San Francisco and the *Al Kasas* from Egypt, and spread a message of revolution among the migrants from the colonies. White Canadian discrimination affected all migrants irrespective of their religion, and Hindus, Muslims and Sikhs joined in opposition to these unequal laws.

For the protection of their own interests, the Sikhs had organised themselves into a Khalsa Diwan Society in 1907. The following year, they built the Vancouver gurdwara (a building of worship for Sikhs) where they could gather together and decide on a common course of action. It became a rallying point for people

---

[10] Barrier (1975).

[11] Weekly Report of Director of Criminal Intelligence (DCI), 13 October 1914, in NAI, Home Poll B, December 1914, File No. 218–222.

of all religions – Sikh, Hindu and Muslim. They appointed two highly literate teachers, professors Teja Singh and Hari Singh, to represent their case in England and mobilise support in liberal British circles. Later, a delegation from the Khalsa Diwan Society led by Raja Singh and the priest Balwant Singh of the Vancouver gurdwara approached the home government in London and the viceroy in India for the removal of the restrictions on the Sikhs.[12] The delegation also included Nand Singh, who was to act as an interpreter. Nand Singh had arrived in San Francisco from Punjab a year earlier and was very close to Hardayal, the key person in expatriate plots against the British in San Francisco.[13] However, in reply to the letter of Raja Singh of the United India League in Victoria, S. H. Slater, the under-secretary to the government of India, pleaded his inability to press for the entry of persons 'other than those who have come on a continuous voyage'.

## The Strategy for Exclusion

The strategy behind this reply had been worked out as far back as 1908 by the three secretaries – the secretary of state for India, the secretary for the colonies and the secretary for foreign affairs – when W. L. Mackenzie King, the deputy minister of labour from Ottawa and the head of the Royal Commission into recruitment methods for oriental labour, had visited them. They understood that it was impossible to deny entry to the Indian immigrants or their families without a rude jolt to the semblance of equality for all British subjects throughout the British dominions. The requirement for 'a continuous passage' had therefore deliberately been woven into the immigration clause to disable Indian immigrants, who could not book a continuous passage from Calcutta. There was no shipping company in Calcutta that would take them directly to Canada; the passengers from Calcutta always had to disembark at Hong Kong and book yet another passage to Canada. The three secretaries of state took shelter under this clause to bar the way to the Indian immigrants and their families without having to reveal the blatant discrimination that lay behind it. The tacit support of the British government for this stand was made clear by the declaration of the Marquess of Crewe, the secretary of state for India, at the Imperial Conference of 1911, that the

---

[12]   Malcolm R. J. Reid, dominion immigration agent, to W. W. Cory, deputy minister of interior, Ottawa Immigration Branch, Department of the Interior, Canada, Vancouver, BC, 17 March 1913, in NAI, Home Poll B, August 1913, Proceedings 37–39. An evening paper, the *Vancouver Daily Province*, reported on this on 17 March 1913.

[13]   W. C. Hopkinson to W. W. Cory, deputy minister of the interior, Canada, Vancouver, BC, 29 April 1913, in NAI, Home Poll B, August 1913, Proceedings 37–39.

'self-governing dominions' had the right to frame their own immigration policies.[14] Lord Minto, the viceroy of India, clarified his government's stand yet further in a letter of 1 March 1909, where he clearly denied 'any intention of raising questions regarding them'.[15]

Indian immigrants could neither hope for justice from the authorities in Canada nor get the necessary support from the government of their own country. India was not yet a free country, and matters affecting Indians abroad were not looked after with the same degree of sympathy that could be expected from rulers of their own race. The colonial government in India had more concern for the interests of the rulers of self-governing colonies than those of the downtrodden subjects in India. They did nothing to press the point of view of the Indian settlers in Canada. Diwan Singh, an Indian immigrant to Canada, wrote to Thakur Singh, the *subedar* (a middle-grade military rank above the sepoy but below the commanding officer) of the 36th Sikhs Dilkhusa Battalion in Lucknow, in early 1914:

> What can be done? Arbitrary laws are made to stop the entry of Indians because they belong to an unprotected nation. If other nations have any trouble their King at once takes steps to remove it. But our King pays no attention to our troubles. Everywhere Indians are governed by arbitrary laws.... The Canadians are trying to stop the immigration of Indians entirely, and there is now necessity of union among us.[16]

## The Predicament of the Aspiring Immigrants

The Canadian, imperial and Indian governments warned all shipping companies against advertising passages to Canada and the lucrative employment opportunities awaiting the Indians in that continent. They were persuaded to withdraw such notifications from gurdwaras, where earlier they had been circulated. Many prospective immigrants had reached Hong Kong with the hope of boarding a ship to British Columbia, but no shipping company would sell tickets. They were thus stranded for years in Hong Kong and forced to eke out a precarious existence in gurdwaras there.

---

[14]  Josh (1975), pp. 14–15.

[15]  Josh (1975), pp. 14–15.

[16]  Diwan Singh to Sardar Thakur Singh, *subedar* of the 36th Sikhs (Dilkhusa Battalion), Lucknow, in letters intercepted at Bombay on 30 January 1914, in H. Wheeler, Criminal Intelligence Office, Government of India, to J. G. Cumming, Chief Secretary to the Government of Punjab, in West Bengal State Archives (WBSA), Intelligence Branch (IB) File No. 586/1914, Sl. No. 47/1914.

On 26 November 1913, Chief Justice Hunter of the High Court at Ottawa passed a judgment in favour of 39 immigrants who had arrived by the Japanese ship *Panama Maru* and succeeded in obtaining a writ of habeas corpus against the Immigration Department's order of deportation. Sikh immigrants were encouraged by this judgment. Mit Singh, who had been secretary to the Khalsa Diwan Society for the past 18 months, wrote to Bishen Ram, a tailor in the village Gojra in the Lyallpur district, about the various disputes between the immigration authorities and Indians. When he proudly stated that 'Indians reside in Canada by force of shoes through law', he probably referred to this case.[17] However, to neutralise the effects of the Hunter judgment, the governor-in-council passed two new orders, on 8 December 1913 and 31 March 1914, prohibiting the entry of artisans or labourers, skilled or unskilled, in any port of British Columbia. The government of Canada expected to discourage immigration even more by raising the minimum amount of money that should be in the possession of the immigrants from 25 dollars to 200 dollars in one go.[18]

## The Ill-Fated Voyage of the *Komagata Maru*

Gurdit Singh was not aware of these orders when he chartered the Japanese ship *Komagata Maru* and sold tickets to the passengers stranded in Hong Kong to take them directly to Canada by a continuous passage. The ill-fated ship had to beat a retreat and was directed to disembark its passengers at Budge Budge *ghat* (a flight of steps leading down to a river) towards the south of Calcutta. Special trains were kept ready to transport the passengers immediately to the Punjab to prevent them from getting further embroiled with the local Sikhs in Calcutta.

The Sikh question was particularly sensitive for the British because of the close connection of the Sikhs with the British army. Since 1857, the British had been forced to shift their traditional recruiting ground for their Indian sepoys from the Awadh or the North-West Provinces to the Punjab, and the Sikhs had come to constitute the backbone of their armies in India and abroad. However, since the canal colonies' agitation of 1907, the unflinching loyalty of the Sikhs had become suspect.

---

[17]  Mit Singh, Vancouver, BC, to Bishen Ram, Tailor, village Gojra, Lyallpur in H. Wheeler, Criminal Intelligence Office, Government of India, to J.G. Cumming, Chief Secretary to the Government of Punjab, in West Bengal State Archives (WBSA), Intelligence Branch (IB) File No. 586/1914, Sl. No. 47/1914.

[18]  Translation of the gist of a conversation with Captain T. Yamamoto and Chief Engineer Y. Shiozaki of the *SS Komagata Maru* on 2 October 1914, with reference to the voyage of his ship under charter to Gurdit Singh, in NAI, Home Dept. Political Branch A, November 1914, File No. 97–177, Proceedings No. 138, Appendix M, p. 117.

The government had tried to alter the conditions of the settlement of smallholders of canal land by an amendment to the Punjab Colonisation of Land Act of 1893 and introduced a canal water rate of 25 per cent in the Sikh districts of Amritsar, Gurdaspur and Lahore. The rates were often doubled for cash crops such as sugarcane and cotton. The rise in labour costs due to a scarcity of hands following a large incidence of bubonic plague deaths was an added irritant. Poor cotton harvests after an influx of bollworms proved to be the last straw on the camel's back, and the Punjab peasant became ready fodder for the Congress agitators Lala Lajpat Rai and Ajit Singh. On 3 February 1907, 10,000 colonists passed a resolution at Lyallpur, calling upon Hindus and Muslims to unite with each other against the British, and Prabh Dayal, the editor of the *Jhang Sayal*, recited the song 'Pagrisambhal O Jatta' (Take Care of Your Prestige, O Jat), emphasising the threat posed by the new Bill to the Jat colonists of the region. In a meeting at Rawalpindi on 21 April 1907, Ajit Singh called upon the Hindus and Muslims to unite: 'We are 30 crores, they are a lakh and a half. A puff of wind would blow them away.'[19] He tried to excite the Sikhs in the local regiments and persuaded them that if the government could go back on its word with the colonists, it was quite capable of breaking faith with the soldiers and denying them the promised pay and pension. Riots followed in Amritsar, Lahore and Rawalpindi. Deporting Ajit Singh and Lajpat Rai to the Andamans did not bring the situation under control. Finally, George Curzon's successor, Lord Minto, had to revoke the new Act on 26 May 1907 and release Lajpat Rai on the request of the secretary of state on 30 October 1907.[20]

## The Tat Khalsa Movement

British faith in Sikh loyalty had received yet another blow with the Tat Khalsa movement. Founded by the aristocratic and conservative section of the Sikhs, the Tat Khalsa movement was an attempt to rouse the Sikhs against the Chief Khalsa Diwan, which had been formed in 1902 as an organ of the leading personages among the Sikhs with the blessings of the government. It was regarded with suspicion by the government due to its spreading of radical ideas. Khalsa College in Amritsar became the focus of the aspirations of an emerging class of middle-class and professional men. The government was worried over the way its students went into raptures receiving the Congress politician Gopal Krishna Gokhale during the canal colonies agitation in 1907. It therefore set up a new council under

---

[19]  K. Singh (1999), pp. 218–219.
[20]  Barrier (1967).

rigid government control, consisting mostly of government officials such as the commissioner of the Lahore Division, the deputy commissioner of Amritsar, the director of public instruction of the Punjab, the political agent of the Phulkian States and the principal of Khalsa College. The property of the college was vested in a managing committee composed of 15 members, six of whom were elected by the states, six by British districts and three were government nominees. Of the last three, the Lahore commissioner and the Amritsar deputy commissioner were the chairman and the vice-chairman respectively. This provoked a strong reaction among the educated or the neo-Sikhs, and the publication of the pamphlet 'Ki Khalsa Kalaj Sikhan Da Hai?' (Does Khalsa College Belong to the Sikhs?) in 1909, authored by Sundar Singh Lyallpuri of the Khalsa School, Lyallpur, alleged that the government was trying to undermine the national character of Khalsa College.[21]

Among the persons identified with the radicalism of Khalsa College, Amritsar, by the CID were Trilochan Singh, an Arora Khatri and a leading spirit of the Tat Khalsa movement; Thakur Singh Giani, possessed of a military background and employed as a *granthi* (an interpreter of the sacred text of the Sikhs) in Rawalpindi before joining Khalsa College as a teacher; Jodh Singh, a professor of mathematics and divinity at Khalsa College, who was in close touch with extremists abroad and circulator of a Berlin extremist newspaper and other organs published from London's India House (run by Shyamaji Krishna Varma); and Narain Singh, the head master of Khalsa College School in Amritsar, who was reported to have circulated photographs of Lachman Singh, the person accused of the murder of British officers in Gujranwala, among the students. He was also detected by the government inspector to be reading out loud from Max Arthur Macauliffe's *History of the Sikhs* during an arithmetic class.

Other men, such as Teja Singh, an inspector (*upadeshak*) of Singh Sabhas employed by the Chief Khalsa Diwan, were found to be fraternising with the Aryas and took part in meetings where anti-government speeches were made in 1907. Jagat Singh, an *upadeshak* of the Chief Khalsa Diwan, was forced to resign for his support of Ajit Singh and Lajpat Rai in 1907 when they came to Amritsar. He praised the Arya Samaj for its sympathy for the agrarian agitation of 1907 and was cut short by the president of the Tarn Tarun Singh Sabha in the midst of a disloyal speech. An occasional contributor to the *Sacha Dhandhora*, a Lyallpur newspaper renowned for its radical views, he visited

---

[21]  D. Petrie, Assistant Director of Criminal Intelligence, Simla, Memorandum on Recent Developments in Sikh Politics, 11th August 1911 in WBSA, Serial No. 22/1911, IB File No. 204/1911.

Khalsa College, Amritsar, and was photographed with the students. Yet another Gurumukhi newspaper disapprovingly mentioned by the CID was the *Prem* from Ferozepore, notorious for the Gurumukhi rendering of the writings of Ajit Singh and his Bharat Mata gang of Lahore. They were ultimately silenced by a series of press prosecutions in 1909–1910.[22]

Many of the Tat Khalsa intellectuals – such as Harbans Singh of Atari, the vice-president of the Chief Khalsa Diwan and Bhai Vir Singh, working in the Khalsa Tract Society with Trilochan Singh and publishing the *Khalsa Samachar* from Amritsar – had targeted the Golden Temple of Amritsar as a hotbed of corruption. The income from the land attached to the gurdwara had received a huge boost since the introduction of canal irrigation in the area, and the land settlement of the British had made the *mahant* (priest) the owner of this property. With so much money at his command, the *mahant* became debauched and corrupt. The *Dodhara Khanda*, a Gurumukhi monthly published by Suchet Singh, addressed the issue of corruption among the *mahant*s and the *pujari*s (priests). These *mahant*s and *pujari*s often played into the hands of the government by accepting all government orders and confirming them. Such orders thus acquired a kind of legitimacy in the eyes of the local people, who held these *mahant*s and *pujari*s in great veneration. Another grievance of the Tat Khalsa was the continued worship of Hindu idols with Hindu rituals on temple premises. Reformers such as Labh Singh, himself a Tarkhan, wanted access for *mazhbi* (untouchable) Sikhs in the sanctum sanctorum of the temple. The inclusion of the *mazhbi*s among the Sikhs had assumed particular importance because of the census operations that were being conducted by the government. The Tat Khalsa was not impervious to the strength of numbers under the new dispensation, and it led to the acquisition of all kinds of political privileges for the community that had thus been reinforced in numbers.[23]

## Seditious Tracts

The tracts authored by these intellectuals sometimes worried the CID. Labh Singh's *A Hundred Years' Calendar: Mughal Persecution of Sikhs* seemed to

---

[22] D. Petrie, Assistant Director of Criminal Intelligence, Simla, Memorandum on Recent Developments in Sikh Politics, 11th August 1911 in WBSA, Serial No. 22/1911, IB File No. 204/1911.

[23] D. Petrie, Assistant Director of Criminal Intelligence, Simla, Memorandum on Recent Developments in Sikh Politics, 11th August 1911 in WBSA, Serial No. 22/1911, IB File No. 204/1911.

indirectly refer to British tyranny. Similarly, Jodh Singh's comparison of British rule to Aurangzeb's oppression and call for the sacrifice of heads and property in the name of religion sounded alarm bells in CID circles. Jodh Singh's book *Jathe Bandi* exhorted the Sikhs to gird their loins to protect their house against foes by using the Chief Khalsa Diwan and the Singh Sabhas. He was probably warning against government intervention when he used the analogy of a thief entering a house and having a free run of the place. He wanted the Sikhs to steadfastly follow their pristine ideals and pointed out the everlasting nature of these ideals. The valour exhibited by a Sikh woman, Daler Kaur, in response to the Mughal invasion was the subject of a book named after the very woman. The purpose of this book was also to remind the Sikhs of their past vigour and to shake them out of their stupor. It followed the recurring strategy of using an analogy of the past to rouse the Sikhs in their present-day battle for education and social progress.[24] Tracts such as *Chamak De Lal*, based on the exploits of Hari Singh Nalwa, who had terrorised the frontier Pathans in the days of maharajah Ranjit Singh, or *Sachi Yadgar*, which narrated the brave sacrifices of the tenth Guru Gobind Singh, were also suspected by the CID of trying to cultivate a spirit of defiance of authority in the Sikhs.[25] Of particular significance for the British authorities was the tract *Guru Ke Liye*, which contained the story of the remission of all revenues for the followers of Guru Amar Das by emperor Akbar after an attempt at the enhancement of the revenue of the Sikh settlements had been tried by the Rajput lieutenants of the Mughals. The CID interpreted it as a tacit encouragement to the canal colonists to refuse to pay the enhanced rates.[26]

## The Sikh Educational Conference

The neo-Sikhs, or the Tat Khalsa, also took the initiative to found a Sikh Educational Conference, which first met at Gujranwala in 1908. The conference owed its origin to a discussion between Tikka Sahib, a member of the Chief Khalsa Diwan and a

---

[24] D. Petrie, Assistant Director of Criminal Intelligence, Simla, Memorandum on Recent Developments in Sikh Politics, 11th August 1911 in WBSA, Serial No. 22/1911, IB File No. 204/1911.

[25] D. Petrie, Assistant Director of Criminal Intelligence, Simla, Memorandum on Recent Developments in Sikh Politics, 11th August 1911 in WBSA, Serial No. 22/1911, IB File No. 204/1911.

[26] D. Petrie, Assistant Director of Criminal Intelligence, Simla, Memorandum on Recent Developments in Sikh Politics, 11th August 1911 in WBSA, Serial No. 22/1911, IB File No. 204/1911.

representative to the viceroy's council, and his Bengali and Marathi colleagues in the council. A Sikh national educational fund was set up by the conference, and all were invited to contribute generously to it. However, the organisation soon passed into the hands of more radical elements, and Tikka Sahib was later heard to have fought Trilochan Singh concerning the mismanagement of funds and the fanning of disloyalty among Khalsa College students. Jagat Singh went to Berlin to collect contributions for this educational fund. Attar Singh, a *cheema* of Rawalpindi, despite being a man of little education, toured through Manjha, Malwa and the Sikh states, lecturing on Sikhism and asking women to give up their jewellery. He was an impressive speaker and collected 5,000 rupees for the national education fund, turning it over during the Rawalpindi Educational Conference. The fund was kept in the Punjab and Sind Bank under the care of the *arora* Trilochan Singh.[27]

Yet another source of Sikh discontent was the way the government had demolished the walls of Rakabgunje gurdwara in Delhi (purportedly housing the ashes of the martyr Guru Teg Bahadur) to make room for a government house. The Sikhs had initially consented, but later a protest was registered by the wife of the former *granthi* of the gurdwara against trespassing on its land. Harchand Singh of Lyallpur made it the subject of a pamphlet, and the matter was given wide publicity among the Sikhs as encroachment upon gurdwara properties. The issue agitated the Sikhs so much that the Chief Khalsa Diwan at Amritsar was compelled to call a meeting to discuss the matter. Harchand Singh of Lyallpur took the matter abroad, and on 8 March 1914, a big meeting of the Khalsa Diwan was held in Hong Kong gurdwara to discuss the Rakabgunge affair. The indignation of the Sikhs may be judged by the letter in Gurumukhi that they addressed from Hong Kong to the *granthi* of the 19th King George's Own Sikhs at Peshawar inciting them to rebel.[28]

## The Radicalisation of Students in Canada and America

These radical and revolutionary ideas were carried abroad by Sikh intellectuals and students. The free atmosphere of Canada and the United States (US) encouraged them to try to build up a resistance movement in response to the tyranny of the imperialists at home. Men such as Hardayal had already come into contact with like-minded students and revolutionary groups all over the world. In London, the India House student hostel run by Shyamaji Krishnavarma, the editor of the

---

[27] D. Petrie, Assistant Director of Criminal Intelligence, Simla, Memorandum on Recent Developments in Sikh Politics, 11th August 1911 in WBSA, Serial No. 22/1911, IB File No. 204/1911.

[28] Weekly Report of Director of Criminal Intelligence (DCI), 28 April 1914, in NAI, Home Poll B, May 1914, File No. 137–140.

*Indian Sociologist*, had been the meeting ground of revolutionary men such as V. D. Savarkar, an ardent follower of the extremist leader Bal Gangadhar Tilak, and Madan Lal Dhingra, who later assassinated Curzon Wyllie, the aide-de-camp of the secretary of state in 1909. Hardayal and others had celebrated the 50th anniversary of the mutiny of 1857 alongside the publication of Savarkar's book *The First War of Indian Independence* in 1907.[29] Hardayal also met the Parsee lady, Madame Cama, who was the founder of the Bande Mataram group in France and was in touch with Sardar Singh Rewabhai Rana. She had attended the International Socialist Congress at Stuttgart in Germany, where she spoke for the dumb millions of Hindustan, from whom English capitalists were taking away 35 million pounds annually. As a result of this exploitation, she claimed, the people of India were dying of poverty at the rate of half a million every month. She ended her speech by unfurling an Indian national flag bearing the words 'Bande Mataram'.[30]

Hardayal was the moving spirit of the Hindusthan Association. The latter was founded in the US and had about 250 members, mostly students and educated men. A member of this association, Surendra Mohan Bose, returned to India to attract more students to the US in order to train them in nationalist, revolutionary and even anarchist doctrines. Among the office bearers of the Indian Association were men who had earned notoriety for their activities in opposition to the British government, including Chandrakanta Chakravarti, the printer of the *Yugantar* leaflet; M. P. T. Acharya, the printer of the seditious Tamil paper *India*; Tarak Nath Das, the editor of *Free Hindusthan*; and Sarangdhar Das, an associate of Hardayal.[31] Surendra Mohan Bose went to Paris to get hold of a manual of explosives and sent it to Victoria through Harnam Singh.[32] Kartar Singh of Ludhiana studied chemistry at Berkeley and intended to use his knowledge for the manufacture of explosives. He drew his inspiration from Krishna Varma's *Indian Sociologist* and *Speeches from the Dock*, which contained the speeches of the convicted Irishman, Parnell. He had found these books and journals in the library of the Yugantar Ashram. Kartar Singh was an inspiring example of the generation of Indian students in America tutored in revolutionary ideology by Hardayal.[33]

---

[29] Barrier (1975).

[30] History sheet of Madame Bhikhaji Rustom K. R. Cama, Criminal Intelligence Office, May 1913, in NAI, Home Poll B, August 1913, File No. 61.

[31] Weekly Report of DCI, 13 October 1914, in NAI, Home Poll B, December 1914, File No. 218–222.

[32] Weekly Report of DCI, 12 May 1914, in NAI, Home Poll B, June 1914, File No. 142–145.

[33] Weekly Report of DCI, 27 October 1914, in NAI, Home Poll B, December 1914, File No. 218–222.

The name of another person also figures among the agitating students in America – that of G. D. Kumar, who collected funds in Manila and Kobe for fomenting sedition in India.[34]

The Pacific Coast Hindu Association, in comparison, was purely an organisation of labourers and was built through the efforts of Hardayal and the Sikh Khalsa Diwan. It had its headquarters at Stockton, California. In an article in the Egyptian journal *Al Kasas*, published from Geneva, Hardayal explained what the movement stood for:

> The movement is entirely one of the people. The members of the party are peasants or working men. There are only about half a dozen educated men to edit the paper, carry on correspondence and to think out plans.[35]

For Hardayal, these men of the labouring class were 'men poor in wealth but rich in courage':

> When the common people understand something, they want to risk their life in order to realize the ideal. They have no property to make them cowards ... men far and near came to see it and then offer offerings as in a temple.... They desire economic as well as political freedom. They hate princes, landlords and capitalists.... They want a democratic rearrangement of conditions in India.[36]

They decided to bring out a weekly eight-page journal in three languages, the *Ghadr*, and smuggle it into China, Japan, East Africa and wherever they could find sympathetic readers. Ram Chand Peshawari, formerly the editor of *Akash* in Delhi and an intimate associate of Ajit Singh, came to San Francisco on 13 January 1913 to help in the editorial work of the Urdu edition of the *Ghadr*.[37] It was proscribed in India, but they hid copies in the private letters of immigrants, thus bringing it to the notice of their brethren at home: 'In California is being prepared the power that will reduce the Empire to dust and ashes.' Hardayal called it the 'revenge of the exile against the powers of darkness that drive men away from their homes'.[38]

---

[34] Weekly Report of DCI, 27 October 1914, in NAI, Home Poll B, December 1914, File No. 218–222.

[35] Weekly Report of DCI, 12 May 1914, in NAI, Home Poll B, June 1914, File No. 142–145.

[36] Weekly Report of DCI, 12 May 1914, in NAI, Home Poll B, June 1914, File No. 142–145.

[37] Weekly Report of DCI, 27 October 1914, in NAI, Home Poll B, December 1914, File No. 218–222.

[38] WBSA, Sl. No. 47/1914, File No. 586/1914.

## Students' Sympathy for the Problems of the Immigrants

From early 1914, the postal censor in the various port cities of India began to seize a large number of copies of the *Ghadr* tucked in the envelopes of letters addressed by Punjabis to their friends and relatives at home.[39] The *Paisa Akhbar* of Lahore, dated 19 September 1914, reported that large meetings were held in six different places in California and other parts of America in which Muslim and Sikh propagandists lamented the condition of the Indian settlers in America, Canada and Africa.[40] In May 1914, Muhammad Barkatullah, a professor of Urdu in Tokyo, was persuaded by Bhagwan Singh, who had served as *granthi* in Hong Kong for three years from 1910 to 1913, to come to San Francisco to help with the spread of propaganda urging the Indian settlers to return to their native land and take part in a rebellion.[41] Appeals were made for a National scientific education fund, and a sum of 20,000 dollars was collected. Barkatullah was also the author of the pamphlet *Feringhiki Fareb* (The Deceit of the English), which received wide publicity in Hong Kong.[42] Rumours circulated among the sepoys and police lines in Hong Kong that the British had become suspicious of the Sikhs, and they were soon to be repatriated. Stories of the outbreak of a mutiny among the Sikhs in India also did their rounds, and it was said that four regiments of Sikhs were being trained at Kabul. The revolutionaries of the Yugantar Ashram presented an explicit threat in a leaflet entitled 'An Open Letter to the British Public by the Hindusthanees of North America':

> If the Hindustanees refuse to handle the muskets and to fill the barracks and dignifiedly refuse to be martyrs for the protection of the British Empire, where they are treated no better than slaves, will the Japanese and the handful of British soldiers be sufficient to protect British interests in the Orient? What will be the internal situation in British India if loyal Sikhs who saved the British Empire in India in 1857 and who are now so much ill-treated in the British colonies, especially in Canada, refuse to shoot down their own countrymen for the interests of their overlords who have not the slightest intention of protecting their rights in the British Empire?[43]

---

[39]  Weekly Report of DCI, 22 September 1914, in NAI, Home Poll B, December 1914, File No. 216–217.

[40]  Supplement to the Weekly Report of DCI, 17 August 1915, in NAI, Home Poll B, 1915, File No. 552–556.

[41]  Weekly Report of DCI, 12 May 1914, in NAI, Home Poll B, June 1914, File No. 142–145.

[42]  Weekly Report of DCI, 6 October 1914, in NAI, Home Poll B, December 1914, File No. 218–222.

[43]  Weekly Report of DCI, 6 October 1914, in NAI, Home Poll B, December 1914, File No. 218–222.

It bore the signatures of nine notorious revolutionaries, including Husain Rahim, the editor of the *Hindustanee*, who had taken over the charter of the *Komagata Maru* from Gurdit Singh, Tarak Nath Das, Balwant Singh, Bhag Singh and Harnam Singh. The pamphlet then asked:

> If these 352 Hindustanees (in the *Komagata Maru*) returning to Hong Kong can succeed in inducing at least the same number of their friends and relations, who are now serving in infantry, artillery and police force, to desert their posts, what will be the moral effect of such an act?

## Sikh Residents of Calcutta and the Suburbs

It was no wonder that the return of the *Komagata Maru* to Calcutta alarmed the local administration in Calcutta. Initially, it was unknown where the ship was going to land. The reply from the superintendent of police, Faridpur, epitomises the reaction of the provincial administration; the home secretary sent urgent messages to the officers in the districts to alert them of the presence of several emissaries of the Hindusthan Association and the Student League in Bengal:

> It is almost utopian to hope that this determined gang won't find some loop hole. The fact is it is the northern races that provide us with our recruits for the Indian army that are the present object of these desperadoes.[44]

Calcutta in 1914 had a teeming Sikh population. They were mostly concentrated in the Howrah, Burra Bazar and Bhowanipore areas. The extracts from the personal diary of L. M. Sen, a sub-inspector in the Intelligence Branch, engaged in tracing the whereabouts of Sikhs to whom a copy of the *Ghadr* had been addressed, give some details of the lives of the Sikh residents of Calcutta and its surroundings. The foremost among them was Gul Charan Singh, a Brahmin *pujari* in a garden temple in Narkeldanga. Gul Charan was in charge of the Guru Granth Sahib that was placed in the temple. Some eight or nine Sikhs – all small shopkeepers – resided in the garden and greatly respected Gul Charan. He sometimes went and lived with another brahmin called Ram Singh at 153/54 Mechua Bazar Street, where there was another temple called Tara Singh Ka Sangat. Ram Singh was in charge of this temple and had great influence among the Sikhs who visited it. The Sikhs had two other *sangats* (congregations) in Burra Bazar: the Burra Sangat in 79 Cotton Street, headed by Amar Singh and Man Singh, and the Chhota Sangat, headed

---

[44] S. P. Faridpur, no. 871, dated 24.7.14, in IB File No. 586/1914 Sl. No. 47/1914, in WBSA, Kolkata.

by Kalu Singh. These places were visited mostly by Sikh traders and shopkeepers. Gul Charan was in close touch with all these men.

Another interesting person mentioned in L. M. Sen's diary was Bawa Singh Mistry, who was working in the Kanchrapara Loco workshop. Some 250 Sikhs worked there, and 100 of them were directly under Bawa Singh. His father, Sirdar Nehal Singh, was a retired military *subedar* who had served the workshop as a contractor for some time after his retirement. However, he was a man of 'an independent spirit'[45] and left the workshop after some friction with the European officers there. Thereafter, he went to reside in Kharagpur.

In Kharagpur lived an unusual person, a Bengali brahmin named Promotho. Born and brought up among the Sikhs in the Punjab and a convert to Sikhism, he had become a Sikh missionary and assumed a Sikh name. Promotho was known to Sirdar Nehal Singh, the father of Bawa Singh. He visited Kanchrapara twice in the year preceding Sen's report at an interval of six months and held mass meetings among the Sikhs, delivering lectures on Guru Nanak and the Sikh religion. While in Kanchrapara, Promotho stayed with Ratan Singh (a pattern maker in a fabric workshop), Chandra Singh and Asha Singh (a contractor). Promotho was prone to suddenly touching upon certain seditious subjects at the end of his religious discourses, which won him an overwhelming response from the local Sikhs, many of whom greeted him by touching his feet when the lecture ended.[46]

## Circulation of Seditious Materials into Punjab through the Agency of the Calcutta Sikhs

The Calcutta Sikhs were a worldly and politically engaged community, having constant communication with the land of their origin in the Punjab. They often visited their native villages and retained relatives and properties there. Sometimes they possessed agricultural land and travelled home during the *rabi* harvest (spring harvest) to claim their share of the crop. If copies of the *Ghadr* reached these people, they could be circulated all over the Punjab to their brethren. The official prohibition of the entry of the paper into India under Section 19 of the Sea Customs Act[47] was circumvented by concealing the letters in various ways with personal letters. L. M. Sen's list of those who had received the *Ghadr* was

---

[45]  Extract from personal diary of Sub Inspector (SI) L.M. Sen (14.7.14), in WBSA, IB File No. 586/1914, Sl. No. 47/1914.

[46]  Extract from personal diary of Sub Inspector (SI) L. M. Sen (14.7.14), in WBSA, IB File No. 586/1914, Sl. No. 47/1914.

[47]  Government of India, Department of Commerce and Industry, notification no. 212-C, dated 22 December 1913.

extensive and indicative of his meticulous care; every class of Indian had been addressed – villagers, police, members of the Provincial Civil Service, pleaders, barristers, doctors, school masters and even students at colleges at Lahore. The majority of these people were the residents of districts that had sent emigrants to America and Canada.

The message of the letters containing copies of the smuggled journal was quite clear and unambiguous. They underlined the grievances of the immigrants alongside those residing in India and exhorted them to rebel. An anonymous letter to Bhagwan Singh, Narangwal village, Ludhiana, said:

> There would be no country to equal ours if the English could only be turned out of it. Kill the white man wherever you meet him. It is admitted that the white people are irreligious. They are cunning and deceitful also. Begin to kill them. Read this paper to other people.[48]

Chanda Singh of British Columbia pointed out in his letter to Harnam Singh of Chhima Thenbwale village, Amritsar, that the country's poverty was due to the drain of 50 crore of rupees every year to England.[49] Puran Singh of California, writing to Pal Singh, a *naik* (a military rank below the *subedar*) with a B Company Regiment of Punjabees in Nowshera, squarely put the blame for the outbreak of the plague on the prevalence of poverty and malnutrition in the country.[50] The missive addressed to Sundar Singh of Ruzka Khurd village, Jullunder (present-day Jalandhar), showed the despair and indignation of the writer:

> They have taken our grain and money to England and have given famine and sickness to India. The white men have opened their mouths for grain and money, but we will fill them with filth.[51]

Puran Singh of California also touched upon the grievances of the Sikhs regarding the usurpation of their cultural and educational institutions by the rulers:

---

[48] Anonymous letter to Bhagwan Singh, Narangwal village, Ludhiana, in H. Wheeler, Secretary, Government of India, to J. G. Cumming, Chief Secretary to Government of Punjab, 24 November 1913, in WBSA, IB File No. 586/1914, Sl. No. 47/1914.

[49] Letter of Chanda Singh, British Columbia, to Harnam Singh, Chhima Thenbwale village, Amritsar, in WBSA, IB File No. 586/1914, Sl. No. 47/1914.

[50] Letter of Puran Singh, California to Pal Singh, Naik No. 299, British Company Regiment No. 82, Punjabees, Nowshera, in WBSA, IB File No. 586/1914, Sl. No. 47/1914.

[51] Anonymous letter to Sundar Singh, Ruzka Khurd village, Jullundher, in 'Abstract of Gurumukhi letters captured in Bombay, 9–10 February, 1914', in WBSA, IB File No. 586/1914, Sl. No. 47/1914.

The Sikh community has fallen and can do nothing, for the community whose sacred places are taken from them are worthless. The greatest Sikh temple is at Amritsar, and has been taken by the English. Before this the Khalsa College, at which the sons of all Sikhs were studying, was taken away.[52]

Sardar Sundar Singh Majithia was condemned for making an Englishman the principal of Khalsa College, Amritsar:

You are a leader of the Panth but you are like Satan. Either drive the English out of the College, raise the nation and prepare yourself to relieve India or your days are numbered.

What becomes of the income of the *Har Mandir* (Golden Temple) which was made by the Guru? The wall of the Gurdwara Rakabganj had been leveled to the ground, but you do not care.[53]

## The Working Together of Hindus, Muslims and Sikhs

The immigrant revolutionaries wanted the Hindus, Muslims and Sikhs to work together to face the colonial authorities. Kartar Singh of Victoria, British Columbia, wrote to Kher Singh, Mangeval village, Ferozepur, about how 'these people [white men] eat beef and pork and the meat of sheep and goat and still they rule over us while we quarrel over cows and pigs'.[54] Syed Ali Khan from Seattle, Washington, asked the editor of *Vakil* to promote unity between communities in the same manner as Zafar Ali, the editor of the *Zamindar*, did:

The Sikhs and Muhammadans of this place have sworn an oath to forget the animosities of the past and to live as brothers in the future. We will not rest until we have driven the English tyrants from India and have relieved our Egyptian brothers from oppression.[55]

[52] Letter of Puran Singh, California to Pal Singh, Naik No. 299, British Company Regiment No. 82, Punjabees, Nowshera, in WBSA, IB File No. 586/1914, Sl. No. 47/1914.

[53] Anonymous letter in mail of 20 February 1914, in WBSA, IB File No. 586/1914, Sl. No. 47/1914.

[54] Kartar Singh to Kher Singh, village Mangewal, in interception of newspaper *Ghadr* in private letters mentioned by H. Wheeler, Secretary to Government of India, to J. G. Cumming, Chief Secretary to the Government of Punjab, 24 November, 1913, in WBSA, IB File No. 556/1914 of Sl. No. 47/1914.

[55] Letter of Syed Ali Khan of Seattle to the Editor of the *Vakil* of Amritsar, in IB File No. 1105/1914, Serial No. 57/1914, in WBSA, Kolkata.

In another letter to Feroze Din, Sasuli village, Hoshiarpur, Syed Ali Khan wrote:

> We are making preparations here for a mutiny and all Hindu, Muhammadan and
> Sikh brothers have joined together in the movement. Some of our party have reached
> Afghanistan and the Punjab and the work has commenced in Bengal. It will soon
> begin in the Punjab. After killing the English our own Raj will be established on
> principles of equality. You should preach stealthily and prepare soldiers for the
> mutiny who will help us on arrival. Our number is increasing day by day. Work on
> fearlessly; you will get assistance from hidden sources.[56]

Chaudhuri Jaimal Khan, Mansurpur village, Jullunder, was also informed about
these 'preparations of a mutiny in America and Canada':

> A good deal is being done in Bengal and parties have been prepared. Revenge for
> Turkey should now be taken.[57]

Lala Devi Chand, headmaster, Arya School, Hoshiarpur, was requested to read
the *Ghadr* to the students and teachers and prepare the students for mutiny:

> You see how Bengal is improving. Students obtain money for national schools and
> colleges by committing dacoity and by plundering Government treasuries. These
> students are trained by their teachers. If you will also preach through several students,
> the students of all classes will be able to relieve the whole of Punjab.[58]

The letters were so ardent and imploring that they were bound to move their
readers to action. 'Do not regard it [the letter] as written on paper in ink,'
M. R. Singh wrote to Mit Singh, Havildar, Bidipur village, Jullunder. 'It has been
written with the life blood of the heart.' They conjured up the vision of a new
dawn and tried to carry with them as many as they could lay hands on:

> This is not the work of one man; lakhs of men are engaged upon this work. There are
> several workshops where guns and cannons are made. All sorts of work is going on.

---

[56] Letter to Dr Feroze Din, Sasuli village, Hoshiarpur district, from Syed Ali Khan, c/o L. Danz
and Sons, 211 Occidental Avenue, Seattle, Washington, USA, in letters captured in Bombay,
13 March 1914, in WBSA, IB File 586/1914, Sl. No. 47/1914, in WBSA, Kolkata.

[57] Letter of Chaudhuri Jaimal Khan of Mansurpur village, Jullundur, in WBSA, Kolkata.

[58] Letter to Lala Devi Chand, Head Master, Arya School, Hoshiarpur, from J. Ram, c/o
L. Danz and Sons, 211 Occidental Avenue, Seattle, Washington, USA, in WBSA, IB File No.
586/1914, Sl. No. 47/1914.

We shall beat the Feringhees, the bastards and drive them to destruction. We will not leave a trace of them in India.[59]

## Conclusion

Three different places – Punjab, Canada and Calcutta – divided from each other by several hundreds and thousands of miles, seemed to be connected in the singular scheme of Sikh revolutionaries. They had identified the source of the Indian discontent as the British imperialist exploitation of India that had compelled the Indians to go and seek work abroad. The newly expanding economy of Canada squeezed the immigrants dry as long as their services were indispensable for settling the prairie waste, but as soon as the wastes were transformed into green fields well-connected by a sprawling railway network, the need for immigrant labour ceased. Canada then wanted to remain 'white Canada forever' and tried to obstruct the further influx of immigrants by raising the barrier of a requirement for 'continuous passage' from one's place of origin to the port of disembarkation at Canada. Rebuffed from his promised El Dorado in the former British colonies and deprived of his erstwhile privileges in the canal colonies in the Punjab, the 'loyal Sikh' could no longer stick to his impeccable loyalty. Sikhs began to question the attempts of the government to dominate their intellectual and cultural institutions such as Khalsa College and the Golden Temple by packing the management of these institutions with the government's own protégés and nominees. The Tat Khalsa movement was not only a movement to bring about reforms in the Sikh community; it also attempted to rouse the Sikhs from their blind faith in the government backing of all their aspirations. Since the days of the Sepoy Mutiny, Sikhs had been the backbone of the British army in India and other colonies of the British in Asia and Africa. However, the failure of the British to protect their rights in the dominion of Canada shook the Sikhs out of their euphoria about their privileged position. In this way events abroad began to influence those within India. Politicised Sikhs began to organise themselves into the United India League in which Hindus, Muslims and Sikhs, all, would be equal members. Students in San Francisco and California, who had formed a Hindusthan Association in San Francisco, also took the initiative of organising Indian labourers in a Pacific Coast Hindu Association, with its headquarters at Stockton, California. Ram Chand Peshwari, an intimate associate of the leader of the canal colonies agitation, Ajit Singh, came to San Francisco to help with the

---

[59] Letter of M. R. Singh to Mit Singh, Havildar, Bidipur village, Jullundur, in mail of 30 January 1914, in WBSA, Kolkata.

editing of the Urdu *Ghadr*. The *Ghadr* sold a dream of united action by Hindus, Muslims and Sikhs, which terrified British officials out of their wits. The First World War had already started when the ship *Komagata Maru* landed on the shores of Calcutta. The CID had information about the attempt of German consuls at different British colonies, such as Egypt, Singapore and Malayasia, to connect with disaffected elements and to instigate trouble by propping them up with arms. The *Komagata Maru* had been refuelling at various ports and, not impossibly, gathering together more of the unwanted characters. British officers had pathetically run out of all ideas and could meet the challenge only with brute force. The violence directed at the voyagers returning by the *Komagata Maru* at the Budge Budge *ghat* on the river Hooghly demonstrated a failure of nerves on the part of the British military and the British intelligence. So far as the immigrants were concerned, they had successfully pushed matters to a head and demonstrated before the whole world that they were being discriminated against in the self-governing British dominions. They were being called upon to mobilise for the defence of the empire and lay down their lives as equal subjects, but when it came to earning better wages in distant British dominions it appeared that some were more equal than others.

## Bibliography

Anderson, Clare. 2010. 'The Transportation of Narain Singh: Punishment Honour and Identity from the Anglo-Sikh Wars to the Great Revolt'. Modern Asian Studies 44: 1115–1145.

Barrier, N. G. 1967. 'The Punjab Disturbances of 1907: The Response of the British Government in India to Agrarian Unrest'. *Modern Asian Studies* 1(4): 353–383.

———. 1975. 'Mass Politics and the Punjab Congress in the Pre-Gandhian Era'. *Punjab Past and Present* 9(2): 353–354.

Fox, Richard G. 1985. *Lions of the Punjab: Culture in the Making*. Berkeley and Los Angeles: University of California Press.

Innes, Arthur D., and Charles Gough. 1897. *The Sikhs and the Sikh Wars: The Rise Conquest and Annexation of Punjab State*. London: AD Innes & Co.

Jackson, Isabella. 2012. 'The Raj on Nanjing Road: Sikh Policemen in Treaty Port Shanghai'. *Modern Asian Studies* 46(6): 1672–1704.

Johnston, Hugh. 1988. 'Patterns of Sikh Migration to Canada'. In *Sikh History and Religion in the Twentieth Century*, edited by Joseph T. O'Connell, Milton Israel and Willard Gurdon Oxtoby, pp. 296–313. Toronto: Centre for South Asian Studies, University of Toronto.

Josh, Sohan Singh. 1975. *Tragedy of Komagata Maru*. Delhi: People's Publishing House.

Juergensmeyer, Mark. 1979. 'The Ghadar Syndrome: Immigrant Sikhs and Nationalist Pride'. In *Sikh Studies: Comparative Perspectives on a Changing Tradition*, edited by M. Juergensmeyer and N. G. Barrier, pp. 173–190. Berkeley: Berkeley Religious Studies Series.

Metcalf, Thomas. 2007. *Imperial Connections: India in the Indian Ocean Arena, 1860–1920*. Berkeley and Los Angeles: University of California Press.

Singh, Narindar. 1999. 'Canadian Sikh Identity'. In *Punjabi Identity in a Global Context*, edited by Pritam Singh and S. S. Thandi, pp. 387–401. New Delhi: Oxford University Press.

Singh, Khushwant. 1999. *History of the Sikhs*, vol. 2: *1839–1988*. New Delhi: Oxford University Press.

# Part II

# Remigration

# 6

# The Remigration of Hindostanis from Surinam to India, 1878–1921*

*Chan E. S. Choenni*

The Dutch colony of Surinam (present-day Suriname), situated on the northern tip of South America, was one of the last colonies to introduce indentured labour from India. In 1870, after extensive negotiations, the Dutch and British governments signed a 26-article treaty, agreeing to the employment of indentured Indian labourers in Surinam. This Coolie Treaty (*Koelietractaat*) was not implemented for another three years, and it was only on 5 June 1873 that the ship *Lalla Rookh* arrived in Surinam with 410 emigrants, having left the port of

---

*   My thanks to Professor Crispin Bates for his advice and comments. This chapter is based on extensive archival research and an oral history study carried out between 2011–2015, when I was the Lalla Rookh professor of Hindostani migration at the Vrije Universiteit Amsterdam (Free University Amsterdam). It resulted in a voluminous book published in Dutch, in 2016, entitled *Hindostaanse Contractarbeiders 1863–1920* (Hindostani Indentured Labourers), and included an extensive bibliography of primarily Dutch sources (pp. 707–725). Besides the annual reports and proceedings collected and published by L. Sarup-Gajadhar in various volumes (by Aldrich International, Kolkata), the most important sources are the yearly colonial reports (*Koloniale Verslagen*) for the Dutch Parliament, published in 1870–1930. The Immigration Department in Surinam, headed by the agent-general, compiled these *Koloniale Verslagen* reports and reported in detail (including demographic statistics) on the British Indian (Hindostani) indentured labourers. An important Dutch report was written in 1903 by major (retired) P. Wiersma. Wiersma was sent to India in 1902 from Jakarta (then the capital of the Dutch East Indies) by the Dutch government to study the recruiting system for indentured labourers. I have also consulted the relevant files of India Office Records (IOR) in the British Library, London. A database of Hindostani indentured labourers contains the records of 26,249 persons, which amounts to 76.5 per cent of the total arrivals, with the other records having been lost. These records reveal who remigrated to India and who returned to Surinam. The fieldwork reports of G. A. Grierson in 1883 (on Bihar) and D. G. Pitcher in 1882 (on Uttar Pradesh) are also informative about returnees in India. I have also interviewed more than a hundred children and grandchildren of indentured Hindostani labourers in Surinam and the Netherlands, often in Hindi. Part of these interviews were in cooperation with my sister, Gharietje Choenni (Choenni and Choenni, 2012). Most of the data in this article are based on these sources.

Calcutta (present-day Kolkata) in February. Within one year (between June 1873 and April 1874), seven ships followed, bringing almost 4,000 Indian emigrants to Surinam. In total, 34,304 Indian emigrants were received across 64 ships between 1873 and 1916.[1] It is important to note that these Indian emigrants remained British subjects in Surinam. Their descendants did not become Dutch subjects by law until 1927, and by that point the majority had been born in the colony. They designated themselves as Hindostanis ('Hindostanen' in the Dutch language) in reference to their land of origin – Hindustan being one of the original names for India.[2] Due to their status as strangers in a foreign colony, special arrangements protected them. According to Article 9 of the Coolie Treaty, the Indian labourers indentured to Surinam had the right to a free return passage after five years. It also stated:

> If he consents to contract a new engagement he will be entitled to a bounty and will retain his right to return-passage at the expiration of such second engagement. The right of the immigrant to a return-passage extends to his wife, and to his children who quitted India under the age of ten years, as well as to those born in the Colony.

More than a third (11,512) of the 34,304 Indian emigrants returned to British India at the expense of the Dutch government.[3] Yet, significantly, in

---

[1]  De Klerk (1953), pp. 72, 73, 176.

[2]  Choenni and Choenni (2012), p. 51. While in the Caribbean, East Indian is the common designation, the term 'Hindostanis' refers specifically to the Indians of Suriname. This is because in the Dutch language, East Indians can be considered persons from the former Dutch colony, East Indies, now Indonesia. This designation is not used in Surinam. Furthermore, in Surinam there were some indentured lasbourers from the East Indies. They were referred to as Javanese, from the main island of Java. We cannot use the designation 'Indo-Surinamese' like 'Indo-Guyanese' or 'Indo-Trinidadian' because that will refer in Suriname to the Javanese. 'Hindo-Surinamse' would be the best designation. 'Innians' means in Dutch language the so-called Indians, the indigenous Amerindians. All in all, 'Hindostanis' is an unique designation. We prefer 'Hindostanis', and not 'Hindustanis', because Hindustani is also a variant of the Hindi language.

[3]  This calculation is based on the period 1878–1926 covered by a catholic priest, J. M. M. De Klerk (1953, p. 159). De Klerk (b. 1903) was sent to Surinam to convert Hindostanis to Catholicism and wrote a PhD thesis on orthodox Hinduism, followed by a seminal book on the immigration of Hindostanis to Surinam. He was acquainted with many indentured labourers and could speak Hindi. However, he did not write extensively on remigration to British India. Almost one in ten, approximately 3,000 Indians (formerly indentured labourers), settled in Surinam as free colonists from other Caribbean colonies between 1873 and 1920 (De Klerk 1953, p. 177). The primary reason was that they could easily obtain land in Surinam.

spite of the gratis opportunity to return, the majority of the emigrants settled permanently in Surinam. They received approximately 5 acres of fertile land free of rent for six years and 100 guilders (equivalent to the cost of the return passage).[4] Furthermore, over a quarter (9,725) of them signed a second contract for an additional five years in Surinam and received an extra premium of 100 guilders.[5] After settling, these Indians and their descendants became successful small farmers in due course. This chapter intends to explore the remigration of this group of indentured labourers and their offspring from Surinam back to India.

Compared to the other colonies, Surinam provided more favourable conditions for remigration to India. The Indian emigrant could return to India after five years of service, with his wife and any children born in Surinam, at the cost of the Dutch government. The Dutch government and the planters wanted to extend the work required to gain the right to free return to 10 years' service, as had been the practice in the British colonies since 1890. The British government, however, refused; this would have meant repealing the Coolie Treaty of 1870. In particular, the protector of emigrants, D. W. D. Comins, who had visited Surinam in 1892, was against altering the treaty. The third agent-general of Surinam, C. Van Drimmelen (protector of the Hindostanis between 1903 and 1920), was also against the extension to 10 years. He had stated that favourable return conditions made it easier to recruit labourers in India for Surinam, an opinion that was confirmed by the Sanderson Commission.[6] However, Van

---

[4] An able-bodied man could earn 60 cents in Surinam (12 *annas* or *bara-annas*), which was equivalent to 25 dollar cents in the British colonies. Surinam's 64,000 square miles, including a fertile coastal area, were sparsely populated. In 1862, the population was 52,963. This rose to 72,144 in 1900, including the Hindostanis. The Dutch government encouraged the permanent settlement of Hindostanis in Surinam; on so-called government land (*gouvernementsplaatsen*), plots had been prepared for agricultural use by Indian settlers since 1895.

[5] Calculated from the data of the *Koloniale Verslagen* (see Choenni 2016, p. 462), around 1878, one rupee was worth 1.20 guilders (or ƒ1.20 [ƒ is for florin]), and one Guyanese dollar was 2.40 guilders (*Koloniaal Verslag* 1879).

[6] *Report: Minutes of Evidence* (1910); De Klerk (1953), pp. 151–152, 162–163. See IOR/L/PJ/3/201, File 842, Proposal to place Surinam on the same footing in regard to the return passage of immigrants from India as the British West India possessions, 23 May 1881; IOR/L/PJ/6/79, File 1277, Emigration to Surinam: Renewed application of the Netherlands for extension from 5 to 10 years of the final contract entitling Indian coolie immigrants to a free return passage to India, 1 August 1882; IOR/L/PJ/6/79, File 1277, Emigration to Surinam: Renewed application of the Netherlands for extension from 5 to 10 years of the final contract entitling Indian coolie immigrants to a free return passage, 1 August 1882;

Drimmelen was also fiercely against the return of Indian emigrants to India. He maintained that they had more freedom and a higher income in Surinam than in India. Furthermore, he was convinced that some emigrants took up a free passage to India only to return to Surinam within a short period of time, sometimes in less than a year. He pleaded in vain that children born in Surinam should not be allowed free passage to India.[7] Other colonies placed more limitations on obtaining free passage. In Fiji and Jamaica, Indian emigrants lost the right to free passage if they had not taken it up within two years of the expiration of their contract, and in some colonies – for example, British Guiana (present-day Guyana, its modern name after 1966) – the returnees had to cover part of the costs.[8] The returnees from Surinam retained a full free passage unless they accepted the premium of 100 guilders. A small group who remained in Surinam never accepted the premium and therefore retained their right to return to India at the expense of the Dutch government until the 1930s.

## A Comparison

Despite the more favourable conditions in Surinam for returning to India, there is little variation in the number of returnees between most colonies. On the whole, around a third of emigrants travelled back to British India. Fiji, where immigration had started in 1879, six years later than in Surinam, had a slightly higher percentage of returnees. Trinidad and British Guiana had marginally lower return percentages as did Mauritius and South Africa (Natal) where the proportion of returnees was 31 per cent and 28 per cent, respectively. It is crucial to bear in mind the parameters framing Indian emigration to these colonies. Under the influence of Mohandas K. Gandhi, South Africa stopped the recruitment of indentured labourers in 1908, and concerns about increasing the Indian population meant that white South Africans were against further immigration.[9]

---

IOR/L/PJ/6/41, File 842, Emigration to Dutch Guiana (Surinam) Question of extending the period of entitlement for a free return passage to India [a term of ten years instead of five years indenture], 23 May 1881; IOR/L/PJ/6/82, Files 1493–1494, Emigration to Surinam: Question of extending from 5 to 10 years the period of contract in the colony entitling to free return passage; IOR/L/PJ/6/104, File 1386, Reports of the British Consul for 1880, 1881 and 1882; question of extending from 5 to 10 years the period of residence entitling coolies to a free return passage, 15 August 1883; IOR/L/PJ/6/780, File 3364, Indian immigrants in Surinam; proposed modification of the conditions of repatriation, 5 October 1906. See also Nota (Report) Van Drimmelen 1906, nr. 1153, Immigration Department, Paramaribo.

[7]  Nota Van Drimmelen, 13 October 1906, nr. 1153.

[8]  Roopnarine (2009), pp. 74–75.

[9]  Northrup (1995), p. 130.

In Mauritius, by 1911 a large Indian population had already settled, and further recruitment in India for this colony was no longer necessary. The last labourer transport to Surinam arrived in 1916, with the timing of the cessation being dictated by a shortage in available ships during the First World War rather than a surfeit of labour (see Table 6.1).

In other colonies, such as Malaysia and Burma (present-day Myanmar), the return migration was much higher, namely 90 per cent and 71 per cent, respectively. However, these colonies did not have indenture systems but *maistry* or *kangani* systems. This meant that the Indian labourers were recruited and employed by an Indian *sardar* (headman), who often returned with them to India after their labour contract had ended.

There were several reasons to return to India. Most Indian emigrants went to the colonies purely to earn money and always intended to return to India. Therefore, the primary reason for remigration to India was to return with the money they had earned and saved. Some returned unexpectedly, having had bad experiences in the colonies and becoming homesick. They had no doubt compared their life in the colonies with life in India and decided to return. A third group returned to their *janmabhumi* (land of birth) to die, because they considered the colony only as their *karmabhumi* (land of work). Assistant captain C. White, who witnessed one of the last return transports from the Caribbean and the

**Table 6.1** Number of Indian labourers arriving in the colonies and returning to India

| Colony | Arrivals | Returnees | Percentage of returnees |
|--------|----------|-----------|-------------------------|
| Surinam | 34,304 | 11,512 | 34 |
| Mauritius | 453,063 | 134,870 | 31 |
| Trinidad | 145,000 | 43,500 | 30 |
| Guyana | 238,000 | 66,140 | 30 |
| Jamaica | 36,412 | 12,109 | 33 |
| South Africa (Natal) | 152,184 | 42,610 | 28 |
| Fiji | 60,000 | 22,800 | 38 |
| Guadeloupe | 42,000 | 10,500 | 25 |
| Martinique | 20,000 | 4,000 | 20 |

*Sources*: Shepherd (1992); Mansingh and Mansingh (1999); Laurence (1994); Choenni (2016).

embarkation in Trinidad, remembers that the returnees were dressed in their best clothes and observed:

> Old men sat around, youngsters crowed, and women jingled their bracelets. All seemed happy at the prospect of seeing India ... some of the East Indians of Trinidad had not seen Calcutta for fifty years, and one old fellow told me that he had arrived on the island with his father when he was twelve years old, and that now, at the age of sixty-eight, he was returning to Calcutta for the first time. He said he would wait at Calcutta 'till death come', and he seemed to regard this as a jolly prospect. Many of these emigrants were like that – returning to the banks of the Ganges to retire on their savings after a life-time of labour on the plantations of Trinidad. Others, more well-to-do, were travelling to the land of their fathers for a holiday and were accompanied by their women and children.

Others returned with the intention to visit their family before going back to the colonies. It is estimated – based on the statistics in the yearly colonial reports on Surinam – that 20 per cent of the Hindostani returnees succeeded in migrating again to Surinam (approximately 900 returnees) and to other colonies.

Among the returnees from Surinam, there was a special category; the Dutch government also implemented the remigration of those who were destitute, paupers and unwilling to work. More than 10 per cent of the returnees from Surinam to India belonged to this group. Other colonies treated this category similarly. Between 1838 and 1859, for example, the Guianese government remigrated 3,584 Indians, and among this number were 'blind persons, lepers, criminals and sick persons'.[10] After 1920, these 'paupers' were forcibly remigrated. On the steamer *Sutlej*, which left Georgetown (the capital of British Guiana) in 1929, 97 of the 520 returnees were allocated as 'paupers'. In 1931, more than half (56 per cent) of the returnees from Trinidad were 'destitutes' being remigrated at the expense of the Trinidad government.[11]

The majority of the approximately 12,000 returnees from Surinam were men (61 per cent), while one-fifth were women (21 per cent). It is clear that fewer

---

[10] Cross (1996), p. 17.

[11] See IOR/L/PJ/6/626, File 289, Proposed repatriation of Indian lepers from Paramaribo, 13 February 1903; IOR/L/PJ/6/630, File 554, Return to India of lepers, paupers and lunatics from Surinam, 19 March 1903; IOR/L/PJ/6/705, File 23, Repatriation of Indian immigrants in Surinam, 2 January 1905; IOR/L/PJ/6/744, File 137, Indian immigrants in Surinam, 28 December 1905; IOR/L/PJ/6/744, File 137, Repatriation of lepers and lunatics, 28 December 1905; IOR/L/PJ/6/756, File 1052, Repatriation from Surinam of British Indian lepers and lunatics, 6 April 1906; IOR/L/PJ/6/839, File 4283, Repatriation from Surinam of lepers and 'lunatic' immigrants, 13 December 1907.

women (35 per cent of arrivals versus 21 per cent of returnees) returned to British India than arrived in the colony. Regardless of the opportunities to settle in the colonies, for indentured women such as widows and 'fallen women' (prostitutes or those who had committed adultery) the option to return was obsolete. As Rosemarijn Hoefte remarked, many would be 'despised and mobbed' in their village, or they would have to spend significant amounts of money to be reinstated in their caste. Remarkably, almost one-fifth of the returnees (18 per cent) were children born in Surinam who were also entitled to a free passage.[12]

## Return Transports and Savings

The 22 return transports to India prior to 1921 were mainly ships that had also brought Indian migrants to Surinam or British Guiana. Steamers made the journey shorter and more comfortable than sailing ships. However, almost two-thirds (7,263, or 63.8 per cent) of Hindostani returnees travelled back to India on the latter, while only 4,128 (36.2 per cent) went by steamer. Arrivals in Surinam were by much the same modes of transport, with two-thirds coming by sail, but the return journey was on average longer than the journey from India to Surinam.

The returnees who saved money or invested it in jewellery and coins took it to British India. The amount of money deposited by them and the value of the jewellery and coins handed over to the ship's surgeon for safekeeping were recorded. The money was transferred to the Hong Kong Shanghai Bank in Calcutta, and upon arrival returnees presented a cheque to collect it. The jewels and coins were handed back at the Surinam depot in Calcutta. In order to get an indication of the average sum of money taken back to India, it is possible to compare the records of two years: one ship carrying a high value of savings and one ship with a low amount of money deposited. Only the men have been included in the calculations, as it is assumed that the women belonged to families and had a male partner. In 1894, the returnees on the ship *Silhet* deposited 115,387.56 guilders in cash and 9,218 guilders worth of jewellery and coins. On average, the men took back more than 350 guilders. In 1911, the returnees on the ship *Sutlej* deposited much less money: 57,995.86 guilders and 10,800 guilders worth of jewellery and coins. On average, the men among the returnees on this ship possessed more than 130 guilders.[13]

---

[12]  Hoefte (1998), p. 164.

[13]  McNeill and Chimman Lal (1914), p. 180.

Over the course of the whole period from 1878 to 1921, the total amount of money recorded across the 22 return transports is 1,501,628 guilders (see Table 6.2). When this figure is divided between the total number of returnees (11,351), it means that the average amount saved by a Hindostani

**Table 6.2** Return transports and value of jewellery and coins carried (in guilders), 1878–1921

| Year | Ship | Men | Women | Children | Total | Money carried | Jewels/ Coins |
|------|------|-----|-------|----------|-------|---------------|---------------|
| 1878 | *Philosopher* (1) | 265 | 114 | 107 | 486 | 44,100.25 | 2,203.65 |
| 1879 | *St. Kilda* (2) | 207 | 80 | 46 | 333 | 23,110.85 | 2,350.– |
| 1884 | *Silhet* (3) | 298 | 131 | 108 | 537 | 115,387.575 | 9,218.– |
| 1886 | *British Peer I* (4) | 331 | 136 | 156 | 623 | 78,287.425 | 8,900.– |
| 1887 | *John Davie* (5) | 290 | 98 | 92 | 480 | 37,908.015 | 10,333.– |
| 1889 | *Jumna I* (6) | 237 | 142 | 148 | 527 | 95,126.345 | 20,045.– |
| 1890 | *Jumna II* (7) | 333 | 116 | 121 | 570 | 71,675.18 | 10,746.– |
| 1891 | *British Peer II* (8) | 360 | 122 | 119 | 601 | 86,034.095 | 16,563.– |
| 1895 | *Grecian* (9) | 339 | 142 | 124 | 605 | 89.687.37 | 15,501.35 |
| 1897 | *Foyle** (10) | 131 | 49 | 33 | 213 | 26,837.37 | 3,697.60 |
| 1898 | *Arno* (11) | 434 | 157 | 152 | 743 | 91,588.72 | 14,750.– |
| 1899 | *Clyde** (12) | 157 | 36 | 21 | 214 | 35,933.765 | 2,501.50 |
| 1900 | *Erne** (13) | 142 | 49 | 38 | 229 | 40,600.30 | 5,572.25 |
| 1903 | *Rhone** (14) | 236 | 50 | 32 | 318 | 48,245.54 | 5,673.– |
| 1904 | *S.S. Indus** (15) | 189 | 41 | 35 | 265 | 27,787.425 | 5,099.– |
| 1905 | *Avon* (16) | 485 | 134 | 115 | 734 | 80,084.71 | 11,433.50 |
| 1907 | *S.S. Mutlah I** (17) | 182 | 29 | 20 | 231 | 33,311.00 | 4,322.50 |
| 1909 | *S.S. Mutlah II* (18) | 371 | 76 | 54 | 501 | 38,700.325 | 4,026.50 |
| 1911 | *S.S. Sutlej* (19) | 418 | 105 | 80 | 603 | 57,995.86 | 10,800.– |

*(Contd)*

Table 6.2   (*Contd*)

| Year | Ship | Men | Women | Children | Total | Money carried | Jewels/ Coins |
|------|------|-----|-------|----------|-------|---------------|---------------|
| 1913 | *S.S. Mutlah III* (20) | 488 | 106 | 74 | 668 | 70,323.45 | — |
| 1920 | *S.S. Madioen* (21) | 586 | 205 | 183 | 974 | 187,874.71 | 29,625.– |
| 1921 | *S.S. Sutlej II* (22) | 513 | 199 | 174 | 886 | 201,113.00 | 25,000.– |
| Total | 22 return ships | 6,992 | 2,317 | 2,042 | 11,351 | 1,501,628.– | 197,388.– |

*Source*: Choenni (2016), p. 509.
*Note*: *These ships left from Georgetown (British Guiana).

returnee is 132.29 guilders. However, we must detract the destitute (10 per cent) and children (20 per cent) from the total number of migrant passengers. This leaves the average amount of money saved per adult at almost 200 guilders. These figures can be compared with the data mentioned by Lomarsh Roopnarine. According to Roopnarine, the amount saved by indentured labourers from Surinam was slightly lower than this calculation. Returnees from Surinam arrived in Calcutta with an average of 77 dollars (1873–1916), while those from British Guiana had 51 dollars (1875–1910), those from South Africa (Natal) had 48 dollars (1902–1907), and those from Trinidad possessed 67 dollars (1899–1907).[14] These sums converted into guilders (1 dollar was 2.40 guilders) means that the average Hindostani returnee from Surinam took home 184.80 guilders. It is clear that those returning from Surinam deposited on average the highest amount of money. Payment in Surinam might have had been low, and sometimes lesser wages were paid than agreed, but it is evident that this still allowed for significant savings. These were attained through thrift and very sober lifestyles – or *phet kat kat*, which meant cutting back on your stomach – and supplementing incomes by selling agricultural products, for example.

## Returning after 1921

Most of the 22 return transports departed from Paramaribo (the capital of Surinam). Six left from Georgetown, as when it was apparent that there were not enough prospective returnees for a full transport, they were sent to the coolie depot in Georgetown and waited to embark there. This could take some days.

---

[14]   Roopnarine (2012), p. 137.

During the First World War, there were no return transports, and returnees had to wait until 1920, when a Dutch steamship was chartered to bring Javanese indentured labourers from Java to Surinam. In the meantime, an influenza epidemic broke out in Surinam, reaching its height in 1918 and claiming the lives of a small group of migrants waiting to return. In 1921, the steamer *Sutlej II* embarked upon the last voyage carrying labourers back to India directly from Surinam. Its passengers returned with the highest recorded savings in money and jewellery.

After 1921, very small numbers of returnees returned from Surinam via British Guiana at their own expense. In 1922, 150 migrants wished to return to India, but only 15 succeeded in paying for their voyage. In 1924, on 29 August, 38 Hindostani returnees embarked in Georgetown for India, arriving in Calcutta on 18 October 1924.[15] A larger group of Hindostanis, comprising of 39 men, 11 women and 30 children, managed to return in 1926 on the steamer *Chenab*. Many gave the reason for their return as a desire to visit family and specifically parents.[16] Out of the adult passengers, 18 had deposited a total of 9,566.62 guilders, and 13 possessed jewellery with an average value of 2,873 guilders. By 1929, only 20 Hindostani returnees journeyed back to India.[17] One of the last return, transports from the Caribbean colonies on the new steamer *Ganges* was arranged in 1936. Almost a third (254 out of 865 returnees) of those travelling were older than 50, and many had left India more than 30 years ago.[18] The majority of them were from British Guiana and Trinidad, which were much larger colonies, and only a small portion of 18 hailed from Surinam.[19] The respective sizes of the different Caribbean colonies are evident in the numbers of expectant returnees. For example, in 1930 in Trinidad, 42,000 Indians emigrants wanted to return to India, but the provisions, including ships, were not available. In 1931, 1,012 of them were actually able to return.

---

[15]  *Koloniaal Verslag* (1925).

[16]  *Koloniaal Verslag* (1927).

[17]  De Klerk (1953), p. 159.

[18]  Roopnarine (2009), p. 76.

[19]  It was notable that for the first time the ship's doctor (surgeon superintendent) on the return voyage was someone who resided in the Caribbean and was qualified as a surgeon, having qualified at the University of Edinburgh in 1917. J. B. Singh was married in Paramaribo, in 1910, to Alice Bhagwandy, the daughter of the first Hindostani leader and head interpreter, Sitalpersad Doobay, the aide of the agent-general. After their marriage and the Hindu wedding party in the Koelie depot, they moved to British Guiana. J. B. Singh and Alice Bhagwandy became leaders of the Indo-Guianese community. See also Seenarine (1998) and Mangru (1996), p. 229.

During the Second World War, return voyages ceased entirely. In the 1930s, returns to India from Surinam organised by the Dutch government definitively closed down, despite protests from some Hindostani organisations. The demand for them remained high, and in 1948, around 1,500 Indian immigrants in Surinam were still registered as desiring repatriation. After the end of the Second World War, the last return voyage from the Caribbean colonies was in 1954. The Indian government was not happy with the arrival and settlement of returnees in India. When the 1954 return transport arrived, prime minister Jawaharlal Nehru commented disapprovingly, 'Thetar log agaye' (The stubborn people have come).[20] He had strongly advised the Indians in the colonies to settle there and become good citizens, whilst maintaining that they must not forget India and keep the name of 'Mother India' (Bharat Mata) in high regard.

On the journey back, the returnees wore tin plates marked with their identification numbers around their necks. Both a representative of the Surinamese government and a Surinamese surgeon accompanied them; yet the passengers were subject to poor health on board, with outbreaks of diseases such as measles and a high death rate. Remarkably, however, in regard to Surinam, the average death rate on the return voyages was lower than for those arriving in Surinam, despite the presence of the destitute among the returnees. There was some variation depending upon the mode of transport. On the sailing ships, the average percentage of migrants who did not survive the return journey was 1.6 per cent, while among arrivals it was 2.6 per cent. The death rate on steamers was less variable, with 0.96 per cent of returnees dying, compared to 1.3 per cent of arrivals in Surinam. In total, the death rate on the 22 return voyages was 1.2 per cent (138) comparable with 2.1 per cent (714) on the 64 ships that arrived with indentured labourers.[21] Interestingly, the birth rate was also lower on return voyages rather than arrivals. For the former, the birth rate was 0.90 per cent on the sailing ships and 0.16 per cent on the steamers. On ships arriving, it was 0.56 per cent and 0.83 per cent, respectively.[22] According to P. C. Emmer, few pregnant women were on board steamers returning to India, accounting for the low percentage of births.[23] It should be remembered that there was a low percentage of women on return voyages in general – only 20 per cent of returnees were female and above 10 years old, compared with the 30 per cent present on ships arriving in Surinam.

---

[20]  Bahadur (2013), p. 169.

[21]  Calculated from the *Koloniale Verslagen* (1873–1927).

[22]  These percentages are calculated as the percentage of those born out of the total number of emigrants on the ships to and from Surinam.

[23]  Emmer (1989), p. 413.

Upon travelling back to their 'homeland', some of the returnees believed that they should arrive as Indians and behave as such – for example, their clothing should be changed appropriately. Marianne Ramesar includes the observation of Linton Gibbon, an assistant to the quartermaster on a return voyage from Trinidad to India in around 1904.[24] He recorded upon nearing Calcutta:

> All the Indians communicated that they did not want to set foot in India looking like Trinidadians (i.e. in dress). They wished to look like Indians, like Hindus ... so they were given all kind of cotton to make cotton capras (clothes). They insisted on shaving their heads, leaving only a little top-knot or chorkee. There was no one to save them, and the captain refused to let the Indians use the razors of which there were some 50 on board. Instead the sailors were ordered to shave the Indian's heads. The sailors were novices, unaccustomed to this 'barbering' so they took a few days to finish the task, shaving a few heads per day of the 500–600 men (not the women).[25]

Gibbons mentioned that many Indian men were bleeding after the shaving. The returnees disembarked on the banks of the Hooghly at Garden Reach, where the depots of the recruiting agencies were situated. It must have been a curious spectacle to see hundreds of Indians disembarking with shaven heads and *choorkis* (topknots) at the port of Calcutta. They were housed in the depots of Calcutta for some days in order to make administrative arrangements, and then they could leave.

One problem faced by indentured Indians was that after finishing their labour contract, whether of five or ten years, they often had to wait for a return voyage due to the difficulties in chartering return ships. Delays occurred when a ship was not immediately available for a group of emigrants who had arrived on the same ship in Surinam and therefore commenced and ended their contracts simultaneously. For example, those labourers who had arrived in April 1898 and finished their five-year contract in 1902 had to wait until 1903 for a ship to be chartered. The relatively small number of returnees in Surinam were not sufficient to justify a yearly voyage to India. In the meantime, the returnees had to wait in Surinam, and the Dutch government had to take care of them, rather than the planter they had worked for. The British consul residing in Paramaribo protected them. Still, few official complaints were lodged at the British consul office about these delays. Instead, the returnees complained that they had to spend their savings to live. According to the writers of the report of 1914, J. McNeill and Chimman

---

[24] Ramesar (1994), pp. 63–64.

[25] Ramesar (1994), p. 63.

Lal, who were mandated by the British government to evaluate Indian emigration to the Caribbean and the living conditions there, few complaints were made about the return voyages themselves. This scarcity of grievances is confirmed by the yearly colonial reports of the Dutch government. According to the Coolie Treaty of 1870, it was obligatory that the protector of immigrants interviewed the returnees about their return voyages and reported back to the Dutch government. The archives, including the yearly colonial reports on Surinam, turn up little directly about the return voyages. One return voyage from Surinam in 1898, with the sailing ship *Arno*, is described as having had 'troubles' (*moeilijkheden*). The *Arno* arrived in Calcutta on 6 January 1899, more than half a year after its departure from Paramaribo. It had docked in the port of Pernambuco, Brazil, shortly after leaving Surinam, and the British consul there had to mediate between the returnees and the ship's captains. The troubles themselves are not described.[26] The return ships were British ships, mostly of the Nourse Line shipping company, which specialised in 'coolie transport'. Only one return voyage was with a Dutch steamer, the *Madioen*, in 1920; it is reported that this voyage to Calcutta ended very satisfactorily.[27]

Once in Calcutta, those who had a cheque went to collect their money from the bank in rupees and *anna*s and were addressed as *chequewallah*s. Many returnees stood out with their strange behaviour and clothes. This was not without its dangers – some Calcutta gangs specialised in robbing the returnees immediately after they had collected their money. They particularly targeted those who hired *tanga*s (horse-drawn carriages) to go to the bank.[28] After these robberies, it was suggested that paying the cheques out in the districts of the returnees' villages would perhaps be more practical, but administrative complications meant that this proposal did not materialise. Those who had collected their savings in Calcutta were also afraid, with good reason, to then travel onwards to their villages due to fears of being robbed on the way. However, some needed no help in dispensing with their earnings and dissipated them in a short time, becoming poor again in India.[29]

Returnees were called *tapuhua*s in India. This meant somebody from the *tapu*, or island, as many thought that the colonies were synonymous with islands. As already remarked upon, the *tapuhua*s could often be recognised by their strange 'non-Indian' behaviour and clothes. One of the identified changes in

---

[26] De Klerk (1953), p. 155.

[27] *Koloniaal Verslag* (1921).

[28] Ramesar (1994), p. 62.

[29] Pitcher (1882), p. 105.

character was that they had become too self-assured and independent. For example, the immigration agent of Trinidad and Fiji, O. W. Warren, remarked that there was a difference 'between a Cooly leaving India and a returned Cooly', when he gave evidence at the Sanderson Commission in 1910. He said that coolies leaving India would approach him and touch his feet, but those returning would shake his hand and ask, 'How are you?' He also supplied the information that many returnees chose to leave India again because they considered it 'too unhealthy'.[30] Benarsidas Chaturvedi conducted research among returnees and in particular with those from the Caribbean. He concluded that not only had the returnees changed during their time away, but India had changed too.[31]

Some returnees might have lived for some time in their villages prior to departure for the colonies, but their changed behaviour due to their time away made it difficult for them to re-accustom themselves with the hierarchical caste rules in India. This could lead to friction, and sometimes returnees decided to re-emigrate. J. M. M. De Klerk recalled the story of the paternal grandfather of a prominent Hindostani family in Surinam belonging to the Chamar (leatherworkers) caste:

> When he rested after his return in his village he sat before his house on a khatiyá or carpai [a light bedstead consisting of a web of rope or tape netting]. He had been accustomed to sit in that manner in Surinam. But he had not realized that the tyranny of the caste hierarchy still existed in India. A Chamar – that was his caste – was not allowed to sit on a khatiyá, but only on the floor or the ground. A Brahmin [someone belonging to the highest caste] of the village saw this violation of caste rules. He approached him and knocked him as a punishment with his kharao [wooden sandal] on his head. After this beating this returnee reconsidered his decision. He realized that social sphere in his country of birth was too oppressive for him. He decided to return to Surinam and acquired a new agreement. He became later a businessman in Surinam. Interestingly his descendants became highly educated and some married Brahmins in Surinam.[32]

Many returnees became stranded in a pitiable situation in their birthplace. Some were not recognised because they had changed their name from that

---

[30]  *Report: Minutes of Evidence* (1910).

[31]  Sannyasi and Chaturvedi (1931), p. 17. They stated: 'Such a journey would anyway entail a relaxation of social strictures on caste purity. However, what often happened on their return was being accorded a status of an outcaste.... at least one-fifth of all returnees from the colonies became stranded in Calcutta. Many of them were old, infirm and destitute often unable to trace their villages kinsfolk or reintegrate into caste proud communities.'

[32]  De Klerk (1953), p. 157.

of their father's or they were not believed because they were considered to be dead – after hearing nothing from the person in more than five years, this conclusion was not unreasonable. Others could no longer locate their families; they might have moved villages, or sometimes the address itself or even the name of the village had changed. In other cases, their parents were already dead. Poverty was another reason to leave home-villages again and go back to the colonies. Some returnees never made it back to their villages due to the fear of rejection. This was especially the case among returnees who had left their family without any notice or following conflicts.

Returnees who reunited with their family could be initially exploited and then repudiated. For example, a young emigrant who returned to his village was expelled as a *pariah* (outcast) after he had spent all his money and was declared *maila* (filthy forever) because he had crossed the *kala pani* (sea).[33] Due to his *maila* status, it was assumed that nobody would marry him or marry into his family. Others were shunned from the village because they no longer fitted within the social structure there. Many returnees were not only weak after their travails, but they could also be perceived as a nuisance. A familiar example in Surinam is the story of a female returnee who was not accepted anymore by her family in India. She retreated as an outcast into the jungle of the Sundarbans ('Achut ban ke Sundarban men chalge').[34] Another example is of women belonging to a higher caste who had married a man from a lower caste. They had lived 10 years in Surinam and returned together to India. Yet, once there, he was repudiated by her with the remark, 'You low-caste man, I have nothing more to do with you.'[35] In some cases, a reconcilement ritual was performed when a family member who had fled to the colonies returned and was reunited with their relatives. Often these rituals cost money, however, and not everyone could afford them or were willing to pay the priests (*pundits*) for the performance. Even if you were accepted by your family and village, it could be difficult to find employment (lack of it having been a common reason for departure in the first place). Those returnees who no longer had relatives and friends in India were still confronted with fewer opportunities in an already overpopulated country.

The returnee Totaram Sanadhya, from Fiji, mentioned the case of the brahmin Guljari Lal, who returned in 1914 to India, in his autobiography. Guljari had with much effort saved 800 rupees during his eight years in Fiji. A practising *pundit* and brahmin, he regularly obtained *sidha* (alms, such as food) from pious

---

[33]  Weller (1968), p. 109.

[34]  Choenni (2016), p. 532.

[35]  Roopnarine (2009), p. 28.

Hindus and could save money. However, his brother insisted that he return to India. Guljari decided to acquiesce, and the Hindus in Fiji gave him extra donations when they heard that he would return to the holy land of India. When he arrived back in his village, he handed over all his savings to his brother for safekeeping:[36]

> Guljari told the villagers about his journey to Fiji and stated that this journey could be considered as a pilgrimage. Still he had to pay for the rituals to be re-instated in his caste and a *katha* [holy reading] meeting from the Bhagvat Gita [the holy Hindu scripture] would be organized. People from five or six neighbouring village would be invited. The religious feast would cost 700 to 800 rupees. When Guljari asked his brother to give him his savings back, his brother refused to give him his money. Soon he learned that the villagers had outcasted him, because he was not able to pay for a *katha* meeting. His brother became his enemy and Guljari was now hated in his village. The returnee Guljari experienced that he was cheated. He wrote a letter to his friends in Fiji explaining his problems and his wish to return to Fiji. Hindus in Fiji collected money for him. Guljari was able to go back to Fiji paying a passage with this money and settled permanently in Fiji.

Not all returnees experienced a downturn in their fortunes in India. Some returnees became successful and bought land there. A couple of them gradually even became *zamindars* (big landowners) and inspired others to emigrate to the colonies.[37] A familiar example is the case of a rich returnee from Trinidad. He brought not only his Indian wife with him to India but also his Creole *sautan* (co-wife).[38] However, the overall impression is that the majority were not successful.

Some returnees, disappointed about the living conditions in India, tried to qualify for a new agreement. How many returnees regretted their decision and resettled themselves back in the colonies is unclear, but it is evident that a large number of these returnees failed to get a new agreement. Not all returnees had intended to stay in India permanently and planned to re-recruit themselves under false names. Fraudulent claims within the recruitment process were not unheard of – Hindus, for example, might have claimed to be Muslim or Christian to avoid caste restrictions. Returnees were not in high demand by the plantation owners; therefore recruitment in India was very stringent for them, necessitating the falsehoods described here. Many returnees were weakened by their previous labour and were considered critical towards accepting orders. Still, on most ships

---

[36] Sanadhya (2003), pp. 71–72.

[37] Committee on Emigration from India and Sanderson (1910), p. 83.

[38] Weller (1968), pp. 107, 109.

to the Caribbean, a proportion of the emigrants were re-emigrating from India with a new agreement. For example, in the year 1887, more than 13 per cent of the Indian emigrants that went to Trinidad consisted of returnees (285 of the 2,185 emigrants). On the ships to British Guiana, 7 per cent of the emigrants between 1890 and 1902 were returnees that had served in other colonies.[39] Many returnees from Surinam in vain tried to come back there on a new agreement and in the end headed elsewhere. Between 1885 and 1894, some 175 returnees from Surinam in India succeeded in acquiring agreements for Trinidad.[40] Others resorted to paying for their own passages.

### The Queen of Sheba

On board the ships, returnees who had obtained new agreements were not popular among the crew and the first-time emigrants because they were often considered instigators and dishonest, having sometimes resorted to enrolling themselves under another name. It is also alleged that some returnees abused the system by using their free passages to see India again before travelling back to the colony on a new agreement. One returnee even openly stated at his embarkation for India, 'I will come back.'[41] The Queen of Sheba, an Indian, provides an interesting case study. In 1877, on the coolie sailing ship *Sheila*, a rich and very handsome woman of 40 years returned at her own expense from India to Trinidad. A widow, she had made a fortune as a businesswoman in Trinidad and was named the Queen of Sheba by the ship's crew. Upon travelling back to India, she was not allowed to retain her caste because she refused to pay the high price that was demanded. She left India and told Captain Angel that 'India is a just place for only coolies.' When the ship stopped at the island of St Helens, she bought the whole catch of fish there and treated the emigrants to a fish feast. This rich and independent Indian lady was clothed in luxurious Indian dress and wore expensive jewellery. Her picture is on the front page of Captain Angel's book.[42]

It must be mentioned that the returnees who disembarked in Calcutta were often not desired as permanent settlers there. Most of the returnees who tried to obtain a new agreement in Calcutta had to stay temporarily on the banks of the Hooghly River and watch the ships depart. They retained the idle hope that they would obtain new agreements for the colonies, where living conditions were better than in India. According to the ambassador, Maharaj Singh, who

---

[39] Bahadur (2013), p. 68.
[40] Weller (1968), p. 165.
[41] Weller (1968), p. 110.
[42] Angel (1995), p. 90.

visited British Guiana, the emigrants had a better life than their companions who
stayed behind in India. He concluded that in the colony they were more
independent, the burden of castes was extinct and there was no purdah (the
practice of isolation of women from public life). According to the researcher
Chaturvedi, the personality of these emigrants might have changed during their
stay in the Caribbean, making them less servile, but they lived in Calcutta in
pitiable circumstances. They settled in the area of Matiaburz, a suburb of Calcutta
opposite the port area of Garden Reach where the depots were situated. According
to Chaturvedi, one-fifth of all returnees were stranded in Calcutta, and they
became 'outcasts' in Indian society. They lived there, 'dispersed among this district
in bustees, infected by malaria, without work, care and medical treatment'.[43]
A Surinamese delegation consisting of the head interpreter, Sitalpersad, and
*pundit* Ramharakh, companions of the returnees on the return voyages,
came across ex-indentured labourers from Surinam who lived like outcasts in
Matiaburz in the 1920s. Many of them could not go back to their birthplace or
had been driven from it, and were attempting to obtain new labour agreements.[44]
Many returnees had become physically weak and even disabled and were
therefore considered burdens upon society. Even without physical changes,
it was difficult to mentally adjust back to the old customs, particularly for
women, and they became homesick for Surinam, regretting their decision to
leave. They pleaded in vain to Hindostani representatives for them to request
that the Dutch government organise their return there.

The disillusioned returnees who settled in Calcutta became a problematic
group for the Indian authorities. Gandhi and the influential minister
C. F. Andrews complained about the costs of feeding the returnees and
inducting them back into normal life in British India.[45] Gandhi described the fate
of these returnees in pathetic terms. According to him, they had jumped from
the frying pan (the colonies) into the fire (India). It was considered better that
they be sent outside of India.[46] In the beginning, the British government had
vainly tried to block the plans of the colonies to allow the emigrants to return to
British India because the assumption was that the returnees would claim the
jobs of the Indians who had never left. This was also one of the reasons behind

[43] Sannyas and Chaturvedi (1931), p. 17.

[44] De Klerk (1953), p. 156. De Klerk quotes a study by Etienne Dennery *Foules d'Asie* (1930, pp. 212–214), who, while in Calcutta, met some hundred returnees from British Guiana who had been very disappointed in their expectations.

[45] Shepherd (1992), p. 102.

[46] Shepherd (1992), p. 103.

the liberal Indian politician Gopal K. Gokhale pleading for the cessation of Indian emigration. In 1912, Gokhale had introduced a resolution in the Indian parliament prohibiting indentured labour. He stated that the indenture system deprived the people of their freedom. The famous woman poet Sarojini Naidu agreed that the indenture system was merely a replacement for slave labour. The nationalists believed that it should be seen as the transitional stage between slave labour and free labour.

## Cessation of Indian Emigration

Besides the problems caused by returnees, the recruitment and emigration of strong and healthy Indians was objected to. Madan Mohan Malaviya and Gandhi, in particular, insisted on stopping emigration as soon as possible. Gandhi was markedly against the returning of emigrants to India because, afraid of the social repercussions and possible unrest, he wanted to prevent those in South Africa from coming back. This was despite the fact that he himself had lived in South Africa and returned to India. The British government reluctantly agreed to end the indenture system on 12 March 1917.[47]

The cessation was severely regretted by the Surinamese government and the Hindostani community in Surinam. Quoting the British report of McNeill and Lal from 1914, they pleaded that the indenture system and immigration to Surinam had more advantages than disadvantages. On the Dutch steamer *Madioen*, a Hindostani delegation left in 1920 to plead for the reopening of immigration. Members of the delegation were H. N. Hajari, an official of the Immigration Department; head-interpreter Sitalpersad; son-in-law of Sitalpersad; the aforementioned J. B. Singh; and the wealthy businessman Lutchman Singh, a prominent Hindostani leader. They had a meeting in Varanasi with Malaviya and talked with Gandhi and the Muslim leader Shaukat Ali in Ahmedabad. They also pleaded with Lal, then mayor of the city of Meerut. However, according to the delegate Hajari, their counterparts were impressed by the good treatment and position of Hindostanis in Surinam, and they rejected a reopening of immigration. Only Lal was in favour.[48] When, on 18 March 1918, the Coolie Treaty of 1870 was repealed by the British government, it was stated in an authoritative publication in Surinam that 'we have had the opportunity during 45 years to populate Suriname with British Indians, but compared to Demerara we have profited less'.[49]

---

[47]  Tinker (1974).

[48]  De Klerk (1953), pp. 178–179.

[49]  Translation mine.

In 1922, a new effort was made to restart emigration from India. A few hundred emigrants left for the island of Mauritius – most of them were returnees from the Caribbean, South Africa and Fiji. However, afterwards, emigration from India based on the indenture system stopped forever. In 1922–1924, the immigration agency of Surinam and the main barrack (depot) in Calcutta was liquidated. In 1927, the Hindostanis in Surinam, who were until then British subjects, became Dutch subjects. The protection extended by the British government ceased and the British consul left Surinam. The immigration department in Paramaribo was liquidated in 1932, along with assistance for Hindostani returnees.[50]

## Conclusion

We must bear in mind that the indenture agreement between the Dutch government and the emigrant was signed voluntarily in order to supply temporary labour. Of course, some were misled, but the majority took the opportunity to earn money, possibly initially with a view to returning to India with their savings. There were also those who knowingly left India permanently for a better life compared to the oppressive situation there; two-thirds of Indian emigrants settled in Surinam and did not use their free passage to India. This proves that life for them was economically better there than in British India. Surinam might not have had been a British colony, but as British subjects, emigrants could easily obtain land after finishing their service. Furthermore, many of those who did return home regretted their decision and spent time and energy attempting to reengage for Surinam.[51] Thus, the remigration of Hindostanis from Surinam to India was hardly a success. Further research on the disillusioned returnees and their offspring in India, as well as their memories of the colonies, is necessary.

---

[50]  De Klerk (1953), pp. 180–181.

[51]  For example, the protector of emigrants in Calcutta stated, on 18 February 1893, to the government of Bengal that 'many Indians were induced to emigrate only because they would eventually be able to return to their country, friends and family'. The Indian government was of the opinion that 'if the return passage was completely abolished, then the Indians probably would not wish to emigrate' (see Weller 1968, pp. 101, 103). Desai and Vahed (2010) refer to the disillusion of the Indian returnees from South Africa (pp. 2–4). In Surinam, I detected the myth of the *bharmai deis* (inveiglement). In total 52,330 emigrants were recruited for Surinam, but only 34,395 embarked at Calcutta for Surinam. The dropout rate was 34.3 per cent (17,935). The most important reason for dropping out was the several stringent medical tests. The emigrants then had to sign an agreement with the Dutch government. The (assistant) magistrates in India were responsible for the procedure and the protector of emigrants in Calcutta reaffirmed it (Wiersma 1903).

# Bibliography

Angel, W. H. Captain. 1995. *A Return to the Middle Passage, the Clipper Ship 'Sheila'.* Trinidad: CIS.

Bahadur, Gaiutra. 2013. *Cooliewoman: The Odyssey of Indenture.* London: Hurst & Company.

Bates, Crispin. 2003. 'Courts, Ship-Rolls and Letters: Reflections of the Indian Labour Diaspora'. In *Creating an Archive Today*, edited by T. Awaya, pp. 131–158. Tokyo: Tokyo University of Foreign Studies, 21st Century COE Programme, Centre for Documentation and Area-Transcultural Studies.

Bhagwanbali, Rajinder. 1996. *Contracten Voor Suriname.* Den Haag: Amrit.

Bhagwandy, Alice. 1958–1962 (1997). *Autobiography of Alice Bhagwandy Sital Persaud*, edited by Sushila Patil and Moses Seenarine. http://mosessite.blogspot.nl/2011/05/autobiography-of-alice-bhagwandy-sital.html. Accessed on 29 April 2021.

Choenni, Gharietje G., and Chan E. S. Choenni. 2012. *Sarnami Hindostani 1920–1960.* Amsterdam: KIT Publishers.

Choenni, Chan E. S. 2016. *Hindostaanse Contractarbeiders 1873–1920.* Volendam: LM Publishers.

*Koloniaal Verslag* (Colonial Report). 1863–1930. Bijlagen van Tweede Kamer der Staten-Generaal, Ministerie van Koloniën. 's-Gravenhage.

Comins, D. W. D. 1892. *Note on the Immigration from the East-Indies to Surinam or Dutch Guiana.* Calcutta: Bengal Secretariat.

Committee on Emigration from India, and Thomas Henry Sanderson. 1910. *Emigration from India to the Crown Colonies and Protectorates: Report of the Committee on Emigration from India to the Crown Colonies and Protectorates*, vol. 27, parts 1–2 (appendix). Westminster.

Cross, Malcolm. 1996. 'East Indian–Creole Relations in Trinidad and Guiana in the Late Nineteenth Century'. In *Across the Dark Waters*, edited by David Dabydeen and Brinsley Samaroo, pp. 14–38. London: Macmillan Publishers.

De Klerk, C. J. M. 1953. *De Immigratie der Hindostanen in Suriname.* Amsterdam: Urbi et Orbi.

Desai, Ashwin, and Goolam Vahed. 2010. *Inside Indenture: A South African Story.* Cape Town: HSRC Press.

Emmer, P. C. 1984. 'The Importation of British Indians in Surinam'. In *International Labour Migration*, edited by Shula Marks and Peter Richardson, pp. 90–111. London: Maurice Temple.

———. 1989. 'The Coolie Ships: The Transportation of Indentured Labourers between Calcutta and Paramaribo, 1873–1921'. In *Maritime Aspects of Migration*, edited by Klaus Friedland, pp. 402–426. Köln: Böhlau Verlag.

Grierson, G. A. 2011 (1883). 'Report on Colonial Emigration from the Bengal Presidency'. In *Facts about Indian Indentured Labour*, edited by Leela Gujadhur Sarup. Kolkata: Aldrich International.

Hoefte, Rosemarijn. 1998. *In Place of Slavery: A Social History of British Indian and Javanese Laborers in Suriname*. Gainesville: University Press of Florida.

Lal, Brij V. 2004. *Girmitiyas: The Origin of the Fiji Indians*. Lautoka: Fiji Institute of Applied Studies.

Laurence, K. O. 1994. *A Question of Labour: Indentured Immigration into Trinidad and British Guiana, 1875–1917*. London: James Currey Publishers.

Look Lai, Walton. 1993. *Indentured Labor, Caribbean Sugar: Chinese and Indian Migrants to the British West Indies, 1838–1918*. Baltimore, MD: John Hopkins Press.

Lubbock, Basil. 1955. *Coolie Ships and Oil Sailors*. Glasgow: Brown, Son & Ferguson.

Mangru, Basdeo. 1996. 'Indian Government Policy towards Indentured Labour Migration to the Sugar Colonies'. In *Across the Dark Waters*, edited by David Dabydeen and Brinsley Samaroo, pp. 162–174. London: Macmillan Publishers.

Mansingh, Laxmi, and Ajai Mansingh. 1999. *Home away from Home: 150 Years of Indian Presence in Jamaica, 1945–1995*. Kingston: Ian Randle Publishers.

McNeill, J., and Chimman Lal. 1914. *Report on the Condition of Indian Immigrants in the Four British Colonies and Surinam or Dutch Guiana*. Simla: Government Central Press.

Northrup, David. 1995. *Indentured Labor in the Age of Imperialism, 1834–1922*. Cambridge, UK: Cambridge University Press.

Pitcher, D. G. 1882. 'Report on Colonial Emigration from the North West Provinces and Oudh'. In *Facts about Indian Indentured Labour*, edited by Leela Gujadhur Sarup Kolkata: Aldrich International.

Sarup, Leela Gujadhur. 2010 (comp.). *Annual Reports and Proceedings: Colonial Emigration 19th & 20th Century*. Kolkata: Aldrich International.

———. 2011. *Facts about Indian Indentured Labour*. Kolkata: Aldrich International.

Ramesar, Marianne. 1994. *Survivors of another Crossing: A History of East Indians in Trinidad, 1880–1946*. St Augustine: University of the West Indies, School of Continuing Studies.

———. 1996. 'The Repatriates'. In *Across the Dark Waters*, edited by David Dabydeen and Brinsley Samaroo, pp. 175–200. London: Macmillan Publishers.

*Report: Minutes of Evidence*. 1910. Part II. Westminster.

Roopnarine, Lomarsh. 2009. 'The Repatriation, Readjustment, and Second Term Migration of Ex-Indentured Indian Laborers from British Guiana and Trinidad to India, 1838–1955'. *New West Indian Guide* 83(1–2): 71–97.

———. 2012. 'Regulations and Remittances from British Indian Indentured Guianese'. *Comparative Studies of South Asia, Africa and the Middle East* 32(3): 662–673.

Sanadhya, Totaram. 2003. *My Twenty-one Years in the Fiji Islands*. Suva: Fiji Museum.

Sannyasi, Bhawani Dayal, and Benarsidas Chaturvedi. 1931. *A Report on the Emigrants Repatriated to India under the Assisted Emigration Scheme from South Africa and on the Problem of Returned Emigrants from All Colonies*. Calcutta: Pravasi Press.

Seenarine, Moses. 1998. *Voices from the Subaltern*. New York: Columbia University Press.

Shepherd, Verene. 1992. *Transients to Settlers: The Experience of Indians in Jamaica, 1845–1950*. Kingston: Peepal Tree.

Tinker, Hugh. 1974. *A New System of Slavery: The Export of Indian Labour Overseas 1830–1929*. London: Oxford University Press.

*Traktaat Staatsblad van het Koninkrijk der Nederlanden* (The Official Gazette of the Kingdom of Netherlands), 17 March 1872. Den Haag: Staatsdrukkerij en Uitgeverij.

Weller, Judith Ann. 1968. *The East Indian Indenture in Trinidad*. Río Piedras: Institute of Caribbean Studies, University of Puerto Rico.

White, L. G. W. 1936. *Ships, Coolies and Rice*. London: Sampson Low.

Wiersma, P. 1903. *Verslag Eener Zending Naar Britsch-Indië*. Paramaribo: El Dorado.

# 7

## Not So Anchored

### The Remigration of Indians within the Caribbean Region

*Lomarsh Roopnarine*

Caribbean migration studies have focused overwhelmingly on the forceful and semi-free movements of Africans and Asians during the period of slavery and indentureship as well as the extra-regional movement of Caribbean nationals to Europe and North America following the Second World War.[1] These studies have done remarkably well in excavating the dynamics so associated with the aforesaid patterns of Caribbean migration, namely how migrants were uprooted from their homeland and transported across the Atlantic and Indian oceans to provide the oxygen of labour on the Caribbean plantations. Studies of migration from the Caribbean following the Second World War show how Caribbean nationals have been pushed out of the region and pulled to developed destinations. Moreover, these studies have provided the fundamental reasons for the leaving and settling of the migrants. They have revealed how the migrants have adapted, settled and even reconfigured the demographics, economics and cultures of the receiving enclaves.[2] Howbeit, studies of migration within the Caribbean pale in comparison to the larger influx during the period of slavery and indentureship as well as out-migration following the Second World War. Still, even when studies are conducted on migration within the Caribbean, they are ethnically imbalanced, focusing largely on Africans and Hispanics.[3] Yet when studies are conducted on Asians, the remigration of them within the Caribbean is largely absent.

The academic exclusionary treatment of Indians in the general Caribbean migration narrative is rather unfortunate since Indians have been on the move since the mid-nineteenth century from India to the Caribbean, within the Caribbean, from the Caribbean to Europe and North America and back

---

[1] Curtin (1969); Look Lai (1993); Roopnarine (2007); Andersen (2018).

[2] Foner (2001); Thomas-Hope (2009).

[3] Marshall (1982); Putnam (2002); Duany (2011).

to the Caribbean.[4] Crispin Bates and Marina Carter ask, 'Why did such a large number of Indian labour migrants who had completed one term of service overseas return to India, and then remigrate, or move from one colonial territory to another?'[5] These scholars espouse that 'the frequency of remigration, and of onward migration to other colonies suggests considerable enterprise and strategic thinking on the part of labour migrants seeking out opportunities within the interstices and constraints of the colonial labour economy'.[6] Until we understand how wide and complex the remigration of Indians has been, one important aspect of their migratory experience will remain a puzzle and buried in the lower depths of Caribbean migration. The non-remigration thesis is a misrepresentation of Caribbean Indians since they have historically and contemporarily reacted in the same way as other ethnic groups, albeit in their own unique fashion. Moreover, the remigration of Indians has shaped, contributed as well as invoked institutional change in the sending and receiving islands within the Caribbean. If these points are not recognised and addressed, then the migratory patterns of Indians within the Caribbean will be grossly misrepresented in the migration historiography of the Caribbean.

The goal of this chapter is not to merely trace, recover or reconstruct the past and present remigration of Indians within the Caribbean, but to also examine under what circumstances and with what methods Indians have migrated to achieve better livelihood opportunities. Additionally, the purpose is not just to put remigration in the historical and contemporary narrative of the Caribbean, which had been left out, but to also provide categories of analysis so that proper recognition is given to ways in which remigration coda provides a vital understanding of how Caribbean Indians have been structured, ordered and organised in a relatively small island space where race, color and class matter. This chapter pulls together the waves of remigration of Indians to analyse the individual and cumulative impact they have had on sending and receiving destinations in the Caribbean from indenture to the modern period. The main argument of this chapter is that the remigration of Indians has been more active and wider than previously discussed. The contention is that while some segments of the Indian Caribbean population have been subdued by colonial regulations, poverty and political parochialism, other segments have remigrated for better life opportunities against tremendous odds and, in so doing, have formed mini-Indian diasporas within the Caribbean. Structurally, this chapter divides the analysis

[4] Roopnarine (2018).
[5] Bates and Carter (2021).
[6] Bates and Carter (2021).

of Caribbean Indian remigration into four sections. The first section provides a background of Indians in the Caribbean in terms of migration. The second examines remigration during indenture. The third assesses remigration during the post-indenture period up to the pre-independence period. The fourth delves into remigration following the independence period after the 1960s and the 1970s. The final section summarises the findings. Sources for the chapter have been drawn from archival and secondary sources as well as from informal interviews and conversations.

## Overview of Indian Migration

The limited literature on the remigration of Indians within the Caribbean region during the period under discussion suggests that when indenture immigration ceased from India in 1917 and indenture was abolished in 1920, so did Indian migration in the Caribbean. This characterisation is a misnomer. Indians were not non-migratory people but quite on the contrary showed myriad migration dynamics that have unfortunately escaped analyses. The mere thought that Indians travelled thousands of miles to labour in foreign colonies would imply that they would continue this movement looking for better livelihood opportunities. Their indenture-contract obligation did not pin them down to a specific spot in a specific colony as narrated elsewhere. Likewise, Indians did not remain on their adapted island or country during the post-indenture and modern periods. They were actively involved in migration, demonstrating that their lives had not been one-dimensional.

Indian Caribbean migration can be divided into two broad overlapping phases: during indenture and the modern period. There are seven recognisable phases of Indian migration, from 1838 to 1920. The first is the movement in India before the indenture system. Millions of Indians were moving from rural to urban areas in India as well as to nearby European colonies looking for work and religious inspiration.[7] The movement was seasonal and circular, determined by the rhythm of agriculture and the marketplace. The second is the movement of Indians during the period of indenture from 1838 to 1920. An estimated 500,000 Indians were shipped to the Caribbean.[8] A majority went to British Guiana (present-day Guyana), Trinidad and Surinam (present-day Suriname), and a smaller number went to Jamaica, the Windward Islands, and French and Danish West Indian Islands. The third is the return migration of Indians who had successfully served

---

[7]  Mongia (2018).

[8]  Tinker (1974); Laurence (1994); Hoefte (1998).

their terms of indenture service. An estimated 175,000 returned to India when their labour contracts expired in the Caribbean. Although the indenture system ended in 1920, the return migration of Indians continued until 1955.[9] The fourth is the remigration of Indians who had served indenture in the Caribbean and returned to India and then contracted themselves for a second or even a third time to labour on the Caribbean plantations.[10] The size of this movement is unknown, but an estimated 500 every year during indenture remigrated from India to the Caribbean. The fifth is the movement, during the early post-indenture period, of those Indians who did not sign labour contracts to work on the plantations. They paid their passage to come to the Caribbean. An estimated 10,000 arrived in British Guiana between 1920 and 1940.[11] The sixth is the trans-colonial movement, which involved movement from one indenture colony to another.[12] For example, some indentured Indians spent over 15 years indenturing themselves: five years in British Guiana, five years in Mauritius and another five years in Natal, South Africa. The seventh is the movement from the estates to settlements in each Caribbean colony. Thousands of Indians moved from the estates to land settlements, which was larger than the movement from the Caribbean to India.[13]

Caribbean Indian migration in the modern period can be divided into four phases. The first is the rural–urban movement – for example, from the countryside to Georgetown in British Guiana, Port of Spain in Trinidad, Paramaribo in Surinam and Kingston in Jamaica.[14] The former are the capital cities of the latter islands or countries. This movement has always been small. An estimated 20 per cent have been actively involved in this rural–urban migration. The second is the movement within the Caribbean, notably from one Caribbean island to another, although the movement is more visible in the southern English- and Dutch-speaking Caribbean.[15] The third is the extra-regional migration from the Caribbean to Europe and North America[16] as well as a small movement from the Caribbean to India. The latter movement has always been small in comparison to

---

9   Samaroo (1982); Roopnarine (2006).

10  Roopnarine (2009).

11  British Guiana: Immigration Agent Report 1921–1940, Guyana National Archives, Georgetown.

12  Roopnarine (2016).

13  See Potter (1975).

14  Shepherd (1986).

15  Roopnarine (2018).

16  Choenni (2013); Premdas (2014); Gowricharn (2015).

pre-1955 return migration from the Caribbean to India. The fourth is the return and transnational migration from destinations back to the Caribbean.[17]

Two analyses are warranted regarding these phases of Indian migration. They have not occurred in isolation from each other. There are overlaps, which can be labelled as criss-crossed migration. For example, in- and out-migration during indenture occurred at the same time. Some migrations were not period-specific. Rural–urban, intra-regional and transnational migrations have been ongoing from indenture to the modern period. Unfortunately, statistics for each movement are rare and imbalanced, which adds to blind spots in Caribbean Indian migration studies. Indian migration has expanded to include more phases, namely the movement of non-indentured Indians since the Second War World to the Caribbean[18] and the migration between the diasporas in Europe and North America. We know little of these migratory patterns.

## Remigration during Indenture

The remigration among Indians during the indenture period can be divided into two categories: illegal and legal. The illegal category of migration reveals unexpected aspects of Indian migration. It shows a determination among some segments of the indentured population to achieve a better life against colonial constraints. To recall, Indians were shipped to the Caribbean on a strict labour-contract system that allowed practically no out-migration options from their stationed plantation base on their terms. The labourers were required to work on a particular plantation until their contracts expired and then returned to India. Any deviation from their contractual obligations resulted in heavy fines for the labourers. Moreover, if anyone was found assisting Indians to move away from their plantation, they were subjected to fines and imprisonment.[19] The Caribbean sugar planters ensured that the contractual engagement was carried out to reap the maximum benefits from their investment. The colonised Indian government insisted that the Indians remain and serve their contracts on specifically assigned plantations, fearing that any movement away from their contractual obligations would result in the abuse of the labourers. The indentured labourers themselves did not possess the knowledge of their surroundings, at least in the first years of indenture, to engage in illegal migration from their plantation base. Even those that did out-migrate illegally in the form of desertion ended up worse off from their

---

[17]  Gowricharn (2009).

[18]  Hanoomansingh (1996).

[19]  British Parliamentary Papers (1989 [1904]), p. 30.

departed domicile. Some became vagrants and beggars in urban areas, while others inadvertently re-engaged themselves with abusive employers who took advantage of their illegal status. Put together, these aforesaid dynamics placed the living and working conditions of the labourers in a state of servitude that allowed little escape from the demands of the labour ordinances to an alternative environment where a different life could be fulfilled.

While the Indian labourers complied with their contractual obligations, some defied them and sought ways to create livable opportunities by themselves and for themselves, beyond the bound plantation yards. Emerging literature shows that when a labouring community is suppressed, or when their aspirations towards a better life regarding basic rights, fair wages and their conditions of employment are denied, they will use any means they can find, including migration, to improve their living circumstances.[20] Through insurgency and resistance, the labouring class or the subaltern uses its own daily experiences to challenge structural domination. Within this context, the indentured Indians developed and applied a variety of innovative strategies to improve their lives through migration in a controlled and conflict-habituated plantation environment. They were not total captives to a paternalistic plantation economy in which institutional and ideological forms of domination prevailed.

There was small and steady illegal migration in the form of desertion among indentured Indians to other Caribbean regions: from Trinidad to the coca plantations in northern Venezuela, from British Guiana to Dutch Guiana and from the French Caribbean islands to other islands. The size of this illegal migration is not precisely known, but it was continuous during indenture. Data do exist on desertion from plantations in specific colonies. For example, between 1865 and 1890, 13,988 Indians deserted the plantations located in British Guiana, while in Martinique 741 Indians deserted the plantations between 1862 and 1874. Desertion was not restricted within each island, given the small size and proximity of the islands. These geographical features encouraged remigration since the size of the islands would not have guaranteed a safe hideout from authorities, and the short distance between the islands made migration more feasible. Likewise, many Indians deserted from their coastal plantation base to the interior regions of British Guiana and Surinam, places that constituted another region because of the distance and tough terrain. Those remigrating by deserting were comparatively few when compared to those that remained on the plantations. Nevertheless, the significance of desertion is more important than the actual population size of the deserters.

---

[20] Scott (1990, 1985); Spivak (1985); Foucault (1972).

The illegal movement reveals another side of the indenture system that cannot be summarily dismissed as a mere flight from the plantations. The movement represented the first significant attempt by Indians to escape their insular island environment, which demonstrated an attempt to move from a controlled to an independent survival. The movement also laid the foundation for further movement, demonstrating that there existed an alternative, however limited and risky, to indentured labor, which disappointed indentured Indians could emulate if so desired. Some desertions occurred based on desperation to escape the yoke of exploitation, and so they were not pre-planned, which added to the underbelly of the indenture system. Some deserters were stranded in urban slums or exploited by their new employers. Some patterns of desertion, however, exhibited knowledge and innovation. The deserters utilised the proximity of the Caribbean islands to each other to escape – for instance, from Venezuela to Trinidad or to British Guiana's forested terrain. Like under slavery, the indentured deserters understood that the closeness and natural environments of the islands provided opportunities for a secure survival, however temporary. The deserters recognised that the planters were constrained by the very environment they were attempting to conquer and colonise. British Guiana's forested terrain was too insuperable for the planters to deal with desertion.

The illegal remigration in the form of desertion within the Caribbean revealed patterns and practices among the indentured not seen in archival or secondary sources. From the viewpoint of indentured Indians, their remigration might have had been illegal, but it was justified. To some indentured Indians, the system offered far too few opportunities for family and personal development. To a labourer living in such difficult circumstances, the idea of desertion offered the possibility of an escape from their labour obligations on the plantation to an entirely new environment where they could start over. In this regard, desertion was a form of migration based upon an aspiration for freedom from oppressive regulations and patterns of work. The movement was an instinctive reaction to the unique drudgery and hazards of life on the plantations. Remigration occurred within the confines of the indenture system in an attempt to transform situations and circumstances to the advantage of the workers, looking for the weakest links in the system of indenture and using them to their advantage. The more militant indentured deserters sometimes even took huge risks to acquire the freedom they desired. These dynamics contributed significantly to the complexity of the movements and settlement of Indian labourers during indenture. The pattern of desertion was more individualistic than collective, more reactionary to plantation conditions than pre-planned and more consistent, even though fewer labourers were involved in comparison to those who remained working on the plantations. The practice of desertion as a form of migration is evidence that some Indians were not willing to be cowed into indenture even when they signed indenture contracts.[21] Their desire to desert showed a considerable degree of determination to live autonomous lives against tremendous odds. Some had a great sense of pride in their achievement of 'freedom' within an environment that was specifically designed to control them.

The legal remigration began in the 1870s when Indians completed their contract and began to settle in the Caribbean. The planter-inspired exchange of return passages for small parcels of land was instrumental in the formation of a cluster of Indian settlements around the sugar plantations. The objective was to provide some economic security for time-expired Indians and to have a steady supply of cheap labour on the plantations. Some Indians used their new settled environment to live a stable life, engaging in full-time employment with the sugar industry, working the available land independently to bring in additional income and rearing livestock. The settlements allowed Indians to reconstruct their homeland culture with some modifications. Indians became comfortable with rural life, which in many ways were similar to their homeland in terms of the climate and peasant life. Despite challenges of the land settlement scheme regarding limited support from the colonial government, Indians were able, for the first time following their arrival in the Caribbean, to break out of their insular plantation domains to a life of independent survival. The option to have a settlement in a new land with their own ethnicity provided them with the opportunity to weigh the advantages of barrack living and India.

To Indians, the land settlement schemes held possibilities for a gradual and better future compared to remaining on the plantation permanently or returning to India. The out-migration from both places was a mark of progress. The land settlement schemes created more possibilities for a stable life for the Indian settlers. As time progressed, Indians became more cognisant of the opportunities related to remigration to other destinations in the Caribbean, encouraged by the movements of other ethnic groups and time-expired Indians. It was not shocking then that as soon as the contracts of the first batch of Indians that arrived in Jamaica in 1845 expired, they followed other post-emancipation workers and remigrated to Cuba. In the first few decades of the twentieth century, an estimated 3,000 Indians from Jamaica migrated to Cuba.[22] The remigration of time-expired Indians among

---

21   See Mahase (2008).
22   Sarusky (1989).

islands during indenture occurred in almost every place where Indians were indentured. By the 1860s, Indians were remigrating from the Windward Islands to British Guiana and Trinidad, from St Kitts and Nevis to Danish St Croix; from the 1870s, from British Guiana to Surinam and between British Guiana and Trinidad; from the 1880s, from Belize to Jamaica; and from the 1890s to the 1920s, mostly from British Guiana to Surinam.[23] The Surinamese historian Maurits Hassankhan stated that about 2,500 Indian migrants went from British Guiana to Surinam during the period of indenture and until 1926. These migrants were integrated into the Hindostani community and became small-scale farmers.[24]

The Indian remigration was not all based on providing manual labour. Some Indians remigrated within the Caribbean islands for trading and educational purposes, although more research is needed to quantify the size and impact of these activities in the sending and receiving colonies of Indians. What is certain is that they did travel, although temporarily, for religious reasons. The remigration was largely influenced by Christian missionaries – mainly from Canada – in the Caribbean. To convert Indians to Christianity, the missionaries provided Western forms of education and the needed social services to the Indian communities. Over time their impact on Indian communities was very noticeable in the areas of socio-economic development and Christian-influenced education. However, the mission was met with opposition from Hindu and Muslim leaders for imposition on the general welfare of their children and community. The mission also faced internal challenges, particularly in reaching the Indian community at large. To get around this challenge, the mission appointed some Indians to the priesthood and encouraged many others to become teachers and catechists. Their aim was to use the experiences of Indian workers to make the process of their conversion to Christianity less cumbersome. What emerged from this program was that migratory Indians spread the doctrines of Christianity. Brinsley Samaroo writes that from Trinidad, the Christian mission was extended to Grenada in 1884 and then to St Lucia and British Guiana in 1885.[25] In 1894, Indian pastors were also dispatched to Jamaica to help the Presbyterian church to reach the indentured workers living there. Similarly, Hindus and Muslims also sought to reinforce cultural–religious beliefs among themselves, which in turn stimulated a modest remigration among Indians in the Caribbean region.

---

[23] Roopnarine (2003).

[24] Maurits Hassankhan, email communication and interview with the author, Suriname, 6 April 2015.

[25] Samaroo (1975), p. 93.

## Remigration of Indians in the Modern Period

As already noted in the previous sections, the remigration of Indians began during indenture and continued up until the 1960s when some countries with a high Indian population became independent. During the colonial period, Indian remigration was driven by stern indenture regulations, cultural and economic aspirations, proximity, ethnic tensions, civil unrest and economic stagnation. The remigration of Indians within the Caribbean following the 1960s and the 1970s was driven by push and pull factors so associated with migration. Indians were pushed out of their home countries by political turbulence, ethnic tensions and economic deprivation and pulled to better livelihood opportunities in other Caribbean islands within the developing world. The remigration of Indians was also determined by geographical closeness, common history, culture, language, family networks in the receiving destinations and favourable immigration laws for skilled workers to meet the overall Caribbean integration initiative. During the early 1970s, governments within the independent English-speaking Caribbean countries came together and developed a free movement clause within the Caribbean Community (CARICOM), called CARICOM Single Market and Economy (CSME), which allowed for skilled persons to be granted the right to move and work freely throughout the Caribbean region. This new development regarding the movement of Caribbean people within the Caribbean was welcomed by some countries with struggling economies. The Indo-Guyanese, for example, took advantage of this liberal immigration clause and remigrated to Trinidad and Barbados, where they have formed noticeable minority populations. This movement was dictated and determined by respective national governments rather than precipitated by the migrants themselves.

The remigration of Indians within the Caribbean has revealed some interesting patterns. First, Indians preferred to move to other Caribbean islands or countries that are closest to them because it was less costly and more manageable. For example, the Indo-Guyanese have been migrating to Suriname and Trinidad. Second, Indians have been migrating to countries that have a larger population of Indians, motivated by the desire to join communities of similar ethnic composition and tradition that makes them feel at home. Third, Indians will remigrate to the growth poles in the Caribbean, irrespective of the ethnic background in the receiving destination. The size of the Indian remigration population in each Caribbean country is unknown. An estimated 120,000 have remigrated from their original indenture base to another Caribbean island following the 1960s. Most of the remigrants are of Guyanese Indian descent, while a minority of them are Indo-Trinidadians and Indo-Surinamese. Trinidad has been more politically and economically stable than Guyana and Suriname, which has stymied remigration from Trinidad because of economic stability. There are about 40,000 and 30,000 Indo-Guyanese living in Suriname and Trinidad, respectively. The remigration of the Indian population to the receiving destination is not homogeneous, however. The time of entrance to the receiving destination generally determines and dictates the differences in status. For example, in an interview, an Indian female Suriname vendor, selling mainly Indian CDs, at the New Nickerie Market, stated that she is half-Guyanese and half-Surinamese since her father came from Guyana and met her mother in Suriname in the 1970s.[26] There are many types of Indian Caribbean remigrants in the receiving destinations: (*a*) those who have migrated and settled, (*b*) those who have migrated and married other Indians, (*c*) those who have migrated and married other ethnicities and formed hybrid families, and (*d*) those who have been living permanent remigration lives, travelling regularly between the sending and receiving countries on a short-term basis.

The remigrants' experience in the Caribbean varies according to their social status and the ethnic make-up of the islands they choose to reside in. Upper- and middle-class Indians are well received in practically any Caribbean island, since their skills are welcome in the drive to promote growth and development. The working-class Indian remigrants do not receive similar treatment like their upper- and middle-class counterparts. They are seen as a burden to the host island, placing unnecessary pressure on limited resources. The ethnic make-up of the island that the remigrants enter fundamentally determines the kinds of treatment they receive. If they remigrated to islands and countries where there is a large concentration of Indians, they tended to face fewer challenges of integration, although this observation is not axiomatic. Guyanese Indian remigrants have done remarkably well in Suriname and Trinidad since they have been remigrating from an ethnologically similar environment to the ones they have left behind. Their adjustment to and the ill-treatment by the wider society are minimal. They are generally free to express their mannerisms, speech and cultural ways, such as the Hindu religion. This is not to suggest that the Indo-Guyanese do not face challenges in their new Indian communities. They still find it difficult to integrate themselves and lack the appropriate channels to negotiate for better treatment and available services, and therefore feel constrained, confused and demoralised in their new environment.

Of all places that Indians have remigrated to within the Caribbean, they face the worst treatment in Barbados. The Council on Hemisphere Affairs (COHA)

---

[26] Anonymous Indian female Suriname vendor, interview with the author, New Nickerie Market, Suriname, 25 June 2015.

reveals that as soon as Guyanese remigrants arrived in Barbados, they were placed on designated benches at the airport 'in an effort to single out illegal Guyanese refugees'.[27] Guyanese migrants in Barbados experience cultural and racial discrimination, especially Guyanese individuals of Indian ethnicity. Racial consciousness and social extremes are rather acute in Barbados, going back to colonial times when light skin was seen as a symbol of social superiority and dark skin quite the opposite. The Indo-Guyanese, being overwhelmingly low-class and brown, fit in the lower end of the inferiority category. Anti-Guyanese feelings have taken many forms in Barbados, ranging from inflammatory remarks from politicians and talk-show hosts to newspaper editorials seeking electoral capital and political mileage that portray immigrants as a threat to the demographic, cultural and national unity. The immigrants are perceived as infringing on sovereignty and changing the racial composition, as evidenced by one report indicating that 'there is discrimination against Guyanese of all ethnic groups, but this anti-Indian feeling seems to be more pronounced and prominent' in Barbados.[28]

The steady influx of Indo-Guyanese has stirred up ethnic feelings in Barbados. Bajans are concerned that the racial African and Indian tensions in Guyana would be imported to Barbados. Unlike in Trinidad, where Indo-Guyanese migrants generally feel at home, the circumstance in Barbados is different. Indo-Guyanese migrants face more challenges of adjustment not only in Barbados but also in the predominantly Creole Caribbean. However, the rural Indo-Guyanese tend to face challenges of adjustment the most because of their insular ethnic upbringing as well as the lack of an established base in their new environment with limited supporting networks. Moreover, the Guyanese Indian population are first-generation migrants who are not always cognisant and confident enough to push for rights and representation because of the fear of identification and deportation. Some associations help with the difficulties of leaving their homeland, but they are concerned with the preservation of national culture through the revival and resuscitation of Guyanese holidays. These associations do not represent or address exclusive ethnic interests. They are symbolic, lacking the forceful tendencies so needed to challenge the bureaucracy and demand rights. The mindset of the Indo-Guyanese migrants, too, in Barbados presents its own set of adjustment problems. These are economic migrants who are uninterested in assimilating into Creole norms or sensibilities. They were familiar with the Creole culture in the Caribbean before remigrating. Still, some migrants are also skeptical and suspicious of the

---

[27]  Associated Press (2009).

[28]  Niles (2006).

Creole culture, especially those Indians who were hurt by Forbes Burnham's racial politics in Guyana. Additionally, the Indo-Guyanese migrants are first-generation migrants who tend to retain their culture. Cultural retention among first-generation migrants is generally strong and persistent. Subsequently, the perception of Indo-Guyanese cultural ways in Barbados is anti-patriotic. Bajans identify with Africanness and view the newcomers with suspicion. It is the first time that Bajans have made significant contact daily with an ethnic group that is Asian Caribbean and different from their own. Naturally, misplaced or misguided feelings do surface, such as the fear that the immigrant group will take over. Ethnic tensions are, however, sporadic rather than the norm.

Indo-Caribbean people have been remigrating beyond the CARICOM region, practically to almost all islands in the Caribbean. Outside of the CARICOM region, remigration of Indo-Caribbean has been less fluid and more regulated and restricted. Remigration to the still dependent colonies such as the United States (US) Virgin Islands requires a visa according to US immigration laws. This explains why the population of Indians is relatively small on these islands. The arrival of these migrants coincides with an upsurge in growth and development in tourism, construction and industry in the microstates of the Caribbean, which have opened a wide array of opportunities for jobs and investment. While there are only a few recognisable Indo-Caribbean communities in the predominantly Creole Caribbean beyond the CARICOM, Indo-Caribbean people have found employment in the private and public sectors, occupying high-level positions. They have also been successful in transferring their Indian culture, culinary and construction skills. In the US Virgin Islands, they have established Hindu *mandirs* (temples) and Indian restaurants, while in Dutch St Maarten, they have dominated the construction industry, particularly during the period of rebuilding after hurricanes.

The children of these Indian remigrants, too, have been pursuing university education, taking advantage of various governmental reforms and opportunities in the dependent colonies. This younger generation will, over time, depart from the weight of oppression that their grandparents and parents carried because of the uprootedness from their homeland and the challenges of integration in their new domicile. They are more eager to unwrap themselves from negative stigma and seize the opportunities arising from the processes and sacrifices of their previous generations. They will eventually become the new generation of model citizens of their new environment through individual motivation, dedication and hard work.

## Conclusion

The objective of this chapter is to assess the remigration of Indians in the Caribbean during and after indenture. The remigration of Indians within the Caribbean is multifaceted and complex, grounded and driven by strict indenture immigration ordinances, economic deprivation, religious zeal, ethnic tensions, political turbulences, personal ambitions, proximity, diverse immigration regulations, governmental policies and uneven levels of development in the Caribbean region.

Four patterns of remigration have been identified. First, during the period of indenture, the remigration of Indians in the Caribbean was driven by the strict indenture ordinances intended to constrain them from seizing opportunities beyond their bound indenture yards. While most of the indentured servants complied with their indenture contracts, some ten per cent of them defied indenture regulations and out-migrated from their insular plantation base to other Caribbean islands. This movement demonstrated that the indenture experience of all Indians was not uniform but diverse, revealing characteristics of resistance and accommodation in a transplanted plantation world. Second, as soon as their indenture contracts expired, a third of the Indians returned to India, while two-thirds of them remained in the Caribbean but not necessarily on the indenture plantations. Some 15 per cent out-migrated legally from their country or island to other destinations in the region, notably between Guyana and Suriname. This remigration movement reveals that Indians were aware of the region close to them in terms of cultural connection and job opportunities. This movement was driven by the need to re-establish or even establish new cultural and economic ties based on ethnicity. Third, the remigration of Indians in the Caribbean following the Second World War was dictated by government policies of economic integration to promote regional growth and development. Indians in Guyana, more so than any other country with a sizable Indian population, have been actively involved in this encouraging remigration program. Guyana is one of the poorest countries in CARICOM, dogged by decades of bad politics and corruption. The Indo-Guyanese have adjusted and assimilated well in countries such as Suriname and Trinidad with similar ethnicity. In contrast, remigration of Indians to the Creole Caribbean has been more challenging in terms of adjustment and settlement as they have been seen as an immigrant group coming to take over, place a burden on social services and transform the demography of the receiving island. Fourth, remigration of Indians has been to the developed dependent colonies of Europe and the US such as the Dutch Caribbean and the US Virgin Islands due to the job opportunities in tourism. Although there are no known visible enclaves in these regions, Indians have transferred their culture and made significant contributions in the private and public sectors.

Taken together, these remigration patterns have shown that Indians have been on the move since they arrived in the Caribbean, contrary to the thought that they were contained in the cyclical movement between India and the Caribbean. Moreover, as these remigration dynamics continue, they have demonstrated that the once dominant movement between India and the Caribbean, and even from the Caribbean to Europe and North America, has shifted to within the Caribbean, although unequally. The movement within the Caribbean has displayed a similar motivation of survival, and that is to use whatever means possible to achieve better livelihood opportunities rather than being trapped in a one-dimensional circumstance. The prediction is that remigration will continue in the Caribbean because a culture of this movement has been formed with significant populations of migrants-turned-citizens in their new domicile. Incoming migrants will fare better than their predecessors since the latter group will act as pioneers and ambassadors that will make adjustment and integration less cumbersome. It is expected that the receiving destinations, irrespective of ethnic differences, will be more tolerant of the newcomers because of a longer period of exposure to and association with them. Finally, remigration of the Indians will continue because of unequal development in the Caribbean.

## Bibliography

Andersen, Astrid N. 2018. 'The Reparations Movement in the United States Virgin Islands'. *Journal of African American History* 103(1–2):104–132.

Associated Press. 2009. 'Caribbean islands Cracking down on illegal Immigrants'. 5 September.

Bates, Crispin, and Marina Carter. 2021. 'Remigration of Indian Subalterns in the Colonial Indian Ocean'. *Journal of Colonialism and Colonial History* 22(1). DOI: 10.1353/cch.2021.0010.

British Parliamentary Papers. 1989 (1904). *Coolie Immigration: Immigration Ordinance of Trinidad and British Guiana*. London: Her Majesty's Stationary Office.

Curtin, Phillip. 1969. *The Atlantic Slave Trade*. Madison, WI: University of Wisconsin Press.

Choenni, Chan E. S. 2013. 'Happy in Holland: The Hindostani Elders in the Netherlands'. *Sociological Bulletin* 62(1): 40–58.

Duany, Jorge. 2011. *Blurred Borders: Transnational Migration between the Hispanic Caribbean and the United States*. Chapel Hill, NC: University of North Carolina Press.

Foner, Nancy (ed.). 2001. *Islands in the City: West Indian Migration to New York*. Berkeley: University of California Press.

Foucault, Michael. 1972. *The Archaeology of Knowledge*, translated by A. M. Sheridan Smith. New York: Pantheon Books.

Gowricharn, Ruben. 2009. 'Changing Forms of Transnationalism'. *Ethnic and Racial Studies* 32(9): 1619–1638.

———. 2015. 'Sociability Networks of Migrant Youngsters: The Case of Dutch Hindustanis'. *Current Sociology* 65(5): 1–18. DOI: 10.1177/0011392115605628.

Hanoomansingh, Peter. 1996. 'Beyond Profit and Capital: A Study of the Sindhis and Gujaratis of Barbados'. In *Ethnic Minorities in Caribbean Society*, edited by Rhoda Reddock, pp. 273–342. Trinidad: Zenth Services Limited.

Hoefte, Rosemarijn. 1998. *In Place of Slavery: A Social History of British Indian and Javanese Laborers in Suriname*. Gainesville, FL: University Press of Florida.

Laurence, Keith. 1994. *A Question of Labor: Indentured Immigration into Trinidad and British Guiana, 1875–1917*. New York: St Martin's Press.

Look Lai, Walton. 1993. *Indentured Labor, Caribbean Sugar: Chinese and Indian Migrants to the British West Indies, 1838–1918*. Baltimore, MD: Johns Hopkins Press.

Mahase, Radica. 2008. 'Plenty a Dem Run Away: Resistance by Indian Indentured Labourers in Trinidad, 1870–1920.' *Labor History* 49(4): 465–480.

Marshall, Dawn. 1982. 'Migration as an Agent of Change in Caribbean Island Ecosystems'. *International Social Science Journal* 34(3): 482–498.

Mongia, Radhika. 2018. *Indian Migration and Empire: A Colonial Genealogy of the Modern State*. Durham, NC: Duke University Press.

Niles, Bertram. 2006. 'Are Guyanese Welcome in Barbados?' BBC Caribbean, 7 September. http://www.bbc.co.uk/caribbean/news/story/2006/09/060906_guyaneseinbdos.shtml. Accessed on 20 October 2021.

Potter, Lesley. 1975. 'The Post-Indenture Experience of East Indians in Guyana, 1873–1921'. In *East Indians in the Caribbean: Colonialism and the Struggle for Identity*, edited by B. Brereton, pp. 1–92. Millwood, NY: Kraus International Publications.

Premdas, Ralph. 2004. 'Diaspora and Its Discontents: A Caribbean Fragment in Toronto in Quest of Cultural Recognition and Political Empowerment'. *Ethnic and Racial Studies* 27(4): 544–554.

Putnam, Lara. 2002. *The Company They Kept: Migrants and the Politics of Gender in Caribbean Costa Rica, 1870–1960*. Chapel Hill, NC: University of North Carolina Press.

Roopnarine, Lomarsh. 2003. 'Indo-Caribbean Migration: From Periphery to Core'. *Caribbean Quarterly* 49(3): 30–60.

———. 2006. 'Return Migration of Indentured East Indians from the Caribbean to India 1838–1920'. *Journal of Caribbean History* 40(2): 308–324.

———. 2007. *Indo-Caribbean Indenture: Resistance and Accommodation*. Kingston: University of the West Indies Press.

———. 2009. 'The Repatriation, Readjustment, and Second-Term Migration of Ex-Indentured Indian Laborers from British Guiana and Trinidad to India 1838–1955'. *New West Indian Guide* 83(1–2): 71–97.

———. 2011. 'Indian Migration during Indentured Servitude in British Guiana and Trinidad, 1850–1920'. *Labor History* 52(2): 173–192.

———. 2016. 'Transnational Migration during East Indian Indenture in British Guiana and Trinidad'. In *The Legacy of Indian Indenture: Historical and Contemporary Aspects of Migration and Diaspora*, edited by Maurits Hassankhan, Lomarsh Roopnarine and Hans Ramsoedh, pp. 15–36. New Delhi: Manohar.

———. 2018. *Indian Caribbean: Migration and Identity in the Diaspora*. Jackson, MS: University Press of Mississippi.

Samaroo, Brinsley. 1975. 'Missionary Methods and Local Responses: The Canadian Presbyterian and the East Indians in the Caribbean'. In *East Indian in the Caribbean, Colonialism and the Struggle for Identity: Papers Presented to a Symposium on East Indians in the Caribbean, The University of the West Indies, June, 1975*, pp. 93–116. Saint Augustine, Trinidad and Tobago: Institute of African and Asian Studies, University of the West Indies.

———. 1982. 'In Sick Longing for the Further Shore: Return Migration by Caribbean East Indians during the Nineteenth and Twentieth Centuries'. In *Return Migration and Remittances: Developing a Caribbean Perspective*, edited by W. F. Stinner, K. D. Albquerque and R. S. Bryce-Laporte, pp. 45–72. Washington, DC: Research Institute on Immigration and Ethnic Studies Smithsonian Institution.

Sarusky, Jaime. 1989. 'The East Indian Community in Cuba'. In *Indenture and Exile: The Indo-Caribbean Experience*, edited by Frank Birbalsingh, pp. 73–78. Toronto: TSAR Publications.

Scott, C. James. 1985. *Weapons of the Weak: Everyday Forms of Peasant Resistance*. New Haven, CT: Yale University Press.

———. 1990. *Domination and the Arts of Resistance: Hidden Transcript*. New Haven, CT: Yale University Press.

Shepherd, Verene. 1986. 'From Rural Plantations to Urban Slums: The Economic Status and Problems of East Indians in Kingston, Jamaica, in the Late Nineteenth and Early Twentieth Centuries'. *Immigrants and Minorities* 5(2): 130–142.

Spivak, Gayatri Chakravorty. 1988. 'Can the Subaltern Speak?'. In *Marxism and Interpretation of Culture*, edited by Cary Nelson and Larry Grossberg, pp. 271–313. Hemel Hempstead, UK: Harvester Wheatsheaf.

Thomas-Hope, Elizabeth (ed.). 2009. *Freedom and Constraint in Caribbean Migration and Diaspora*. Kingston: Ian Randle Publisher.

Tinker, Hugh. 1974. *A New System of Slavery: Export of Indian Labour Overseas, 1830–1920*. London: Oxford University Press.

# 8

## On the Move

### Remigration in the Indian Ocean, 1850–1906*

*Yoshina Hurgobin*

On 21 September 1909, the acting protector of immigrants in Mauritius wrote to the Inspector General of Police of the colony the following about Boodhun, who was now living in Seychelles:

> I am informed by the bearer of the letter that an old immigrant named Boodhun who had left the colony [Mauritius] for Seychelles has returned & was on board the French Mail and that is considered as an undesirable & prevented from landing. It is to my knowledge that his son is a labourer in the service of the Beau Bassin & Rose Hill Board [in Mauritius] & he has asked me to interfere to get his father's [repeal] ... as he is willing to receive & to maintain him at his expense. In these circumstances, I hope you will issue orders accordingly.[1]

The aforementioned story is an illustration of remigration – that is, mobility[2] – between supposedly minor colonies without returning to India. Boodhun, an indentured worker from India, had completed his contract of five years, had probably spent many more years in Mauritius and had eventually become an 'old immigrant'. Time and familiarity in Mauritius had shaped his information networks in such a way that he was aware of the populations in neighbouring

---

* Archival records used for this chapter were consulted at the National Archives of Mauritius (NAM) in Coromandel, Mauritius, and at the Mahatma Gandhi Institute (MGI) in Moka, Mauritius. I am deeply grateful to Crispin Bates for his numerous insights and kind support. I could not have completed this chapter without the precious support of Sheela Hurgobin. At the NAM, Sangeeta Mohun provided me with much support. Dharmendra Mukool's demise was unexpected. He was most helpful and encouraging during my archival trips at Coromandel. All translations are mine.

[1] National Archives of Mauritius (NAM), PA 295, Acting Protector to Inspector General of Police, 21 September 1909, 300 (in pencil).

[2] By mobility, I mean how oceans facilitated movement of persons. I am not referring to 'absence as well as presence' as understood by E. Ho (2006, p. 10).

colonies such as Seychelles. Colonial discourse emphasises how he was 'undesirable' in Mauritius, thus possibly rendering Seychelles a refuge for all unwanted immigrants. However, this could not be further from the truth since Seychelles had a significant population of 22,409 persons in 1909 and was a major exporter of vanilla and coconut oil.[3]

The presence of Boodhun in Seychelles is not to reify the exotic undertones of islands as spaces of violence, disease or penalisation. Rather, his presence suggests the economic possibilities that remigrants pursued, despite the constraints of colonial administrations (here, those of Seychelles and Mauritius). This chapter uses passenger logs and colonial reports to examine Indian labour remigration within various nodes[4] of the Indian Ocean between 1847 and 1906. Remigration, as pointed out earlier, refers to the process whereby labour migrants moved across colonies (and their dependencies) without returning to India or making the three main ports of embarkation (Calcutta, Madras and Bombay [present-day Kolkata, Chennai and Mumbai, respectively]) the points of departure. The chapter further queries the profiles of those who pursued remigration and their motivations. It suggests the term 'return' could have multiple meanings and follows the development of remigration, charting its decline until the early twentieth century. It finally uses the passenger logs sample to suggest that remigration in the south-west Indian Ocean was the highest between 1847 and 1865. The aim is to disentangle a causative linkage based on a crude materialist analysis, correlating growths in production to the arrival of remigrants so as to focus on the subjective world of the workers and their desires and fears.

---

[3]  Board of Trade (1909), p. 116. The figure for 1909 is an estimated population. For 1891, the total population (including females and males) was 16,440. By the census of 1901, the total population was 19,237 (I could not track down the source of this figure). Though Seychelles is often subsumed as a dependency of Mauritius, it became financially independent in 1872: 'Up to the year 1871 inclusive, the Seychelles finances were controlled entirely by the Mauritius Government, and its Customs revenue was collected in Mauritius. But the Order in Council of the 22 April, 1872, which created a Board of Civil Commissioners, with the chief civil commissioner as president, transferred this control, subject to the Governor's instructions, from Mauritius to Seychelles.' Great Britain Parliament House of Commons (1901), Report on the Seychelles Blue Book for 1900, No. 333, p. 5.

[4]  Sugata Bose refers to the Indian Ocean as an inter-regional arena that 'lies somewhere between the generalities of a "world system" and the specificities of particular regions' and an arena 'tied together by webs of economic and cultural relationships, [which] had flexible internal and external boundaries' (Bose 2006, p. 6). The inter-regional arena framework is useful to frame circular migration of returnees between India and Mauritius. However, it does not consider how returnees, old immigrants and Creole Indians could move diversely between various nodes such as Mauritius, Seychelles, Madagascar, Réunion and nearby islands.

## Contexts and Debates

Studies on indentured labour abound. One of the earliest works in the field highlighted the way high imperial imperatives had led to the development of the indentured labour system.[5] More recent works have underlined the importance of studying Indian emigrants' 'social worlds and changing fortunes' both in 'India and overseas', as well as the state's role in overseeing migration.[6] Ultimately, one can identify three approaches to the field that have coalesced uneasily. The first approach highlighted how indentured labour was similar to slavery and how the abuse of indentured workers was produced and reproduced in various social intersections (gender, caste and class) in societies that received indentured labour.[7] A second approach emerged from disagreements with the slavery thesis. Scholars of this latter approach posited that indentured workers were the epitome of rational decision-making because they actively sought to leave India. Votaries of the first approach have dominated the field of indenture studies. A prime example of the first approach is Hugh Tinker's influential work, *A New System of Slavery: The Export of Indian Labour Overseas, 1830–1920*.[8] Tinker equates indentured labour to slavery and describes, in the following unflattering terms, the life of Indians embracing indentured labour:

> The majority of the Indians who emigrate gain little from their emigration: they exchange one situation of casual intermittent, poorly paid labour for a similar situation in the new country.... The coolies who crossed the seas a hundred years ago or more, died without issue.[9]

Adherents of the second approach criticised Tinker's 'new system of slavery' thesis and argued for the informed actions of the indentured worker.[10] Brij Lal, for example, painted indentured workers as 'actors in their own right who were

---

[5] Cumpston (1953).

[6] Kumar (2017), p. 12; Mongia (2018), p. 1.

[7] Tinker (1974); Das Gupta (1981); Breman (1989); Behal and Mohapatra (1992); Daniel, Bernstein and Brass (1992), p. 5.

[8] Tinker (1974).

[9] Tinker (1974), p. xiii. The second sentence in the quote is from this longer sentence: 'This book is a study of the forerunners of these Indian workers of the present day: one cannot say their ancestors, because most of the coolies who crossed the seas a hundred years ago or more, died without issue.'

[10] Hazareesingh (1975), pp. 20, 26. Kissoonsingh Hazareesingh, similarly to Lal, seems to straddle the free–unfree positions (Lal 1980, p. 66; Ali 1980, p. 5).

consciously aware of their situation'.[11] Lal, too, however, occasionally, meandered between rational decision-making and the slavery path.[12]

A third approach emerged in the work of Marina Carter, who argued that both the previous approaches ignored the preponderant role of *sirdars* (overseers). In her 1995 work, she

> sought to emphasise those areas of the migrant experience which were outside the realm of cognizance of the official world, for example the effects of the use of returnee migrants or sirdars in the creation of semi-independent chain migration streams.[13]

Thus, the *sirdar* was crucial in recruiting new indentured workers and shaping patterns of circular migration between Mauritius and India. In a later work, Carter argues that the returning process was often interlinked with remigration to new places beyond India:

> Nevertheless, at least two-thirds of all migrants failed to return to India on completion of their indentures. Some went elsewhere: time-expired labourers in Réunion went to Mauritius, old immigrants in Mauritius went to Natal and Madagascar, Indians in the West Indies travelled between the islands, and some overseas Indians even journeyed from Mauritius to Brazil and China.[14]

In the same work, Carter excavates notions of remigration as stated in a 1874 report of the protector of emigrants examining the Mauritius agency at Calcutta: 'In his report on the working of the emigration depots in 1874, the protector noted that a special feature of the Mauritius depot was that there was always "a comparatively large number of old returned emigrants about to re-emigrate with their families and friends" [from India]'.[15] In the aforementioned work, it is clear that Carter has underlined two types of remigration: one from colony to colony

---

[11] Lal (1980), p. 54.

[12] Lal, Munro and Beechert (1993), pp. 187–188. The actual quote I am referring to reads: 'The two Fiji strikes were spontaneous movements, local in scope and lacking in firm leadership and strategy. Being essentially defensive actions to protest the withholding of some privileges to the workers or the abuse of the labour ordinances by the employers, they were quickly and effectively put down by the authorities. Hugh Tinker observes aptly that the "coolies hardly ever took action in support of demands for new gains: almost always, they protested because the management tried to take away some existing portion of their agreed conditions".'

[13] Carter (1995), pp. 6, 35–67; Carter (1996), p. 62.

[14] Carter (1996), p. 54.

[15] Carter (1996), p. 33.

and the other where the migrant returns to India and re-indenture to either the same colony or another colony.

Crispin Bates and Carter have expounded on return and remigration in two later works. They have juxtaposed the *sirdar* figure of indentured labour historiography with the *sardar* (recruiter) and jobber figures much discussed in Indian labour historiography. They suggest that 'it was certainly the case that not all *sirdars* were returnee migrants sent for the purpose of recruitment'.[16] The process of return then unveils all its complexities and possibilities.

More recently, Bates and Carter explicitly addressed the remigration issue by asking the following question: 'Why did … a large number of Indian labour migrants who had completed one term of service overseas return to India, and then remigrate, or move from one colonial territory to another?'[17] They answered this by examining anecdotal evidence drawn from the Indian Ocean region and concluded by providing a typology of remigration: 'distress, criminalization, familial and contractor-inspired remigration'.[18] They have also highlighted the quandaries of 'subaltern careering', a remigration to two or more sugar colonies elaborated in the paper of Reshad Durgahee.[19] Durgahee later uses the novel lens of historical geography to 'examine the experiences of labourers' in two spaces (Mauritius and Fiji) and to underline the process of remigration – that is, one where 'indentured labourers, who having completed one tenure of indenture in a specific colony, returned to India and then enlisted for another tenure of indenture either in the colony in which they had previously served or in a new colony'.[20] However, Durgahee is incorrect in his assertion that remigration between 'sugar colonies and the wider colonial world' has been 'unexplored'.[21] The aforementioned discussion thus suggests return and two types of remigration coexist on a longer migratory spectrum.

Though the issue may seem to be semantic in nature (the use of returnee and remigration), remigration seems buried within the returning process mostly because of the nature of colonial archives and intent. Colonial governments – especially that of Mauritius – were dependent on the labour of *sirdars* to funnel new labour for sugar-cane plantations. Meanwhile, analysing remigration on its own merits within the south-west Indian Ocean indicates that sugar plantations

---

16  Bates and Carter (2017), p. 472.
17  Bates and Carter (2021), p. 1.
18  Bates and Carter (2021), p. 25.
19  Durgahee quoted in Bates and Carter (2021), p. 15.
20  Durgahee (2021), p. 14.
21  Durgahee (2021), pp. 2, 15.

(though dominant) were not the only plantations that thrived. Seychelles, Agaléga and Diego Garcia were not mere dependencies of Mauritius since they produced significant amounts of vanilla, coconut and coconut oil. Moreover, an easy embrace of the category 'minor dependencies' would be an uncritical reading of the colonial document. As Frederick Cooper has stated, 'the categories by which we understand the colonies' past and the ex-colonies' future were shaped by the process of colonization'.[22]

## Role of Returnees and Two Meanings of Return

The beginnings of the indentured labour system in Mauritius were intricately connected to chattel slavery and its eventual dismantlement in the plantation complexes of the British Caribbean. The early indenture system began with some fits and starts. The overlap between indentured labour and slavery was so intricate that abolitionists, humanitarians, liberal parliamentarians and Indian industrialists equated the system with slavery. Temporarily halted in 1838 (just four years after its beginning in 1834), the indenture system did not have much to look forward to.

After the system reopened in early 1842,[23] new regulations were implemented whereby an immigration department and the position of a protector of immigrants were created. Once Indian immigrants completed their initial contract of five years in the colony, they actively sought to return to India. This was evident in the correspondence between the colonial secretary of the colony and the protector of immigrants, which contains admissions of this fact, such as in a letter dated 28 February 1845 stating that 'time expired Indians at the depot ... were desirous to return to their country [that is] India'.[24] Colonial missives with similar language became very frequent after 1845. However, the term 'return' in this colonial language of the indenture system had two meanings.

From quite early on, the colonial government of Mauritius was aware of the potential role of returnees. In his report to William Nicolay, the governor of Mauritius, Thomas Hugon, a civil servant in the Bengal Service – and later to become a protector of immigrants in Mauritius – who had studied 'the question

---

[22]  Cooper (2005), p. 3.

[23]  Queen's Order in Council of 15 January 1842 is later invoked several times. See Mahatma Gandhi Institute (MGI), PL 57, Colonial Secretary to Stipendiary Magistrates, 8 January 1843.

[24]  NAM, PA 2, Colonial Secretary to Protector of Immigrants, 28 February 1845.

of Cooly emigration from India to this colony in all its bearings'[25] had highlighted how 'the further introduction of Indian labourers [could] in fact be effected almost only by those already in the Island'.[26] By the mid-nineteenth century, the population of Indian immigrants in Mauritius increased from 35.5 per cent in 1846 to 43.1 per cent in 1851. The colonial government in Mauritius acknowledged this steady increase in the census of 1851: 'It is almost superfluous to add that the disproportionate increase in the latter class [Indians] has been caused by Immigration.'[27] Though the government scrupulously tracked the demographic change wrought on by the immigrant influx, it seemed unaware of the clout of the returnees, the extent of their remittances and, more crucially, their roles in shaping the arrival of new immigrants in the colony. This, however, did not go unnoticed by some observers. As early as 1852, Frederic J. Mouat noticed the different allure of the returnee migrant:

> The immediate influence of this wealth is, however, of minor importance compared with the intelligence, freedom from prejudice, knowledge of improved modes of agriculture, and habits of industry brought back by the return coolie to his benighted home.[28]

For Mouat, returnee migrants played a larger role than simply bringing remittances to India. A returnee migrant was more seasoned and supposedly had become more 'intelligent' having rid herself or himself from possible primordial biases and ties. More broadly, according to Mouat, the returnee migrant brought with him new agricultural notions to India, a colony that could not extirpate itself from the quagmire of socio-economic darkness.

However, the term 'return' had another meaning in official colonial parlance. Workers wanted to return to India for various reasons. For instance, if they had

---

[25]  British Parliamentary Papers (BPP) 1840 (331) 37.539, Volume 37, Correspondence relative to Introduction of Indian Labourers into Mauritius, Report of Commissioners of Inquiry into the present condition of those already located in that colony, Thomas Hugon to William Nicolay, 29 July 1839, p. 184.

[26]  Thomas Hugon to William Nicolay, 29 July 1839, p. 190.

[27]  NAM, Census of 1851, under para. 'Proportions', p. 2. Alongside the socio-economic category of 'Indians', two other categories existed: 'General Population' and 'Ex-apprentices'. 'General Population' referred to people while 'Ex-apprentices' referred to former slaves who had resettled off sugar plantations after the abolition of slavery. The percentage referring to 'General Population' declined from 1846 to 1851 (from 33.4 per cent to 30.2 per cent); the same trend could be seen for the category of 'Ex-apprentices' (from 31.1 per cent to 26.7 per cent).

[28]  Mouat (1852), p. 96.

not been paid, workers would actively seek to leave the colony. Such was the case of workers on Laborde's estate, 'L'Union', who 'in consequence of the delay and difficulties of recovering [the] arrears [of their wages], ... had expressed a desire to return to their country'.[29] In some other cases, indentured workers could afford their return passages and wanted to leave Mauritius. Immigrants also sought to return to India when the local colonial government would not provide vital medical treatment (medical care in an estate hospital) to them. Besides its unwillingness to provide health facilities to indentured workers and female immigrants, the colonial government in Mauritius had started producing colonial labels highlighting workers' lack of productivity and their unsuitability for agricultural labour. If workers were allowed to remain in Mauritius, the colonial administration reinforced their inability to earn a livelihood or to return to India at their own expense.

While workers sought to return to India, the colonial government in Mauritius attempted to control workers' mobilities and their contractual terms. It soon realised that workers could, in several cases, leave before the end of their contracts. The governor of the colony, William Gomm, affirmed the same in his letter to Frederick Stanley (also known as Lord Stanley) on 15 September 1845, when he wrote the following: 'The sacrifices actually incurring by the colony, and monthly recorded, through the early return of immigrants at their own charge, I have endeavoured to lay distinctly before your Lordship.'[30] This return to India was specifically linked to the abuse and exploitation common to the early phase of the indentured labour system. Thus, the Immigration Department in Mauritius would often report return passages to India in the early 1840s. For example, on 4 March 1845, the protector reported that 199 passengers returned to Calcutta and Madras. Of these, 56 immigrants paid their own expense.[31] Simultaneously many 'time expired Immigrant labourers ... really desirous of returning to India ... were actually detained at the Depot [in Mauritius]', and this in effect was 'an account of the difficulties they have met with in obtaining from their former

---

[29]  NAM, PA 2, Colonial Secretary to Protector of Immigrants, 31 October 1845.

[30]  BPP 1846 (691), Papers in continuation of those presented last year (Sessional Paper, No. 642, of 1845) relating to the Labouring Population of the British Colonies (West Indies and Mauritius), part I, copy of Despatch from William Gomm to Frederick Stanley, 15 September 1845, p. 171.

[31]  NAM, PA 2, Protector of Immigrants to Colonial Secretary, 4 March 1845. The detailed statistics are as follows: for Calcutta, 100 immigrants returned at government's expense; 45 returned at their own expense; for Madras, 43 immigrants returned at government's expense; 11 at their own expense.

employers the means of paying their back passage'.[32] The coexistence of migrants who could pay for their passage (returnees) and those who encountered more difficulties in doing so indicated that information networks might have had overlapped.

## Overlap and the Nature of Information Networks

Return, at this stage in 1843, could be interpreted as an element of the structure of the indenture system still in motion. On the one hand, the colonial government was mobilising returnees to recruit new migrants, and, on the other, indentured workers were leaving Mauritius because of the iniquities they faced in the colony. More importantly, the mobilities of returnees illustrated the India–Mauritius circuit in the Indian Ocean (especially from the main ports of embarkation: Calcutta, Madras and Bombay). Over time, this circuit would overlap with others. For example, Soobrayen reached Mauritius on 12 February 1847 'as a passenger on board the ship "Roberts" from Moulmein' (present-day Mawlamyine in Myanmar). Soobrayen did not operate within the larger indenture system since he did not have a contract and had probably found himself by accident in Mauritius. However, he remained in the colony, and by 1864, he was a 'labourer on the Roads'.[33]

After 1842, indentured workers sought more information on the conditions tied to the return passage. For example, the labour intermediary, Ramasawiny, 'a native of Madura', had informed recruits that they 'would be entitled to a free passage back to India' after one year in Mauritius. The emigration agent in Madras promptly sought to correct this information for the emigrants:

> It was likewise explained to the Emigrants that they would not be entitled to a free passage back to India until they had served 5 years at the Mauritius; but that they could return at any period, at their own expense.[34]

---

[32] MGI, PL 57, Colonial Secretary of Mauritius to Stipendiary Magistrate, 11 April 1843.

[33] NAM, ZD2 9, 19 November 1864, Assistant Surveyor General to Inspector General of Police, No. D/569. 'Sir, I have the honor to request that you will grant a ticket free of charge to the Indian Soobrayen, who has been employed as a labourer on the Roads; his ticket appears to have been either lost of misplaced in this Office. He arrived here as a passenger on board the ship "Roberts" from Moulmein, on the 12th February 1847.'

[34] MGI, PL 57, 24 February 1843, Captain C. Biden, Emigration Agent at Madras to J. F. Thomas Esq. Chief Secretary.

Upon hearing this explanation, the 'Emigrants ... appeared to be dissatisfied, and consequently no passports were issued'.[35] The evidence further illustrates how the bureaucratic strictures of indenture circumscribed the possible subsequent actions of workers.

Having faced the brunt of harsh criticism concerning the indentured labour system between 1838 and 1842, the colonial government of Mauritius came to rely on the Immigration Department's possible protections for workers. However, by doing so, it also controlled the mobilities of immigrants after 1842. The colonial secretary expressly conveyed to the chief commissary of the colony that 'natives of India are not allowed to embark for countries other than their own, not even to the islands Dependent on Mauritius'.[36] Planters, however, ignored this injunction, and in the 1840s, it was common for planters to petition the protector of immigrants for indentured workers to accompany them to Réunion. This enabled immigrants to know of other nodes in the south-west Indian Ocean. However, very often, planters' petitions were denied. Such was the case of P. Elias who had requested that 'an Indian Immigrant be allowed to accompany [his wife] to Bourbon [Réunion]'. However, the colonial secretary replied that 'under the Instructions of the Government of India, [his] request [could not] be complied with'.[37] The level of mobility of the workers were to change later on, as the study of passenger logs in this chapter will demonstrate.

Information networks of indentured workers (returnees and the two types of remigrants mentioned earlier) were vast, widespread and unconfined to one ocean. Such networks were boosted by the routes that the ships took. For example, on 8 January 1859, 429 'Indian emigrants' from Pondichéry (present-day Puducherry) stopped in Mauritius before proceeding to Guadeloupe in the Atlantic Ocean.[38] Information networks of indentured workers included knowledge of nearby colonies in the south-west Indian Ocean ('dependencies' in colonial discourse) but also included spatial knowledge. Madoo, a native of Sattara, brought 'back people of their own villages' to Mauritius.[39] In May 1851, he had returned to India for 18 months. The circumstances described as follows were such that Madoo resorted to ingenuity to return to Mauritius with new migrants.

---

[35]  MGI, PL 57, 24 February 1843, Captain C. Biden, Emigration Agent at Madras to J. F. Thomas Esq. Chief Secretary.

[36]  NAM, PA 1, Colonial Secretary to Chief Commissary of Police, 21 June 1844.

[37]  NAM, PA 2, Colonial Secretary to P. Elias, 21 April 1845.

[38]  NAM, Z2D 37, Return of Passengers arrive on board the Ship 'Suger,' Arrival in Port Louis, Mauritius, 8 January 1859, p. 41 (in pencil).

[39]  NAM, RA 1121, Protector of Immigrants to Colonial Secretary, 7 May 1851.

[He] left Sattara for Bombay with 20 men and 10 women, but finding there no vessel bound for Mauritius, he kept only as many as he could support with his means and told the others to return to their village; after waiting 8 months, he embarked with 7 men and 4 women to go to Cochin [present-day Kochi], where he was aware frequent communications existed with this colony, [Mauritius].[40]

Those who accompanied Madoo to Mauritius 'processed by land from Cochin to Madras' and 'state[d] that many others from their country would embark for this [island], if a less distant Port than Madras was available to them'.[41] The example of Madoo sheds light on the returning process (of returnees). To reach Mauritius, Madoo and the new recruits walked from Cochin to Madras. Second, in expressing that they would have departed from a closer port of embarkation than Madras, newly recruited migrants were already demonstrating their understanding of distance and the accumulation of knowledge about places from which they could depart to sugar colonies. Often workers did not yield to the hegemony of the ports of embarkation of Calcutta, Madras and Bombay. For instance, Soornum did not hesitate to write to the protector of immigrants 'to be good enough to allow [her] to proceed to Pondichéry on board the ship Diogène although [she] came from Madras to Mauritius by a coolie ship'.[42] The reason she provided for her request was as follows: 'My brothers are going on leave on urgent private business & I should like very much to accompany them.'[43]

Remigration, defined in this chapter as migration from Mauritius to a nearby colony, was entangled with the returning process since migrants who returned to the same destination in India could have met those shuttling to nearby colonies. However, remigration remains an obscure process because the focus of colonial administrators was ultimately on the returnees' contribution in bringing new recruits and stabilising the labour force of the colony. Meanwhile, remigrants were burrowed away from the officially recorded returning process of returnees and only appeared anecdotally in the colonial archive.

## A Study of Passenger Logs (Réunion, Diego Garcia, Agaléga and Seychelles)

The increased population of Indian immigrants in Mauritius was connected with its booming sugar production. Sugar-cane acreage and cultivation in Mauritius

---

40  NAM, RA 1121, Protector of Immigrants to Colonial Secretary, 7 May 1851.

41  NAM, RA 1121, Protector of Immigrants to Colonial Secretary, 7 May 1851.

42  NAM, PA 43, Soornum to Protector of Immigrants, 30 June 1880, p. 448 (in pencil).

43  NAM, PA 43, Soornum to Protector of Immigrants, 30 June 1880, p. 448 (in pencil).

had increased from 58,500 acres in 1841 to 123,000 acres in 1861.[44] The increased influx of immigrants into Mauritius meant that they developed a familiarity with possibilities of travel within the south-western Indian Ocean. They came to know of travel to Tamatave (in Madagascar), Seychelles, Natal (in present-day South Africa), Agaléga, Diego Garcia and Réunion. However, the reverse was also true, and migrants (emigrants either indentured and/or passengers) in the neighbourhood of Mauritius also travelled to the island. While the sample in Table 8.1 is dominated by arrivals from Réunion, Diego Garcia and Seychelles, the list shows three arrivals from further away in the Indian Ocean (Moulmein, Coringa and Lombock). Using a series of passenger logs, Table 8.1 is a compilation of the arrivals of 54 Indian migrants into Mauritius between 1847 and 1865. They were relatively young (aged 15 to 50). Only two women (Amiraude, a French subject who 'wishe[d] to reside' in Mauritius, and Sintong, a 'Malay woman' born in Bally [present-day Bali]) appear on the list.[45] In order of importance, the arrivals are as follows: 24 arrivals from Réunion, 10 from Diego Garcia, 6 from Agaléga, 5 from Seychelles, 3 from St Brandon, 2 from Singapore and 1 each from Coringa, Moulmein, Lombock and Tamatave.

Réunion, an old colony of the French Empire, saw the first arrival of indentured workers in 1826 while slavery was still present in the colony.[46] By 1830, 3,012 Indians were living in Réunion,[47] but their lives were full of hardships. The colonial government could not obtain more indentured workers from India, and according to the French colonial theorist Paul Leroy-Beaulieu, workers faced struggles in adjusting to a new society because of 'language, religion, customs'.[48] The impending abolition of slavery in the French Empire in 1848 led to the renewal of indentured labour in 1848, and even before the abolition, indentured workers started reaching the colony.[49] Soon in November 1850 (see Table 8.1), informed remigrants from Réunion came to Mauritius to labour in its booming sugar estates. For instance, on 9 November, two 'labourers', Shaik Coda Bux and

---

[44] Lamusse (1964).

[45] For Amiraude, see NAM Z2D 16, Return of Passengers Arrived on Board the Barque *Ariel*, Arrival in Port Louis, Mauritius, 13 November 1859. For Sintong, see NAM Z2D 37, Return of Passengers Arrived on Board the Brig *Melbourne*, 25 March 1859.

[46] Tinker (1974), p. 61; Northrup (1995), p. 60.

[47] Leroy-Beaulieu (1874), p. 246.

[48] Leroy-Beaulieu (1874), p. 246.

[49] Govindin (2004), p. 53, cited in H. Q. Ho (2004), p. 13. The quote reads: 'Le trois-mâts le Mahé de la Bourdonnais y débarque 500 coolies indiens. Le 8 avril 1849, La Julie ramène 433 émigrants indiens et un mois après, le Mazagran dépose 448 émigrants.'

Shaik Salar Bux, both from Calcutta, who held French passports, travelled from Réunion to Mauritius on the barque *Ariel* and indicated that they 'wishe[d] to reside in the Colony'.[50] It could well be that both had lived in Réunion since 1826 and considered Mauritius a hop away. Moreover, it was also not unusual for migrants to afford their passages by 1850. However, most immigrants to Réunion were ethnically from southern India. The names of Shaik Coda Bux and Shaik Salar Bux suggest otherwise, and they might, thus, have reached Réunion between 1848 and 1849. Except for two instances, all 22 remigrants from Réunion to Mauritius either 'wishe[d] to reside in the colony', were 'in search of work' or 'wanted to reside' in Mauritius.

Diego Garcia, an island in the Chagos Archipelago, is mostly – if not only – invoked in connection to the creation of the British Indian Ocean Territory in 1965 and to the presence of a United States (US) military base in Chagos. However, the history – albeit still colonial – of Diego Garcia does not start in 1965.[51] In his 1826 account on islands and islets, Marie Claude Antoine Marrier (also known as Baron d'Unienville) relates how Lapotaire, Cayeux and Dédier acquired the island in May 1809 on the condition that it would house persons who contracted leprosy in Mauritius. While the three island owners lived in Mauritius, Diego Garcia was used for coconut cultivation and partially to receive lepers. The island 'produced a lot of coconuts' that were then sent to the absentee island-lords in Mauritius for oil manufacturing.[52] In the 1850s, Diego Garcia still required labour. However, the legal structure did not always support the plantation owners' capitalistic demands. On 21 April 1856, Dumas thought he could request '50 Indians' directly from Calcutta to labour in Diego Garcia and Peros Banhos (another island in the

---

[50] NAM, Z2D 16, Return of Passengers Arrived on Board the Barque *Ariel*, Arrival in Port Louis, Mauritius, 13 November 1850, p. 16. It was also for the case of 40-year-old Maduane from Calcutta and 40-year-old Soobrayah from Madras who left Réunion for Mauritius on 13 July 1850 via the schooner *Egle*.

[51] For a discussion of Chagos in the contemporary context, see Jeffery (2011) and Carter (2017).

[52] BPP 1827, p. 110, A Return of the Number of all the Islands which come under the denomination of Dependencies of Mauritius, showing their Geographical position in reference to that Island; the Extent of their Territory; any Census which may have been taken of their Population, together with their Civil and Military Establishments; and the description of Naval Force which may have been stationed there at any time since the conquest of the Colony, (Etat Des Isles et Islots compris sous le nom 'De Dépendances de L'Isle Maurice; énoncant leur position Géographique, l'étendue de leur Territoire, leur Population, leur Etablissemens Civils et Militaires, quand aucun il y a', p. 3. Under section '3. – Diego Garcia', 'Etablissemens' is spelt incorrectly, but it appears as such in the evidence. In 1826, there were 37 lepers out of a total population of 275. Total population was as follows: 204 males, 47 females, 15 girls and 9 boys.

Chagos Archipelago) under 'Ordinance No. 12 of 1835'.[53] The colonial secretary vehemently underlined that accepting Dumas's request would be illegal, but that if he ardently required labour, he could recruit 'Old Immigrants for service in those islands'.[54] Though the colonial government shaped oceanic mobilities and labour of old immigrants, one can surmise that they would often wish to 'reside' in Mauritius (see Table 8.1). This was also the case of Itou, Putchay, Ayagapen, Chiniah, Soubramanien and Papou who remigrated from Agaléga to Mauritius in July 1859.

In 1860, Seychelles, an archipelago comprising 30 islands, was categorised as part of the dependencies of Mauritius. In that same year, four Indian remigrants came to Mauritius seeking 'employment' (see Table 8.1). It was only in 1872 that it would become financially independent from Mauritius.[55] It would be misplaced to embrace colonial discourse and easily state that Seychelles was a simple dependency of Mauritius. By the end of the nineteenth century, the remigration of Indians to Seychelles would cause legal and administrative conundrums to colonial officials in Mauritius precisely because Seychelles was gradually morphing into an autonomous colony. The stories of Rungen and Ellamah illustrate this argument. On 16 August 1879, R. M. Rennards, officer of the civil status in Seychelles, sought a certificate as per 'article 72 of ordinance 17 of 1871' so Rungen could marry in Seychelles.[56] When he received the request, J. G. Daly, the protector of immigrants in Mauritius, opined that the law's mobility meant that he was not the protector in 'that part' of the colony – that is, Seychelles:

> The word 'Mauritius' having been changed into 'Seychelles Islands', I am not Protector of Immigrants in that part of the colony. It is true the Civil Status Ordinance is unchanged, but Art. 72 mentions a 'certificate signed by the Protector of Immigrants of this Colony' – but a later ordinance (No. 12 of 1878) … declares me not to be 'Protector of Immigrants' for Mauritius as enacted by Art 17 of [Ordinance] 12 of 1878 but provides Art. 7 of Proclamation the 'Chief Civil Commissioner' to be so in Seychelles.

---

[53] Piggott et al. (1896), p. 473. This ordinance was 'for the due performance of the duties of the Ministère Public before the Executive Council sitting as a Land Court'.

[54] NAM, PA 4, Colonial Secretary to Protector of Immigrants, 21 April 1856, p. 115 (in pencil).

[55] For further information on Seychelles's independence from Mauritius, see note 2 in this chapter.

[56] NAM, PA 41, Officer of Civil Status Seychelles to Registrar General, Mauritius, 16 August 1879, pp. 27–28 (in pencil).

**Table 8.1** Arrival of passengers in Mauritius between 1847 and 1885

| Name | Age | Profession | Place of birth | Passport | Motive for voyage | Coming from | Date of arrival in Mauritius; name of Ship |
|---|---|---|---|---|---|---|---|
| Soobrayen | | | | | | Moulmein | 12 February 1847; *Robarts* |
| Banigan and female child | 21 | Labourer | Calcutta | French | 'Wishes to reside in the colony' | Réunion | 13 November 1850; barque *Ariel* |
| Shaik Coda Bux | | Labourer | Calcutta | French | 'Wishes to reside in the colony' | Réunion | 13 November 1850; barque *Ariel* |
| Shaik Salar Bux | | Labourer | Calcutta | French | 'Wishes to reside in the colony' | Réunion | 13 November 1850; barque *Ariel* |
| Amiraude (woman) | | Labourer | Calcutta | French | 'Wishes to reside in the colony' | Réunion | 13 November 1850; barque *Ariel* |
| Bidou | | Labourer | Calcutta | French | 'Wishes to reside in the colony' | Réunion | 13 November 1850; barque *Ariel* |
| Amoudalingum | | Labourer | Carical | French | 'Wishes to reside in the colony' | Réunion | 13 November 1850; barque *Ariel* |
| Chauvareemootoo | 15 | Servant | Carical | French | 'Temporary' | Réunion | 13 December 1850; schooner *Egle* |

*(Contd)*

**Table 8.1** (*Contd*)

| Name | Age | Profession | Place of birth | Passport | Motive for voyage | Coming from | Date of arrival in Mauritius; name of Ship |
|---|---|---|---|---|---|---|---|
| Armoogum | | Labourer | Madras | | 'Wishes to reside in the colony' | Singapore | 14 December 1850; barque *Prince Albert* |
| Coopen | | Labourer | Madras | | 'Wishes to reside in the colony' | Singapore | 14 December 1850; barque *Prince Albert* |
| Sinanasagen* | 26 | Labourer | Tranquebar | French | 'Wishes to reside in the colony' | Réunion | 9 March 1851; barque *Norna* |
| Kichnasamy | 25 | Labourer | Tanjore | French | 'Wishes to reside in the colony' | Réunion | 9 March 1851; barque *Norna* |
| Mahina | 28 | Labourer | Madras | | 'To reside' | Diego Garcia | 21 January 1859; brig *Governess* |
| Cardapen | 30 | Labourer | Madras | | 'To reside' | Diego Garcia | 21 January 1859; brig *Governess* |
| Sinasamy | 30 | Labourer | Madras | | 'To reside' | Diego Garcia | 21 January 1859; brig *Governess* |
| Soupraya | 28 | Domestic | Madras | | 'In search of work' | Réunion | 5 February 1859; *Neptune* |

(*Contd*)

**Table 8.1** (*Contd*)

| Name | Age | Occupation | Place | Nationality | Purpose | Destination | Date; Ship |
|---|---|---|---|---|---|---|---|
| Verapin | 40 | Servant | Karical | French | 'To reside' | Réunion | 5 February 1859; *Georges* |
| Savrimoutou† | 40 | Domestic | Madras | French | 'In search of employment' | Réunion | 26 February 1859; *Neptune* |
| Marimoutou† | 18 | Domestic | Madras | French | 'In search of employment' | Réunion | 26 February 1859; *Neptune* |
| Balapouron | 34 | Domestic | Madras | French | 'For employment' | Réunion | 8 March 1859; *Neptune* |
| Sintong (woman) | 16 | 'Malay woman' | Bally | | 'To reside' | Lombock | 25 March 1859; brig *Melbourne* |
| Sangivi, 'vide Mr. Leriche's Passport' | 26 | Servant | Madras | French | 'To reside' | Réunion | 20 June 1859; *Angelina*; 'released from quarantine', 3 July 1859 |
| Carpanin | 25 | Servant | Madras | None | 'To reside' | Réunion | 20 June 1859; *Angelina* |
| Moutousamy | 23 | Servant | Madras | None | 'To reside' | Réunion | 20 June 1859; *Angelina* |
| Amenchetty | 28 | Servant | Madras | None | 'To reside' | Réunion | 20 June 1859; *Angelina* |

(*Contd*)

**Table 8.1** (*Contd*)

| Name | Age | Profession | Place of birth | Passport | Motive for voyage | Coming from | Date of arrival in Mauritius; name of Ship |
|------|-----|-----------|---------------|----------|-------------------|-------------|---------------------------------------------|
| Itou | 39 | Labourer | Bombay | | 'To reside' | Agaléga | 28 July 1859; brig *Ibis* |
| Putchay | 27 | Labourer | Madras | | 'To reside' | Agaléga | 28 July 1859; brig *Ibis* |
| Ayagapen | 48 | Labourer | Madras | | 'To reside' | Agaléga | 28 July 1859; brig *Ibis* |
| Chiniah | 39 | Labourer | Madras | | 'To reside' | Agaléga | 28 July 1859; brig *Ibis* |
| Soubramanien | 29 | Labourer | Madras | | 'To reside' | Agaléga | 28 July 1859; brig *Ibis* |
| Papou | 33 | Labourer | Madras | | 'To reside' | Agaléga | 28 July 1859; brig *Ibis* |
| Delia | 23 | Servant | Singapore | | 'To reside' | Coringa | 17 August 1859; *Daylight* |
| Inguetassamy | 28 | Domestic | Madras | French | | St Denis | 20 August 1859; *Neptune* |
| Paquirmamoude | 28 | Servant | Pondichéry | French | 'To reside' | Réunion | 29 August 1859; steamer *Union* |
| Soundrom | 26 | Servant | Pondichéry | French | 'To reside' | Réunion | 29 August 1859; steamer *Union* |

(*Contd*)

**Table 8.1** (*Contd*)

| | | | | | | | |
|---|---|---|---|---|---|---|---|
| Antony | 25 | Servant | Pondichéry | French | 'To reside' | Réunion | 29 Aug 1859; steamer *Union* |
| Saydoo | 30 | Servant | Madras | French | 'To reside' | Réunion | 31 Aug 1859; steamer *Victoria* |
| Peleravou | 21 | Servant | Karical | French | 'To reside' | Réunion | 27 December 185; brig *Marie Angélique* |
| Ramsamy | 27 | Labourer | Madras | None | 'Employment' | Seychelles | 6 April 1860; *Alexander Auguste* |
| Cassim | 24 | Labourer | Madras | None | 'Employment' | Seychelles and Providence | 6 April 1860; *Alexander Auguste* |
| Ongamoutou | 39 | Labourer | Madras | None | 'Employment' | Seychelles and Providence | 6 April 1860; *Alexander Auguste* |
| Ramsing | 45 | Labourer | Madras | | 'Employment' | Seychelles and Providence | 6 April 1860; *Alexander Auguste* |
| Peera Samy | 18 | Servant | Madras | | 'Temporary' | Tamatave | 22 April 1860; barque *Walter Scott* |

(*Contd*)

**Table 8.1** (*Contd*)

| Name | Age | Profession | Place of birth | Passport | Motive for voyage | Coming from | Date of arrival in Mauritius; name of Ship |
|------|-----|-----------|---------------|----------|-------------------|-------------|--------------------------------------------|
| Ravau | 40 | Labourer | Madras | | 'Residence' | Diego Garcia | 5 May 1860; *Zoel* |
| Jalapa | 50 | Labourer | India | | 'Residence' | Diego Garcia | 5 May 1860; *Zoel* |
| 21 labourers | | Labourer | India | | 'Residence' | Diego Garcia | 5 May 1860; *Zoel* |
| Sinna | 31 | Labourer | India | | 'Residence' | Diego Garcia | 29 May 1860; *Australia* |
| Sinnapaya | 16 | Labourer | India | | 'Residence' | Diego Garcia | 29 May 1860; *Australia* |
| Moutien | 36 | Labourer | India | | 'Residence' | Diego Garcia | 29 May 1860; *Australia* |
| Cader Buccus | 22 | Labourer | India | | 'Residence' | Diego Garcia | 29 May 1860; *Australia* |
| Lal Mahamood | 35 | Servant | Calcutta | | 'Residence' | St Brandon | 5 June 1860; *Martigaon* |
| Ramlagan | 30 | Servant | Calcutta | | 'Residence' | St Brandon | 5 June 1860; *Martigaon* |

(*Contd*)

**Table 8.1** (*Contd*)

| | | | | 'Residence' | St Brandon | 5 June 1860; *Martigaon* |
|---|---|---|---|---|---|---|
| Jonger Maha | 30 | Servant | Coringa | 'Residence' | St Brandon | 5 June 1860; *Martigaon* |
| Dourga | 17 | Servant | Calcutta | 'Residence' | Seychelles | 8 October 1865; schooner *Vistulas* |

*Source*: Information for Soobrayen is from Z2 D9, p. 118; information for passengers from Banigan to Coopen is from Z2 D16; information for Sinanasagen and Kichnasamy is from Z2 D17, p. 103; information for Mahina to Sintong is from Z2 D 37, pp. 69, 132, 136, 186, 226, 271; information for Sangivi to Saydoo is from Z2 D 38, p. 522, 714, 856, 870, 938, 972; information for Peleravou is from Z2D 39, p. 441; information for Ramsamy to Peera Samy is from Z2D 40, pp. 268–269, 344; information for Ravau to Jonger Maha is from Z2D 41, pp. 15, 92, 123; information for Dourga is from Z2D 61, p. 49.

*Note*: *The format of the Z2 D registers changes over time. 1850 registers had a column titled 'Names of Persons to whom recommended'. I did not include such a column in the table since there was no information for the passengers that I am interested in. However, Sinanasagen was recommended to Pavaday'. National Archives of Mauritius (NAM), Z2D 17, Return of Passengers Arrived on Board the French Barque *Norna*, 9 March 1851, p. 103. †Savrimoutou and Marimoutou were on the same passport. The blank columns indicate that no information was available in the original sources.

Daly wrote to the registrar general of Mauritius and invoked an inane legality that ignored how in 1879 Seychelles was territorially and judicially part of Mauritius.[57] Further, Daly underlined that Rungen was 'no longer an Immigrant at all within the meaning of the [aforementioned] Labour Ordinance' and was 'a resident at Seychelles' and '[should] be governed by the labour law as read there'.[58] The registrar general of Mauritius disagreed with Daly. E. Pellereau, the acting substitute procureur general, had to intervene. For Pellereau, the matter was clear: 'I do not think that practically the difficulty is at present of any importance.'[59] Daly relented and produced the marriage certificate for Rungen.

By the early twentieth century, indentured workers who had established multi-generational families in Mauritius remigrated close by. For instance, on 29 April 1901, J. F. Trotter, the protector of immigrants, elaborated on Ellamah's desire to meet with her husband in Seychelles. Writing to the administrator of Seychelles, Trotter narrated:

> Ellamah who has two grown up daughters and a grandchild ... wishes to join her husband Munusawmy ... who went to Seychelles with Mr. Dupont and is engaged to your Government. Ellamah and her two daughters are able and willing to work.[60]

Having outlined Ellamah's, as well as her two daughters' desire to work, Trotter proceeds to ask whether the administrator of Seychelles would 'authorise [him – that is, the protector of immigrants in Mauritius] to pay the passage of these women and the infant to Seychelles at the expense of the Government [of Seychelles]'.[61] Harkening back to the nineteenth-century governmental attempt to regulate the female-to-male immigration ratio, Trotter adds: 'It seems to me desirable that there should be some women with the men who emigrated to Seychelles.'[62]

---

[57]  Sermet (2009), p. 207. Seychelles obtains its name from viscount Jean Moreau de Séchelles in 1756. By 1777, the French established their presence in the archipelago. It remained under the administration of Mauritius when the British took over in 1810 until 1903 when it became a crown colony of its own.

[58]  NAM, PA 41, Protector of Immigrants to Registrar General of Mauritius, 1 September 1879, p. 30 (in pencil).

[59]  NAM, PA 41, Report 943 of E. Pellereau, Acting Substitute Procureur General, 13 October 1879, p. 36 (in pencil).

[60]  NAM, PB 40, Trotter, Protector of Immigrants to the Administrator, Seychelles, Entry 552, 29 April 1901. I would like to thank Sheela Hurgobin for drawing my attention to this source.

[61]  NAM, PB 40, Trotter, Protector of Immigrants to the Administrator, Seychelles, Entry 552, 29 April 1901.

[62]  NAM, PB 40, Trotter, Protector of Immigrants to the Administrator, Seychelles, Entry 552, 29 April 1901.

Munusawmy first emigrated from India to Mauritius and remigrated from Mauritius to Seychelles. That Munusawmy is now a government employee indicates that he became socially mobile when he shifted from indenture work on a Mauritius sugar plantation to other positions until he landed in the situation with Dupont. Often times, old immigrants would have formed families in Mauritius, and geographical proximity to them was crucial.

By the late 1870s, the passenger logs registering the arrival of passengers into Mauritius were also printed differently and did not contain the 'Motive' column. Because of this bureaucratical change in the format of the passenger logs, it is difficult to ascertain the nature of voyages made by passengers. For example, B. Verissamy and P. Verisamy, carpenters, both in their late 20s and born in Mauritius, returned from Natal on board the barque *Umgeni* on 10 September 1878.[63] It is unclear whether the two Mauritius-born Indians were remigrating or simply traveling between Natal and Mauritius.

## Contingencies and Remigration

Remigration was occasionally not the result of economic pursuits or for the betterment of an immigrant's life. Contingencies and matters of the heart could shape the decision to depart Mauritius for neighbouring lands. On 13 August 1880, Latchoomoo Chengelayen left Mauritius for Réunion with Ramsamy Ramalingum, a painter. Left behind were her husband, Vencatachellum Appoo, and a three-year-old child. Infuriated, Appoo petitioned the protector of immigrants to intervene in the matter since Latchoomoo 'is now living and committing adultery' and that

> she took away with her ... the property of your petitioner a sum of hundred dollars composed of one hundred rupees and ten sovereigns of five dollars each, four gold ear-rings & one gold ring.[64]

Appoo was very well informed not only of his wife's whereabouts in Réunion but also of the possibilities of international law. He hoped the protector would

> take such measures as well be consistent with the international law passed between England and France and will at the same time protect the interests of your

---

[63] NAM, Z2D 105, Return of Passengers Arrived on Board the Barque *Umgeni*, Arrival in Port Louis, Mauritius, from Natal, 10 September 1878, p. 40.

[64] NAM, PA 43, Petition of Vencatachellum Appoo to Protector of Immigrants, 23 August 1880, pp. 499–501 (in pencil).

unfortunate petitioner by causing the said Latchoomoo Chengelayen be arrested at Bourbon and be sent back to Mauritius.[65]

Unfortunately, the protector erred on the side of caution 'who, after carefully considering [the case], [was] of opinion that he [could not] assist the applicant in any way whatever'.[66] In the aforementioned case, Chengelayen was able to craft a new life in Réunion not only because of the circumstances but also because of the long-standing familiarity that circulated within immigrant communities in Mauritius by the late 1870s.

## The Late Nineteenth Century and the Early Twentieth Century: Economic Vicissitudes and the Erosion of Remigration

As much as the remigrants sought new economic avenues and used the demand for their labour to seek new horizons, much of this process was connected to the volatile economic patterns within the Indian Ocean. In 1900, distinctive categories of workers existed for plantations and mines in Perak in the Federated Malay States. The labour market was not strictly geared towards sugar plantations, and therefore sugar planters there had to compete with mine owners for labour. However, the lack of Chinese labour was severely felt when the bubonic plague increased quarantine restrictions. As a result of this, planters and mine owners rushed to employ Indians rather than Chinese, as had been the case on Chinese-owned mines. The employment of Indians coincided with a boom in sugar cultivation: 'Judging from the demand for sugar land, and the success which has attended the majority of planters in Perak, there is reason to expect an extension of sugar cultivation'.[67] So while in 1900, Mauritius was starting to suffer from the long-standing cultivation of sugar cane and the saturation of a tired and forlorn sugar industry, the Federated Malay States were auguring a boom in the sugar industry. There was also a sense within British colonial circles, as expressed here by Frank Swettenham, the acting high commissioner of the Federated Malay States:

---

[65] NAM, PA 43, Petition of Vencatachellum Appoo to Protector of Immigrants, 23 August 1880, pp. 499–501 (in pencil).

[66] NAM, PA 43, Petition of Vencatachellum Appoo to Protector of Immigrants, 23 August 1880, pp. 499–501 (in pencil).

[67] BPP 1900 (Cd. 382), Reports on The Federated Malay States for 1899, Frank Swettenham Report of 16 March 1900, Enclosure 2, 'Perak Administration Report for the Year 1899', para. 53, p. 20.

[T]he local conditions of the Federated Malay States, which are easily accessible both from India and China, and in which the labour rates are still comparatively low, should render it possible for them to compete with other cane sugar producing districts such as the West Indies and Mauritius, situated at a much greater distance from any source of cheap labour supply, and which have a local 'gold' standard.[68]

However, Swettenham was inaccurate. The late nineteenth century saw a depression of wages in sugar colonies such as Mauritius, which was in stark contrast to the buoyant mid-nineteenth century. During that time, remigration patterns in the Indian Ocean were characterised by a mix of long-distance mobility (trans-oceanic and trans-colonial – for examples, from Mauritius to Fiji and from Trinidad to Mauritius) and relative proximity to India (intra-oceanic).[69] Remigrants would journey to India first and remigrate to another sugar colony then. However, by the early twentieth century, remigration patterns had changed significantly, in part because local labour markets such as those of Mauritius did not offer much either in terms of employment or high wages. The case of Dersady, a *dhobi* (washerman), illustrates this best. He traveled to Mombasa in late 1899 and 'had since not been heard of by his parents in the island [of Mauritius]'.[70] They did not 'know whether he [was] alive or dead'.[71] Writing on behalf of Dersady's parents, the protector enjoined the consul to 'obtain this information required from some of the other *dhobies* [washermen] living in Mombasa'.[72] The Cape was equally close to Mauritius. Jaul Oomar[73], an 'inmate of the Barkly Asylum', petitioned the poor law commissioner in Mauritius for 'a free passage ...

---

[68]  BPP 1900 (Cd. 382), Reports on The Federated Malay States for 1899, Frank Swettenham Report of 16 March 1900, Enclosure 2, 'Perak Administration Report for the Year 1899', para. 53, p. 20.

[69]  Hurgobin and Basu (2015), p. 25.

[70]  NAM, PB 38, J. F. Trotter, Protector of Immigrants to British Consul, Mombasa, Zanzibar, 13 October 1899, No. 1045, p. 72 (in pencil). I am grateful to Sheela Hurgobin for drawing my attention to this missive. Trotter made a mistake in his note since he addressed it to the British consul at 'Mombasa, Zanzibar'.

[71]  NAM, PB 38, J. F. Trotter, Protector of Immigrants to British Consul, Mombasa, Zanzibar, 13 October 1899, No. 1045, p. 72 (in pencil). The full sentence reads as follows: 'I shall be much obliged if you can give me any information about him as his parents do not know whether he is alive or dead.'

[72]  NAM, PB 38, J. F. Trotter, Protector of Immigrants to British Consul, Mombasa, Zanzibar, 13 October 1899, No. 1045, p. 72 (in pencil).

[73]  The name appears to be Jane Oomar in the primary document.

to return to India or the Cape'.[74] It is uncertain how Oomar reached Mauritius. He could have indentured in Natal and then remigrated from Natal to Mauritius or could have come to the island as a passenger.

Though the sugar industry in Mauritius was lacklustre[75] in the early twentieth century, some migrants from India still hoped for wondrous economic opportunities in the sugar colony. Boutte Khan, a former sepoy in the 17th Bengal infantry, was discharged at his own request on 30 April 1907 and came to Mauritius as 'a passenger in June of the same year and obtain[ed] a situation as prison warden'.[76] In his statement at the Immigration Department, Khan relates the following:

> On or about the 14 October 1908, I was dismissed from that post [at the Mauritius prison] on a charge brought against me by a prisoner who alleged that I had given him a 'rotin' [beating]. I now apply to the Protector either for employment or for a free return to Colombo, where I wish to seek for employment.[77]

Khan was 'very anxious to be sent away at once as he [had] no money and [was] living on the charity of a friend'.[78] The protector of immigrants in Mauritius offered a woodcutter position to Khan, who refused it. He was then keen for Khan

---

[74] MGI, PL 75, Poor Law Commissioner to Acting Colonial Secretary, 19 April 1904, MP 3029.

[75] Swettenham and Mauritius Royal Commission (1910 [1909]), app. B: 'Minutes of Proceedings and Evidence, Cd. 5186'. Alexander Lethbridge Banbury, the receiver general, attributed the poor economy to the sugar industry: 'There was a very serious depression of the sugar industry during the year 1906–7 which paralysed the whole of the trade of the colony' (answer to question 48, p. 6). Graham John Bower, the colonial secretary of Mauritius, attributed it to 'excessive expenditure' of the government and the 'indebtedness and high interest' of the population (para. 1668, p. 41). William Newton, an elected member of Port Louis from 1888 to 1911, attributed it to 'the difficulties with which the sugar industry has been confronted for many years past, and which reached a culminating the last 7 years' (answer to A.1., p. 102).

[76] MGI, PL 31, Statement of Boutte Khan, 17 November 1908.

[77] MGI, PL 31, Statement of Boutte Khan, 17 November 1908. The term that Khan probably used is *rotin*, meaning a bamboo stick that has been sharpened. The *rotin* was used in the nineteenth century. See Frere and Williamson (1875), app. H (No. 1), para. 17: '102 Indiens'. 'Les plaignants au nombre de 102 se plaignent d'avoir reçu des coups de rotin a différentes époques au bureau du Protecteur des Immigrants' (102 Indians have complained to have received beatings with the *rotin* at different periods at the protector of immigrants' office).

[78] MGI, PL 31, Protector of Immigrants to Colonial Secretary, 2 June 1909.

to leave since he '[would] probably become a burden to the Colony if not sent away' and was only ready to send Khan back to Calcutta instead of Colombo.[79] Finally, the government of Bengal paid 40 rupees for the deck passage of Khan and the protector advanced 10 rupees for Khan's 'maintenance during the voyage'.[80] Khan's case demonstrates that despite the paltry economic situation of some migrants from India and the equally sad economic situation of Mauritius, they still hoped for better avenues in another colony instead of returning to India.

Old sugar-cane plantation complexes in Mauritius and Réunion as well as in the West Indies 'adapt[ed] ... in the nineteenth century to emancipation and the central factory system'.[81] The boom in sugar cultivation was most evident in the case of Mauritius, which witnessed an exponential increase in sugar-cane acreage between 1841 and 1861.[82] The direct corollary of this economic boom was an increase in the number of returnees (between India and Mauritius) and remigrants (across colonies) in terms of both intra-Indian Ocean and trans-ocean. Remigration was already difficult to trace in the nineteenth century. In the twentieth century, it became yet harder to ascertain whether remigration rates decreased or increased. It was still present, as can be seen in the report of Arthur R. Coates, the agent-general of immigration of Fiji. In 1907, he indicated that 117 immigrants had 'worked or lived previously in other colonies'. Of that figure, 14 returnees had been to Fiji earlier. The remaining remigrants had been to Natal, British Guiana, Jamaica, the Straits Settlements, Mauritius, Rangoon (present-day Yangon), Ceylon (present-day Sri Lanka), Surinam (present-day Suriname) and Trinidad before reaching Fiji.[83] One year of statistics is, however, insufficient to assess trans-oceanic remigration (Indian Ocean to Pacific Ocean). Two years later in the Atlantic Ocean, William Heron Coombs, the protector of immigrants for Trinidad and Tobago, explained how 'there were no less than

---

[79]  MGI, PL 31, Protector of Immigrants to Colonial Secretary, 18 November 1909.

[80]  MGI, PL 31, Chief Clerical to Protector of Immigrants, no date available.

[81]  Galloway (1989), p. 218.

[82]  Lamusse (1964). In 1841, sugar-cane acreage was 58,500 acres, while in 1861 it was 123,000 acres.

[83]  MGI, PL 21, *Annual Report on Indian Immigration to, Indian Emigration From, and Indentured Indian Immigrants in the Colony [Fiji] For the Year*, 12 July 1907, p. 5. Natal (33), British Guiana (30), Straits Settlements (15), Ceylon (10), Mauritius (4), Jamaica (3), Rangoon (3) Trinidad (1). The number of returnees to Fiji is 14. This leaves 103 from other colonies.

96 who were "Returns" from this and other Colonies'.[84] Coombs did not distinguish between returnees (those who returned to Trinidad and Tobago) and those who remigrated from other colonies. He especially railed against the influence of the 96 'Returns':

> These are, as a rule, very undesirable people. They may be acclimatised, and know the work as some argue, but my experience is that they know too much, and taint the minds of the other immigrants during the voyage with their bad advice. Nearly all the troubles we have had on estates can be traced to the influence of 'Return Immigrants'.[85]

One could readily believe that it was returnees – who had been to the colony earlier – who caused a ruckus on estates. However, out of the 96 'Returns', the majority came from other colonies. Thus, while remigrants sought better economic opportunities, colonial governments did not always consider their presence benevolently.

## Conclusion

While much scholarship on indentured labour has focused on return and two types of remigration (return to India and remigration to the same sugar colony or a different colony and remigration from a sugar colony to another sugar colony), this chapter has examined remigration that happened between sub-clusters of the Indian Ocean. This remigration operated between sugar colonies (Réunion and Mauritius) and colonies termed 'minor dependencies', such as Diego Garcia, Seychelles and St Brandon. Though colonial discourse has reified the lesser economic nature of dependencies, a study of passenger logs has demonstrated the

---

[84] NAM, PA 296, Protector of Immigrants, Trinidad and Tobago, to Protector of Immigrants, Mauritius, 30 August 1909, *Annual Report of the Protector of Immigrants for 1908–9 for the Colony of Trinidad and Tobago*, p. 3. The calculation behind 96 is as follows: the ship *Ganges* that reached the colony on 20 July 1908: 7 from Fiji, 1 from Surinam, 18 from Natal, 2 from British Guiana and 3 from Trinidad and Tobago; the ship *Indus* that reached the colony on 12 August 1908: 18 from Natal, 4 from British Guiana, 1 from Fiji, 1 from Mauritius and 21 from Trinidad and Tobago; the ship *Mutlah* that reached the colony on 4 September 1908: 3 from Natal, 1 from Fiji and 2 from Trinidad and Tobago; the ship *Sutlej* that reached the colony on 1 October 1908: 3 from Natal, 1 from British Guiana and 10 from Trinidad and Tobago.

[85] NAM, PA 296, Protector of Immigrants of Trinidad and Tobago to Immigration Department of Mauritius, 30 August 1909, *Annual Report of the Protector of Immigrants for 1908–9 for the Colony of Trinidad and Tobago*, pp. 3–4

variety of destinations that remigrants chose. Recent scholarship on the South Asian diaspora has queried the 'migration strategy' adopted by Indian immigrants and the role of 'individual ingenuity'.[86] Though this chapter focuses on the Indian Ocean, it suggests that the mobilities of remigrants were often a product – not of set migration strategies but of personal initiative, colonial bureaucratic largesse and contingencies. Remigration did not function dialectically in relation to return migration but was imbricated within the process of return while simultaneously developing its own dynamic. Further, the chapter demonstrates that far from operating as a web[87] (with India in the center and colonies connected to the subcontinent), the Indian Ocean contained sub-clusters of nodes that facilitated migrant mobilities.

## Bibliography

Ali, Ahmed. 1980. *Plantation to Politics: Studies on Fiji Indians*. Suva: University of the South Pacific.

Ballantyne, Tony. 2003. 'Rereading the Archive and Opening Up the Nation State'. In *After the Imperial Turn: Thinking with and through the Nation*, edited by Antoinette Burton, pp. 102–121. Durham, NC: Duke University Press.

Bates, Crispin. 2017. 'Some Thoughts on the Representation and Misrepresentation of the Colonial South Asian Labour Diaspora'. *South Asian Studies* 33(1): 7–22.

Bates, Crispin, and Marina Carter. 2017. 'Sirdars as Intermediaries in Nineteenth-Century Indian Ocean Indentured Labour Migration'. *Modern Asian Studies* 51(2): 462–484.

———. 2021. 'Remigration of Indian Subalterns in the Colonial Indian Ocean'. *Journal of Colonialism and Colonial History* 22(1): 1–30.

Behal, Rana P., and Prabhu P. Mohapatra. 1992. '"Tea and Money versus Human Life": The Rise and Fall of the Indenture System in the Assam Tea Plantations 1840–1908'. *Journal of Peasant Studies* 19(3–4): 142–172.

Board of Trade. 1909. *Colonial Statistics, 1909: Alphabetical List of the British Self-Governing Dominions, Crown Colonies, Possessions, and Protectorates*. London: Commercial Department, Board of Trade, Great Britain.

Bose, Sugata. 2006. *A Hundred Horizons: The Indian Ocean in the Age of Global Empire*. Cambridge, MA: Harvard University Press.

Breman, Jan. 1989. *Taming the Coolie Beast: Plantation Society and the Colonial Order in Southeast Asia*. Oxford: Oxford University Press.

---

[86] Chatterji and Washbrook (2013), p. 4; Bates (2017), p. 7.
[87] Ballantyne (2003).

Carter, Marina. 1995. *Servants, Sirdars, and Settlers: Indians in Mauritius, 1834–1874*. Delhi and New York: Oxford University Press.

———. 1996. *Voices from Indenture: Experiences of Indian Migrants in the British Empire*. New York: Leicester University Press.

———. 2017. 'Towards a Workers' History of the Chagos Archipelago'. *Journal of the Indian Ocean Region* 13(2): 213–233.

Chatterji, Joya, and David Washbrook (eds.). 2013. *Routledge Handbook of the South Asian Diaspora*. New York: Routledge.

Cooper, Frederick. 2005. *Colonialism in Question: Theory, Knowledge, History*. Berkeley and Los Angeles: University of California Press.

Cumpston, I. M. 1953. *Indians Overseas in British Territories, 1834–1854*. Oxford: Oxford University Press.

Daniel, E. Valentine, Henry Bernstein and Tom Brass (eds.). 1992. *Plantations, Proletarians, and Peasants in Colonial Asia*. London: Frank Cass & Co Ltd.

Das Gupta, Ranajit. 1981. 'Structure of Labour Market in Colonial India'. *Economic and Political Weekly* 16(44, 46): 1781–1806.

Durgahee, Reshaad. 2021. *The Indentured Archipelago: Experiences of Indian Labour in Mauritius and Fiji, 1871–1916*. Cambridge (UK), London and New Delhi: Cambridge University Press.

Frere, William Edward, and Victor Alexander Williamson. 1875. *Report of the Royal Commissioners Appointed to Enquire into the Treatment of Immigrants in Mauritius: Presented to Both Houses of Parliament by Command of Her Majesty, 6 February 1875*. London: William Clowes and Sons.

Galloway, J. H. 1989. *The Sugar Cane Industry: An Historical Geography from Its Origins to 1914*. Cambridge (UK) and London: Cambridge University Press.

Govindin, Sully-Santa. 1994. *Les Engagés Indiens: Ile de La Réunion 19eme Siècle*. Sainte-Marie: Azalées Editions.

Great Britain Parliament House of Commons. 1901. *Parliamentary Papers: Colonies and British Possessions*. Colonial Reports (Annual), Hong Kong to Turks and Caicos Islands, Session 16 January 1902 to 18 December 1902, vol. 65. London: HM Stationery Office, Darling & Son Ltd, Bacon Street, E.

Hazareesingh, Kissoonsingh. 1975. *History of Indians in Mauritius*. Hong Kong: Macmillan Publishers.

Ho, Engseng. 2006. *The Graves of Tarim: Genealogy and Mobility across the Indian Ocean*. Berkeley and Los Angeles: University of California Press.

Ho, Hai Quang. 2004. *Histoire Economique de l'île de La Réunion (1849–1881): Engagisme, Croissance et Crise*. Paris, Budapest and Torino: Editions L'Harmattan.

Hurgobin, Yoshina, and Subho Basu. 2015. '"Oceans without Borders": Dialectics of Transcolonial Labor Migration from the Indian Ocean World to the Atlantic Ocean World'. *International Labor and Working-Class History* 87 (Spring): 7–26.

Jeffery, Laura. 2011. *Chagos Islanders in Mauritius and the UK: Forced Displacement and Onward Migration*. Manchester: Manchester University Press.

Kumar, Ashutosh. 2017. *Coolies of the Empire: Indentured Indians in the Sugar Colonies, 1830–1920*. Cambridge (UK), London and New Delhi: Cambridge University Press.

Lal, Brij V. 1980. 'Approaches to the Study of Indian Indentured Emigration with Special Reference to Fiji'. *Journal of Pacific History* 15(1): 52–70.

Lal, Brij V., Doug Munro and Edward D. Beechert (eds.). 1993. *Plantation Workers: Resistance and Accommodation*. Honolulu, HI: University of Hawaii Press.

Lamusse, Roland. 1964. 'The Economic Development of the Mauritius Sugar Industry – I: Development in Field and Factory'. *Revue Agricole et Sucrière de L'île Maurice (Organe Officiel de La Société de Technologie Agricole et Sucrière de l'Ile Maurice)* 43(1): 22–38.

Leroy-Beaulieu, Paul. 1874. *De La Colonisation Chez Les Peuples Modernes*. Paris: Guillaumin et Cie Libraires.

Piggott, Francis Taylor, Louis Arthur Thibaud, Furcy Alfred Herchenroder, George Guibert and William Newton. 1896. *The Laws of Mauritius*, vol. 2. Mauritius: Gabriel Bouic.

Mongia, Radhika. 2018. *Indian Migration and Empire: A Colonial Genealogy of the Modern State*. Durham, NC: Duke University Press.

Mouat, Frederic John. 1852. *Rough Notes of a Trip to Réunion, the Mauritius and Ceylon: With Remarks on the Eligibility as Sanitaria for Indian Invalids*. London: Thacker, Spink and Co.

Northrup, David. 1995. *Indentured Labor in the Age of Imperialism, 1834–1922*. Cambridge (UK) and London: Cambridge University Press.

Sermet, Laurent. 2009. *Une Anthropologie Juridique des Droits de l'homme: Les Chemins de l'Océan Indien*. Paris: Editions des Archives Contemporaines.

Swettenham, Frank Athelstone, and Mauritius Royal Commission. 1910 (1909). *Report of the Mauritius Royal Commission, 1909*, part 2. London: Eyre and Spottiswoode Ltd.

Tinker, Hugh. 1974. *A New System of Slavery: The Export of Indian Labour Overseas, 1830–1920*. London and New York: Oxford University Press.

# Part III

# Gender and Family

# 9

# Intimate Lives on Rubber Plantations

## The Textures of Indian Coolie Relations in British Malaya*

*Arunima Datta*

On 13 September 1935, Muthusamy, an Indian coolie from the Haron Estate, Klang, in British Malaya (henceforth Malaya), was charged with enticing away a married woman, Thavakka, who was a coolie and the wife of Rengasamy, another coolie at the same estate. During the trial, it was established that Rengasamy married Thavakka in India in 1927, just before they arrived in Malaya at the Haron Estate. In his statement, Rengasamy claimed that Muthusamy had begun taking his meals with the couple from August 1934, and in March 1935 the latter enticed Thavakka away from him. Muthusamy, on the contrary, claimed that during the previous year he had been depositing all his earnings with Rengasamy for safe keeping, and in March 1935, when he demanded the money back from Rengasamy, the latter offered his wife instead of the money. Furthermore, Muthusamy tried to establish that he had initially refused the offer, but upon the pleas and eagerness of Thavakka, he agreed, and they proceeded to an estate in Ipoh where they began to live as 'husband and wife'. After hearing the case, the magistrate convicted Muthusamy and sentenced him to three years of rigorous imprisonment.[1]

---

* Certain parts of this chapter were originally published as an article titled '"Immorality", Nationalism and the Colonial State in British Malaya: Indian "Coolie" Women's Intimate Lives as Ideological Battleground' in the journal *Women's History Review*, vol. 25, no. 4 © Taylor & Francis Group Pvt Ltd 2016. All rights reserved. Reproduced with the permission of the copyright holder and the publisher, Taylor & Francis Ltd; see Datta (2016). It also later appeared in the author's book, *Fleeting Agencies: A Social History of Indian Coolie Women in British Malaya*, published by the Press, in 2021; see Datta (2021).

[1] *Singapore Free Press and Mercantile Advertiser*, 17 September 1935, p. 6.

The investigation and verdict on the Muthusamy and Rengasamy case was covered in a number of local newspapers, as were most 'enticement' cases in Malaya.[2] Such cases were not uncommon in transnational migrant labour communities in colonial plantation societies. Colonial administrators, while dealing with incidences of domestic trouble, kidnapping, crimes of passion and other misdemeanors often used stereotypical labels of 'victim' and 'enticer' to categorise colonised subjects, but stereotyping did not always prove helpful for either administrators or their subjects. The frequent recurrence of incidents involving acts of 'wife enticement'[3], sexual jealousy and partner or spouse desertion amongst immigrant Indian coolies[4] in Malaya sparked intense debate amongst colonial administrators both in India and Malaya from 1900 to 1940. The discourses that arose in the wake of such incidents offer many clues about the nature of Indian coolie life in British Malaya, particularly the nature of intimate gender relations.

Due largely to the demographics of early Indian immigration, historical research on Indian coolies in Malaya has tended to focus on male immigrants and their work as coolies, *kangani*s and *chettiar*s.[5] This emphasis has resulted in complete silence regarding Indian coolie women or gender relations between coolie migrants within colonial plantation societies.[6] An examination of the

---

[2] 'Enticement' in Malaya, as in other British plantation colonies, was understood as an act of enticing away a spouse from his or her partner. While in reality these cases were very similar to adultery, the administrators took on a gendered approach in judging these cases where almost always the woman was seen as a passive victim and the man an enticer, cancelling out any chance of conscious adultery from both subjects involved. For further discussion, see Datta (2021).

[3] Important to note here is that wife-enticement was not a criminal offence amongst the British and was in legal terms not the same as 'adultery'. The very existence of such an offence reveals that Indian women were seen differently from British women, who might have had been victims of rape or guilty of adultery but were not seen as subjects participating in 'enticement'.

[4] I use the term 'coolie' consciously but in a non-derogatory manner to refer to the professional category that is the subject of this study. I understand that using the term 'coolie' as a professional category, as archival records suggest, is contentious since the term in the present day carries a heavy derogatory baggage.

[5] The Tamil term *kangani* refers to the profession of an overseer or labour-leader. *Chetty* or *chettiar* is a 'title' or surname used by various mercantile, agricultural and land-owning castes in south India, particularly in Tamil Nadu. During the late nineteenth and twentieth centuries, many *chettiar*s migrated to colonial plantation colonies to venture into the money-lending business and even tried to become planters themselves.

[6] Kelly (1991); Jain and Reddock (1998); Ramachandran (1994); Sandhu (1969); Sinappah (1970); Jain (1970); Jackson (1961); Mahajani (1960); Kaur (2006). There has been a marked absence of work on Indian coolies in Malaya since the 1970s, and this is reflected in Kaur's (2006) work, as even she does not refer to any recent literature.

complex interactions and intimacies between Indian coolie men and women in Malaya can present new insights into Indian–Malaysian history, offering a better understanding of the textured realities of everyday life on plantations and the factors that could bring uncertainty, fear and, sometimes, violence into the lives of migrant coolies. While historians have hinted at the existence of unique forms of gender conflict and relations between coolie men and women, none have explored the subject in depth.[7]

The paucity of women in early Indian migrant communities in Malaya, as in other plantation colonies, had implications for gender relations that have often been misrepresented in colonial discourses in which women have been painted as perpetual victims and men as perpetual perpetrators. Whilst there is clear evidence that women were sometimes victims of male violence and kidnapping, the idea that they were victims rather than participants in 'enticement' or 'seduction' is, I suggest, a product of colonial gender stereotypes that downplayed the agency of women and their active engagement in sexual and conjugal relationships. Such presumptions, and the stereotypical representations on which they were based, had the effect of removing responsibility for structural imbalances from colonial administrative systems and blaming the ensuing problems on generically 'violent' and 'immoral' coolie men and 'subservient' coolie women. When such cases came before courts, such stereotypical views often had perverse effects on verdicts. Using a selection of reported trials concerning intimate or conjugal problems amongst Indian coolies in Malaya, this study considers how scarcity of women and loopholes in colonial administrative policy created new possibilities for intimate relationships between Indian coolie men and women, many of whom exhibited patterns of behaviour and interaction with each other that were significantly different from those back in the Indian subcontinent.[8]

This chapter begins with a brief history of Indian coolie migration to British Malaya. Next, it moves to explore the textured realities of Indian coolie lives in British Malaya through readings of various case studies. It then analyses the ways in which colonial administrators and judges tried cases wherein both coolie men and women exhibited non-conventional and fleeting forms of agency

---

[7] Ramachandran (1994); Sandhu (1969); Jain (1970); Mahajani (1960).

[8] The chapter primarily relies on newspapers such as the *Malaya Tribune*, the *Morning Tribune*, the *Perak Pioneer*, the *Times of Malaya* and the *Straits Times*. It also uses colonial administrative documents, including census reports, India Office records on 'Indians in Malaya' and reports of the agent of the government of India in Malaya as sources of statistical data to analyse the demographic profiles of Indians in Malaya and the frequency of such incidences.

in their intimate and conjugal relations. The chapter concludes by showing how studying the volatile nature of gender dynamics opens up new understandings of community and identity formation among subjugated immigrants within the colonial context.

## Indian Coolie Migration to Malaya

With the opening of the Suez Canal in 1869, Malaya, previously ignored by the British Empire, became a crucial maritime link between the West and the East and a valued colony. Concurrently, with the abolition of slavery, many planters from coffee-producing British colonies relocated to Malaya, mostly to the Federated Malay States (FMS), but encountered challenges resulting from tropical plant diseases and shortages of skilled labour.[9] Faced with poor production returns, most planters had switched to rubber (introduced to Malaya in 1897) by 1900, but labour shortages remained a prime concern. Planters found local men 'too lazy' for labour-intensive estate jobs, whilst political complications made it difficult for planters to employ Javanese coolies from neighbouring Dutch Indonesia.[10] Planters also avoided employing immigrant Chinese labourers as this would have made them dependent upon Chinese networks of labour recruitment. Lacking other alternatives, planters turned to immigrant Indian labourers, who were considered docile, were accustomed to tropical conditions and had been successfully deployed in older British plantation colonies including Fiji, Surinam (present-day Suriname), Jamaica and British Guiana (present-day Guyana).[11]

Initially, coolie migration to Malaya was transient and predominantly male. By the 1890s, planters had realised the disadvantages of relying on transient labourers. First, a transient labour force increased the cost of production. Second, relying on such a labour force made the planters vulnerable to political instability arising from the increased complexity of relationships between British India and Malaya following the 1867 separation of the two governments, which affected the regularity of the labour supply from India. These concerns pushed planters to establish a locally settled pool of labour by encouraging the immigration

---

[9]  Forthwith, by 'planters', I refer to the European rubber planters in colonial Malaya unless stated otherwise. FMS was a federation of four Malay states under British protection – Selangor, Negri Sembilan, Pahang and Perak – established in 1895 and dissolved only in 1946 when the FMS was merged with the rest of the Malayan states: the Straits Settlement (SS) and the Unfederated Malaya States (UMS).

[10]  See Arkib Negara 1957/0103354, *Correspondences Regarding Recruiting of Indian Labor from Northern India*, 1902, National Archives of Malaysia, Kuala Lumpur; Jackson (1961).

[11]  Sandhu (1969).

of coolie women and families.[12] The Malaya census reports from 1911 to 1931 reflect this marked demographic change. In 1911, coolie women constituted 25 per cent of coolies on rubber plantations, whilst by 1931 they constituted 39 per cent of the coolie population.[13] Nonetheless, an imbalance in the sex ratio amongst coolies remained. As Piya Chatterjee and Janaki Nair insist, colonial plantations regarded women labourers primarily as labour reproducers rather than producers and as servicing agents for plantation society at large.[14] Whilst coolie women provided individual labouring bodies no less skilled than male coolies, they were always paid lower wages than their male counterparts for the same work. Planters rationalised lower wages and the non-allowance of rations or bonuses to women, irrespective of marital status, on the grounds that coolie women were secondary wage earners for a family.[15]

Most migrants to Malaya came from Madras (present-day Chennai), which, at the turn of the twentieth century, was still struggling to recover from disastrous recurring famines between 1866 and 1881. Increased pressure on land and resulting unemployment encouraged lower-caste Tamils to migrate to escape hardships at home.[16] Women, however, migrated for varied reasons, not limited to economic factors. While many women migrated as 'wives' of coolie men, there were others who migrated alone to escape abusive marriages, family quarrels or lives as widows or prostitutes.[17] Coolie women who migrated alone became so numerous that lady inspectors were appointed to act as chaperones on board the ships that transported coolies from south India to Malaya.[18] Single women migrants were a minority compared to the number of accompanied women but still constituted a significant presence in estate societies. In fact, the Labour Commission appointed by the government of Madras (1916), to review the condition of Indian labour in the Malay Peninsula and Ceylon (present-day Sri Lanka), stated that most of the south Indian workers coming into Malaya did not bring their womenfolk from India but rather developed contract alliances locally.[19] Since most of the coolie

---

[12]  Datta (2016), p. 588. Also see Datta (2021).

[13]  Vlieland (1932), pp. 85–86.

[14]  Chatterjee (2001), pp. 80–82; Nair (1996), pp. 99–104.

[15]  Datta (2016).

[16]  Kaur (2006), p. 430.

[17]  Pool and Singh (1999).

[18]  Office of the Honorary Commissioner for Depressed Classes for SS and FMS (1926), pp. 2–3.

[19]  Office of the Honorary Commissioner for Depressed Classes for SS and FMS (1926), pp. 2–3.

women were presumed to be married, the statement seems to be either that they engaged in adulterous relations or that many coolie marriages were questionable. It further reported that while most of the women coolies migrating to Malaya were married, some were no doubt prostitutes.[20] Validation of such perceptions can be found in cases wherein women and men admitted to having contracted marriages or were coerced into marriage by recruiters in order to be eligible to migrate.[21] Despite the gendered nature of migration, wages and social life, coolie men and women often collaborated with each other in estate labour politics, especially in strikes, and also in social activities such as toddy drinking as well as 'immoral activities'. Reductionist colonial views of coolie men as exclusively miscreants and coolie women as exclusively victims thus seem highly improbable to be true.[22]

## Textured Realities of Coolie Intimacies in Malaya

Even after the substantial influx of Indian coolie women into British Malaya, a considerable gender imbalance persisted. While this imbalance among Indian coolies was never as extreme as it had been for the Chinese community, Indian coolie women were still outnumbered by Indian coolie men in Malaya, and this has been seen by many to have had been a source of sexual jealousy and violence among the coolie community.[23] Annual reports of the agents of the government of India in Malaya during the 1920s and the 1930s documented the high frequency of domestic troubles being brought to the courts in Malaya by coolies, and in all such reports, the agents candidly blamed the administrators of Malaya for the gender imbalance among Indian coolies and hence for the alarming increase in social offences.[24] In 1929, agent S. R. Naidu documented 272 cases of marital offences and violence amongst Indian coolies. Similarly, agent Rao S. M. K. Nair recorded 380 such cases between November 1930 and December 1933. And in 1934, agent K. A. Mukundan reported 735 cases, the majority of which involved

---

[20] *Straits Times*, 23 March 1917, p. 12. Such instances led to India's stationing protectors of emigrants at ports of emigration at Negapatnam and Madras (Avadi) to examine emigrants' background, health, motives, marital status and awareness concerning their planned employment. Often single women were detained for a later shipment to Malaya to ensure that they were not enticed away by recruiters and were not of 'bad' character.

[21] Datta (2016, 2021).

[22] Datta (2016, 2021).

[23] Warren (2003a, 2003b).

[24] Henceforth, the agents are referred to by their name (with the prefix 'agent') and respective years.

'wife enticement'.[25] Further, the local British administrators in Malaya claimed, in their annual reports of crime in the FMS and in newspapers during 1934–1938, that more than half of the murders in the FMS were caused by Tamil coolie men. They even asserted that as most of these murders were unpremeditated and committed in a fit of fury or passion, they were not preventable by police actions.[26]

Several case files, inquests and newspaper details about case trials of domestic violence, sexual jealousy and enticement demonstrate that, faced with a lack of female companionship, some Indian coolie men resorted to desperate measures to consort with coolie women, who commonly experienced advances, sometimes welcome and sometimes unwelcome, from coolie men as a part of their daily lives in Malaya. Incidents involving enticement did not always end as peacefully as the case discussed earlier; sometimes they turned violent. In June 1937, an inquest and trial were held in the Selangor assizes concerning the death of Rengasamy, an Indian coolie man who allegedly died accidentally while trying to confront Devasagayam, another coolie who had attempted to entice away Perumal's wife, Meenachie. Perumal and Meenachie worked alongside Rengasamy and Devasagayam on the Sepang Estate in Kuala Lumpur. Perumal and Rengasamy both testified that Devasagayam had repeatedly propositioned Meenachie to desert her husband and run away with him. On the day of the incident, Meenachie, feeling herself subjected to what we would now call sexual harassment, reported Devasagayam's 'unacceptable advancements' to her husband and Rengasamy. In their testimonies, both Perumal and Rengasamy – who recorded his testimony just before dying of his injuries – stated that Devasagayam had been making such propositions for several years and that they chased after Devasagayam to discipline him, but the latter took out a knife and stabbed Rengasamy.[27] Available records reveal that the court decided that Devasagyam was guilty of trying to entice Perumal's wife Meenachie and was sentenced to rigorous imprisonment for five years. However, the records give us no answer as to what the verdict was on the act of manslaughter and how the court decided on that account.

Indian coolie husbands and wives in Malaya often learned to be 'careful' and on guard against single male coolies, who were often close acquaintances

---

[25] *Annual Report of the Agent of the Government of India in Malaya* (1929), p. 21; *Annual Report of the Agent of the Government of India in Malaya* (1931); *Annual Report of the Agent of the Government of India in Malaya* (1932), pp. 20–21; *Annual Report of the Agent of the Government of India in Malaya* (1934), p. 20.

[26] *Straits Times*, 29 August 1935, p. 7; *Report of the Commissioner of Police for FMS* (1937); *Straits Times*, 19 September 1938, p. 3.

[27] *Malaya Tribune*, 8 June 1937, p. 14.

working on the same estates and either boarded with coolie couples or 'messed' with them regularly.[28] 'Enticers' were rarely known criminals and were sometimes close friends, as in the 1935 case in an estate in Ipoh concerning a coolie man, Sinnasamy, who was a close friend of another coolie, Perumal, and had repeatedly attempted to seduce Perumal's wife. On the ill-fated day of Thaipussam in 1935, Perumal, upon returning home, saw Sinnasamy trying to 'touch his wife when she was sleeping'. Enraged at this, Perumal dragged Sinnasamy into the street where the fight attracted police attention. During the trial, the magistrate decided that as no substantial evidence could be produced against Sinnasamy, he would only be fined three dollars or receive three days of imprisonment.[29]

Sometimes, such obsessions went beyond 'enticement' and elopement, involving the kidnapping of women by obsessed coolie men. Several inquests provide evidence of attempted kidnapping by Indian coolie men who took advantage of isolated workspaces or sometimes different working hours of different kinds of coolies on rubber estates.[30] On 10 December 1931, Naraina, a rubber tapper on the Eaglehurst Estate, Pondok Tanjong, approached Urukumani, a coolie woman and the wife of Doraisamy, another coolie, with the intention of enticing her. On her refusal, Naraina gagged her and carried her off to the Chemor Road, where she was discovered with Naraina five days later by Doraisamy. In his defence, Naraina claimed that Urukumani and he had been intimate and physically close and that he had only kidnapped her because she pled with him to take here away. However, based on the evidence of witnesses and circumstantial evidence, the magistrate sentenced Naraina to a fine of 75 dollars or rigorous imprisonment.[31] Whether this case was one of a victimless elopement we can never know for sure, although the detail of gagging suggests otherwise. Annual administrative crime reports from British Malaya make it evident that such incidents were frequent,

---

[28]  'Messing' refers to the communal dining arrangements in coolie residential quarters. Planters in British Malaya from the late 1800s, and particularly from 1900 onward, encouraged coolie women on their plantations to not only cook for their households but also engage in communal cooking in return for extra earnings. Thus evolved the communal messing infrastructure in coolie lines. While there was no written law to force coolie couples to engage in such entrepreneurial activities, the meager pay coolie couples earned and the constant encouragement of such arrangements by plantation authorities often influenced coolie couples to capitalise on the demand for such enterprises. See Earl (1861).

[29]  *Times of Malaya*, 23 January 1935, p. 2.

[30]  Some coolies such as tappers would finish work by 9 a.m., and others such as weeders and factory workers would work from 9 a.m. until the evening.

[31]  *Times of Malaya*, 18 January 1932, p. 13.

but they seldom explain whether such cases were really cases of kidnapping or elopement.[32]

Interestingly, such superficial documentation of these cases ignored the agency of women involved in the cases of elopement and simultaneously ignored the socio-economic realities behind such behavior of coolie women. In the aforementioned cases, the Indian coolie men who attempted to entice or abduct coolie women were single men, raising the question of whether feelings of jealousy or emasculation resulting from not having a wife or partner drove them to such behaviour . As many scholars studying abuse and harassment of women in contexts of unbalanced sex ratio have shown, unbalanced sex ratio does not automatically explain incidents of rape, abduction and other forms of violence.[33] They have shown that such acts of intrusion or harassment are not necessarily a product of sexual arousal but rather about affirming some kind of status, 'manhood' and power through conquest and intimidation.[34] Historian Albert Hurtado, in the context of nineteenth-century California, has shown that sexual harassment and abuses against women by men were results of situational stress and can be read as attempts by the perpetrators to compensate for feelings of inadequacy in a given situation.[35] Likewise, it can be argued that the coolie men who attempted to abduct, abuse or entice the wives of other coolie men were disheartened by their economic prospects in Malaya and sought to assert their masculinity and power through the subjugation of women, who happened to be the wives of other Indian coolies who in the eyes of the perpetrators were at least nominally more successful than they were.

While coolie women were often the victims of 'enticements' and resulting crimes of passion, there were several cases wherein the concerned coolie women were consensual parties in many kinds of socially unacceptable intimacies. When caught in unfavorable circumstances, these coolie women capitalised on the colonial perception of Indian coolie women as passive victims to escape social or legal sanctions. Moreover, 'enticements' and kidnappings did not always involve married couples; sometimes single women were reported to have been enticed away from their parents and relatives. On 28 April 1910, Arulanandan, a coolie

---

[32]  See Datta (2016).

[33]  Groth (1975), p. 5; Sanday (1981), pp. 5–27; Brownmiller (1975); Schwendinger and Schewendinger (1983), pp. 27–46.

[34]  Groth (1975), p. 5; Sanday (1981), pp. 5–27; Brownmiller (1975); Schwendinger and Herman Schewendinger (1983), pp. 27–46.

[35]  Hurtado (1988), pp. 182–186.

on the Chankat Salak Estate, was accused at an assize court in Ipoh of kidnapping Nagamal, a daughter of fellow coolies. During the trial, Arulanandan claimed that Nagamal was not a 'child' and that both had consciously decided to elope and get married. While Nagamal, according to various newspaper reports, looked 'well grown for her age', the court did not investigate her real age and accepted the claims of her parents that she was a child who had been taken away by force.[36] The court did not seek any further details regarding Nagamal's relation with the accused and quickly decided that Arulanandan was guilty as charged and sentenced him to rigorous imprisonment for three years.

In March 1938, Ramasamy, a rubber tapper on an estate in Sitiawan, Perak, was charged in the Perak assize court for enticing and kidnapping a Tamil girl of 16 years from the same coolie line.[37] In his defense, Ramasamy claimed that they had been intimate for several years and that they both consensually agreed to elope from the estate. He further explained that due to their intimacy, the girl had often been teased by her friends on the estate about being Ramasamy's mistress, and being frustrated with the situation, she began pleading with Ramasamy in December 1937 to elope. Ramasamy claimed that he had initially refused but eventually gave into her pleas. He also asserted that many people on the estate were aware of their intimate relations, although some, including the girl's parents, might have disapproved. When the girl was summoned for questioning, she denied having any intimate relations with Ramasamy and also denied going anywhere willingly with him. Medical evidence collected during the course of the trial revealed that the couple had been physically intimate and that there was no sign of coerced intimacies. Interestingly, however, neither the medical evidence nor the statements of witnesses from other estate coolies were taken into consideration by the court. The public prosecutor, R. M. Cluer, apparently finding himself on weak ground regarding the particular case, shifted his argument to a more general level, claiming that kidnappings and enticements had become far too common among coolies in Malaya, and suggested to the magistrate that 'something should be done to put a stop to it'. The magistrate, J. M. Aynsley, accepted this argument from social necessity and convicted Ramasamy of kidnapping, fining him 100 dollars each year for two years.[38] As in Nagamal's case, the magistrate showed little interest in the evidence relating to the specific case before him.

It was not only single girls such as Nagamal's and Ramasamy's 'victims' who might have had been willing partners in cases of 'enticement'. In a case presented

---

[36] *Times of Malaya*, 28 April 1910, p. 6.

[37] *Morning Tribune*, 17 March 1938, p. 3.

[38] *Morning Tribune*, 17 March 1938, p. 3.

before the Klang magistrate in February 1935, Periasamy, an estate coolie from Batu Tiga, charged a fellow coolie, Muthusamy, with enticing away his wife, Muthamma, in October 1932. During the trial, Muthamma, in her witness statement, claimed that after consuming some curry offered by the accused, she did not know what had happened and had instantly become obsessed with Muthusamy and followed him to Teluk Anson, where they lived as a married couple. Muthusamy, denying allegations that he had served drugged or magical curry, stated that, in fact, 'it was Muthamma who enticed him' and that he had been unaware that Muthamma was ever married as she had 'begged him to be her husband and not being able to withstand her entreaties he took her away'.[39] When the magistrate demanded proof of marriage, Muthamma's father claimed that she was married to Periasamy. Word of mouth, uncorroborated by any documentary evidence, was proof enough for the magistrate to find Muthusamy guilty of wife-enticement and to sentence him to two years of rigorous imprisonment. The evidence given by witnesses in this case appears contradictory and implausible. While Muthusamy feared imprisonment and fines, Muthamma feared violence from her husband and chastisement from her family, who lived in Malaya. It appears likely that this was a case of two consenting individuals in a victimless act of 'immorality'. On being dragged to court, both played victims, and as a result of colonial perceptions of coolie women as victims of enticement rather than as enticers themselves, it was Muthamma's story that was believed. In such cases, more than 'enticement', what we witness is how coolie women could easily 'fake' character through their courtroom performances and particularly sway judges' emotions. Such cases also highlight how magistrates and administrators used widely held notions and presumptions of Indian coolie men being immoral and violent towards their women to excuse what appeared to have been rather sloppy judicial and police work on the case. Moreover, it is not difficult to see that in most cases of enticement, judges agreed with popular notions that were felt most conducive to social stability, regardless of the actual rights and wrongs of the case. This reveals that these stereotypes about coolie men and women were not necessarily blind prejudice but served a colonial purpose of maintaining 'order' amongst colonial subjects.

There were also innumerable instances wherein magistrates and investigators presumed enticement to be a male initiative and made interrogations along those lines, even when there was significant evidence to indicate that the concerned coolie women were actively involved in the 'enticements'. On 18 September 1933, the Klang magistrate found Karuppen, a coolie man, guilty of enticing away a fellow

---

[39] *Singapore Free Press and Mercantile Advertiser*, 16 February 1935, p. 3.

coolie's wife, Nagamah, and sentenced him to a fine of 50 dollars or three months of rigorous imprisonment. Annamalay, the husband of Nagamah, reported to the police that while he was hospitalised, his fellow coolie, Karuppen, enticed away Nagamah. Subsequently, Nagamah in her witness statement argued that she was ill-treated by Annamalay, and thus, in his absence, she asked Karuppen to take her away with him without informing the latter that she was married. Thereafter, they both left the estate and lived in Segamat as husband and wife for three years. Interestingly, the Klang magistrate did not order the marriage between Nagamah and Annamalay to be proven; nor did the magistrate give any consideration to the fact that Nagamah consciously chose to leave her 'husband'.[40] Regardless of such evidence, the Klang magistrate found Karuppen guilty of wife-enticement.

Cases such as these show that while Indian coolie women were vulnerable to attacks from scheming countrymen and subject to facile characterisations by colonial administrators as helpless and passive victims, they also wielded significant power and agency. They managed to exercise substantial control over a major aspect of their lives – their intimacies. As I have argued elsewhere, coolie women often capitalised on such gendered presumptions to escape with new partners and abandon unsuitable marriages or oppressive relationships.[41]

The failure of colonial judges in such cases to take account of female agency[42] and their gendered reading of the evidence can be understood as a product of both their stereotypes of coolie households and their own patriarchal values and assumptions and a product of administrative convenience. Thus, gender and racial profiling was understood to provide information about a person's character, likely guilt or innocence and degree of moral responsibility. Such perceptions are clearly visible in records of court proceedings. As the historian Jeffery Weeks has convincingly argued, a community's idea about what is moral is subjective and based on what they consider or are taught to consider as moral, irrespective of the views and the lived realities of those being judged.[43]

## Conclusion

While both judicial administrators and newspapers reporting trials focused on coolies' 'moral failings', ranging from the lack of modesty, trustworthiness or honesty to a propensity for violence, a re-examination of the cases raises questions

---

[40]  *Straits Times*, 21 September 1933, p. 12. Also see Datta (2016).

[41]  Datta (2016, 2021).

[42]  For the definition of situational agency, see Datta (2016, 2021).

[43]  Weeks (1991).

about both the basis for such stereotyped views and the integrity of the colonial courts that relied upon them. By questioning the basis for the judgements of the courts, it exposes, in the recorded events of 'immorality', 'enticement' and real violence, the underlying colonial structures manifested in the colonial system of gendered labour recruiting, a gender-biased judiciary and, ultimately, the dependence of the plantation economic system on the exploitation of raced and gendered coolie labourers.

This chapter on gender relations in the immigrant Indian coolie community in Malayan colonial plantation society has shown that when the intimate relations of coolies commanded the attention of colonial administrators in Malaya, which was invariably when they posed a threat to the 'order' amongst the colonised, they were dealt with in terms of the gendered stereotypes of 'enticing' male agents and 'enticed' female subjects, occluding the complex textures and agencies of real coolie life on the plantations.

The chapter also highlights a form of intra-ethnic conflict that historians have only recently begun to explore: the fissures between married and single men within the community and the internalised mistrust towards fellow coolies that it generated. Cases from British Malaya bring into view the contrasting lives of 'married' and single coolie men. Some single coolie men demonstrated tremendous frustration with their inability to obtain a partner who often was more than a spouse and would act as a symbol of 'property' and social standing, and they took their frustration out on women and other men. These examples indicate the need to expand research on the complexities of marital status and intimate relations within immigrant communities under colonial rule. Furthermore, the internal community turmoil uncovered through the cases in this chapter indicates the presence of a distinctive form of the hope and aspiration of intimacy for coolie immigrants which at its core placed a high premium on intimate relations. For Indian coolie men, success in Malaya had little definition in the context of plantation societies and thus very soon came down to achieving and maintaining an intimate partner.

Intimate lives of immigrant coolies in Malaya long buried in the archives help us reconstruct the hidden history of Indian immigrant coolies' gender relations in Malaya and show how labour migration across the British Empire had disruptive effects on the lives of many Indian coolies who settled in plantation colonies during the early twentieth century. Analysing the volatile nature of gender dynamics opens up new understandings of community and identity formation among immigrants. It underscores the ways in which gender conflict along with emergent marital-status conflict fractured ethnic and class solidarity in the early stages of the Indian coolie settlement across colonial plantations under the British Empire. Such analysis also reveals the processes through which ordinary men and women acted in unexpected ways to claim and carve out new lives for themselves in an unfamiliar land. Above all, this chapter suggests the need for a sensitive understanding of how subjugated individuals reacted to complex sociocultural contexts produced by British colonialism and colonial plantation societies.

## Bibliography

*Annual Report of the Agent of the Government of India in Malaya.* 1929–1934. British Library, India Office Record (IOR) V/24/1184.

Brownmiller, Susan. 1975. *Against Our Will: Men, Women and Rape.* New York: Simon & Schuster.

Chatterjee, Piya. 2001. *Time for Tea: Women, Labor and Post-Colonial Politics on an Indian Plantation.* Durham, NC: Duke University Press.

Datta, Arunima. 2016. 'Immorality, Nationalism and the Colonial State in British Malaya: Indian "Coolie" Women's Intimate Lives as Ideological Battleground'. *Women's History Review* 25(4): 584–601.

———. 2021. *Fleeting Agencies: A Social History of Indian Coolie Women in British Malaya.* New Delhi: Cambridge University Press.

Earl, George Windsor. 1861. *Topography and Itinerary of Province Wellesley.* Pinang: Pinang Gazette Printing Office.

Groth, A. Nicholas. 1975. *Men Who Rape: The Psychology of the Offender.* New York: Plenum Press.

Hurtado, Albert L. 1988. *Indian Survival on the California Frontier.* New Haven, CT: Yale University Press.

Jackson, R. N. 1961. *Immigrant Labour and the Development of Malaya: 1786–1920.* Kuala Lumpur: Government Print Office.

Jain, Ravindra. 1970. *South Indians on the Plantation Frontier in Malaya.* New Haven, CT: Yale University Press.

Jain, Shobita, and Rhoda Reddock (eds.). 1998. *Women Plantation Workers: International Experiences.* Oxford: Berg Publishers.

Kaur, Amarjit. 2006. 'Indian Labour, Labour Standards, and Workers Health in Burma and Malaya, 1900–1940'. *Modern Asian Studies* 40(2): 425–475.

Kelly, John D. 1991. *A Politics of Virtue: Hinduism, Sexuality and Counter Control Discourse in Fiji.* Chicago: University of Chicago Press.

Mahajani, Usha. 1960. *The Role of Indian Minorities in Burma and Malaya.* Bombay: Vora & Co.

Nair, Janaki. 1996. *Women and Law in Colonial India*. New Delhi: Kali for Women (published in collaboration with the National Law School of India University, Bangalore).

Office of the Honorary Commissioner for Depressed Classes for SS and FMS. 1926. *Report on the Traffic between South Indian Ports and Malaya 1926*. Kuala Lumpur: Government Print Office.

Pool, Gail R., and Hira Singh. 1999. 'Indentured Indian Women of the Empire: Between Colonial Oppression and the Brahmanical Tradition'. *Journal of Plantation Society in the Americas* 6(1): 1–46.

Ramachandran, Selvakumar. 1994. *Indian Plantation Labor in Malaysia*. Kuala Lumpur: S. Abdul Majeed & Co.

*Report of the Commissioner of Police for FMS*. 1937. Cornell University Kroch Library (CUKL), Ithaca, NY. Film 9186.

Sanday, Peggy Reeves. 1981. 'The Socio-Cultural Context of Rape: A Cross-Cultural Study'. *Journal of Social Issues* 37(4): 5–27.

Sandhu, K. S. 1969. *Indians in Malaya: Some Aspects of Their Immigration and Settlement (1786–1957)*. Cambridge, UK: Cambridge University Press.

Schwendinger, Julia, and Herman Schewendinger. 1983. *Rape and Inequality*. Beverly Hills, CA: SAGE Publications.

Sinappah, Arasaratnam. 1970. *Indians in Malaysia and Singapore*. Bombay: Oxford University Press.

Vlieland, C. A. 1932. *British Malaya: A Report on the 1931 Census and on Certain Problems of Vital Statistics*. London: Malayan Information Agency.

Warren, James F. 2003a. *Ah Ku and Karayuki-San: Prostitution in Singapore 1870–1940*. Singapore: Singapore University Press.

———. 2003b. *Rickshaw Coolie: A People's History of Singapore*. Singapore: Singapore University Press.

Weeks, Jeffery. 1991. 'Invented Moralities'. *History Workshop* 32(1): 151–166.

# 10

## Labouring under the Law

### Exploring the Agency of Indian Women under Indenture in Colonial Natal, 1860–1911

*Nafisa Essop Sheik*

Eighteen-year-old Votti Veeramah Somayya arrived in Natal in May 1890 from Madras (present-day Chennai). She apparently 'fought' to be allocated to a sugar estate in Ifafa with two men she had met aboard ship, Govindsamy Veerasami Naik and Bappu Ponnusami. She lived together with Naik as his 'wife' until he died by suicide in November the same year. Shortly after his death, she began 'living with' Bappu on the same estate but would frequently disappear 'for six to eight days at a time', causing Bappu and their employer, Gavin Caldwell, to report her disappearances to the protector. Votti claimed in 1893 that she had never been married to Naik. 'He was not my husband. I was only living with him,' she told the protector of Indian immigrants. She said that after Naik's death, Caldwell had refused to keep her in his employ 'unless I got a husband and I said I did not want a husband and my Master became disagreeable.... I have no husband in the colony although I have been living with Bappu.... I do not wish to live any longer with him.'

At Caldwell's request, the protector transferred Votti into the employ of a 'free Indian', Charlie Nulliah, who had completed his own indenture and bought freehold land that he turned into a profitable sugar-farming enterprise. However, Votti refused to work for him. She deserted his estate repeatedly on the grounds that he made sexual overtures towards her. She was imprisoned numerous times for between a week and a month at a time for desertion and 'being without a pass' that employers were responsible for providing to authorise the public movement of their indentured workers. In spite of repeated imprisonment, Votti remained defiant: 'I am not ready to go back and I will not go back. You can cut my throat but I will not go back.... I came to work, not to be a wife.'[1]

---

[1] Pietermaritzburg Archives Repository (PAR) II, 1/68, 1521/1893.

In looking at the discourses surrounding Indian women and gender under indenture in colonial Natal from 1860 to 1911, the primary intention of this chapter is to grapple with the agency of indentured Indian women. The opening anecdote conveys a distinct set of ideas concerning the manner in which the decisions and actions of women who immigrated to Natal as indentured workers confounded a colonial administration that held particular beliefs about gender and the expected roles of men and women – both of English men and women in Victorian England and of Indians they had come to 'know' through the colonial encounter on the subcontinent. As such, it departs from the argument proposed by many scholars of Indian women's history – on the subcontinent and in the Indian diaspora – that the weight of subalternity shouldered by the Indian woman was compounded by her position as a racial and gendered other and that, as a result, 'there [is] no reprieve from the structures of domination'.[2] There are layers that have not been explored. The thicket of discourses produced by the sexual, social and administrative interactions amongst men and women around women's labour and the place of Indian women in the colony belies the straightforwardness of arguments such as that made by Jo Beall in her article on indentured Indian women in Natal.[3]

Women came to be constituted as subjects in these discourses not simply by virtue of their sex but more importantly due to the historically specific social meanings attached to the idea of their 'womanhood'. With the advent of indenture in the mid-nineteenth century at the end of the Atlantic Ocean slave trade, the British Empire sought moral legitimacy for this new system of waged labour that purported to acknowledge the humanity of its subjects. The manner in which the social reproductive role of women was viewed under this system meant that women who indentured in Natal were uniquely placed in relation to both their slave counterparts and women who remained on the Indian subcontinent. Not only were they subjects in the law under indenture, but in Natal they were – for a time at least – outside of the struggles between colonial and Indian men on the Indian subcontinent that ascribed their subordination to 'tradition'.[4]

In Natal, an arguably tenuous but necessary dichotomy juxtaposed women's productive (waged) and reproductive (mainly unpaid domestic labour including,

---

[2]  Pillai (2004).

[3]  Beall (1990).

[4]  The effects of these struggles on women are detailed by numerous scholars of Indian history, most notably in the subaltern studies school. See, for example, Bhattacharya (1996); Spivak (1988); Mani (1998); Chatterjee (1989a, 1989b).

for example, the provision of food and caring for children and the sick) labour. This was the discursive axis around which debates about the presence of Indian women turned. It becomes clear from the documentary evidence of the colonial state that colonial officials and Indian men were, to different degrees, the main proponents of views about women and their productive and reproductive labour. While the 'voice(s)' of women is (are) not immediately apparent, it is by analysing the discourses within which indentured Indian women were imbricated that one may attempt to access the many ways in which they existed within them and the ways in which resistance and accommodation took place and sometimes even how these discourses might have had been manipulated and moulded by their subjects.

Colonial patriarchal discourses were themselves negotiated and reformed in the various British colonies as officials and indigenous patriarchs encountered each other.[5] It was also the case that colonial administrators shared many patriarchal understandings and socially constructed ideas of gender with newly arrived Indian men in Natal. However, it is a point of my argument that these ideas were often seized upon by Indian women to create spaces of autonomy and opportunities for resources – however small these might have been – for themselves and sometimes for their children. The ways in which Indian women in this region interpreted, acted and resisted the circumstances and various discourses of gender and colonial law that they encountered were neither uniform nor unambiguous. Any study that seeks to explore the possibilities that existed for them to exert some measure of control over their own bodies, lives and destinies must acknowledge this. Yet it is my argument that despite the patriarchal 'collusions' between colonialists and Indian men to which Jo Beall refers – and sometimes even because of it – women, although ultimately subordinate, were able to negotiate spaces for themselves and secure important economic and emotional resources.[6]

## From Slavery to Indenture: The Importance of Women

The British cross-ocean slave trade had come to an end by the 1830s, and the ensuing labour shortage left British capitalists in particular searching desperately for a reservoir of cheap and plentiful labour for plantations in the Caribbean. John Gladstone – a plantation owner in British Guiana (present-day Guyana) and the father of the British liberal prime minister William Gladstone – attempted to set up an indentured labour system in 1836 that would compensate for the loss of

---

[5]   Guy (1997).
[6]   Beall (1990), p. 166.

labour incurred by the abolition of slavery.[7] This new system, however, had to be clearly distinguished from the old one in order for it to be accepted by a British parliament that was under immense pressure from abolitionist groups and social reformers to reject all forms of slavery.[8] The fact that indenture involved wage labour would not be enough; this new system had to concede and uphold the fundamental humanity of the labourers who contracted under it. Property had to become human in a fuller sense – workers were now rights-endowed human beings who deserved the opportunity to live and engage freely in familial and social life.[9]

Many of the arguments against the institution of slavery had condemned the effects that it had on family life. Anti-slavery campaigns were often family-centric, highlighting the sanctity of the family and the moral and physical violence that slavery did to family units and to colonial culture more generally.[10] Criticisms included the break-up of marriages and households in many African societies from which slaves were taken and the high male-to-female ratio on plantations that resulted in short-term unions, independent women and children out of wedlock without the support and authority of fathers.[11] Abolitionists also pointed to the absence of protection against the breaking up of slave families by slave sales, and as Donald Matthews points out, slavery was, in the arguments of most abolitionists, a 'legalised system of licentiousness'.[12]

John Gladstone proposed to the British parliament that both male and female indentured labourers be imported from Bengal in an attempt at overturning the unequal sex ratio that had been a feature of Atlantic slavery.[13] Indenture could be distinguished from slavery and attain some measure of moral legitimacy if labourers were accompanied by their wives and families and were able to secure some measure of social stability. This precondition was unable to prevent the ensuing disparity in the sex ratio on estates in all of the colonies where indentured labour was contracted and placed, increasing pressure on employers of labour and colonial administrators in these places.

Early on in the indenture system, the issue of the sex ratio – and the shortage of women more generally – was a crucial argument in the politics of anti-slavery

---

[7]  Checkland (1954).

[8]  Kale (1998).

[9]  Kale (1998); Northrup (1995).

[10]  Green (1983).

[11]  MacDonald and MacDonald (1973).

[12]  Matthews (1967).

[13]  Kale (1998).

groups and Indian nationalists.[14] Both groups argued that the continuation of a slavery-style demographic arrangement meant that the supposed recognition of the humanity of former slaves, and now indentured workers by a system of paid labour that no longer regarded them as property but as people, was a compromised principle. As long as labourers were constrained in their social reproduction (especially given that any offspring produced by women under indenture would not necessarily contribute positively to the labour supply as was the case in most slave contexts), they could not be deemed to be any freer than they might have been under slavery. The continuing legitimacy of this new 'free' labour system therefore depended largely on the increasing numbers of women being indentured.

## Ratios and Recruitment: A Perpetual Shortage of Women

In Natal, debates over the importation of women would simmer for the duration that the system existed in the colony. The Indian government had set a quota of four women for every ten men shipped to the colony in the first year of immigration, with the quota rising to 50 per cent women by 1863.[15] As the indenture system came into being, however, these ideals were never quite realised. Indian men and women were shipped in disproportionate numbers, and the immigration of women would become a sticking point in the making of, and discussions around, the indenture system in Natal in the nineteenth century. The premise of not breaking workers' kindred ties was undermined at once, given the relative reluctance of Indian men, especially on grounds of caste, to immigrate with their wives.[16] Those who did were in the minority. The overwhelming majority of female workers recruited in India were single women.[17] Both married and single men indentured, but it was sometimes the case that married men came over by themselves, leaving their wife or wives and families behind.

The female-to-male ratio set by the Indian government would turn out to be impracticable for various reasons. Emigration agents in Calcutta (present-day Kolkata) and Madras, the two main ports of embarkation to Natal, constantly complained to the Indian Immigration Trust Board of Natal of the difficulty of recruiting women in fulfilment of the sex ratio. It was most often the case that

---

[14]  Matthews (1967).

[15]  Document 21, 'Proceedings of the Madras Government', in Meer (1981), p. 51.

[16]  PAR, Colonial Secretary's Office (CSO), 1760, 1904/3996. See also Beall (1990).

[17]  Essop Sheik (2003). See also reports of the Coolie Commission (1872) and the Indian Immigrant (Wragg) Commission (1887) in Meer (1981), pp. 118–169, 246–633.

ships sailed from Indian ports without the required numbers of women and with the understanding that the shortfall would have to be made up in subsequent shipments. When Gladstone proposed that at least half the Bengali men he imported to British Guiana be married and that their wives 'be disposed' to work in the fields, he could not have anticipated the problems this would pose to recruiting and emigration authorities or the complications that female labour would lend to the tenuous legitimacy of indenture as a new and 'free' labour system.

Emigration recruiters in Madras and Calcutta complained at length about these difficulties, including the fact that given women's role in field labour in India and the caste of women who were most ready to emigrate, it was only during periods of famine that a supply of 'reliable' female labour could be procured for Natal.[18] More often than not, as the deputy protector, Charles Manning, pointed out in his evidence to the Wragg Commission in 1885–1886, the proportion had to be made up by 'touting the cities just before the ship leaves India'.[19] As a result there were frequent complaints about the character of single women recruited for indenture.

There was a general concern in the colony about the shortage of Indian women, especially married or marriageable women and the 'immorality' that was believed to result from this. The 1872 Coolie Commission took up the matter in their report and impressed upon the administration of the colony the need for a greater proportion of women with subsequent shipments of workers from India. While the commissioners acknowledged 'the difficulties with which the subject is surrounded', they argued that the evils arising out of the scarcity of women were so serious (including prostitution, assault and murder) and the complaint was so prominent that it required urgent government attention.[20]

## The Question of Women's Labour

Crucially, employers in Natal did not pay the colonial administration for female labourers in the same way that they did for men. The cost of employing women (besides rations and wages) was, according to the protector of Indian immigrants (a post set up after numerous complaints of abuses by employers of indentured labour), included in the cost of employing men in the colony.

---

[18] Correspondence among the Colonial Office, the Natal government, the Indian government and the government emigration agents for Natal, 1904. PAR, CSO, 1760, 104/3996.

[19] 'Indian Immigrants Commission Evidence: Examination of Mr. C. Manning', in Meer (1981), p. 340.

[20] See the report of the Coolie Commission in Meer (1981), pp. 118–169.

As the protector Louis Mason wrote to the colonial secretary in 1890, '[T]he cost of the introduction of females is included in that of the males. Employers therefore pay nothing whatever directly for these women.'[21]

Labour contracts, it would turn out, were expected to be rather flexible in the case of women. Women had to be given food rations whether or not they performed labour on estates. If they did work, they were given half the wages of men as stipulated in their contracts. There were numerous complaints by employers regarding women's refusal to work. On the 24 February 1875, the resident magistrate of Pinetown imprisoned 13 Indian women with hard labour for refusing to work, prompting an immediate flurry of correspondence between the acting protector at the time and the colonial secretary. Within a day, the Colonial Secretary had declared the sentence illegal and ordered the release of the women.[22]

The proliferation of complaints around women's field labour led the colonial secretary of Natal to inquire about the work that women were assigned in other colonies. The administrators of indentured labour in Jamaica, Demerara in British Guiana, Mauritius, Trinidad and Fiji all concurred with the opinion of the medical officers in Natal whom the colonial secretary had consulted. They argued that despite the fact that many women helped their husbands in the fields, most forms of field labour were particularly 'unsuited' to women's physique and that in all the colonies women were not compelled to work. The attorney general of British Guiana went so far as to say:

> With respect to the general treatment of women, I may point out that the tendency in this Colony is to keep in view the fact that the woman is the complement of the man, and is against being too exacting in respect of their work. Major Comins, in dealing with this question remarked that 'even when under indenture, the labour laws should not be strictly enforced again them', and this opinion has not been lost sight of.[23]

Occasionally it was the husbands, especially those who claimed to be of higher castes, who would object to their wives doing field labour. One employer even attempted to claim sixpence a day from two married men who objected to their wives working on the estate.[24] Some colonial officials such as the assistant

---

[21] PAR, Indian Immigration Files (II), 1/58, I1256/90, Protector of Immigrants, Louis Mason, to Colonial Secretary, 18 November 1890.

[22] PAR, CSO, 509, 681/1875, Telegraph from Protector (Mitchell) to Colonial Secretary and Telegraph to Resident Magistrate Pinetown, 24 February 1875.

[23] PAR, II, 1/161, I1618/08, Working of Indian women.

[24] PAR, II, 1/58, I1254/1890, T. G. Colenbrander, New Guelderland: Regarding Conditions of Employment of Indentured Indian Women.

protector, who made regular visits to estates, used sex differences to justify their support of women's exemption from 'any occupation unsuited to their sex', explaining that the physical labour demanded by some employers was 'decidedly harmful'. Instead, he advocated that greater opportunity be afforded to women 'to attend to their household duties…. The health of estates depends on the number of females free to attend to their husbands' comforts – at least to a large extent.'[25]

The mandatory provision of food rations to women also became an issue, with many women complaining of the withholding of rations by employers. As the acting protector stated in his correspondence with the colonial secretary, '[E]mployers state that they are not bound to supply food unless the women work, and urge that if they have to do so it will have the effect of causing a lot of ill women on the estates to turn into common prostitutes.'[26]

The colonial bureaucracy quickly became aware of the problems associated with the contracts entered into by female labourers. The colonial secretary circulated a memorandum acknowledging the questions around women's work and confirming the flexibility of women's indenture contracts:

> It seems quite clear … that female Indian immigrants cannot be compelled to work against their will, but that when they do work they are entitled to half wages. Of course, it is optional with the employer to employ these or not.[27]

The last sentence is misleading in that employers less often 'chose' to employ women than they had women allocated as partners to the men whom they employed. Some women were especially requested as servants involved in childcare and similar tasks, but Indian women were rarely employed in their own capacity even though they were made to sign indenture contracts upon their arrival in the colony.[28] Many arrived with their husbands from India and were 'given' to employers along with the male labourers. Most often single women were 'accepted' by employers along with a group of males whose labour had been contracted by virtue of being 'attached' to a man in the group. The underlying presumption – something that would become clearer the longer the indenture system endured – was that women were brought to Natal less for the purposes of procuring labour

---

[25] PAR, II, 1/160, I1428/1908, Circular from Protector of Indian Immigrants to Estates Concerning How Estates Employ Female Indentured Indians as Labourers.

[26] PAR, CSO, 510, 735/1875, Correspondence between Acting Protector and Colonial Secretary, February 1875.

[27] PAR, CSO, 510, 735/1875, Memorandum 736/1875.

[28] Badassy (2005).

for the colony than to fulfil the sexual 'rights' of men and for the women's reproductive capabilities.

## The Work of Reproduction: 'She Is About as Much Use as a Blister on a Wooden Leg'

In attempting to gauge the worth and significance of women's labour, there is a danger of accepting the views of colonists and employers of women at face value. While there is no question that female labourers were not what planters and the colonial state envisaged when the indenture system was established, there is considerable evidence to suggest that for all the complaints about their 'laziness', women's labour was extracted for both 'heavy' and 'light' work and was particularly important at key moments of production cycles, such as during the harvesting process. It was particularly at these moments that women chose to withhold their labour. This was a situation that made life difficult for employers of female Indian labour as the terms on which the government of India had allowed the indenture labour migration to Natal to go ahead did not allow for the forced labour of women; nor did it permit punitive action against women who refused to fulfil the terms of their contracts.

Perhaps the main aspect of women's reproductive labour, childbearing (including pregnancy, birth and rearing), was often regarded by employers as an impediment to productive field labour. Employers were not always sympathetic to pregnant women, as the colonial administration required that pregnant women – especially those whose pregnancies were advanced – be exempted from almost all forms of field labour. Indian women's domestic reproductive labour in the colony is even more significant when one considers the rate at which the Indian population of the colony increased. The reports of the protector of Indian immigrants recorded a steady annual increase by birth – with the rate increasing every year.[29] It is notable that despite a high infant mortality rate, the increase reported in the protector's returns are uniformly high, especially when one considers that Indians were often fined or remonstrated for not reporting the birth of children to the protector. Given the fact that the proportion of women imported in relation to men averaged, in practice, less than 30 per cent for the entire period of indenture, a relatively small number of women were responsible for a hefty annual population increase.

A typical example of the amount of time and energy that indentured women spent on childbearing may be demonstrated by the testimony of men and women

---

[29]  PAR, II, 8/6, Annual Reports of the Protector of Indian Immigrants.

who sought to register their marriages and legitimate the birth of their children. One particular couple had failed to register their marriage within the 30-day period stipulated by the 1872 Coolie Law Amendment Act and gave depositions to the protector explaining their situation:

> My name is Sellam. I am indentured to Mr Colenbrander. I am the wife of Ramasami. I married him of my own free will and consent. I have borne him three children. I married him four and a half years ago. I was married to him in the usual manner under Hindu custom.
>
> My name is Ramasami. I am indentured to Mr Colenbrander. My wife's name is Sellam. I was married to her four and a half years ago according to Hindu custom. I did not register my marriage because I was indentured but I reported it to my master. I have three children now. They have been born since my marriage to Sellam.[30]

The woman had been present in Natal for approximately six months before she married Ramasami. The testimonies of the couple indicate that the woman was pregnant for about half the duration of her presence in the colony. The protector of Indian Immigrants often had to emphasize to employers the illegality of forcing women to work while they were pregnant, were breastfeeding or had infant children to care for and that this time could not be made up for by lengthening indenture contracts. This meant that for women such as Sellam, the time spent fulfilling the terms of indentured labour contracts was relatively small in comparison to the work of reproducing families and carrying out other forms of domestic labour (especially when one considers the simultaneity of productive and domestic reproductive labour, as women who worked on estates also cooked, cleaned and cared for their husbands and children). The fact that women's usefulness to employers was limited for significant periods of time due to pregnancy and child-rearing is noteworthy in the context of the aforementioned debates around women's labour.

## Deserting Estates, Deserting Homes

The hidden labour that women were responsible for became most evident at times when it was contested by men. Women's domestic labour was often an issue with Indian men who were hardly different from colonists in expecting such work of women, while at the same time they often derided it and complained about its inefficiency. Violence in the home and the instability of personal relationships

---

30  PAR, II, 1/53, I1134/90, Depositions of Ramasami and Sellam.

could often be seen as stemming from struggles around women's domestic labour. Women often left partners they thought too coercive and demanding of their domestic labours for other men they considered more amenable, with officials observing that marriage ties were decidedly 'loose'. It is no surprise that charges of bigamy abounded in this context and was perhaps more common amongst women than men.

Many of the cases of bigamous men were about sexual competition, but they were also, more importantly, related to the domestic labour of women. Bigamy and multiple relationships outside of registered marriages were almost as common a charge amongst women, both those who had come to Natal already married as well as those who arrived as single women. Cases of bigamy were often discovered by the protector when desertion occurred on estates. Cases of desertion were referred to the protector's office for investigation. More often than not, the women in question were found to be living with other men as wives or in some kind of domestic relationship. The depositions of these women testify to the trials of economic and emotional dependency. Some deserted with their children, while others left them behind. Most often violence and ill-treatment were cited as reasons for deserting their husbands and thereby the estates to which they were assigned. Desertion might have had been considered by employers to be a violation of labour contracts and has often been interpreted by historians – especially Marxist labour historians – as symptomatic of the problems associated with labour exploitation, such as overwork and mistreatment. In the case of indentured women in this region, it is evident that desertion was, more often than not, linked to problems within the domestic unit.

Desertion reflected not only the resistance of women to difficult, often violent domestic situations, but also the agency that they demonstrated in actively seeking out alternative sources of economic and emotional resources. In the case of women, especially, it appears to be more a case of deserting abusive or unsupportive husbands or men rather than deserting employers on the estates where women might have themselves performed waged labour. Underlining the reality that desertion was closely linked to personal and familial problems is the fact that it was one of the prominent issues that colonial officials would have to contend with in dealing not with women's contracted labour on estates but with disputes that arose around marriage.

## Situating Marriage

The indentured labour contract and the contract of marriage that indentured women and men entered into in the colony were closely bound together.

Employers often complained to the protector about the propensity of women to simply refuse to work once they became 'attached to men'. There are a number of cases in which the status of women's labour contracts was contested on the basis of newly contracted unions. In theory, an indentured immigrant entering into a legal marriage with another on a different estate did not alter the labour contracts of either party. In practice, however, employers often expressed a willingness to release women from contracts (which did not compel women to estate labour at all) in order that they might be married and 'become dependent on somebody else'.[31] In a great many cases where employers refused permission to transfer women who wished to marry or 'take up' with men on other estates, women would 'become difficult', refusing to work as they might previously have had done and demonstrating 'insolence' in order that employers would concede to their wish for a transfer. In one case, a woman described by her employer as 'decent' and 'a good worker' resorted to exposing herself to other workers and to her master's children, with the result that the employer hastily agreed to her transfer.[32]

In many instances, women claimed to have been told by emigration agents and recruiters in India that married women were preferred emigrants. Some women also complained that they were duped into relationships with men who told them that the Emigration Agency had 'allotted' them to the men as wives.[33] This no doubt accounted for a significant number of the marriages registered at the Immigration Depot at the point upon disembarking in the colony.[34] Marriages between arriving men and women were recorded and registered before their allotment to estates to ensure that families did not become separated, although these 'families' in the case of many Indians were men and women with whom they were acquainted for a short time and who had arrived in Natal to similar personal and social uncertainty.

Employers concerned about the 'morality' of Indians on their estates would very often send couples – men and women described as 'friendly toward each other' or living together in some form of domestic arrangement – to register their 'marriage' with the protector, whether or not the Indians themselves considered

---

[31] PAR, II, 1/127, 1974/1904, Correspondence among Cuthbert Phipson, A. R Holme and the Protector, April 1904.

[32] PAR, II, 1/69, 1881/93, A. T Button to Protector, November 1893.

[33] PAR, II, 1/162, I2154/1908, Sonarie Deposition, 17 September 1908.

[34] The protector's annual marriage returns often reflected a comparatively high number of marriages registered upon disembarkation. Along with unions that new arrivals stated they had entered into during the voyage, this process of registration also included marriages that had been entered into as civil contracts in India as well as those solemnised by Hindu and Muslim religious authorities on the subcontinent.

themselves married.[35] The protector often found, upon enquiry at registration, that the man had a wife in India and the woman had 'taken up' with him. Considering the insecurity and danger of the situations in which the majority of indentured women found themselves, marriage would become a keenly contested legal and moral issue during indenture.

## Validating Indian Marriages

The first official indication of concern over demographic gender disparities and the resulting sexual mores in the colony, as well as the need for regulating personal relationships between Indian men and women, came with the publication of the report of the Coolie Commission in 1872. The report suggested the need for 'legislation regarding Coolie marriages, and the settlement of disputes arising out of the seduction of married women'. It recommended, also, that a careful register be made of women in the colony, distinguishing married women from 'concubines', and that the validation of marriages by registration be made compulsory.[36] Registration of marriages, the report claimed, would ensure the possibility for redress in the case of disputes and was expected to function as a check on immorality.

As the protector later explained to the colonial secretary, many migrants 'who eagerly desired on their first arrival to live together no less eagerly demanded to be separated from one another in the course of a month or two'.[37] The limited definition of marriage in colonial common law meant that keeping record of what could officially be termed 'marriages' did not necessarily enable officials to keep track of highly mobile women. The civil register of women was an attempt to compensate for the indeterminate status of many early marital unions.

The registration of Indian marriages thus became a legal requirement in Natal in 1872. It is clear from letters amongst officials and employers and from the testimony of Indians themselves that many Indians did not regard registration as constituting a binding union. It was far more common that men would register marriage with one woman but remain living with another under customary rites, and when a dispute arose among the parties, they would claim the second woman as their wife.[38]

---

[35] See, for example, CSO, 1538, 8033/1897, Magistrate of Lions River to Honourable Attorney General, 6 November 1897.

[36] Report of the Coolie Commission in Meer (1981), pp. 118–169.

[37] PAR, II, Protector to Colonial Secretary, 11 June 1877.

[38] PAR, II, 1/141, I285/06, Protector of the Indian Immigrants to Attorney General, Durban, 2 February 1906.

Both Indian men and women had difficulties adjusting to the different status of their marriages in India and Natal. Most were unaware for a long time that polygynous marriages were contrary to the law of the colony. Colonial officials in Natal began grappling with issues of Indian marriage as these were raised by the various commissions and by the complaints of the protector and employers of Indians, many of whom sat on the colony's legislative council. They had hoped that requiring the registration of Indian marriages would be as much intervention as was necessary but were proved wrong early on.

## Polygyny and Colonial Law in Natal

Polygynous marriage was identified early on as an obstacle in the administration of Indians in the colony. It was widely practised by Indian men in India, and Natal legislators were determined that such a practice had no place in the colony.[39] The Natal government had effectively outlawed the practice for all people who fell under the civil laws of the colony, with the first marriage ordinance passed in 1846.[40] This piece of legislation dealt specifically and exclusively with marriage in the newly annexed territory of Natal. It was an extraordinary piece of legislation that, by its provisions, repealed previous 'laws, customs or usages' that might have had been considered 'repugnant to or inconsistent with' the idea of Christian marriage (monogamous, heterosexual and permanent unions) that the ordinance envisioned as the legal norm, not just in the colony but for a number of 'colonies, plantations and possessions' of the British Empire.

African men in Natal were practising polygynists long before the arrival of Indians, and like the Indians, as non-citizens they were not subject to the civil laws of the colony. The Marriage Law of 1869 was a measure that attempted to deal with polygyny amongst Africans as the regulations taxed every marriage contracted by Africans, restricted the practice of *lobola* (bride-wealth) and required that brides publicly express their assent to the marriage.[41] The secretary for native affairs, Theophilus Shepstone, expressed that the 1869 law could 'only favour the operation of natural causes to achieve the extinction of polygamy'.[42] Jeremy Martens quotes lieutenant governor Robert Keate in illustration of the

[39]  PAR, Natal Colonial Publications (NCP), 2/1/1/5, Legislative Council Debates, 1883, Indian Divorce Bill.

[40]  PAR, NCP, 5/5/4, Ordinance 17, 1846.

[41]  Welsh (1971), pp. 67–96.

[42]  PAR, Secretary for Native Affairs (SNA), 1/7/8, pp. 18–23, T. Shepstone, 'Memorandum: Registration of Native Marriages', 22 March 1869, p. 23, cited in Martens (2003).

Natal administration's approach to dealing with polygyny amongst Africans. Keate argued that instead of tackling polygyny directly, the legislative course adopted was prudent, as 'all that could be done by Legislative interference [is] to help on and remove obstructions to the natural causes which are leading, however slowly, to that result'.[43] He also claimed that the marriage tax would encourage 'labour habits among the male portion of the native community upon which more than anything else the practice of polygamy depends'.[44] Africans were thus expected to be 'weaned of [*sic*]' polygynous practices, and this process was intended to be tied to changes in the sexual division of labour brought about by colonial interventions.

The introduction of Indian indentured labour as a migrant labour force in 1860 would complicate the Natal administration's strategy around polygyny. The Natal government would, until the 1890s, pass laws governing Indians as laws of indenture – that is, laws relating to labour. Piecemeal laws concerning aspects of personal law such as marriage were to be included in 'Coolie Consolidation Laws' until the end of the nineteenth century. There was no parallel system of law, such as 'Native Law', governing Indians. Further, they did not fall under the 'ordinary' civil laws of the colony. Administrators such as the attorney general would infer that polygyny was prohibited by the 'morality' of the colony, and as such, polygynous Indian marriages would not be recognised.[45] For the better part of 30 years, however, there would be no legislation forbidding the practice amongst Indians.

The colonial administration prohibited the registration of polygynous marriages specifically amongst Indians in a legislation passed in 1891. Before this time, the protector and resident magistrates were confronted with numerous cases of men attempting to register multiple marriages and were advised by the attorney general to refuse registration to all but the first marriage. The biggest loophole in the law was that it did not make provision for polygynous marriages that had been contracted in India (where these marriages were validated by British authority) and that disputes often arose that could not be dealt with in the absence of legislation that dealt with the status of these relationships. The problems are apparent in one particularly heated exchange when the attorney general remonstrated with the protector for registering both wives of a newly arrived male immigrant. The protector argued that

---

[43]   Keate quoted in Martens (2003), p. 6.

[44]   Keate quoted in Martens (2003), p. 6.

[45]   PAR, II, 1/141, I285/06, Correspondence between the Attorney General and the Protector.

it would be a distinct breach of faith to bring these people here and then on arrival cast adrift one of the wives because of the interpretation of a section of the law which has never been tested by the Supreme Court of the law. Polygamous marriages are valid in India and when we recruit Indians for labour in Natal we are bound by simple justice to admit them with the same privileges as are accorded them in India in this connection. In view however of your opinion in this matter it appears to me that it would be more advisable and to the point to cause the Agents of India to be instructed not to recruit men with more than one wife. This would obviate any necessity for further action.[46]

Unlike Africans in the colony who were subject to 'Native Law', Indians were not governed by a separate legal code. It was the original intention of the colonial administration that Indian personal law would apply as it did in India, where it had begun to be codified and tied to legal precedent since 1772. The administration suggested that the personal laws of Hindus and Muslims could be applied for the duration of their residence in the colony. However, this proved impracticable in a colony where the settler population, including British officials, saw Indian personal law as 'repugnant' and contrary to their 'moral sense'.[47] The rejection of Indian custom as 'repugnant' in Natal, coupled with the reluctance to legislate due to the attempts by the Natal government to repatriate Indians after their 'temporary sojourn in the Colony', meant that legal uncertainty around issues of Indian customary law would persist until the end of the nineteenth century.[48]

The law around polygyny was not fully resolved, and the question of polygyny and the validity of marriages would become even more prominent when women took up legal claims. The status of polygynous unions was keenly debated amongst the colony's officials during indenture, resulting in the passage, repeal and amendment of marriage laws within relatively short periods of time. While the Natal administration categorically denied legal recognition to polygynous marriages at first, in 1891 the legislature acceded to the calls of the protector and other officials directly involved in the resolution of disputes among Indians and retrospectively legalised polygynous marriages that had been contracted in India before the arrival of the immigrants to Natal.

Many scholars have described British administrative interventions in the personal law and lives of its Indian subjects at length, concluding more often than not that British action was contradictory and inconsistent.[49] The arena of

---

[46] PAR, II, 1/141, I285/06, Correspondence between the Attorney General and the Protector.

[47] PAR, NCP, 2/1/1/5, Legislative Council Debates, 1883, Indian Divorce Bill.

[48] PAR, NCP, 2/1/1/5, Legislative Council Debates, 1883, Indian Divorce Bill.

[49] Mani (1998); Liddle and Joshi (1986); Sarkar (1993).

personal law would prove to be the foremost battleground on which battles of colonial politics and anti-colonial nationalism would be fought. Almost invariably, women became the signifiers of these struggles, as symbols of contested tradition. For all the apparent concern with women, these debates rarely offered women a voice as subjects themselves; nor did they admit women's possession of any power of agency.[50] Rather, they stressed the weakness and ignorance of women. As Lata Mani argues, this was because the real point of contest in these debates was not women at all, but the status of Hindu tradition and the legitimacy of colonial power.[51] Thus, in India, women came to represent tradition in the arguments conducted among colonialists, Hindu liberals, reformers, conservatives and, ultimately, nationalists.

## From Recalcitrance to Resistance

The presumption of a body of unchanging ritual, custom and belief carried around by all Indians regardless, even, of their context would be challenged in the colonial outposts to which Indian labourers were sent under indenture. State intervention in personal law on the subcontinent usually led to the consolidation and conservation of husbandly power. In the case of Natal, however, legislative vacillation in the area of personal law for the first four decades of indenture presented women with opportunities to resist practices regarded as 'traditionally Indian'. It was outside of the context of Indian political struggles, and in a new context of legal uncertainty, that women were afforded more space to take advantage of access to the law.[52]

One particular aspect of personal law that caused a good deal of litigation was the registration of marriages, with cases frequently having to be decided by the protector of immigrants. The office of the protector was tasked with resolving disputes amongst Indians who soon became acutely aware of the protections afforded to them under the law. Women, too, took advantage of this to resist marriage and its accompanying 'traditional' practices. The acting protector complained in his annual report for 1877 that

> the Protector is compelled to register all marriages which may be reported, Indian Immigrants being also required, under a penalty of 5 Pds., to report their marriages to him within one month of their occurrence.... The result is that,

---

50  Spivak (1988).

51  Mani (1998).

52  Carroll (1989).

with the custom common amongst these people of contracting their daughters in marriage at a very early age, when the time comes for the ratification of the contract the girl as often as not refuses to live with her husband, and in the absence of the strong public opinion, so to speak, which would act upon her were she in India, obtains her own way. The Protector is appealed to ... but he has no power, even were it desirable, to compel the girl against her inclinations.[53]

Colonial officials soon observed the differences in women's participation in ritual and customs between India and Natal. The traditional role of women, as British colonialists had come to understand it in India, was being reconfigured in mid-nineteenth century Natal. Crucially, the difference in social context between the subcontinent and Natal meant that women – many of whom had arrived single, some due to reasons of caste prejudice and other well-documented cases of shame – were free of many of the strictures placed upon them by extended family, religious institutions and the nascent nationalist discourse in India. The force of 'public opinion' to which the Major S. Graves alluded in 1877 is no doubt a reference to the strong contestations around issues of personal law that British administrators encountered in India. Outside of the Indian national context of struggle for 'tradition', women were beginning to claim space to resist customary practices on their own terms with Indian men, although these would become increasingly limited as the Natal colonial administration exercised greater legal intervention in Indian personal law as indenture wore on into the twentieth century.

Access to the law in general, via the protector's court, enabled women to seek redress for such affronts as desertion or assault. This was certainly the case in Natal, with Indian women often seeking legal protection from abusive husbands and even the dissolution of marriages registered by the protector. In his report for the year 1876, the protector of Indian immigrants, noting his inability to provide relief for Indians seeking divorce, remarked, 'I am frequently besought by the women to grant them divorces, but never by men.'[54] He further remarked in 1880:

The laws do not appear to call for any amendments, except the ordinance regarding that most important question, the Law of Marriage and Divorce, and which should not be lost sight of, as I cannot help being of the opinion that the rigidity of the law in this respect is responsible for many of the crimes which would not be committed were the Protector empowered to grant divorces.

---

[53]  Report of Major Graves, 1877, Acting Protector of Immigrants, in Meer (1981), p. 592.

[54]  PAR, II, 8/4, Protector's Annual Report, 1876.

The fact that Indians could only obtain divorces from the Supreme Court of the colony was a point of concern for the protector of Indian immigrants in Natal who had to deal daily with the problem of the dearth of laws of divorce for Indians and the resultant physical abuse (including assault and murder) and the desertion.[55] Correspondence between the governments of India and Trinidad bear testimony to the difficulties of decisions around intervention in the personal law of indentured Indian immigrants.[56]

A bill providing for divorce amongst Indians was tabled for the first time in 1883. It was withdrawn at the second reading after objections by members of the legislative council who, while acknowledging the great necessity for this law, claimed that the legislation was too complex and that they could not, in all good conscience, legislate for divorce when 'there [is] no definition of what constitutes marriage between Indians in this country'.[57]

In 1891, a general attempt was made to address Indian personal law including marriage, the age of consent, adultery, bigamy and divorce.[58] It was a wide-ranging law, encompassing a variety of issues such as health, labour contracts and the like, and its somewhat general nature allowed for divorce proceedings to be instituted by both men and women. It was an important piece of legislation, considering that non-intervention would have favoured religious personal law as was the case in contemporary India, thereby restricting the ability of women to seek divorce (as in the case of Muslim marriages) or preventing them from doing so altogether (as in Hindu personal law).

In the midst of this legal ambiguity around Indian personal law in the colony, women often took the opportunity of asserting themselves. One such example is the much-publicised case of Tulukanum, an Indian woman who sued for nullification of her marriage on the grounds that it was polygynous and therefore against the law of the colony.[59] It is an illustration of the advantage that some women took of the early uncertain status of Indian personal and customary law in Natal. The case was reported at length in most of the colonial newspapers and merited a detailed analysis in the protector's annual report for 1899.

---

[55] PAR, NCP, 2/1/1/5, Legislative Council Debates, 1883, Indian Divorce Bill.

[56] Meer (1981), pp. 594–610.

[57] PAR, NCP, 2/1/1/5, Legislative Council Debates, 1883.

[58] PAR, NCP, 5/2/18, Law 25, 1891, 'To Amend and Consolidate the Laws relating to the introduction of Indian Immigrants into the Colony of Natal, and to the regulation and government of such Indian Immigrants'.

[59] PAR, II, 1/141, I452/1900; PAR, II, 1/141, I447/1899; PAR, II, 1/141, I309/1900; Natal Advertiser, 8 March 1900, 'Important Local Decision Affecting Indians'.

The case of Tulukanum, brought against her husband, Munusami, was particularly remarkable as she had arrived from Madras together with her husband and their child, as well as with his first wife. Their marriage was recorded at the Emigration Depot in Madras, and her name was listed – correctly or not as the case might be – *after* that of Thoyi, the other women to whom her husband was married. She appealed, under the laws of Natal, for nullification of the marriage and custody of their three children, two of whom she had borne with her husband whilst in the colony. The magistrate ruled in favour of Tulukanum, stating that the registration of their marriage by the protector after their arrival in Natal contravened the laws prohibiting bigamy in the colony. Tulukanum, recorded as the second wife, was therefore entitled to an annulment. Tulukanum's actions were without precedent in Natal. Neither party in the case owned property, making it unlikely that Tulukanum would have benefited materially from nullification of her marriage while retaining custody of her children. It is, nonetheless, a notable example of women's acknowledgement of their legal rights of access to courts (although this was most often mediated through interpreters, the protector's office and other legal representatives) and their willingness to use it in the social and political context of Natal.[60]

The 1891 legislation was intended to 'provide relief' for the Indian population in general, given the instability of Indian domestic life in the colony at the time, but offered considerable relief to Indian women who had the possibility of legal recourse where it was denied in India and where separation from the husband would likely have resulted in severe ostracisation and, in some cases, even death.[61] So while they might not have enjoyed equality within marriage, women had the opportunity to – and did – creatively wield the colonial legal system in Natal to get away from neglectful or abusive husbands and to extricate themselves from traditional practices that they might have had been unable to defy in India.

## Conclusion

It is abundantly clear that women laboured, both on plantations and in the homes that they set up. It is also clear that regardless of the legal and philosophical justifications for their presence in the colony, the discourses in which they were implicated were based overwhelmingly on expectations of women's productive and reproductive labour. The importance of this is that women should not be seen simply as a way of legitimating a system of labour, but also as agents in a system

---

[60]   Badassy (2002).

[61]   Liddle and Joshi (1986).

that derided their existence and yet still expected – and at times even depended on – their labour.

Women's consent to labour was a key issue around which colonial discourses about them pivoted, and this consent was often a tool that women used to negotiate access to the resources held largely by men. As with women under slavery, they used their sexuality as a commodity to improve their own situation and that of their children.[62] However, unlike slavery, as women's legally sanctioned presence in the colony was primarily an attempt at legitimating indenture as a system of 'free' labour (in opposition to slavery) rather than being about extracting their productive labour, indentured women could in some limited ways use both their productive and reproductive labour to negotiate resources and better emotional and economic security in Natal.

As I have demonstrated, British law in the colony also offered avenues for women to assert themselves in the face of discourses that implicated them in 'traditional' practices by claiming their acquiescence to culture. It is perhaps also relevant to consider the change in the legal and social context between India and Natal in order to more fully interrogate gender under indenture.

Equally, it is necessary to place the situation of indenture in Natal within the larger British imperial project. The rise of utilitarianism in the late eighteenth and early nineteenth centuries significantly influenced debates around law, subjecthood and citizenship in British colonies. British thinkers such as John Stuart Mill made arguments connecting British rule, citizenship and the subjection of women in England, India and the British Empire more broadly. Metropolitan contestation around marriage, property, women's work and women's suffrage influenced the views of British colonial lawmakers in the eighteenth and nineteenth centuries. In addition, an understanding of how the changing meanings attached to womanhood influenced legal debates around gender in the colonies is essential to an investigation of the kind that I have attempted to undertake here.

It is clear in the case of indentured Indian women in Natal that the law was the primary ideological discourse through which these women were able to exercise some degree of agency. As I have attempted to demonstrate, it was the dearth of decisive and comprehensive legislation vis-à-vis Indian personal law that allowed them to negotiate space for themselves in a way that might not have had been possible for either African women subject to 'Native Law' in the colony or

---

[62]  Wilson (2004).

white settler women constrained by increasing concerns over race and sexuality in late-nineteenth-century Natal.[63]

It was only around the beginning of the twentieth century that Indian nationalist discourses that mobilised around the issue of indenture began to rise to prominence in the colony. We still know too little about how these struggles related to gender when indentured women began to leave India in the middle of the nineteenth century. At various points in the century, though, anti-colonial struggles on the subcontinent appropriated gender in its discourses, and personal law became a highly public and politicised area of intervention and contestation. With regard to Indian personal law, Natal was a legal blank slate onto which the colonial administration had hoped to graft religious personal law as it had been codified in India. This intention did not consider the contingencies that would arise out of the reconstitution of social life by Indian immigrants to the colony. The space between the perception of the character of Indian 'custom' by colonial officials in Natal and colonial officials on the Indian subcontinent, as well as the uncertainty about the immigration status of Indians, effectively halted decisive legislation around Indian personal law in Natal for the first four decades of indenture. It was in this legal fissure that Indian women discovered opportunities for agency.

## Bibliography

Badassy, Prinisha. 2002. 'Turbans and Top-Hats: Indian Interpreters in the Colony of Natal, 1880–1910'. PhD Thesis, University of Natal, Durban.

———. 2005. '"… And My Blood Became Hot": Crimes of Passion, Crimes of Reason – An Analysis of the Crimes against Masters and Mistresses by Their Indian Domestic Servants, Natal, 1880–1920'. Masters Dissertation, Howard College, University of KwaZulu-Natal, Durban.

Beall, Jo. 1990. 'Women under Indentured Labour in Colonial Natal, 1860–1911'. In *Women and Gender in Southern Africa to 1945*, edited by Cherryl Walker, pp. 146–167. Cape Town: David Philip Publishers.

Bhattacharya, Nandini. 1996. 'Behind the Veil: The Many Masks of Subaltern Sexuality'. *Women's Studies International Forum* 19(3): 277–292.

Carroll, Lucy. 1989. 'Law, Custom and Statutory Social Reform: The Hindu Widow's Remarriage Act of 1856'. In *Women in Colonial India: Essays on Survival, Work, and the State*, edited by J. Krishnamurty, pp. 363–388. Delhi: Oxford University Press.

---

[63]  Martens (2002).

Chatterjee, Partha. 1989a. 'The Nationalist Resolution of the Women Question'. In *Recasting Women: Essays in Colonial History*, edited by Kumkum Sangari and Sudesh Vaid, pp. 233–253. New Delhi: Kali for Women.

———. 1989b. 'Colonialism, Nationalism, and Colonialised Women: The Contest in India'. *American Ethnologist* 16(4): 622–633.

Checkland, S. G. 1954. 'John Gladstone as Trader and Planter'. *Economic History Review* 7(2): 216–229.

Essop Sheik, Nafisa. 2003. '"A Beastly Nuisance": An Exploratory Paper on Attempts to Control Venereal Disease among Indian Immigrants in Natal 1874–1891', Honours Essay, University of Natal, Durban.

Green, William. 1983. 'Emancipation to Indenture: A Question of Imperial Morality'. *Journal of British Studies* 22(2): 98–121.

Guy, Jeff. 1997. *Accommodation of Patriarchy*. Unpublished paper, Colloquium, Masculinities in Southern Africa, University of Natal, Durban.

Kale, Madhavi. 1998. *Fragments of Empire: Capital, Slavery, and Indian Indentured Labor in the British Caribbean*. Philadelphia: University of Pennsylvania Press.

Liddle, Joanna, and Rama Joshi. 1986. *Daughters of Independence: Gender, Caste and Class in India*. London: Sed Books.

MacDonald, John Stuart, and Leatrice D. MacDonald. 1973. 'Transformation of African and Indian Family Traditions in the Southern Caribbean'. *Comparative Studies in Society and History* 15(2): 171–198.

Mani, Lata. 1998. *Contentious Traditions: The Debate on Sati in Colonial India*. Berkeley and Los Angeles: University of California Press.

Martens, Jeremy C. 2002. 'Settler Homes, Manhood and "Houseboys": An Analysis of Natal's Rape Scare of 1886'. *Journal of Southern African Studies* 28(2): 379–400.

———. 2003. 'Polygamy, Sexual Danger, and the Creation of Vagrancy Legislation in Colonial Natal'. *Journal of Imperial and Commonwealth History* 31(3): 24–45.

———. 2005. 'The Impact of Theories of Civilization and Savagery on Native Policy in Colonial Natal'. In *African Studies Association of Australasia and the Pacific 2003 Conference Proceedings*, p. 6. www.ssn.flinders.edu.au/global/afsaap/conferences/2003proceedings/martens.PDF. Accessed on 18 March 2005.

Matthews, Donald. 1967. 'Abolitionists on Slavery: The Critique behind the Social Movement'. *Journal of Southern History* 33(2): 163–182.

Meer, Y. S. 1981. *Documents of Indentured Labour, Natal 1851–1917*. Durban: Institute for Black Research.

Northrup, David. 1995. *Indentured Labor in the Age of Imperialism, 1834–1922*. New York: Cambridge University Press.

Pillai, Shanthini. 2004. 'In Gendered Chambers: The Figure of the Indian Immigrant Women of Colonial Malaya'. *Hecate* 30(1): 141–159.

Sarkar, Tanika. 1993. 'Rhetoric against Age of Consent: Resisting Colonial Reason and Death of a Child Wife'. *Economic and Political Weekly* 28(36): 1869–1879.

Spivak, Gayatri Chakravorty. 1988. 'Can the Subaltern Speak?'. In *Marxism and The Interpretation of Culture*, edited by C. Nelson and L. Grossberg, pp. 271–313. London: Macmillan Publishers.

Welsh, David. 1971. *The Roots of Segregation: Native Policy in Colonial Natal, 1845–1910*. Cape Town: Oxford University Press.

Wilson, Kathleen. 2004. 'Empire, Gender, and Modernity in the Eighteenth Century'. In *Gender and Empire*, edited by Philippa Levine, pp. 14–45. Oxford: Oxford University Press.

# 11

## Gujarati 'Passenger Indians' in the Eastern Cape since 1900

### Business, Mobility, Caste and Community

*Sheetal Bhoola*

This sociological and anthropological study of the Mochi,[1] or Kshatriya, caste-based community living in Port Elizabeth, South Africa, contributes to the dearth of literature on this sub-ethnic grouping globally and to the existing historical studies on Gujaratis in South Africa. The chapter discusses the social and financial mobility of a Mochi community that immigrated to South Africa primarily to improve their lives and escape a hierarchical caste system that predetermined their status and occupations in society.[2]

Migrants and their descendants in South Africa sought to attain financial security through establishing caste-based businesses and other entrepreneurial initiatives. Narratives of prosperous Gujarati entrepreneurs are widely available, often contributing to misplaced stereotypical notions of affluence and Gujaratis being 'inherently entrepreneurial'. Dharam P. and Yash P. Ghai, in their article 'Asians in East Africa: Problems and Prospects', explain that Asians have had a monopoly of both wholesale and retail trade, especially in Uganda and Tanganyika (present-day Tanzania), and both Asian businesses and industrialists are responsible for a substantial amount of investment within East Africa.[3] Roli and Daya R. Varma have indicated that the 'entrepreneurial capacity of the Indian immigrants in the United States is notable', with up to 15 per cent of the technology businesses being Indian-owned after the 1990s.[4] In a more recent publication titled *Settled Strangers: Asian Business Elites in East Africa (1800–1900)*, Gijsbert Oonk discusses the entrepreneurial success of these Asian business migrants

---

[1] The term 'Mochi' references a working-class caste grouping of people. The term is derived from *mojadi* (shoes). This group of people engaged in shoemaking as a livelihood and as a result became known as *mochi*s.

[2] See Mandal (2012), p. 197.

[3] Ghai and Ghai (1965), p. 38

[4] Varma and Varma (2009), p. 66.

in new homelands and circumstances after migration to East Africa.[5] Similarly, Manan Dwivedi considers Gujarati migrants and their entrepreneurial and trading skills that have contributed significantly to these migrants being respected as successful businessmen globally in his paper 'Global Platform: Perceptions, Contributions and Experiences'.[6]

The perception that prevails is that most Gujaratis are successful in business, irrespective of locality. Recent media reports available also adhere to this belief. An online news portal, India TV News, published a report revealing the top ten Gujarati businessmen in India and discussed their ability to achieve astronomically high profit margins during financially challenging periods.[7] The tone of the article, however, feeds into a widespread generalisation concerning the alleged inherent spirit of entrepreneurship among Gujaratis. Although this chapter is not an endorsement of this perception, it does, however, concentrate upon a little-known community of Gujarati shoemaker entrepreneurs in South Africa's Eastern Cape province.

Inspiration for this chapter stems from the direct experiences of the author in two former British colonies of the world: South Africa and Fiji. In regard to the South African context, Uma Dhupelia-Mesthrie, in her essay 'Gujarati Shoemakers in Twentieth-Century Cape Town: Family, Caste and Community', points to the successful business stories of Gujarati Mochi men and families. She speaks of their acquisition of multiple properties and their overall approach of involving family members to expand their businesses.[8] A recent visit to the Fiji islands alerted me to the way in which Gujaratis are highly respected by the locals for their business acumen and successful enterprises. International franchises such as the Hard Rock Café and other business initiatives are mostly owned by Gujarati families. For example, Jack's of Fiji is a renowned chain of souvenir and clothing stores situated in four areas of the Viti Levu island, and Harrisons Fiji is a clothing outlet with five branches in Nadi, Denarau Island, Suva and Lautoka.[9]

Other exemplars of successful Gujarati entrepreneurship include the numerous hotel entrepreneurs living in the United States. Arturs Kalnins and Wilbur Chung explain that there are approximately 400 Gujarati families living in Dallas, Texas, of which 95 per cent are engaged in the hotel and lodging business

---

[5] Oonk (2013).

[6] Dwivedi (2010).

[7] India TV (2015).

[8] Dhupelia-Mesthrie (2012), p. 182.

[9] See jacksoffiji.com and harrisonsfiji.com (accessed on 31 May 2017).

between the regions of Virginia and California.[10] This diaspora has become hotel owners even though their livelihoods in the state of Gujarat, in India, were primarily structured around caste-occupational divisions as weavers, shoemakers, goldsmiths, silversmiths and barbers. Some of the most prosperous Gujarati hotel owners have become franchisees of several large American chains. Kalnins and Chung note the following statistics: in the year 1999, Gujaratis owned 69 of 102 Comfort Inns, 22 of 30 Econolodges and 55 of 84 Super Eight Hotels.[11] These figures reflect a positive trend of social and financial mobility within this diaspora, but studies and statistics concerning Gujarati diasporas that have not experienced financial and social growth are few and far between. Therefore, there is a need for studies such as this one, which reflects a range of experience within the Gujarati community in Port Elizabeth (now Gqeberha) and Uitenhage (now Kariega) and forms a significant contribution towards the historical documentation of Indian migrants in South Africa.

'Passenger Indians' from India predominantly emigrated to South Africa with the aim of attaining financial mobility. They entered South Africa under normal immigration laws under British rule, paid their own passage and – unlike indentured migrants – were not bound by any British-regulated contractual labour conditions. Upon arrival, they were allowed to live anywhere in the country. For indentured immigrants, legislature was initially passed to regulate their movement to South Africa. Clause 9 of Law 14 of 1859 indicated that after five years the labourers should be discharged and permitted to engage in the hiring out of their skills and services. This clause served as a stimulus for 'passenger migrants' to come to South Africa during this period.[12] They believed that there would be an opportunity for them to trade without hindrance and engage in varying types of entrepreneurial activities. Indian immigrants came from all regions of India. There was a predominance of Hindus, along with a substantial population of Muslims and Christians.

Scholarly literature has primarily focussed on Indian traders that migrated to Natal, South Africa, but minimal attention has been given to Indian traders that chose to settle in other regions of South Africa. For instance, Vishnu Padayachee and Robert Morrell published a detailed historical account of petty traders and shopkeepers in Natal between 1875 and 1914,[13] Goolam Vahed has researched

---

[10]  Kalnins and Chung (2006), p. 237.

[11]  Kalnins and Chung (2006), p. 238.

[12]  Harris (2010), p. 152.

[13]  Padayachee and Morrell (1991).

Gujarati traders in Durban,[14] and Kalpana Hiralal has examined Indian family businesses in KwaZulu-Natal.[15] If we look to the Western Cape of South Africa, Dhupelia-Mesthrie has engaged in research on the Gujarati shoemakers located specifically in Cape Town.[16]

Literature that focusses on Indian Gujarati migrants that settled in other regions of South Africa such as the Eastern Cape, Mpumalanga and the Free State is scarce, and in the case of the Gujarati community in Port Elizabeth, scholarly literature is non-existent. In addition, there is a dearth of studies concerning the Gujarati community and their histories in other cities and towns of South Africa, such as East London, Port Elizabeth, Queenstown and Uitenhage. Furthermore, little has been done to understand and reflect upon the caste-based art and trade of shoemaking as a means of survival within the Eastern Cape. Many 'passenger migrants' entered various regions of South Africa prepared to become traders; however, others were forced to adopt the small-business approach because they lacked the appropriate educational qualifications, had limited work experience or had little knowledge of the English language. For some, the small-business option offered meagre earnings, but for many it served as a step towards economic betterment. According to Pratap Kumar, 'the laws pertaining to the Indian traders were less oppressive in the Cape Colony', and the discovery of diamonds in the year 1867 on the banks of the Orange River also drew migrants to both the Western Cape and the Eastern Cape.[17] By 1910, there were approximately ten thousand Indians in the Cape, but we are uncertain as to what percentage of these migrants were from Gujarat, north India or south India.[18]

According to a publication distributed by the South End Museum in Port Elizabeth in 2006, the first arrival of Indians in the Cape Colony, especially in Port Elizabeth and East London, was not documented, and the exact dates of settlement can only be assumed through the collation of narratives and oral histories. Indians in Port Elizabeth predominantly settled in South End and North End, with a few families living in other areas of the city. Some reports have indicated that there were Indians living in Port Elizabeth in 1880, and there has been some evidence that lends itself towards Indians disembarking from ships in Port Elizabeth

---

[14]  Vahed (2005).

[15]  Hiralal (2008).

[16]  Dhupelia-Mesthrie (2012).

[17]  Kumar (2013), p. 11.

[18]  Kumar (2013), p. 11.

as early as 1882.[19] This can only be proved correct through the study of sources such as the book *Daan Data Granth*, published by the South African Kshatriya Mahasabha (SAKM), which explains the purpose, goals and origins of the organisation and contains details of events and members of the Gujarati community – and in particular the shoemaker caste, who arrived as 'passenger Indians' in the late nineteenth century – in Port Elizabeth.[20]

## Context and Research Process

This qualitative study uses two formal research approaches and one informal approach. Namely, it utilises a literature survey, face-to-face interviews and informal discussions with family members. The primary aim of the research was to attain in-depth information about Gujarati families and their upward movement from working class to middle class in the Eastern Cape. Other focuses include the development of community life in Port Elizabeth and their caste occupations, including the accordant limitations of the latter, which have continually influenced the steps taken towards financial upliftment. First, the qualitative method is appropriate for studying community dynamics and allows for the incorporation of multiple resources to assist in description and understanding. Second, the use of secondary data – including dated community brochures, publications and various books – has been pivotal in contributing towards the historical context of this chapter and has clarified and reaffirmed information retrieved during interviews. Works such as the *Daan Data Granth* and commemorative brochures of the Port Elizabeth temple celebrations and milestone events have been instrumental in providing dates and time frames during which important events took place.

Third, the selection of interviewees was based on guidance from several tried and tested sampling techniques. According to W. Lawrence Neuman, sampling is 'a process of systematically selecting cases for inclusion in a research project'.[21] Purposive sampling was employed to achieve the objectives of this study. Purposive sampling allows the researcher to make strategic choices in relation to where with whom the research will take place and how to go about the process. Purposive sampling and judgemental sampling methods are mostly employed by

---

[19]   South End Museum Board of Trustees (2006), p. 5.

[20]   A leather-bound publication by the SAKM in honour of all the Mochi families that contributed towards the SAKM Educational Trust. The book was published in 1995 and distributed to every family who donated towards the trust fund. It was dedicated to the upliftment of the Mochi community of South Africa.

[21]   Neuman (1994), p. 96.

researchers because the respondents fall within a certain set of criteria or, often, possess sought-after qualities that can contribute towards the study significantly. Therefore, my sample populace was selected based on certain criteria, including possession of experience of the caste-inherited trade of shoe-repairing and being of at least a second or third generation descent from Gujarat and above the age of 65 years. The interviewees all resided in Port Elizabeth and Uitenhage and were either living with their spouses only or with their children's families at the time of the interviews. They were all of the Mochi caste and in recent years no longer engaged in shoemaking and shoe-repairing; however, all of them began their working lives as Mochis immediately after migration to the Eastern Cape.

The interviews were often prolonged, and each lasted two to three hours at a time depending on the interviewees' recollection of their past experiences. Memories of their family's financial and social progression as well as detailed narratives of events within the community of Port Elizabeth were focused upon. For some respondents, revisiting the memories of their financial struggles led to the resurfacing of a lot of sad and happy emotions. This often resulted in lengthier interviews. Numerous discussions of information and social events not relevant to my study assisted in developing a better overview of life in the Gujarati community of Port Elizabeth during the early 1900s. These discussions were coupled with the sharing of a cup of traditional Gujarati tea and snacks. The narratives collated are in-depth and contribute significantly to the lacuna of studies on Gujaratis in South Africa and, in particular, those on the Mochi caste from Port Elizabeth.

## Understanding Mochis in South Africa

Gujarati shoemaker families were of a caste known as Mochi and were commonly referred to as low-class cobblers. The word *mochi* is more often than not denounced as a pejorative, and in the state of Uttar Pradesh in north India, people can be prosecuted for using the word to refer to others.[22] According to the *Daan Data Granth*, people of this community adopted the livelihood of shoemaking due to historic factors. The shoemaking process involved the use of skins of dead animals, which was perceived as one of the many 'unclean occupations'. Shivani Kapoor explains that unclean occupations are collectively described as work that involved physical contact with human and other dead bodies, their secretions and odours. The touching of refuse, waste or decaying substances was also perceived to be unhygienic. 'This aesthetic judgment of odours is intimately related to caste, race,

---

[22] Yengde (2015), p. 66.

gender, and class positions.'[23] The upper classes were able to maintain their class status by primarily supervising the lower-caste populations that were employed in leather tanneries, beam houses and slaughtering spaces.

Contrary to this, this chapter indicates that initially the ancestral lineage of the members of this community in South Africa were never Mochis but Kshatriyas.[24] However, scholarly evidence and publications to support this notion are virtually non-existent, but this understanding of how the Mochis came about was adopted by many people of this community in Port Elizabeth. There were other caste-based Gujarati communities in South Africa that decided not to accept this notion. This contributed towards the Mochis still being known as Mochis and not Kshatriya from their period of migration to South Africa until now. The term *kshatriya* was used as a formal descriptive term to describe the Mochis in written and published texts and used in organisational names in South Africa. Anecdotal evidence can support this historical trend that is still practised in contemporary South Africa. The *Daan Data Granth* explains:

> In the thirteenth century AD the Muslims invaded India and our ancestors lost the battle. The Muslims annexed Sind in the beginning and started to convert Hindus into Muslims. Our ancestors who had the pride and dignity to be true Hindus, fled their land and trekked forward towards the South of India, finally landing at Kutch, Saurashtra, and various parts of Gujarat. Our ancestors under no circumstances conceded to convert to the Islamic religion and thus, took refuge with the Harijans in each village or town where they finally settled. The Harijan community would gather all dead animals in the villages and use their skins for various household functions. From these skins our ancestors made their first pair of shoes, known as 'mojadi' in those times. Mojadi making soon developed into a trade and the mojadi makers soon became known as 'Mochis'. This is how we, Kshatriyas, came to be known as 'Mochis'. Even today, we have the traditional Kshatriya surnames of 'Parmar', 'Chavda', 'Chudasama', 'Gohil', 'Chauhan, 'Solanki' and many others. We do not denounce the fact that we are born into a 'Mochi' home and we are extremely proud of this.[25]

The caste system is sustained through endogamy and other stringent cultural or religious habits that have become identifiable attributes of varying caste groupings. For instance, the Mochi people of Port Elizabeth predominantly followed the

---

[23] Kapoor (2021), p. 4.

[24] *Kshatriya* is a Sanskrit term used to describe a second-rank caste grouping within the Indian caste system. Their primary function was to be warriors and protect their community.

[25] SAKM (1995), p. 216.

Arya Samaj[26] path within Hinduism, whereas other castes focused on different religious paths.

Caste in India, and in particular the Hindu paradigm of classification, has been stratified into a hierarchy with the priesthood of Brahmins[27] at the top and the Dalits (former 'untouchables') at the bottom. Between these layers lie the Kshatriyas,[28] the Vaishyas[29] and the Shudras.[30] The shoemaker clan fell within the Shudra stratification and is one of many sub-castes within it. Diaspora communities migrated with their respective caste identities, linguistic traits and cultural behaviours. The caste system in India is a complex and multi-dimensional paradigm that includes approximately 3,000 castes and 25,000 sub-castes. Some are specific to an occupation, but this is not always the case.[31] Ambedkar's perspective highlights the fact that the caste system is not only a division of labour but also a hierarchy that stratifies one individual or occupation above or below another. The choice of professional activities is often predetermined by the socio-economic status of the parents.[32]

Established scholars such as Surendra Bhana and Kusum K. Bhoola and Pratap Kumar have indicated in their studies of Indians in South Africa that the Gujaratis in South Africa have practised caste in a systematic and rigid way in comparison to other Indian linguistic groupings.[33] This pattern of behaviour is evident in the formation of a number of caste-based organisations which fall under the Gujarati linguistic umbrella. Other caste groupings have also systematically formed regulatory bodies to sustain and preserve caste-based ethnic traditions and regionally influenced practices. Like the SAKM, the Shree Parsuram Darjee Association was founded in 1919 and remains an active organisation in Durban, KwaZulu-Natal, South Africa. This organisation is representative of the tailoring

---

[26]  The Arya Samaj was a Hindu reform movement that was introduced to South African Hindus by its founder, Swami Dayanand Saraswati. This movement was conceived primarily to uplift those oppressed by the caste system.

[27]  Brahmins are a priestly caste that looks after the religious activities of the Hindu communities. This segment of people were historically educated and primarily vegetarian from birth. Purity and cleanliness have been associated with this caste of people.

[28]  The Kshatriyas were known as the warrior group of the community and primarily protected people.

[29]  The Vaishyas were the trading and farming class of people.

[30]  Shudras refer to labourers and working classes that are assumed and stereotyped to be associated with unhygienic lifestyles, illiteracy and uncomfortable socio-economic positions.

[31]  Pandin (1978), p. 142.

[32]  Mondal (2012), p. 197.

[33]  See Bhana and Bhoola (2011) and Kumar (2012).

caste sect of Gujarati-speaking people living in Durban. At present it is influential among young members of this community despite the prevailing approach of undermining and ignoring caste-consciousness and its influences within the Hindu diaspora of South Africa. An indication of this is that their chairperson is younger than 50 years, at the time of writing, and was born into a tailoring caste community in the late 1970s. Its primary function is to sustain a network and unity among this caste sect. Other objectives include the provision of educational loans to students of the caste sect and engaging in philanthropic work.

As early as 1917, the first Mochi organisation,[34] known as the Shree Kshatriya Gujerati[35] Mandal (SKGM), was established in Port Elizabeth. This spurred on the birth of similar arrangements across South Africa; other Mochi organisations were formed in Cape Town, Durban, Ladysmith, East London, Johannesburg, Pretoria and Pietermaritzburg. At the time of the formation of these organisations, membership was exclusively for Mochi people of Hindu faith living in South Africa. The Port Elizabeth Kshatriya Mandal even encouraged the formation of a similar organisation for Mochis residing in Mumbai – the Surat Valsad Jilla Kshatriya Mochi Gnyati Parishad (hereafter, the Surat Jilla Parishad) – in the year 1925. It was intended to unite the members of the Mochi community residing in the surrounding villages and towns in the state of Gujarat with those in Mumbai city and to assist with poverty alleviation and educational gaps among Mochis. It was mainly funded by the various Mochi organisations in South Africa. For instance, members of the Port Elizabeth Kshatriya Mandal volunteered to raise funds and to transport these funds to the Surat Jilla Parishad almost annually.

The historical account of the formation of numerous unifying organisations in almost every city of South Africa is indicative of the Mochi diaspora being inclined to be caste-conscious in pre-apartheid[36] South Africa and during the apartheid[37] era. Dhupelia-Mesthrie has stated in her paper on Mochis residing in Cape Town that this community had a tendency to exhibit behaviours indicative

---

34  The Port Elizabeth-based organisation is for Mochi members only.

35  Both 'Gujerati' and 'Gujarati' represent people that originate from the state of Gujarat, India. There is a discrepancy in the way these terms are spelt. Academic scholars in their publications and online dictionaries use the term 'Gujarati', whereas brochures, catalogues and other literature produced by the various Port Elizabeth Gujarati organisations use the term 'Gujerati' instead.

36  South Africa was under colonial rule prior to the apartheid regime.

37  During apartheid, the government institutionalised racial segregation and favoured the 'white' citizens of the country, whilst people of other races were marginalised and segregated by regulations.

of being extremely caste-conscious.[38] For Gujarati families of other castes residing within the province of the Eastern Cape, this proved to be an accurate reflection of the Mochi community, especially between the 1970s and the late 1990s. Interviews revealed many narratives of how families forbade the marriage of their Mochi son to a girl of a Darjee (tailor) family based on caste differences between the families, despite both homes speaking the same vernacular and sharing the same community. Another practice that perpetuated both class- and caste-consciousness was the prohibition of Gujarati girls marrying boys that were Hindu but not of Gujarati descent. Narratives collated explained the many romances that never bloomed because of the social taboos of marriages across vernaculars and ethnicities within the Indian diaspora in Port Elizabeth. Interesting to note is that the Mochis who originated from Mumbai city itself saw themselves as different from those who had roots in the towns and villages of Gujarat. Personal opinions expressed through narratives indicated that some Mochi women from Mumbai believed that they were smarter, more educated and more worldly than those from villages in Gujarat. Similarly, a handful of men that had roots in Indian cities claimed that they were more skilled entrepreneurs than their village counterparts. Despite this, interviewees discussed with nostalgia the type of unity this community shared. From the 1930s onwards, weekly Sunday gatherings amongst these men had multiple purposes. Anecdotal evidence reveals that the gatherings provided an opportunity for these migrants to share various enterprising ideas and possibilities, ways in which to be thriftier in their lifestyles as well as means to save money for an uncertain future in South Africa. The discussions were mostly dominated by the men when the families gathered to share traditional chai and Gujarati snacks on a Sunday afternoon. These meetings were replaced at a later stage with larger community gatherings and Hindu events in Port Elizabeth intended to sustain Gujarati ways of life and unity amongst community members.

As a means to sustain communication and business networks among the Mochis and other Gujaratis of varying caste descents in the Eastern Cape, a telephone directory was compiled in the year 1987 titled *The Uitenhage and Port Elizabeth Telephone Directory*. This directory listed all the Gujarati-speaking families living in Port Elizabeth and Uitenhage but failed to include the Gujarati families living in nearby towns and cities within the Eastern Cape. It contained telephone numbers and physical addresses, and a column was created especially for the listing of villages in Gujarat where families originated. This was the first directory that was compiled by the community and was funded by late Nagindas Manibhen Bhana, a Port Elizabeth Mochi entrepreneur, his wife and

---

[38] Dhupelia-Mesthrie (2012).

their family to mark the occasion of his 60th birthday celebration. Six hundred copies of the book were printed and distributed by Gujarati Mochis who were in the printing business.[39] Then, in 1994, an updated version of the directory was compiled and published. This new edition contained details of all Gujaratis residing in the entire Eastern Cape region and included families from Port Elizabeth, Uitenhage, Grahamstown, East London, Alice, Aliwal North, Burgersdorp, Butterworth, Humansdorp, King Williams Town and Queenstown. It also contained the names of each child, parent and grandparent within the households as well as the business names, physical addresses, postal addresses and telephone numbers of each of these families and, in some cases, even the names and details of the firms where one was employed. A column titled 'origin' listed the regions of the world where individuals came from. In cases where a Gujarati man married a woman who was not of Indian descent, the South African city of the woman's origin was listed under the column of origin. For instance, a few Gujarati men married 'Coloured'[40] women from Port Elizabeth, and they were integrated into the society. However, Gujarati women from the Eastern Cape region were rarely listed in the directory if they married a man who was not of Indian descent. There were 238 Gujarati households recorded in Port Elizabeth alone and 41 households in Uitenhage.[41] Approximately 92 per cent of these households were Mochi Gujaratis, and the remaining members of the community were of the Dhobi,[42] tailoring and agricultural castes. Only two families were of the tailoring caste, and they comprised 13 households. At present, these statistics merely indicate a broad insight into the size of the communities, and they have not been formally updated since many of the households featured have split up into two or more households as children have married and made their own nuclear families, and others have relocated outside of Port Elizabeth.

---

[39]  Bhana Printers was one of three Mochi family-owned printing businesses in Port Elizabeth. It was related to the sponsors of the telephone directory and therefore was tasked to print this edition of the telephone directory.

[40]  In South Africa, this term is used to describe a multiracial grouping of people who have roots in more than one ethnic group. Within the South African context, 'Coloured' was used to make reference to people of mixed ethnicity and race. During the apartheid era, the racial categorisation relied on four primary race groups. They were African, Indian, Coloured and White. In a post-apartheid South Africa, these categorisations are still being used as descriptivism and identification amongst people (Posel 2001, p. 57).

[41]  Port Elizabeth Hindu Seva Samaj (1994).

[42]  Dhobi is a caste grouping historically engaged in laundry as an occupation.

Mochi families also found kinship and unity with each other based on which village they came from, grounding the importance of growing and sustaining relationships with other families in the fact that they shared the same village of origin. For instance, families that came from the village Sadervel often referred to each other as family. These extended family relations were frequently given prominence and respect at gatherings such as weddings, house-warmings and other celebrations. Mochis in Port Elizabeth came from as many as 40 various villages in Gujarat; the commonly recurring ones include Kos, Surat, Valsad, Dakwada, Varavel and Bilimora. The only city noted as a place of origin in the directory is Mumbai. However, it is a misnomer that all of these 40 places should be categorised as villages or towns. Interviews revealed that some of these places could have consisted of just one street situated within rural regions in Gujarat. Some of these 'villages' or 'one-street towns' may have more than one name, and some perhaps lie completely vacant and dormant as areas of residence today.

Over the past 50 years, it was a normative practice for the community to be inclusive. For instance, invitations of events hosted either by the community or families were extended to all members of the community, despite the various class and age groups. Furthermore, it was a norm to honour invitations to these. The beginnings of this community life began as early as 1910, when Mochi men were living in Port Elizabeth as bachelors because their wives and children still remained in Gujarat or Mumbai. During the early 1900s, the men would meet on weekends and socialise with each other as a form of recreation and networking. It was during these instances that finances were discussed, and in-depth discussions of how to attain resources for shoemaking or shoe-repairing took place. Arrangements were also made to share shoe-repairing tools, and a unique approach to bartering and money-lending materialised among them. Between 1910 and 1925, it was estimated that there were approximately 12 to 15 Mochi households living in Port Elizabeth. Not all of them included whole families, and it was at the informal gatherings that the men decided to send one person back to Gujarat and Mumbai every three years to transport money and other resources to their families who had remained behind. Parents in India were in awe of their children's financial progress in Port Elizabeth, and this encouraged many others to consider migrating to Port Elizabeth.

Since Mochis were the dominant caste sect within the Gujarati community in Port Elizabeth, they opted to take the reins of most cultural, social and religious activities within the community. Simultaneously, as the mirror organisations of Mochis in other cities of South Africa grew and entrenched themselves further in philanthropy and community and educational developments, the mindset of being far more progressive and philanthropic than other caste sects of the Gujarati community in South Africa emerged. This mindset became synonymous with rapid fiscal mobility and educational advances within selected Mochi families. It was also influenced by the entrepreneurial respect they earned as shoe artisans in Port Elizabeth in comparison to back in Gujarat, where working with leather and raw hides was seen as a demeaning task by most upper-caste Gujarati Hindus. For instance, a respondent – let us call him Respondent A – spoke of how appreciated he felt when clients, who were mostly of other race groups, would express their happiness when a shoe was repaired and restored well. He explained further that in India his father would experience a lack of respect and appreciation when spoken to by a higher-caste Hindu. As the Mochis settled into Port Elizabeth and business initiatives were launched, collective development of the community, cultural and religious sustenance and togetherness became dominating concerns.

## The Shree Kshatriya Gujerati Mandal

The foundation of the SKGM in Port Elizabeth in 1917 ensured the continuation of the performance of Hindu rituals and prayers by community members. Religious and spiritual thinking and practices were encouraged, and members willingly participated in these discourses. They were taught to perform specialised prayers and *havans*[43] (usually only performed by upper castes at that time), and the following of the Arya Samaj was established. Through the SKGM, community members arranged the visit of a renowned spiritual yogi to Port Elizabeth. On the souvenir brochure published in the year 1989 to commemorate the platinum jubilee of the SKGM, key community members were commended for their cultural, economic and social contributions towards the society.[44]

Many social and cultural events were initiated, funded and managed by the leading members of the SKGM. In 1923, the organisation purchased their first property (a community hall) in Leather Lane, in central Port Elizabeth. A total of 400 pounds were donated by Mochi people living in the Eastern Cape towards its purchase. In 1925, further discussions and a proposal took place to purchase additional land for the building of a Gujarati school[45] with a hall for recreational purposes. In 1926, a site was purchased nearby Leather Lane with the intention

---

[43] A *havan* is a Hindu prayer ritual that involves the burning of offerings such as grains, wood and ghee (clarified butter) in fire. This ritual is usually held to mark marriages, births and other religious days of importance in the Hindu calendar.

[44] SKGM (1989).

[45] This was a school that primarily focused on education in the Gujarati language as well as the traditional and customary habits of Gujarati people.

of erecting two buildings: a school and an adjoining hall. Building plans were modified to suit the limited funding collected from numerous donors within the community. Instead of two premises being constructed, one was built with dual purposes. The new hall served as a school and a venue for community gatherings. In addition to the hall structure, the building housed a small separate kitchen, a room for storage, an office and garages beneath the hall at the basement level. The school opened in 1931 and was led by Gurukula Kangdi. All relevant teaching literature was imported from the state of Gujarat. The management of the school attempted to closely align the school's curriculum with that of vernacular schools in Gujarat.

In 1968, the SKGM was forced to sell the school building to the city council due to plans to recondition the suburbs. The roads surrounding the premises had to be widened and adjusted to the requirements of the new city plan. The payment in return was sufficient to build replacement premises for the community in the newly assigned residential area for people of Indian origin known as Malabar. The funds were temporarily banked and accrued interest in the interim. In 1973, a final farewell prayer and gathering were held in the school building prior to its demolition, and community members acknowledged their contribution towards upholding social and cultural practices. The new hall in Malabar (Mount View Drive) was to serve the community as a multi-functional venue. The plans included an adjoining kitchen, dining area, main hall with a stage as well as storage facilities. The hall was spacious enough for religious and recreational activities, such as dancing and drama, as well as indoor sporting activities, such as table tennis and squash. The hall was completed and furnished by 1979 thanks to various fundraising initiatives by individuals in the community. It is still utilised by residents living in Malabar, irrespective of their racial and ethnic grouping, for private functions such as weddings and celebrations and for sporting and social events. The hall rental tariffs are still affordable for people of all income groupings, and the money generated is put towards the upkeep of the premises.

The initiatives of the SKGM continuously strove to upkeep community togetherness through key philanthropic, religious and social activities. The organisation gained responsibility over most public events and festivities within the community and managed to remain active until the late 1980s, when it was dissolved so that new organisations could be formed for people of Gujarati descent, irrespective of whether they were Mochi or not.[46]

---

46   SKGM (1989).

## The Relevance of the South African Kshatriya Mahasabha

Cohesion among Mochi people in Port Elizabeth is evident in the data collated from interviewees, the existence of varying organisations that were created by community leaders, the contents of various publications and the formation of the SAKM.[47] Despite the community being stigmatised and ostracised by Indian citizens and Indian diaspora communities globally, within the South African Indian diaspora they have become respected thanks to their striving for social cohesion and financial mobility. As they strove, this diaspora denounced the label of Mochi and chose to identify themselves as Kshatriyas. The *Daan Data Granth* formalised this new identification in its publication.

As the Mochi community in Port Elizabeth adopted this identity, they paved their way towards social and fiscal mobility. One noteworthy way they did this was by founding organisations that primarily aimed to uplift the community through education and monetary loans for businesses. The SAKM was formed in April 1943 and the Mochis of Port Elizabeth were instrumental in its birth. The purpose of the national body was to standardise cultural and philanthropy practices within the Mochi community. As previously mentioned, the diaspora community also took the initiative to develop and sustain communication with a Gujarati Mochi organisation[48] in India that could assist the Mochi people in the state of Gujarat by donating money in support of its activities. The SAKM and its various educational trusts offered fiscal assistance to members of its caste grouping through loans and bursaries for university study. The funds were donated by numerous families from both the Port Elizabeth and Cape Town communities. The donors are identified in the *Daan Data Granth* lists alongside the amount of South African rands that were contributed. The money collected was placed into fixed investments and the dividends spent on philanthropic projects in both India and South Africa. Between 1952 and 1995, the SAKM Educational Trust awarded approximately 200,000 rands in bursaries to needy students of the Mochi community.

Along with the details of those who donated towards the education funds, the *Daan Data Granth* also records the names of Mochi graduates, their academic achievements and their home region in South Africa. This information is presented with photographs of their families and a brief historical account of where they lived, the type of entrepreneurship they were engaged in and how many children each nuclear family had within an extended family overview. Interesting to note is that emphasis was placed on the type of livelihood these individuals were engaged

---

[47] Founded in 1943 by Mochi men living in Port Elizabeth.

[48] The Surat Jilla Parishad was formed in 1925 in Mumbai in India.

in and, more so, when they diverted from the caste trade of shoemaking. Some Mochi families adopted skills from other caste groups and incorporated those skills into their existing, often shoe-based, businesses. For instance, the background information of the Hari family reveals that Fakirbhai Hari began his tailoring business in 1932. Similarly, the information of the Makan Bhana family showcases their varying business successes and makes no mention of shoe-repairing as a starting point of fiscal growth after settlement in Port Elizabeth. Yet an interview revealed that in 1904, when Makanjee Bhana arrived in Port Elizabeth, he travelled with a few nails, a hammer and a metal tool that was hand-moulded and unidentifiable by the interviewee – let us call him Respondent B. Upon settling, shoe-repairing was his first choice of occupation. After migration to South Africa, some Mochi people desired to deviate from the caste trade of shoemaking as soon as possible. Respondent B explains:

> The mindset among Mochi people was that there was more profit in other types of businesses than in shoemaking, and if people had the funds or skills to start something else other than shoemaking, it was admired and supported. Ultimately, everyone wanted to do something other than shoemaking and shoe-repairing.

The SAKM was pivotal in cultivating a vision of social and financial upliftment that inspired Mochi people to achieve academically and to focus on business expansion and development. A total of 101 graduates are listed within the Eastern Cape segment, and reference is also made to graduates residing in Australia, England, Canada, India, Zimbabwe, New Zealand and the United States. However, this account of Mochi graduates does not record the years in which these graduates completed their studies. Further absences include the inconsistent noting of the names of institutions where degrees were attained, and in the case of graduates living abroad, there is no information to indicate their city of residence. The lack of a time frame within this publication contributes to the misnomer that most Mochi graduates mentioned in this text predominantly graduated during the apartheid era, even though there are some individuals listed that completed their qualifications before then.

Amongst other achievements, the Mochi community of Port Elizabeth celebrated the graduation of their first female medical doctor in 1971.[49] The values that made this event worth celebrating were fostered collectively through the SAKM and its promotion of the importance of education, religious and cultural preservation and philanthropy. As the *Daan Data Granth* states, 'The key to a

---

[49] SKGM (1989).

prosperous future was through obtaining a sound education.'[50] Educational qualifications were appreciated and admired by the community and were seen as a surety for a far more prosperous future. However, tertiary, or university, education was still not accessible to everyone for various reasons. Some families needed their children to remain in Port Elizabeth and assist with or manage their family businesses. This was particularly evident in families where there were many younger siblings that were still in school and the parents of these children were burdened with ailing health. Interviews indicated that only a handful of parents allowed their children the opportunity to study in colonial Natal, whilst others preferred to have their children reside in Port Elizabeth and assist in family businesses. Respondent A explains:

> Sometimes our parents could not foresee their lives being enhanced with a university education of their children. There were some families that placed greater importance on business as a route to a better income and life. I recall some parents who were just not willing to allow their children to live away from them, so sending them to Natal for a degree was not considered. During the apartheid era, we had no other option but to go to the University of Durban-Westville for a tertiary education. I was fortunate, my parents willingly sent me away to study.

It was also revealed by interviewees that families who were not opposed to university education in the late 1960s onwards were more likely to send their sons away to study in India or in Durban rather than their daughters. Some young Mochi women were encouraged to enhance their homemaking and craft skills instead, while others joined the family business and gained business-relevant skills. A number of families were willing to send their children away, irrespective of their gender, but only if they had proven themselves academically during their high-school years and if they could be described as responsible individuals. This criterion was often discussed amongst members of the extended family, and thereafter decisions were made collectively. Mochi girls pursuing a tertiary education were seen as privileged in comparison to Gujarati girls of other castes and more so if they were given the opportunity to reside in another city or country for educational purposes. Interviewees explained that the community, and especially the SAKM, believed that they were being progressive by encouraging their daughters to be educated, even though some families were resistant to the idea.

Prior to the apartheid era, most South African universities allowed people of Indian origin to be enrolled for various degrees. Interviews revealed that some

---

[50]  SAKM (1995), p. 106.

Mochi medical graduates began studying at the University of Cape Town in 1959 and completed their studies in 1965. Tuition fees were 1,000 rands per annum. Some students were forced to take study loans from the SAKM Educational Trust, whilst others were fortunate to receive bursaries from the fund. The apartheid government then enacted the Extension of University Education Act (Act No. 45), 1959. This legislation prohibited South African 'non-white'[51] youth from becoming university scholars at most local and national universities. These universities were reserved for 'whites only'. The University of Durban-Westville in Durban was the only South African university that accepted non-white learners. This university was founded primarily to serve people of Indian origin. Despite this, some parents sent their children to India (Gujarat and other regions) to pursue a tertiary education. Multiple reasons surface from interviews regarding why children were allowed to go back home to study despite financial difficulties. Some families believed that their children were too far removed from the reality of the 'Mochi struggle'[52] in India, whereas others indicated that educational and living expenses were lower there. Other parents preferred that their children spend time with ailing grandparents and extended family in India, and they had hopes that the 'Indian culture'[53] would be further entrenched in their children during their stay. Many families also feared the apartheid regime and felt uncertain about their future prospects in South Africa.

Then there were those families who attained large amounts of wealth during the pre-apartheid and apartheid years, chiefly through retailing and servicing the 'non-white' race groups in Port Elizabeth. They did so with the help of their sharp business acumen and ability to manage money efficiently. Like most Mochi families, they initially ran and managed family-owned shoe-repairing businesses. A trend that can be noted amongst Port Elizabeth's Mochi-owned businesses is that most of them went into shoe and clothing retailing directly after shoe-repairing and thereafter ventured into retailing and wholesaling of other merchandise and fresh produce. Interviewees talked of the wealthy and prominent families with immense pride, especially because they are of the Mochi caste. Particular reference was made to certain families that committed to uplifting their community through continuous donations towards the building of the community hall in Leather Lane

---

[51] A person who is not a member of a race of people who are white-skinned. See Hornby (2000), p. 795.

[52] 'Mochi struggle' is used as a concept that loosely describes the challenges that the Mochi communities face.

[53] 'Indian culture' is used as a concept that only loosely implies social normative practices, and not as a universally acceptable concept.

and to bursaries and other subsidiaries needed for overall growth. An interviewee – let us call him Respondent C – explained:

> I think many families were able to grow rich quickly during the apartheid years because 'non-whites' were denied access to certain shopping facilities, which meant they were forced to visit the small shops. Furthermore, our businessmen knew how to personalise their services and were in general good businessmen.

Gujarati businessmen managed to engage in the retailing and wholesaling of most goods, from furniture, crockery and formal and informal attire to leather accessories and hardware. However, most importantly, these businessmen adapted to the needs of possible consumer trends and demands. The service that these shopkeepers rendered to consumers was personally tailored. For instance, interviewees revealed how they would source anything on request for their customers. This type of service assisted in growing a regular and loyal clientele of whom some were Gujarati. Wholesaling also appealed to a handful of Mochi businessmen. The ability to attain merchandise on credit enabled a few to dabble into and consider wholesaling as a long-term venture. The movement of large quantities of stock meant that businesses needed bigger premises for storage, wholesaling and retailing, and some of these businesses eventually owned the premises that they initially rented. Some attained immense growth and managed to secure themselves numerous properties and other assets of value, whereas others were content with their fiscal improvement that had raised them from their poverty-ridden beginnings.

By the late 1990s, most Mochi families in Port Elizabeth had made significant progress both socially and financially. Many families were well integrated into the broader business society in Port Elizabeth and enjoyed the company of some very successful businessmen. A few brave families dabbled with politics during the apartheid era and eventually became involved in the anti-apartheid coalition in the Eastern Cape region. In 1984, the Mochis from Port Elizabeth had their first representative at the parliament level in the apartheid government. The House of Delegates of South Africa was in existence from 1984 to 1994, and it was reserved for Indian South Africans represented at a national governmental level. Fiscal upliftment created the space for social upliftment and new identities for the Mochi in the Eastern Cape. On the other hand, there were some families that did not prosper, and they had no choice but to live frugal lives and be receptive to the fiscal and social support the community offered through its varying organisations.

However, with this assistance, these families have persevered, and their children have excelled in their respective careers thanks to the attainment of tertiary and further education.

## Conclusion

Gujaratis that migrated to the Eastern Cape settled with a singular vision: to be alleviated from poverty. Central to this was the collaborative approach of organisations that supported educational and fiscal mobility. These goals were not only prioritised by individuals but by community members at large. The ethos shared by this Gujarati community was admirable and unique. They understood each other's hardships and were able to collaborate in business ventures and support one another's educational aspirations. Families excelled in business through the networking opportunities supplied by organisations such as the SKGM and the SAKM. The benchmark of gaining prosperity and reaching a tertiary level of education was set by these groups and encouraged by the Mochi-specific fiscal supporting structure (educational bursaries and loans) that they put into place. This was complemented by the continuous efforts to strengthen human relations among community members through social and religious events managed by leading members.

These organisations played a central role in sustaining the community networks within, first, Port Elizabeth and then, gradually, the entire area of the Eastern Cape. Eventually they created a platform for all Mochis in South Africa to interact. This positively influenced their personal business portfolios as well as the broader commercial network within South Africa. Mochi graduates also gained exposure via varying organisations, philanthropic causes and additional networks, which enhanced their personal position within the South African diaspora. The mobilisation of all Mochis in South Africa to meet annually and bi-annually was often facilitated through the SAKM and its regional sub-sects. The aim here was to collaborate in philanthropic ideas and address inadequacies in the attempt to sustain Gujarati ways of life and religious influences. These events also contributed to the clannishness of Mochis across South Africa and encouraged marriages between them for a number of decades.

The Mochi community of Port Elizabeth grew in solidarity through the common values and goals that individuals shared. These closely knit relationships were further enhanced by the fact that the Mochis were one (the largest and most dominant) of three caste groupings comprising the Gujarati community.

The personal and social benefits enjoyed by an individual from a close-knit community can often be undermined in the broader scheme of things. Fellow Mochis supplied encouragement and support for one another and at times were each other's competition as well. Finally, the shoemaker, or the *mochi*, was seen as a unique artisan in this region of South Africa, and this assisted their transition into the wider business network of Port Elizabeth and then South Africa as a whole. Their reputation contributed significantly to the alteration of their personal identities, their self-esteem and the overall perception of the Mochi community.

## Bibliography

Bhana, Surendra, and Kusum K. Bhoola. 2011. 'The Dynamics of Preserving Cultural Heritage: The Case of Durban's Kathiawad Hindu Seva Samaj, 1943–1960 and Beyond'. *South Asian Diaspora* 3(1): 15–36.

Dhupelia-Mesthrie, Uma. 2012. 'Gujarati Shoemakers in Twentieth-Century Cape Town: Family, Gender, Caste and Community'. *Journal of Southern African Studies* 38(1): 167–182.

Dwivedi, Manan. 2010. 'Gujarati Diaspora on a Global Platform: Perceptions, Contributions and Experiences'. *Diaspora Studies* 3(2): 161–185.

Ghai, Dharam P., and Yash P. Ghai. 1965. 'Asians in East Africa: Problems and Prospects'. *Journal of Modern African Studies* 3(1): 35–51.

Harris, Karen L. 2010. 'Sugar and Gold: Indentured Indian and Chinese Labourers in South Africa'. *Journal of Social Sciences* 25(1–3): 147–158.

Hiralal, Kalpana. 2008. 'Indian Family Businesses in Natal, 1870–1950'. *Natalia* 38: 27–38.

Hornby, Albert Sidney. 2000. *Oxford Advanced Learner's Dictionary*. New York: Oxford University Press.

India TV. 2015. 'Top 10 Gujarati Billionaires'. 1 August. https://www.indiatvnews.com/business/india/top-10-gujarati-billionaires-3732.html. Accessed on 15 March 2023.

Kalnins, Arturs, and Wilbur Chung. 2006. 'Social Capital, Geography and Survival: Gujarati Immigrant Entrepreneurs in the U.S. Lodging Industry'. *Management Science* 52(2): 233–247.

Kapoor, Shivani. 2021. 'The Violence of Odors: Sensory Politics of Caste in a Leather Tannery'. *Senses and Society* 2(2): 1–13.

Kumar, Pratap. 2012. 'Place of Subcaste (Jati) Identity in the Discourse on Caste: Examination of Caste in the Diaspora'. *South Asian Diaspora* 4(2): 215–228.

———. 2013. *Hinduism and the Diaspora: A South African Narrative*. Jaipur: Rawat Publications.

Mondal, Samar Kumar. 2012. 'Caste System and the Present Society: Some Observations on Ambedkar's View'. *Contemporary Voice of Dalit* 5(2): 193–200.

Neuman, W. Lawrence. 1996. *Social Research Methods: Qualitative and Quantitative Approaches*. Boston: Allyn and Bacon.

Oonk, Gijsbert. 2013. *Settled Strangers: Asian Business Elites in East Africa (1800–2000)*. New Delhi: SAGE Publications.

Padayachee, Vishnu, and Robert Morrel. 1991. 'Indian Merchants and Dukawallahs in the Natal Economy, 1875–1914'. *Journal of Southern African Studies* 17(1): 73–102.

Posel, Deborah. 2001. 'What's in a Name? Racial Categorisations under Apartheid and the Afterlife'. *Transformation* 47: 50–75.

Pandin, Jacob. 1978. 'The Hindu Caste System and Muslim Ethnicity: The Labbai of a Tamil Village in South Africa'. *Ethnohistory* 25(2): 141–157.

Port Elizabeth Hindu Seva Samaj. 1994. *Eastern Cape Telephone Directory*. Port Elizabeth: Bhana Printers.

Shree Kshatriya Gujerati Mandal (SKGM). 1979. *Diamond Jubilee Souvenir Brochure, 1917–1979*. Port Elizabeth: Bhana Printers.

———. 1989. *Platinum Jubilee Souvenir Brochure, 1917–1989*. Port Elizabeth: Bhana Printers.

South African Kshatriya Mahasabha (SAKM). 1995. *Daan Data Granth*. Port Elizabeth: Bhana Printers.

South End Museum Board of Trustees. 2006. *Passage from India, a Celebration of Indian Heritage in Nelson Mandela Bay*. Port Elizabeth: Bhana Printers.

Vahed, Goolam. 2005. 'Passengers, Partnerships, and Promissory Notes: Gujarati Traders in Colonial Natal, 1870–1920'. *International Journal of African Historical Studies* 38(3): 449–479.

Varma, Roli, and Daya R. Varma. 2009. 'The Making of Indian Immigrant Entrepreneurs in the US'. *Economic and Political Weekly* 44(3): 64–69.

Yengde, Suraj Milind. 2015. 'Caste among the Indian Diaspora in Africa'. *Economic and Political Weekly* 37(1): 65–68.

# 12

# The Eurasian Female Workforce and Imperial Britain

## Harnessing Domestic Labour by People of Mixed Racial Descent*

*Rochelle Almeida*

## The Invisibility of Eurasian Female Domestic Migrant Labourers in Britain

At the outset of this chapter, I would like to clarify that the term 'Eurasian' to identify 'biracial' people or people of mixed racial descent (Euro-Asian) was in general use throughout the Victorian Age. It was replaced by the term 'Anglo-Indian' in 1911, when members of the community in India made it known through their leaders that they would prefer to be labelled as such in order to distinguish them from the mixed-race offspring of colonials based in other parts of Asia and the Far East. After India's Independence in 1947, the community was more categorically defined in Article 366(2) of the Constitution of India as the progeny of European fathers and Indian mothers domiciled in India (then British India, now among the territories of India, Pakistan and Bangladesh). The perplexing issue of their nomenclature attains significance for the simple reason that they were often erroneously classified: as 'Europeans' when in India and as 'Indians' or 'Asiatics' when outside the colony. Rarely were they correctly labelled as 'Eurasians' or 'Anglo-Indians' – a matter that makes it challenging to isolate them as a distinct ethnic community among Indians and has added to their invisibility.[1] Indeed, as much as India's people of mixed racial descent are 'invisible' in the South Asian diaspora as immigrants in Great Britain today, so too had they remained uncounted among labour forces in England during the decades

---

\* This work was carried out in the United Kingdom (UK) and supported by a generous research grant from New York University. It supported my extended stay as a GRI (Graduate Research Institute) Fellow at New York University, London, in the fall of 2016. Special thanks in absentia to the late director of NYU London, Gary Slapper, who sponsored a Brown Bag lecture by me on this subject, and to the library staff at Queen Mary College of the University of London and the British Library, London.

[1] Since this chapter focuses on the community's doings before 1911, I shall be referring to them as 'Eurasians' throughout.

of the British Raj. The reasons for their 'invisibility' (as I have argued in my book on Britain's Anglo-Indians[2]) are that they had European surnames (either Portuguese, French, Dutch or British, derived from their paternity) and anglicised first names, were 100 per cent Christian by religious affiliation, were either Roman Catholic or Anglican, and employed English as their mother tongue. They were also westernised in terms of dress and lifestyle. This combination of factors served to create the identity confusion that still plagues the community but also serves to single them out in photographs when depicted in diverse groups.

Difficult as it might be to identify people of mixed racial descent from the Indian subcontinent in the United Kingdom (UK) today, it is well-nigh impossible to ascertain their presence in the UK during the colonial era. Although Rozina Visram's extensive research into the issue sheds light on the South Asian presence in Britain from the seventeenth century onwards, her work does not focus closely on female Eurasian presence in Britain.[3] Definitive markers of identity are conspicuous by their absence, but it is easier to point to the presence of Eurasian females than it is to spot their male counterparts. Some evidence of their presence in London is available through pictorial documentation, which I have drawn upon liberally as a resource. Indeed, I daresay that among the hundreds of women who travelled to the metropolitan 'centre' from the colonial 'periphery', either as household help or as *ayah*s (that is, nursemaids or nannies) to provide domestic assistance to upper-class English families, there were undoubtedly some Eurasians. An examination of official documents in the India Office Records (IOR) in London, letters written by Englishwomen during the Raj and photographs from the late nineteenth and early twentieth centuries found in magazines about London corroborate my claim that among the first members of the South Asian labour force in Britain, there were Eurasian women. Indeed, William Dalrymple's scholarship[4] has proven definitively that Eurasian males were sent to England by their upper-class British fathers for education as early as the seventeenth century. If, in like manner, there were Eurasian females in Britain in the same era, not a lot of evidence has been yet unearthed. Yet, from what slight evidence exists, it is clear that they were present in certain clearly demarcated roles. For the purpose of this chapter, I shall focus on the occurrence and agency of domestic helpers and *ayah*s of mixed racial descent as part of the migrant labour pool available in Britain in the Victorian period.

The enormous amount of scholarship that brought attention to indentured labour from the Indian subcontinent in various British colonies has led also

---

[2] Almeida (2017).

[3] Visram (1986, 2002).

[4] Dalrymple (2002).

to its wide use as a fictional backdrop, as seen most prominently in Amitav Ghosh's *Ibis* trilogy.[5] Scholarship on the plight of migrant female domestic labourers from the Indian subcontinent is less prolific but equally worthy of scrutiny. Like indentured labourers, casual domestic workers (Indian and Eurasian) were subject to the mercy of a single employer far from home shores. Unlike their indentured sorority, however, they did not benefit from the panoply of rules, regulations and inspections that governed movement. So fluid was their status that it is difficult even to ascertain their numbers other than through calculated guessing. While one might presume that passenger manifests in outgoing-ship registers in conjunction with passport records might provide definitive proof of Eurasian inclusion among the female labour force from the Indian subcontinent, this resource leads to a dead end. Arunima Datta's recent scholarship shows that

> many of these records, even passage slips and passports, do not give ayahs' names. To those keeping the records, these women were not of sufficient significance to warrant being individually identified, adding an additional layer of difficulty for those seeking to uncover their lives.[6]

Datta's research into incoming passenger lists from 1878 to 1960, outward passenger lists from 1890 to 1960 and the census of 1871, 1891 and 1901 enables one to argue that most *ayah*s who landed in Britain returned to India either through continued employment with the person who brought them to England or by securing employment with other families travelling the reverse journey. However, she writes, 'Exact numbers are hard to determine because ayahs' first names were not recorded in passage lists, rather they were recorded as they [*sic*] servant of their respective employers, making it difficult to track individuals.'[7] If it is so challenging to ascertain the exact numbers of *ayah*s who arrived into, departed from or remained in England at any given time, imagine how difficult it is to determine their ethnicity or to identify the Eurasian women who might have formed their numbers.

## Female Migrant Labourers in Britain: Permanent and Temporary

In her book *Indians in Britain: Anglo-Indian Encounters, Race and Identity 1880–1930*, Shompa Lahiri states that from the middle of the nineteenth century,

---

[5]  Ghosh (2008, 2011, 2015).

[6]  Datta (2021), p. 97.

[7]  Datta (2021), p. 98.

the Indian population in Great Britain consisted of roughly five main transient groups: students, princes, soldiers, *ayah*s and *lascar*s (seamen who provided casual manual labour on ships plying the high seas).[8] Similarly, Visram's pioneering research on *ayah*s, *lascar*s and princes throws light on the presence of Indians in the labour market long before independence came to the subcontinent.[9] Datta states that '[a]yahs were only one group amongst many Indian domestic servants employed in Britain. Some families brought back young boys or girls as companions to their children or as cheap domestic servants'.[10] They joined the British staff in upper-class domestic urban spaces or on country estates to serve as kitchen maids or waitstaff. I would argue that among this migrant labour force were Eurasian women employed as domestic servants in a permanent capacity. The nature of their employment presupposed their systematic integration into British society and negated the hope or possibility of repatriation to India. Many single women would, gradually, have married within the host community and become domiciled in Britain. In doing so, they assimilated more easily into the British mainstream than their male counterparts who were often derogatorily termed WOGs (westernised oriental gentleman) each time they attempted social assimilation in Britain. In English literature, one of the earliest examples of a Eurasian domestic 'servant' – daughter of an English merchant and an Indian princess – is Zillah Le Poer (The Poor) in Dinah Mulock Craik's novella *The Half-Caste*, first published in 1851.[11] It must be noted that while Zillah is sent to England to live with her uncle, his wife and two daughters as a member of their family, she is perceived as fit to be treated, according to Melissa Edmundson, 'as little more than a servant in the household'.[12]

There were also *ayah*s who served their colonial employers as temporary child-minding nursemaids in a more casual mode. Their numbers, which would have included Eurasian women, also remain uncounted. Because legislation with regard to the responsibilities of British employers towards them and their position in British households was either non-existent or subject to interpretation, they lived in an ambiguous twilight zone, subject to the compassion of their employers to repatriate them and, if they found themselves destitute in England, dependent

---

[8] Lahiri (1999), p. 1.

[9] Visram (1986). Please note that by 'princes', Visram means extended members of India's royal families. These wealthy Indian aristocrats did not, of course, form part of India's labour forces in Great Britain.

[10] Datta (2021), p. 97.

[11] Craik (2016 [1851]).

[12] Edmundson (2016), p. 19.

upon organised philanthropy. Their lack of immigrant rights caused immense uncertainty and suffering in their lives and serves to underscore the politics of race, class and gender that affected all migrant female labourers from the Indian subcontinent in Britain. Stripped of all social resources that could have guaranteed their security, they developed social networks and resources of their own that highlight their agency as a group of underprivileged individuals who, despite a plethora of socio-economic disadvantages, made a significant contribution to the empire as they staked their place within it.

## Definition of *Ayahs*, Their Duties and Responsibilities

Lahiri provides an explanation for the word *ayah*, declaring that it originated from the Portuguese word for tutor, *aio*.[13] In like manner, in his article entitled 'Human Birds of Passage', A. C. Marshall explains that

> an ayah is a native nurse or ladies' maid and an essential part and feature of a white mistress' household in India. The actual word is the feminine of *aio*, a tutor, and belongs by all the rights of language to the Portuguese. That it was carried by them to India when they possessed a maritime ascendancy even as long ago as the sixteenth century there is very little doubt.[14]

Indeed, the Portuguese might well have been the first Europeans to hire Indian *aio*s – both in India and on journeys back and forth between India and Portugal when they would have acted as ladies' maids and childminders. Subsequently, as Lahiri also explains, these women served as nurses and attendants to English families on the long voyages to and from India.[15]

The prolonged presence of *ayah*s in Great Britain, at least throughout the nineteenth century, was the result of two factors: First, once they landed on British shores, they were meant to bide their own time until their British employers took them back to India (once, presumably, their vacations at 'home' were over). Or, second, they were abandoned upon arrival in Britain. In many cases, British employers grew fond enough of and attached enough to their *ayah*s to take them back on their return voyages to India, bearing, of course, the personal expense of their passage. However, during the vacation of the employers in varied parts of Britain, *ayah*s were often expected to fend for themselves. To make their situation even more precarious, more often than not the *ayah*'s job was perceived as done

---

[13]  Lahiri (1999), p. 1.

[14]  Marshall (1922), p. 104.

[15]  Lahiri (1999), p. 1.

upon arrival in England, for a rosy-cheeked English attendant would have arrived at the Tilbury or Southampton docks to take over from her. In providing a detailed account of the terms and conditions involved in the hiring of *ayah*s as child-attendants on ships returning to Britain in colonial times, Marshall states that their services were often dispensed with at the very docks where their ship's long journey from the East terminated. Marshall states, 'A pink-faced nurse is there to pounce upon the baby or children.'[16] Datta corroborates this observation. She writes:

> In most cases, employers discharged their ayahs in Britain either immediately upon disembarkation or after the employers settled in. A European nurse would often take charge of the lady and child that they had served throughout the journey immediately upon disembarkation. This abrupt cessation of employment and sometimes outright abandonment was a severe challenge for ayahs.[17]

Thus, substantial numbers of *ayah*s who might be termed 'labour migrants' in England found themselves abandoned by their British employers and left to depend upon their own resources during the period of their employers' sojourn in the UK. This period could last for as brief as a few weeks to the time it would take the *ayah*s (often several months) to find British employers willing to hire them to undertake childcare for their offspring on their return voyage to India and, hopefully, for the continued length of their stay on the Indian subcontinent. In that respect, they found themselves in a position of deep ambiguity. Not being indentured, they ceased to be the responsibility of an employer once their duties on the outgoing vessel ended. Being deprived of the means to support themselves during the period of their employers' stay in England, they often became dependent on charity offered by their host country. It is a matter of admirable resourcefulness on the part of the *ayah*s and an assertion of their agency that they were able to pass time productively until their return to India.

## Eurasian Female Domestic Employees

In attempting to trace the earliest presence of Eurasian female labour in the UK, I used, as the springboard to my inquiry, Visram's statement that often children sent back to England for their education were accompanied by Indian servants.[18]

---

16  Marshall (1922), p. 105.

17  Datta (2021), p. 98.

18  Visram (1986), p. 12.

According to scholars such as Dalrymple and Christopher Hawes, many upper-class Eurasian male children – even as early as the seventeenth and eighteenth centuries – were sent 'home' for an education after being born to Indian women, or *bibis*, in India,[19] accompanied by lower-class women who provided assistance and kept their young charges safe and amused on the voyage. I advocate the view that among these lower-class assistants were females of mixed racial descent not fortunate enough to have been sired by upper-class European fathers. As female children of low-level European soldiers in India – often abandoned by their fathers and raised by poor Indian mothers – they had little choice but to seek independent means of financial survival. Becoming *ayah*s to the wealthier (sometimes mixed-race) offspring of Europeans in India (and then traveling with them on their extended periods of 'leave' in England) was one such avenue of employment available to them. These unfortunate women, like the English working-class Victorian governesses of literary fame such as the eponymous heroines of Charlotte Brontë's *Jane Eyre* and Anne Brontë's *Agnes Grey* and Craik's Cassandra Pryor from *The Half-Caste* and Felicia Lyne from *Bread Upon the Waters*, accepted domestic employment to ward off poverty and were what Edmundson calls 'liminal figures occupying a social no-man's land: not "low" enough to be part of the servant class but not "ladylike" enough to be part of the family employing her'.[20] Indeed, if they were Eurasian women, their position in England was no different from that which prevailed in India – when being neither fully European nor fully Indian, they did not belong in either camp. Katherine Holden's work on the Victorian 'nanny' throws much light on the ambiguity of the governess' situation (whether European or otherwise) and how a Eurasian nanny would have found herself in the same abstruse position.[21] However, given that fictional Caucasian heroines often found deliverance from their condition by marriage either to their employer or a man within his circle, it would be safe to assume (although records are lacking) that Eurasian women in this position might have become permanent expatriates in Britain through similar avenues – marriage with working-class British men – and ceased to be counted either as Indians or as Asiatics. In that regard, their position was infinitely better than that of *ayah*s from the Indian subcontinent, whose limited, indeed temporary, presence in Britain added to their insecurity.

---

[19]  See Dalrymple (2002) and Hawes (1996).

[20]  Edmundson (2016), p. 29.

[21]  Holden (2013).

## The Case of Kitty Johnson and Eliza Fay

Lack of documentation about Eurasian migrant female labourers makes the process of seeking their presence in Britain a relentlessly unrewarding experience. However, some exceptions do exist. We do, in fact, have documented evidence of a Eurasian woman, one Kitty Johnson, being taken to England in the 1700s, soon after the British acquired the colony of Bengal, to work in a domestic capacity. Through a twist of fate, Kitty almost ended up being sold into slavery on the island of St Helena – not by her original owner, one Eliza Fay, but by the British friends to whom Fay had 'gifted' Kitty. An account of this bizarre incident is, in fact, available on record, through one of Fay's own letters from India to her friends in Blackheath, London. So how did Kitty Johnson find herself almost sold into slavery?

It so happened that Eliza Fay, born in 1756, wife of a British lawyer named Anthony Fay, accompanied her husband on his voyage to India in 1779, where he hoped to find a position as a British judge in the newly acquired colony of Bengal. During her tenure in India, Mrs Fay wrote copious letters to friends back home in Blackheath, of which she was a native. Within that time frame, she also made three voyages, back and forth, between Britain and India. Her letters were edited by the novelist E. M. Forster and published in 1925 under the title *Original Letters from India 1779–1815* by Hogarth Press in London.[22] In one of her letters, Mrs Fay expresses her resentment on being considered responsible, by a local British court of law in St Helena, for the safe return of Kitty and her two children to India as it was through Mrs Fay that her English friends had fallen in 'possession' of the unfortunate Kitty. Mrs Fay's friends had attempted to dispose of Kitty by selling her as a slave when their ship arrived on the island of St Helena. Presumably, Mrs Fay was traveling with them on the same ship, because when found responsible for the safe return of Kitty to India, Mrs Fay preferred to abandon her on the island rather than assume any responsibility for her continued safety. When this matter reached the ears of British colonials in India, it caused widespread outrage on the subcontinent, not least because British colonials, in general, as well as their Indian subjects turned a stern eye towards slavery as a source of cheap labour. The work of Indrani Chatterjee and Richard M. Eaton has drawn valuable attention to the issue of colonial slavery in South Asia[23] from the seventeenth century onwards, but it does not lie within the purview of this chapter to elaborate upon their findings with regard to the possible general use of Eurasian female labourers as slaves.

---

[22] See Forster (1925).

[23] Chatterjee and Eaton (2006); Chatterjee (2002).

The case of Kitty is used here merely to highlight the fact that Eurasian women were employed as domestic labourers in Britain but only very rarely identified definitively as such.

## The 'Deposit System' of 1822

Through the eighteenth century and into the nineteenth, the position in Britain of female Indian casual labourers from the Indian subcontinent became increasingly perilous. Abandonment led to destitution, and destitution led to the involvement of local authorities who were frequently called upon to intervene in the repatriation of poverty-stricken *ayah*s. In order to alleviate social concern and decrease the burden placed upon their administrative resources, the East India Company took measures in 1822 to place responsibility upon the shoulders of British employers who hired these women for domestic labour. The introduction of the 'Deposit System' required the employers of Indian servants travelling to Britain to deposit 100 pounds (later decreased to 50) at a government treasury in India to secure the servant's return passage.[24] The practice remained in place until 1844 when the number of *ayah*s travelling to Britain increased so dramatically as to make official administration of their movement a bureaucratic hurdle that was best eliminated.[25] Although no available archival records prove formal abolition of the 'Deposit System', a great deal of correspondence in the IOR in London demonstrate the effects of the confusion that arose following its cancellation. On the one hand, British employers faced ambiguity with regard to their responsibility towards their hired Indian servants, while, on the other, deprived of the financial protection that had guaranteed their repatriation to India, female *ayah*s found themselves facing the increased prospect of abandonment and impoverishment in Britain.

## Legislation Regarding Abandoned Casual Labourers

Much correspondence passed, for example, between British lawyers inquiring on behalf of their clients who had brought Indian servants to England, as to the exact extent of their client's responsibilities. See, for instance, the letter from a certain J. Howard Bowen addressed to J. A. Godley, soliciting advice on the extent of his client's liability regarding his Eurasian female servant. Notice that the document is entitled 'Enquiry as to legal liability of an officer bringing an *Indian* servant

---

[24]  See India Office Records (IOR)/L/PJ/158/1282.
[25]  See *Bengal Almanac*, 1851, 1852, West Bengal State Archives.

to England to provide return passage to India'.[26] Although the document describes her as an 'Indian', in his letter Bowen states specifically that the woman in question is 'an Indian and a Eurasian'.[27] Again, while women of mixed racial descent were part of this migrant labour force, this particular letter, somewhat rarely, actually mentions the word 'Eurasian' in connection with the woman employed as a domestic labourer.

Much scholarship has been undertaken on correspondence pertaining to such cases from the eighteenth century onwards, including many petitions written for and by South Asians in Britain on behalf of their indigent compatriots. See, for example, a letter from Syed Abdollah, a professor at Trinity College, Cambridge, petitioning for the reinstatement of the 'Deposit System' to eliminate the possibility of adding to the number of 'as many as 900 cases in London alone during 1868'.[28] However, despite the abandonment of *ayah*s after their disembarkation, few such migrant workers challenged this inhumane custom as the official policy regarding the return of such servants to India was never spelled out or made clear. Indian employees relied solely on the compassion of their British employers in providing for them once their ships docked in England. Bowen was hired by a client who wished to be apprised of his legal obligations with regards to the Eurasian woman he had hired in India to serve him on his voyage to Great Britain. Few employers cared enough about their *ayah*s to even make such inquiries. The response that Bowen received from the office of the secretary of state for India to his query underscores this ambiguity. It stated:

> It is not the duty of the Secretary of State to advice Solicitors upon questions of Law. There is no absolute law compelling persons who bring native servants to England to take them back; but practically, people bringing them are expected to send them back.[29]

---

26 Letter from J. H. Bowen, Solicitor, of Weymouth, Dorset, dated 15 July 1885, addressed to J. A. Godley, Esq., Under Secretary of State for India, Charles Street, Westminster, entitled 'Enquiry as to legal liability of an officer bringing an Indian servant to England to provide return passage to India', IOR L/P&J/6/158, No. 1282.

27 Letter from J. H. Bowen, Solicitor, of Weymouth, Dorset, dated 15 July 1885, addressed to J. A. Godley, Esq., Under Secretary of State for India, Charles Street, Westminster, entitled 'Enquiry as to legal liability of an officer bringing an Indian servant to England to provide return passage to India', IOR L/P&J/6/158, No. 1282.

28 Datta (2021), p. 99.

29 Letter from Under Secretary of State for India at India Office, Charles Street, Westminster, to J. H. Bowen, Solicitor, of Weymouth, Dorset, entitled 'Enquiry as to legal liability of an officer bringing an Indian servant to England to provide return passage to India', IOR L/P&J/6/158, No. 1282.

Ambiguity regarding the responsibilities of British employers towards their Indian (or Eurasian) employees, which had prevailed since the 1860s, accounts for the fact that *ayah*s were often abandoned without any compunction in the UK. As early as 25 August 1869, a handwritten letter signed 'Argyll' to the governor-general of India in Council had referred to a dispatch dated 24 June 1869 'on the subject of the measures to be adopted for ensuring the provision of a return passage for all Natives engaged in India for service out of the country'[30]. 'Argyll' 'trusted that arrangements' would be made at the various ports in India under instructions issued by the British government to successfully check what they described as 'the serious evil which has for some time attracted attention'.[31] The 'serious evil' was the prevalent practice of abandoning Indian employees in London and forcing them to face destitution.

The letter is followed by a large typewritten document that goes into four pages containing a resolution presented to 'Argyll' by a number of official signatories (Mayo, W. R. Mansfield, H. M. Durand, H. S. Maine, John Strachey and B. H. Ellis) at India Office, London. It addresses the Duke of Argyll, Her Majesty's secretary of state for India, Simla, on 24 June 1869, as 'My Lord Duke' and states that in regard to 'certain natives of India who were received into the Strangers' Home for Asiatics in London in a state of destitution,'[32] the following resolution was passed:

> It appears from the communication from the Government of Bengal that in order to provide, as far as possible against the recurrence of such cases, the Lieutenant-Governor has instructed the Collector of Customs to explain the nature of their position to men taken home under engagements of a similar nature, and to assist them in securing a satisfactory arrangement for their return passage. His Honour seems to have done all that is at present needed, and the ... Government and Administrations will be requested to issue similar instructions to the proper officers at the ports under their control.[33]

[30] Letter signed 'Argyll', the Right Honorable Duke of Argyll, K. T., from India Office, London, dated 25 August 1869, addressed to His Excellency, the Right Honorable Governor-General in Council, IOR L/P&J/6/158, No. 1282.

[31] Letter signed 'Argyll', the Right Honorable Duke of Argyll, K. T., from India Office, London, dated 25 August 1869, addressed to His Excellency, the Right Honorable Governor-General in Council, IOR L/P&J/6/158, No. 1282.

[32] Resolution presented to the Right Honorable Duke of Argyll, K. T., by Mayo, W. R. Mansfield, H. M. Durand, H. S. Maine, John Strachey, B. H. Ellis of India Office, London. It addresses the Duke of Argyll, Her Majesty's Secretary of State for India, Simla, 24 June 1869. IOR L/P&J/6/158, No. 1282.

[33] Resolution presented to the Right Honorable Duke of Argyll, K. T., by Mayo, W. R. Mansfield, H. M. Durand, H. S. Maine, John Strachey, B. H. Ellis of India Office, London. IOR L/P&J/6/158, No. 1282.

The matter of official involvement in this issue ends here, but the social ramifications of providing for Indian migrant labourers (frequently referred to as 'Asiatics' in contemporary texts) attracted the attention of local contemporary Christian Missions in London as in many cases such women (and men, often unemployed *lascars*), abandoned by their employers upon arrival in the UK, were found insolvent in London.

## Asserting Agency in Seeking Succor

Although, for the most part, contemporary documents present *ayah*s as docile creatures, seen but barely heard and powerless against Victorian bureaucracy, occasionally the opposite episode gained publicity. Datta draws attention to the case of a destitute *ayah* found wandering the streets of London until she was picked up by a few 'charitable men' who discovered that she had been abandoned by her employer, one Mrs Kelly from Suffolk Street, who had promised to send her back to India but had reneged on the agreement upon arrival in Britain.[34] When the East India Company House was approached to resolve her situation, they replied that they 'could no longer help such cases legally'. The case made the news in local newspapers such as *The Globe* of 22 October 1852, the *Wells Journal*, the *Herts Guardian*, the *Lloyd's Weekly Newspaper* as well as a number of Irish periodicals.[35]

Not willing to accept the Company's washing of its legal hands in the matter, the *ayah* took to the streets to plead her case. She begged in front of London's East India Company House with a placard that described herself as a 'Poor Ayah' who lacked both rice and milk, had a 'poor baby in Calcutta' and no husband to love her. In broken English, the placard further announced that she had been 'brought here by bad bad woman' who would not send her back to Calcutta. Her placard ended with the words 'Pity. Pity'.[36]

Becoming a public embarrassment to the East India Company, the *ayah* was eventually presented at the Mayor's Court where the magistrate, Alderman Hooper, applied pressure on the Company to see her safely back to Calcutta. I agree with Datta that the enormous courage she would have shown in fighting her case alone on the streets of London was indicative of the agency of some female domestic helpers from India who manipulated public response to achieve their ends. In doing so, at a time when official assistance was held back, they

---

[34] Datta (2021), p. 101.

[35] See *The Globe*, 22 October 1852, in the British National Archives, London.

[36] Datta (2021), p. 101.

appealed to the conscience of the British public. Furthermore, they reminded British officialdom as representatives of the empire, not to ignore the promptings of their moral compass. Poor, illiterate and unprotected as they were, the subcontinent's women domestics were astute and indomitable in recognising their rights and demanding them.

## The Ayahs' Homes of the East End

Datta further states, 'Social responses to destitute ayahs in Britain were markedly different from official responses.'[37] Indeed, individuals and institutions came together to provide succor for the suffering. However, while considerable numbers of *ayah*s depended on local charity, an equal number asserted agency in the choices they made to remain voluntarily in these institutions as paying inmates because they benefitted from the support networks they provided. For example, as Datta explains, 'The Ayahs' Home offered food and lodging and employment brokerage services in securing wage passage to India.'[38] However, much as they might seem to have been run entirely on a philanthropic basis, these homes were not entirely charitable institutions. As Visram notes, 'The rent paid by the ayahs for such a lodging was 16 shillings a week.'[39] Thus, much as the Missions might have supported such institutions financially, most of the *ayah*s seemed to have been paid lodgers in these homes with the rare exception of those who had no means of support in Britain and relied entirely on missionary charity.

Nor were their managers motivated purely by altruism. As Datta states, 'Some who justified efforts to help destitute ayahs by a rhetoric of humanitarianism may also have had more material agendas.'[40] The Ayahs' Home set up in London by one Rogers couple, to whom Visram[41] also draws attention, was one such initiative. Set up originally in Aldgate at 6 Jewry Street, the Rogerses ran out of funds to keep it going. When the London City Mission took it over in 1900, it moved to 26 King Edward Road, Mare Street, Hackney. It is among the records of these philanthropic missions that one finds most accounts of the presence of both male labourers (in the form of *lascar*s) and female labourers (in the form of *ayah*s) from the Indian subcontinent in nineteenth-century London. It is mainly upon their publications that I draw in making inquiries into the presence

---

[37]  Datta (2021), p. 100.

[38]  Datta (2021), p. 102.

[39]  Visram (1986), p. 18.

[40]  Datta (2021), p. 102.

[41]  Visram (1986), pp. 17–18.

and status of women of mixed racial heritage as migrant labourers in Victorian and Edwardian England.

Victorian magazine articles, such as those that appear frequently in the *London City Mission Magazine* in the form of annual reports, throw a great deal of light upon the plight of *ayahs*, among whom, going solely by name and their appearance in photographs, Eurasian women might well be identified. The Strangers' Home for Asiatics in London, referred to by members of the India Office in London as being filled with abandoned Indian migrant labourers, was only one of the many Ayahs' Homes that flourished in London's East End, especially around the dockyards of Limehouse, Aldgate and Hackney during the Victorian Age and into the early twentieth century. Visram's account of the Ayahs' Homes in London is far from heartening. She writes:

> While awaiting reengagement many lived in squalid lodging houses and were grossly exploited. It was believed that while these lodgings for the ayahs were usually 'far more respectable' than for the lascars in Ratcliff Highway [in the East End of London], they too were highly overcrowded. For instance, in one lodging house it was found that 'there were between 50 and 60 ayahs', and another lodging housekeeper assured Colonel R. M. Hughes, Secretary to the Strangers' Home in Limehouse, London, that 'on one occasion there were no less than 32 in her house'.[42]

Marshall, however, describes the Hackney place in far more complimentary terms. He writes, 'There is no word with quite the flavor of "home" to a newcomer of foreign blood from overseas, and this place is a home indeed.'[43]

These homes, however, were not without their own rules and regulations or without strict official supervision. In this working-class district in East London, states Visram, a superintendent, usually with experience of Christian work in the East, was in charge of the home.[44] Marshall draws attention to a certain William Fletcher and his wife, missionaries with experience of working in the East, who ran the home in Hackney (see Figure 12.1):

> Here, there is a superintendent who has laboured in the mission fields of India and who can speak the dialects of many districts. There is his wife, the matron, who has sojourned Far East as well.... To the little brown ladies from the tropics. Mr. Wm Fletcher is always 'fader' and Mrs. Fletcher 'mudder'.[45]

---

42  Visram (1986), pp. 17–18.
43  Marshall (1922), p. 105.
44  Visram (1986), pp. 29–30.
45  Marshall (1922), p. 105.

A group of Ayahs recently domiciled in the Society's Home at Hackney. The Superintendents (Mr. & Mrs. Fletcher) and their daughter in the back row.

**Figure 12.1** 'A group of Ayahs recently domiciled in the Society's Home at Hackney', with the superintendents, Mr and Mrs Fletcher, and their daughter in the back row

*Source*: Marshall (1922, p. 104); British Library, London (public domain).

In the *London City Mission Magazine* of 2 July 1900, as part of the 65th annual report of the mission, there are references to missionary work being done among the foreigners of London, specifically in homes housing *ayah*s and *lascar*s. In this report, there are two pictures of Ayahs' Homes in London. One shows the exterior of a building with the caption 'New Ayahs' Home, Hackney NE' (see Figure 12.2).

**Figure 12.2** New Ayahs' Home, Hackney, London, run by the London City Mission

*Source*: *London City Mission Magazine*, London, June 1922, p. 87; British Library, London (public domain).

The other picture is a close-up of the entrance of another Ayahs' Home with four *ayah*s on the porch and two attendants: one Englishwoman (probably the matron, Mrs Rogers, who is referred to in the article), and one Englishman (the husband, Mr Rogers). It carries the caption 'Front Entrance of the Ayahs' Home' (see Figure 12.3).

The text that accompanies the pictures in the segment entitled 'The Ayahs' Home' refers to it as 'the latest enterprise of the Society'. It explains that

> as Mr. and Mrs. Rogers found the expenses connected with it more than they could raise, they approached the Committee, and offered, whilst handling it over to them, to continue to manage it under their guidance and control, on the same lines as heretofore.[46]

FRONT ENTRANCE OF THE AYAHS' HOME.

**Figure 12.3**  Front entrance of Ayahs' Home at 26 King Edward Road, Mare Street, Hackney, London

*Source*: *London City Mission Magazine*, London, 2 July 1900, p. 173; British Library, London (public domain).

---

[46]  *London City Mission Magazine* (1900), pp. 172–174.

The report continues:

> In this Home the Ayahs find protection, and receive Christian instruction from the Missionary to Orientals, who visits it regularly. Here Anglo-Indians[47] can come and engage them for the outward voyage, and it is hoped that Christian friends, and those ladies and gentlemen who thus benefit by the Institution, will do something for its support. The Society's supporters, and all persons interested in such institutions, are heartily invited to visit the Home any day of the week (except Sunday) when the matron will gladly show them over the premises.[48]

'The Missionary to Orientals' was a familiar figure in these homes. As long as the London City Mission financially subsidised the running of these homes, they saw it fit to send their religious representatives to administer to the spiritual needs of their 'Oriental' inmates (regardless of whether or not they were Christians). Visram also makes reference to the proselytising mission of these homes. She refers, in particular, to one Joseph Salter, stating:

> Joseph Salter, the Missionary to the Asiatics and Africans, found 28 ayahs in one house; and according to him it was by no means unusual to find men also lodging in the same house. This house in question was never free of them, the 'boxes of the ayahs generally formed their bedstead, and they (were) all placed close together, to prevent them rolling out'.[49]

Visram singles out the missionary work of Salter in her book using an illustration depicting Salter 'visiting an opium den' during one of his rounds that appeared in the *London City Mission Magazine* of 1 May 1899 in an anonymous article entitled 'Work among the Asiatics and Africans in London' (see Figure 12.4).

## Pictorial Representations of Ayahs in London Homes

An examination of a picture accompanying a chapter by Alec Roberts entitled 'Missionary London' that appears in the book *Living London*, edited by George R. Sims, would corroborate my contention that some of the *ayah*s in this home were of mixed racial descent (see Figure 12.5).[50]

---

[47] The term 'Anglo-Indians' is used here not to denote people of mixed racial descent but rather British colonials who were officially stationed long-term on the Indian subcontinent.

[48] *London City Mission Magazine* (1900), p. 174.

[49] Visram (1986), pp. 17–18.

[50] Roberts (1904), p. 279.

**Figure 12.4** 'Mr Salter Visiting an Opium Den'

*Source*: 'Work among the Asiatics and Africans in London', *London City Mission Magazine*, London, 1 May 1899, p. 84; British Library, London (public domain).

**Figure 12.5** Inside the Ayahs' Home, Hackney, London

*Source*: Roberts (1904, p. 279); British Library, London (public domain).

Although the history of identifying people by superficial aspects of their appearance is contentious, the picture in this report (Figure 12.5) permits the scholar the opportunity to glean ethnic information about its 'subjects' based on styles of clothing. Seen sewing and reading around a sizeable table, supervised by white English matrons who bend over their work, are a large number of women of varied Asian origins. While the ladies wearing sarees or sarongs are likely to be either from the Far East or of Indian Hindu background, it is arguable that the women in the foreground wearing long skirts and long-sleeved, Western-style blouses are of mixed racial descent. Contemporary photographs of Eurasian women living in India in the same era (that I was privileged to have been given access to during my ethnographic research in Britain by the descendants of such women) depict them wearing similar garb and sporting similar hairstyles. By convention, in India, Eurasian women wore Western clothing in appropriation of the dressing conventions of their paternal side. How many of the women in these Ayahs' Homes, living temporarily between jobs, were of mixed racial descent is impossible to discern as they would uniformly be referred to in official records as 'Indians' or even more generally as 'Asiatics'. Hence, it is only by appearance that we can comment on their ethnicity. I would argue that where the woman in question is draped in a sari, she is quite likely not to have been a Eurasian. On the other hand, if she is in Western attire, she would have descended from mixed racial parentage. And indeed, in England, where these photographs were taken, she would have stuck to the Western clothing with which she had become both familiar and comfortable in India.

The account provided by Marshall specifically mentions one of the inmates of Ayahs' Home by name. He writes, 'She was a widow, Mrs. Anthony Pareira, according to her passport.'[51] Marshall also refers to an advertisement that appeared in a contemporary newspaper: 'Wanted – An Indian ayah to travel with three young children to Colombo. Apply, etc.'[52] Going by Pareira's surname, she could have been either Indian (Goan Christian), Eurasian or even Sinhalese (a Burgher). The mention of Colombo in the advertisement that drew Marshall to investigate the position of *ayahs* in London would bear this out. However, it is customary for the surname to be spelled as 'Pereira' in Goa and as 'Perera' or even 'Prera' in Ceylon (present-day Sri Lanka). Nonetheless, in addition to Pareira, Marshall says that at the Ayahs' Home, he met

---

[51] Marshall (1922), p. 104.
[52] Marshall (1922), p. 104.

besides, Agida Hany Fonseka and Lee Ah Su and Mariambai and Gangoo, and nearly
a score of Indians, Singalese, Javanese, Chinese, Siamese, Japanese, Malays – each
hailing from a strange-sounding city or deep-water port in the mystic East – Bombay,
Hooghly, Hongkong or Singapore, Penang or Bangkok – at home to their friends in
India, Ceylon, Burma, Siam, the Federated States, or China.[53]

Again, if one goes strictly by names and surnames alone, then Fonseka and
Mariambai were likely to have had been poor Christians from India or Ceylon.
Fonseka (spelled also as 'Fonseca') is a Portuguese surname that could have passed
to male progeny of Portuguese mixed-race alliances in India and Ceylon or could
have been taken on as a surname by Christians (not of mixed race) in south India
or Ceylon at their time of conversion to Roman Catholicism by Portuguese
missionaries or proselytising Spaniards.[54] Indeed, among these Christian women,
some of mixed racial descent would have been present. In the picture featuring
superintendent Fletcher and his wife, amidst all the swarthy-skinned women
draped in sarees (probably from south India or Ceylon) there is one woman right
in front wearing Western garb (Figure 12.1). I would suggest that she is a Eurasian
or of mixed European and Sinhalese descent – a 'Burgher' as people of mixed racial
descent are known in Sri Lanka.

More evidence of the kind of atmosphere that prevailed in the Ayahs' Home
in London is provided by Roberts's article entitled 'Missionary London'.[55]
Roberts states:

> Occasionally in London there are missionary gatherings of vivid interest and
> picturesque aspect.... Then you may see men and women from the four quarters of
> the globe – some of them garbed like the native races amongst whom their lot is cast.
> They come from Indian bazaars and zenanas.[56]

## Role of the Zenana Missions

Roberts writes admiringly of the 'Zenana Missions – Church and
Nonconformist – [that] afford a fine example of women's work for women.

---

[53]  Marshall (1922), p. 105.

[54]  A woman with the surname Fonseka or Fonseca could also have been a Catholic from
Goa (not part of the British Empire as it was held firmly by Portuguese imperialists).
However, it is common knowledge that thousands of Indian Goans migrated from Goa
into British India and British East African colonies to seek employment as Goa offered too
few opportunities.

[55]  Roberts (1904), pp. 279, 281.

[56]  Roberts (1904), p. 280.

Lady missionaries, skilled in medicine or nursing, are a blessing to the jealously guarded women of heathen and Mohammedan lands.'[57] I advocate the view that not only were many inmates of this Ayahs' Home of mixed racial descent, but that some of the women missionaries from the Zenana Missions who administered to the needs of 'Orientals' in such philanthropic places were also of similar mixed racial backgrounds. As we have no records of how many of the female migrant work force who arrived on Britain's shores as *ayah*s ever left it at all, there is a distinct possibility that scores might have had been absorbed into the fabric of British society – some even as missionaries themselves. Eurasians were 100 per cent practising Christians by religious affiliation. Christians, through the ages, have perceived the church as a means of finding permanent foothold in foreign lands. In Britain, Christian Eurasians would have expected and received similar succor from the Anglican church and, after benefiting from its assistance, might well have assimilated into the church as ministering do-gooders themselves. This avenue would have provided permanent entry and assimilation into British society and an alternative to marrying a British man and making England a permanent home. Although no documentary evidence exists to confirm this, it is very possible that scores might have become assimilated into British mainstream society through opportunity afforded to them by taking on philanthropic work themselves in churches or in missionary-run sheltered homes for the destitute (such as the Ayahs' Homes). Roberts also writes:

> The foreigner within our gates is an object of as much solicitude as our own people.... At Hackney the City Mission has its Ayah's Home – a great boon to the Indian women who come and go between here and India as nurses or attendants on ladies and their children. In connection with St. Andrew's Waterside Mission there is a mission to Lascars, carried on by native Indian ministers at Victoria Docks.[58]

## Eurasians as Ecclesiastical Ministers

I would argue that a number of the 'native Indian ministers', to whom Roberts referred, who administered to the *lascar*s at the London Docks were, in fact, of mixed racial descent. For just as Visram described Kitty Johnson, who was of mixed racial descent, as an 'Indian' maid, so too Roberts might have included Eurasians when he referred to 'native Indian ministers'. It is impossible, once again, to try to identify Eurasians who arrived in Britain as ministers or clergymen with a philanthropic mission (or indeed those who became ministers after arriving

---

[57]  Roberts (1904), p. 281.
[58]  Roberts (1904), p. 281.

in Britain and partaking of Christian philanthropy) or Eurasian women in Britain who entered missionary service in such institutions. Their European names (derived through their paternity) make such categorisation impossible.

There is evidence that Eurasians – both male and female – were to be found among Britain's domestic labour forces in the Victorian Age in large enough numbers for them to have made a public impression. It would seem that as members of the working-class domestic labour force in Britain, Eurasians had a mixed reputation. Both Eliza Fay and J. Howard Bowen referred to insolence, on board the ship to England, of Eurasians they had hired. Their perception of insolence in their servants had led to a desire on their part to dispense with the services of such employees. If one goes by these accounts, Eurasians hired as domestic migrant labourers were neither docile nor subservient. They contested authority and asserted their individuality and agency. Their tendency to stand up for themselves – a trait that might have been perceived by their white employers, who sought and expected complete obedience and servility from their 'native' servants – might well have been interpreted as a form of defiance or resentment of authority. While we have letters from such employers complaining about the insolence of such Eurasian servants on the one hand, the community as a whole seems to have been held in high regard as domestic employees by contemporary Britons, on the other. In fact, so well were they regarded as domestic servants that some enterprising Britons actually came up with schemes to bring Eurasians into England as members of a major domestic labour force. Like Caucasian Victorian governesses, they occupied an in-between position: they were not perceived to be in a social class as 'low' as 'coolies'; nor would they have had been as highly organised a labour force as indentured servants. However, they were uniformly regarded as a valuable segment of the colonised manpower market whose possibilities for domestic employment in the metropole had not yet been fully exploited.

## A Scheme to Bring Eurasian Domestic Labourers to Britain

By the end of the nineteenth century, however, British colonials began to see the potential of this demographic segment. In 1898, one Jane Warr of Hindhead, Graysholt, Surrey, addressed a letter to the undersecretary of state for India, proposing a scheme to 'bring over Indian women between the ages of 13 and 40 or 45 for service as domestic servants in Britain'.[59] Warr's plans were motivated by the presence in her home of her 'Indian manservant, a "half-caste" whose father was in

---

[59]  Letter from Mrs. Jane Warr to the India Office, London, dated 10 May 1898, IOR L/P&J/6/480, No. 993.

the siege of Lucknow and a prisoner'.[60] So impressed was Warr by her manservant of mixed racial descent that she tried to enlist the help of the India Office, London, in her plans to bring more individuals of his kind – females, in fact – to Britain. She proposed that the India Office should send her 'as an experiment' and 'free of cost' two or three young women who would be willing to be trained in domestic service. Her goal was to coach them well and find them placement in English upper-class homes. Warr appeared quite certain of the future of her scheme for, she stated, that if it proved to be a success, she would 'bring them over by the score and by the hundred before three month[s] elapse'.[61]

What is especially relevant to my inquiry into the presence of Eurasian domestic labourers in Britain in the nineteenth century is the fact that Warr specifies the exact locations from which she would like the women for this experiment to hail. She writes that 'women from the neighborhood of Lucknow, Cawnpore [present-day Kanpur] and Calcutta [present-day Kolkata] are preferred'.[62] Now, as was common knowledge in Britain at the time, these parts of India, comprising large colonial military barracks, were well populated by Eurasians – progeny of British colonial forces and native Indian women – who happened to be fluent in English, Westernised by custom and Christian by religion. The 'half-caste' manservant that inspired Warr's experiment was a Christian himself. She writes, 'He has been ... a member ... of the Church of England 8 [sic] years, is an abstainer and is very well informed.'[63]

I would further argue that Warr had Eurasian women in mind when she floated her scheme. Although her visionary scheme was inspired by a 'half-caste manservant', she categorically expressed her preference for 'two or three young women'. Why women and why Eurasian young women, one might well wonder. It was primarily because they were perceived as being Westernised enough to be incorporated into a British household without too many cultural differences. Their fluency in English would have eliminated any difficulties arising from linguistic incomprehension in the fulfilment of their domestic duties.

---

[60] Letter from Mrs. Jane Warr to the India Office, London, dated 10 May 1898, IOR L/P&J/6/480, No. 993.

[61] Letter from Mrs. Jane Warr to the India Office, London, dated 10 May 1898, IOR L/P&J/6/480, No. 993.

[62] Letter from Mrs. Jane Warr to the India Office, London, dated 10 May 1898, IOR L/P&J/6/480, No. 993.

[63] Letter from Mrs. Jane Warr to the India Office, London, dated 10 May 1898, IOR L/P&J/6/480, No. 993.

She did not, however, bargain for the response she received from one Horace G. Walpole,[64] an assistant undersecretary to the secretary of state for India (not to be confused with Horace Walpole [1717–1797], son of British prime minister Robert Walpole). He responded by stating that Warr's scheme seemed 'impractical, and is certainly not one which the secretary of state for India could support officially'.[65] Furthermore, Walpole had written to Warr stating, 'You do not seem to be aware that native women of the parts mentioned would be absolutely ignorant of the English language.'[66] In this regard, it was Walpole who was unaware of the linguistic fluency of potential Eurasian domestics for if it was Eurasian women who applied and were selected for this mission specifically from the areas that Warr preferred, undoubtedly, English would have been their first language, as they would have had received the rare benefit, at least in India, of an elementary education in English. Probably because he had no immediate knowledge of mixed-race culture in nineteenth-century India, or because he was based in the India Office in London and had no real acquaintance with the use of the English language in India in that era, Walpole was ignorant of the fluency in English of people of mixed racial descent. In actual fact, they were prized by European colonials as interpreters simply because their multilingual skills (in English and vernacular Indian languages) were highly desirable.[67]

Not discouraged by Walpole's response, Warr wrote a second letter, dated 16 May 1898, in which she stated that her young fellow[68] 'speaks *good* English – no grammatical errors – he aspirates his h's also – and uses choice and suitable words in expressing himself. However rapidly I speak he follows without difficulty'.[69] She concluded her letter by insisting that if sent 'women or girls [who] have anything like the common sense he has [they would] get along splendidly and

---

[64]   The name of Horace G. Walpole appears as assistant undersecretary of state in the Office of Secretary of State for India, St James' Park, London SW, in the *India Office List*, dated 1893.

[65]   Walpole responded to Warr's letter of 10 May 1898 with his own letter from the India Office, London, dated 13 May 1898. IOR L/P&J/6/480, No. 993.

[66]   IOR L/P&J/6/480, No. 993.

[67]   Dalrymple (2002).

[68]   When writing about 'my young fellow' in her letter dated 16 May 1898, Warr was referring to her 'half-caste' manservant – the one with whom she was so impressed that she hoped to bring more such people to Britain to train and to place them as domestic servants in middle-class British households. See IOR L/P&J/6/480, No. 993.

[69]   Letter from Mrs. Jane Warr to the India Office, dated 16 May 1898, IOR L/P&J/6/480, No. 993 (emphasis original).

adapt to any varying circumstances or humor (or caprice)'.[70] It is pertinent, of course, to question why Warr used a manservant as a model to further her appeal for official support of her scheme and yet keeps referring to 'young women and girls' as the intended target of her plan. It is possible, in analysing the gender implications of this dichotomy, to presume that she perceived women as being more malleable, less prone to rebellion or defiance of authority and perhaps even more appealing to British working-class men as possible marital partners, thus facilitating permanent assimilation into British society and forming a viable source of ceaseless employment opportunity. If fiction were any indication of common practice at the time, Craik's character Zillah Le Poer in *The Half-Caste* marries Andrew Sutherland, a frequent visitor to the household she serves. The marriage carries her up the class ladder, rescues and distances her from an endless fate as domestic labourer and provides assimilation into mainstream British society that offered permanent domicile in Britain.[71] At the end of her second letter, Warr does state, 'It would be quite immaterial as to what part of India the girls or women came from – as long as they were willing to be *trained*.'[72]

There is no further correspondence on this subject between Warr and Walpole (or any other member of the India Office). The rather ambitious scheme was probably dropped by either Warr or by the India Office who probably saw no future in it or no further need to be involved in the matter. If indeed Warr pursued it independently and without official assistance, no documentary evidence has been found. The failure of this one scheme to bring Eurasian women to Britain to be trained and placed as domestic servants does not negate the fact that those who already found themselves in London (brought to British shores by their colonial employers) might have remained domiciled in Britain as domestic servants in upper-crust London households. They would have served as cooks, kitchen maids, parlourmaids or nursery maids or amidst mainstream white British domestic servants.

The reluctance of the India Office in London to get involved with schemes to bring Indian female domestic labourers to Britain notwithstanding, available documented pictorial evidence proves that women of mixed racial descent arrived in England prior to India's independence and spent varying periods of time in London before either returning to India with British employers or staying on in England. It is the ones who travelled regularly between India and Britain who qualify as

---

[70] Letter from Mrs. Jane Warr to the India Office, dated 16 May 1898, IOR L/P&J/6/480, No. 993.

[71] Craik (2016 [1851]).

[72] Letter from Mrs. Jane Warr to the India Office, dated 16 May 1898, IOR L/P&J/6/480, No. 993 (emphasis original).

migrant labour. According to Marshall's article, these back-and-forth voyages were undertaken repeatedly. In referring to one of the *ayah*s he met while carrying out research for his article, Anthony Pareira, Marshall writes, 'No fewer than fifty-four times had this nurse of the turbulent oceans made the journey betwixt India and Great Britain and once to Holland.'[73] She bided her time in between voyages at the Ayahs' Home in London.

## Ethnic Branding of *Ayahs* in Contemporary Print Media

It is interesting that *ayah*s depicted in photographs – in their white half-saris, heads demurely covered – became symbolic of the fundraising efforts of the London City Mission. Although, from all available evidence, the work carried out on the *ayahs'* behalf was but a small part of the much larger philanthropic London missions' network in the late nineteenth century, *ayah*s – as a symbol of poor, harmless, abandoned and destitute Orientals in England – became 'branded'. Their images were used commercially, through print advertisements, to solicit contributions to the missions' efforts in general. Under a portrait of an Indian *ayah* is the caption 'An Indian Ayah, a study in black and white. Like many others of her race, she is full of gratitude for the service of the Mission.'[74] The portrait was used specifically to advertise and sell a brochure entitled 'The World at Our Doors' where such people were described as 'children of other climes'.[75] The copy that accompanies the advertisement boasts that the brochure is fully illustrated. Furthermore, it urges all people who have 'the Evangelization of the World-City at heart' to order it (see Figure 12.6).[76]

By virtue of their Westernisation, however, Eurasian *ayah*s would not have been of any value to the London City Mission in their attempts at fundraising. While the exoticism of the Oriental *ayah* was exploited in contemporary brand advertising, her Eurasian sister was further marginalised even within this marginalised group in that her appearance was unlikely to warrant public sympathy or evoke donor impulses. Going by her dress (an outfit, half-skirt and half-sari) of the *ayah* in the advertisement, it is not likely that the woman was a Eurasian. A Eurasian childminder was not likely to wear a sari or appear in as 'Oriental' a guise as this woman did. Hence, although Eurasian women might also have been beneficiaries of missionary largess, their images would hardly have made convincing advertising

---

[73]  Marshall (1922), p. 104.

[74]  *London City Mission Magazine*, vol. 88, no. 1039, October 1923, British Library, London.

[75]  *London City Mission Magazine*, vol. 88, no. 1039, October 1923, British Library, London.

[76]  *London City Mission Magazine*, vol. 88, no. 1039, October 1923, British Library, London.

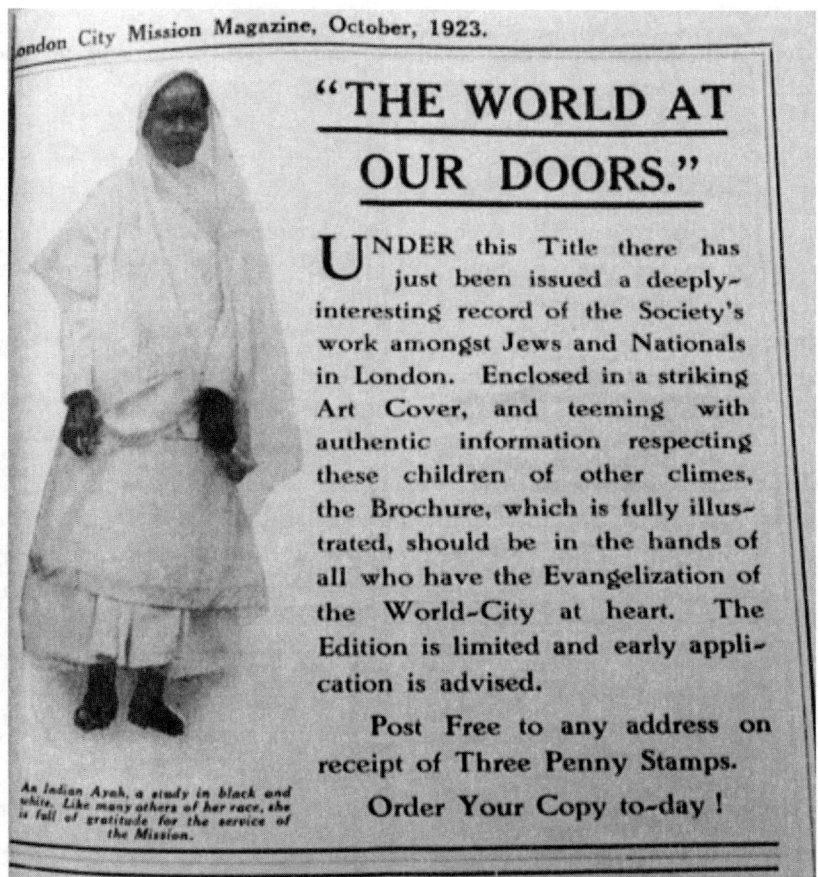

**Figure 12.6** 'The World at Our Doors', an advertisement for a brochure published by the *London City Mission Magazine*, 1923

*Source*: *London City Mission Magazine*, vol. 88, no. 1039, October 1923; British Library, London (public domain).

tools where the attempt was to raise funds for the mission. They would have appeared too pale-skinned, too Westernised in their garb and appearance – in other words, not exotic enough to have evoked an interest in the magazine's readers or to have motivated them to contribute to the missionary cause. In using a swarthy-skinned woman in this print advertisement to champion the cause of Indian *ayah*s and in soliciting funds for their welfare in particular and for the work of the mission in general, ethnic branding was in evidence. London philanthropists kept Eurasian women out of the visuals in print advertising because they were not exotic, foreign or Oriental enough to attract the funds they hoped to raise.

## Conclusion

Where female domestic helpers in Victorian and Edwardian England were not Eurasian, these temporary caregivers never shed their subcontinental identity during the periods of their stay in Britain, sticking to their Oriental garb, manners and habits in spite of the best efforts of Christian proselytizers. In fact, they incorporated their individual national customs and language into the mainstream whole and brought a maternal element into their dealings with their charges. If they were Eurasians, their paternal European bloodlines did not provide them with any privileges in Britain; nor (probably going by the experiences of their community in India) did they feel entitled to expect them. Although their images were not used to solicit funds, going strictly by printed textual and pictorial evidence to be found in contemporary popular print media, it would be fair to say that people of mixed racial descent from the Indian subcontinent lived, worked and made a valid contribution to social life in Britain long before the British Nationality Act of 1948 made their existence ubiquitous. Concentrated mainly in the city of London, they were a fascinating group, as they cohabited with their counterparts from varied Asian cities. Certainly, as migrant labourers and as part of the domestic work force, they were a compelling enough presence in late Victorian and early Edwardian British society to have solicited both evangelical and journalistic interest. Although not recognised as such, they were an intrepid and enterprising segment of the traveling temporary labourers who plied between England and her Eastern colonies, not only making a living through honest means but also adding a rich thread to the pluralistic social fabric of Britain. As independent wage earners, they exhibited a brand of Victorian feminism that was still in a nascent stage even among their white British female counterparts who were also negotiating their place in a society that had become rapidly industrialised. Their influence was strong enough for them to remain in demand until independence in 1947 ended the seafaring back-and-forth sojourns of their employers and the need for them to function as temporary mothers.

## Bibliography

Almeida, Rochelle. 2017. *Britain's Anglo-Indians: The Invisibility of Assimilation.* Lanham, MD: Lexington Books.

Chatterjee, Indrani. 2002. *Gender, Slavery and Law in Colonial India.* Delhi: Oxford University Press.

Chatterjee, Indrani, and Richard M. Eaton. 2006. *Slavery and South Asian History.* Bloomington, IN: Indiana University Press.

Craik, Dinah Mulock. 2016 (1851). *The Half-Caste*, edited by Melissa Edmundson. Peterborough, Ontario and Canada: Broadview Press.

Dalrymple, William. 2002. *White Moghuls: Love and Betrayal in Eighteenth-Century India*. London: HarperCollins Publishers.

Datta, Arunima. 2021. 'Responses to Traveling Indian Ayahs in Nineteenth and Early Twentieth Century Britain'. *Journal of Historical Geography* 71: 94–103.

Edmundson, Melissa. 2016. 'Introduction'. In *The Half-Caste* by Dinah Mulock Craik. Peterborough, Ontario and Canada: Broadview Press.

Forster, E. M. (ed.) 1925. *Original Letters from India 1779–1815*. London: Hogarth Press.

Ghosh, Amitav. 2008. *Sea of Poppies*. New York; Farrah, Straus and Giroux.

———. 2011. *River of Smoke*. London: Hodder & Stoughton.

———. 2015. *Flood of Fire*. New York: Farrah, Straus & Giroux.

Hawes, Christopher. 1996. *Poor Relations: The Making of a Eurasian Community in British India, 1773–1833*. London: Curzon Press.

Holden, Katherine. 2013. *Nanny Knows Best: The History of the British Nanny*. Cheltenham, Gloucestershire: The History Press.

Lahiri, Shompa. 1999. *Indians in Britain: Anglo-Indian Encounters, Race and Identity 1880–1930*. London: Routledge.

*London City Mission Magazine*. 1900. *Sixty-Fifth Annual Report on Ayahs' Home*. 2 July.

Marshall, A. C. 1922. 'Human Birds of Passage'. *London City Mission Magazine* 87, pp. 104–106.

Roberts, Alec. 1904. 'Missionary London'. In *Living London*, vol. 3, edited by George R. Sims, pp. 279–285. London: Cassell.

Visram, Rozina. 1986. *Ayahs, Lascars and Princes: The Story of Indians in Britain, 1700–1947*. New York: Routledge.

———. 2002. *Asians in Britain: 400 Years of History*. London: Pluto Press.

# Part IV

# Legacies

# 13

## After the Long March

### Colonial-Era 'Relief' for Burma Indian Evacuees in Visakhapatnam District, 1942–1948

*Emma C. Meyer*

For diasporic Indian communities living in Burma (present-day Myanmar), the Second World War was a period of massive upheaval. As the Japanese military bombed the colonial capital of Rangoon (present-day Yangon) in December 1941 and conquered large swaths of Burma by the spring of 1942, many Burma Indians fled across the Bay of Bengal by steamship, aircraft or on foot.[1] They, along with much smaller numbers of Anglo-Indians, Anglo-Burmese and Europeans, reached British India's borders, numbering approximately 500,000 in total.[2] Upon their arrival in India, these displaced people became the subject of large-scale relief projects developed by the government, which included limited efforts to employ 'skilled' workers, labour projects to absorb 'unskilled' evacuees and the issuance of repayable loans. The final stage of colonial relief for the Burma evacuees came after 1945, when the government cobbled together a repatriation programme to assist those who wished to return to Burma after the war. By providing an overview of these policies, this chapter will track the colonial administration's changing responses to Burma Indian populations as they went from 'migrants' to 'evacuees' to 'repatriates' during the 1940s. Drawing on historical evidence from Visakhapatnam district,[3] which received the largest number of Burma Indian evacuees of any district in India during

---

[1] I use the term 'Burma Indians' as shorthand to refer to Indian migrant populations or people of Indian descent born in Burma who had economic, social or political ties there.

[2] The total number who attempted to reach India probably was closer to 600,000, and an estimated 80,000 died along the way. See Bayly and Harper (2004), p. 167.

[3] The 'Visakhapatnam' referred to throughout this chapter is the undivided district that included the present-day districts of Visakhapatnam, Srikakulam and Vizianagaram. I have chosen to use the current spelling instead of the colonial-era 'Vizagapatam' to avoid confusion.

the war, the chapter also provides a brief discussion of evacuees' responses to government-run aid programmes.[4]

In recent years, scholars have begun to reappraise the impact of the Second World War on South Asia.[5] One of the outcomes of this new research has been to see the war years not only as the lead-up to national independence, but also as a period that caused massive disruption and social and political change throughout Asia.[6] Within this broader literature, a growing number of authors are now examining the effects that the war had on migratory and diasporic Asian communities. Scholarship from the 1970s onward on Indian communities in Burma, for instance, has presented the regional onset of war and the evacuation of Burma as the start of a precipitous decline for people of Indian descent. For instance, Nalini Ranjan Chakravarti, a Burma Indian Civil Service (ICS) member, wrote of the period from 1942 onwards as 'the end of Indian interests in Burma'.[7] More recent works, however, have argued that while the war ushered in a period of decline for mobile communities, many migrants sought the re-establishment of patterns of movement and social and economic connections between India and Burma after hostilities concluded.[8] Though newer works have discussed the evacuation of Burma and have included first-hand accounts from survivors, scholarship to date has tended to set the evacuation within parentheses, marking it as a dead-end within broader narratives of the war and histories of twentieth-century forced migrations and resettlement in the Bay of Bengal.[9] Perhaps the clearest evidence of this tendency is that only a few fleeting references exist regarding what happened to the Burma Indian evacuees once they reached India's borders.[10] This lack of coverage of the events *following* the long march, after the high drama of the evacuation, overlooks an important chapter within the historical unfolding of colonial administrative policy towards displaced populations in South Asia.

---

[4]  Histories of Burma Indian evacuees and their experiences in India during the war years are covered in more detail in Meyer (2020).

[5]  Basu, Bhattacharya and Keys (1999); Khan (2015); Bayly and Harper (2007); Amrith (2013a).

[6]  Prakash, Menon and Laffan (2018), p. 2; Bayly and Harper (2007), p. 7.

[7]  Chakravarti (1971), p. 169. See also Adas (2011), p. 208.

[8]  See Amrith (2011) and Amrith (2013a).

[9]  Scholars and authors such as Sunil S. Amrith, Parthasarathi Bhaumik, Amitav Ghosh, Jerry Pinto, Yvonne Vaz Ezdani, Bhisetty Lakshman Rao and Mira Kamdar have sought out first-hand accounts as well as fictional representations of the exodus.

[10]  For example, Amrith (2013a), p. 205. See also Khan (2015), pp. 103–106; and Leigh (2018), p. 136.

## Pre-War Indian Migrations to Burma

From the late nineteenth century into the early decades of the twentieth century, the demands of British-ruled Burma's colonial economy, the development of labour recruitment networks and the lure of jobs and higher wages in Burma helped create booming migration patterns across the Bay of Bengal. British forces annexed regions of Burma to British India during the mid-nineteenth century, establishing Burma as a province of colonial India by 1886. To boost their agricultural and industrial pursuits in Burma, colonial officials sought to provide the province with labourers from mainland India. The government of India instituted labour recruitment offices to enlist Indian workers and bring them to Burma under contract, but these efforts met with limited success.[11] Instead, the colonial government resorted to boosting labour migration to Burma through other means, including starting weekly and fortnightly steamship services that would ply southern India's Coromandel Coast.[12] The colonial administration also introduced subsidies and incentives for shipping companies to lower the cost of passage and increase the number of passengers.[13] These policies, coupled with the fact that Burma offered migrants from India comparatively higher wages and more opportunities for employment, facilitated the formation of large-scale patterns of movement, with 12–15 million migrants traveling from India to Burma between 1846 and 1940.[14]

Migrants from India filled a wide range of social and economic roles in Burma in the half-century prior to the Second World War. Perhaps most notable was the labour power they provided in Burma's rice fields, mines, industries and transportation sectors. These labour migrants' patterns of movement were predominantly circular, as most came to Burma as seasonal agricultural labour or settled in Burma for a few years to earn money before returning to India.[15] Men dominated the ranks of working migrants, greatly outnumbering women and children.[16] By the twentieth century, many contemporary observers remarked that colonial Burma had become completely reliant upon Indian workers.

---

[11] Jaiswal (2014), pp. 911–912.

[12] Satyanarayana (2002), p. 93; Andrew (1933), pp. 46–47.

[13] Jaiswal (2014), p. 912.

[14] McKeown (2004), pp. 157–158; Amrith (2013b), p. 133.

[15] Baxter (1941), p. 12.

[16] During the 1920s, women and children composed 8.97 per cent of passengers arriving onboard steamships from the Coromandel Coast in 1921, which was the highest percentage reached during that decade. Their lowest percentage was 6.76 per cent of all passengers in 1925 (A. N. Rao 1933, p. 155).

In 1933, E. J. L. Andrew, a former immigration official at Rangoon, wrote, 'For its industry, its transport and its trade, more especially for the large disciplined industries connected with transport and those located in its cities and towns, Burma is dependent on alien Indian labour.'[17]

The heart of this immigrant workforce came from districts along India's eastern coast, including Ganjam, Visakhapatnam, East and West Godavari and Krishna.[18] Telugu-speakers made up 25 per cent of the total population of Indians in Burma by the 1920s.[19] Especially in Rangoon, Telugus composed a central portion of the city's labour corps as they operated mills and factories, laboured on the docks and worked in the streets as sanitation workers and rickshaw pullers.[20]

Labourers who could save money from their earnings often sent back remittances to family members remaining in India, which formed an important part of many Coastal Andhra household economies prior to the Second World War.[21] Though coming to Burma could be lucrative for some, the colony also held pitfalls for workers. The demand for labour in Burma varied considerably according to season and left many Indians unemployed or underemployed during slack periods. The uncertainty of their work status from one season to the next kept Indian labourers in Burma insecure and disorganised.[22] Systems of labour recruitment could also make workers more vulnerable. The *maistry* system was the most common type of labour recruitment among Telugu speakers. In Telugu, *maistry* referred to the headman or jobber who recruited other individuals and acted as the middleman between employers and workers. These labour recruiters were not 'outsiders' but were often linked through caste or kin relationships to the men and women whom they were recruiting.[23] They also controlled the disbursement of wages and had the power to dismiss workers at will. This arrangement often led to working emigrants being indebted to and dependent upon their *maistry*. Even though they were not bound by a formal contract, workers recruited under this system could easily fall into a perpetual state of indebtedness.[24]

---

[17]  Andrew (1933), p. 11.

[18]  Satyanarayana (2002), p. 95.

[19]  A. N. Rao (1933), p. 50.

[20]  Amrith (2013a), p. 150.

[21]  Andhra Pradesh State Archives and Research Institute (APSARI), Public Works Department, File No. PWD GO 2806, 21–12–1943, Letter from C. H. Masterman to the Secretary to the Board of Revenue, Madras, 5 July 1942.

[22]  A. N. Rao (1933), p. 168.

[23]  Satyanarayana (2002), pp. 100–101.

[24]  A. N. Rao (1933), p. 18.

As the prominent Telugu-speaking Burma Indian labour leader, economist and politician Avatapalli Narayana Rao wrote in the early 1930s, 'So, if the working man migrates to Burma by borrowing at rack interest, he requires public subscription for his funeral, in case of his death here.'[25]

Despite these potential downsides to migration, the flow of Indian labour to Burma remained strong well into the 1930s, when a series of economic and political changes threatened to disrupt existing patterns of movement. During the Great Depression, hostility towards immigrant communities surged in Burma while economic opportunities evaporated as part of a global economic slump.[26] Anti-immigrant riots rocked Rangoon during the months of May and June 1930 and again from July to September 1938, causing deaths, injuries and property damage for Burma Indian communities.[27] The uncertainty of the times led to slackening rates of emigration from India to Burma. More broadly, for the first time in six decades, long-standing patterns of migration throughout Southeast Asia reversed during the 1930s as more Indians departed Southeast Asia than arrived there.[28]

Further complicating matters, the administrative reorganisation of Burma (which had been a province of British India since 1886) under the 1935 Government of India Act resulted in the creation of a new crown colony of Burma.[29] Restricting labour immigration to Burma had been a recurring theme in discussions on the administrative separation of India and Burma, and once the division became effective in 1937, Burma's new government sought to limit unchecked labour migration from India. These efforts culminated in the 1941 Indo-Burma Immigration Agreement between the governments of India and Burma, which instituted a battery of permit requirements, fees and (in some cases) literacy tests for those seeking legal entry into the colony.[30] Although the two colonial governments did not fully enforce the contents of their agreement prior to the war, they wasted no time in carrying out what was arguably the central tenet of the deal – to exert control over the immigration of 'unskilled'

---

[25] A. N. Rao (1933), p. 5.

[26] Amrith (2013a), pp. 184–185. See also Brown (2005).

[27] Adas (2011), pp. 204–208.

[28] Manikumar (2003), p. 169–171; Amrith (2011), p. 239. See also Adas (2011), p. 208.

[29] The Government of India Act and the Government of Burma Act of 1935 went into effect in 1937, separating the province of Burma from India and establishing it as a colony.

[30] The text of the Indo-Burma Immigration Agreement is printed in Baxter (1941).

Indian labourers to Burma.[31] While the agreement was supposed to take effect on 1 October 1941, 'unskilled' immigration to Burma was completely stopped during the 'transition period' starting on 21 July of that same year. After that date, all individuals intending to leave British India by sea for Burma to conduct manual labour there were prohibited 'unless by general or special order of the Central Government'.[32]

The Indo-Burma Immigration Agreement struck a blow to Indian interests in Burma and was thoroughly unpopular in India. Perhaps the most vehement critiques of the immigration agreement emerged from the Madras Presidency, as many Indian communities there had close ties to Burma. On 28 July 1941, the month in which the agreement was announced, a public meeting was held in Gokhale Hall, Madras (present-day Chennai), to express 'feelings of disappointment and dissatisfaction at the recent Indo-Burma Immigration Agreement'. Attendees, who packed the hall to capacity, demanded that the agreement be reconsidered.[33] The immigration pact was disliked outside Madras as well, and numerous individuals and organisations spoke out against it. In August 1941, the *Bombay Chronicle* published a statement by the Indian National Congress leader, Mohandas K. Gandhi, voicing his disapproval and calling the new arrangement 'unhappy' and 'panicky and penal'.[34]

Indian opposition to the Indo-Burma Immigration Agreement forced the colonial Indian government to re-evaluate its stance on the matter. Eventually, the government of Burma agreed to work with their Indian counterparts to modify the pact's harsher restrictions.[35] As the two administrations returned to the drawing board, however, the advance of Japanese military forces into Southeast Asia and the bombing of Rangoon in December 1941 shook the region and temporarily ended debates over immigration. As A. V. Pai, an ICS member in the Department of Indians Overseas, remarked in April 1942, 'It is true that immigration to Burma

---

[31]    In the 1941 report, the agent to the government of India in Burma wrote that 'the most vital item in the Agreement was the immediate stoppage of the immigration of unskilled labour'. See British Library (BL), India Office Records (IOR), File No. IOR L-PJ-8-212, Annual Report of the Agent to the Government of India in Burma for the Period January 1st to December 31st 1941, 10 October 1942.

[32]    National Archives of India (NAI), Department of Indians Overseas (Overseas Section), File No. F.70-12/42-O.S., File Note by Sundram, 8 April 1942.

[33]    BL, IOR, File No. IOR L-J-8-213, Indo-Burma Immigration Agreement All Party Protest, 1941.

[34]    This statement was published in the 25 August 1941 edition of the *Bombay Chronicle*. See Gandhi (2000–2001), pp. 14–18.

[35]    Mohan (1955), p. 168.

at present is of no practical importance whatever.'[36] Though the Indo-Burma Immigration Agreement was a dead letter by the time of the arrival of hostilities, the governments of India and Burma would resurrect it in the post-war period.

## War, Evacuation and Resettlement

The arrival of the Second World War in Burma and other parts of Southeast Asia pre-empted further debate over immigration policy and spurred the exodus of people of Indian descent from Burma to the relative safety of India. After Japanese imperial forces bombed Rangoon in December 1941, civilian populations in the city and surrounding areas began to leave in large numbers. As these events were occurring in Rangoon, the Japanese military continued its advance on other parts of the colony, setting off new chains of forced migration as it went. News spread of the evacuation of Rangoon, coupled with the fall of Moulmein (another port city in lower Burma), and this precipitated further movement of civilian populations out of Burma. As Hugh Tinker writes, the sight of thousands of evacuees surging northward in advance of the Japanese probably also affected residents of upper Burma, triggering further mass movements out of the colony.[37]

Accounts of the evacuation of Burma revealed its brutality. Facing harsh terrain, lacking basic supplies such as food and clean water and suffering from diseases such as cholera and malaria, an unknown number of people died during the trek, though estimates of the deceased have ranged from 10,000 to as high as 100,000.[38] Of those who survived the evacuation, approximately 500,000 people sought refuge in the neighbouring colony of British India, many of whom arrived after passing through the jungles of north-west Burma on foot.[39] Many of the evacuees from Burma arrived in India completely destitute and in need of extensive assistance.

Efforts to rehabilitate the evacuees from Burma were some of the first refugee resettlement programmes developed in India, predating the policies put in place to deal with partition-era forced migrations after 1947. Between 1942 and February 1948, the Indian government organised relief efforts to meet the influx of wartime evacuees from Burma. During the early months of 1942, the colonial

---

[36] NAI, Department of Indians Overseas (Overseas Section), File No. F.70-12/42-O.S., File Note by A.V. Pai, 2 April 1942.

[37] Tinker (1975), pp. 4–6.

[38] Tinker (1975), pp. 2–4. Christopher Bayly and Tim Harper estimate 80,000 died. See Bayly and Harper (2004), p. 167.

[39] Tinker (1975), pp. 2–4.

administration initially believed that the evacuees arriving in India did not need any special assistance beyond what it termed 'reception, feeding and despatch'. These efforts provided transportation and triage, getting the evacuees to their destinations via steamships and special evacuee trains and providing them with food, medicine and medical care for those who had been injured or fallen ill during the evacuation.[40] Much of the work of 'reception' was carried out by volunteers from Indian humanitarian organisations who also raised considerable funds through public donations. In Visakhapatnam district, the Visakhapatnam Prema Samajam met incoming evacuees at the train stations at Waltair and Vizianagaram, and M. Nagabushanam Naidu, then honorary secretary of the organisation, estimated that thousands of evacuees arrived daily in Visakhapatnam in the early months of 1942. According to records taken by Prema Samajam workers, the organisation fed 150,000 evacuees between January and April 1942 in Visakhapatnam and another 43,325 evacuees at Vizianagaram between April and July.[41]

Visakhapatnam district received more evacuees than any other in colonial India as Burma Indians who had been born there returned to Visakhapatnam during the war, and many who had been born in Burma fled to the natal villages of their parents or grandparents. More than 68,400 evacuees settled in the district.[42] In addition, as evacuees were separated from their employment and properties in Burma, they could no longer support family members who had been dependent on their income. In Visakhapatnam district alone, there were an estimated 36,900 of these so-called dependents. Altogether, district officials estimated that 105,348 men, women and children could be counted among the evacuees and their dependents in Visakhapatnam district.[43] The sudden return of so many labourers made jobs scarce, and the war placed enormous pressure on civilian populations

---

[40]  Tamil Nadu Archives (TNA), Public Works Department, File No. PWD GO 209, 1-2-1943, which details amounts spent in individual districts of the Madras Presidency on 'reception, feeding and despatch' for the month of September 1942.

[41]  The Visakhapatnam Prema Samajam was formed in 1930 with the 'main object of serving the poor, the needy and the distressed, without distinction of caste or creed'. See TNA, Public Works Department, File No. PWD GO 1762, 26-8-1943, Letter from M. Nagabushanam Naidu, Honorary Secretary of Vizag Prema Samajam, to D. D. Warren, Secretary to the Government of Madras, Public Works Department, 31 August 1942. See also the Prema Samajam's pamphlet 'Visakhapatnam: Diamond Jubilee Souvenir', n.d., p. 4.

[42]  TNA, Public Works Department, File No. PWD Letter 1178, 22-4-1944, Letter from H. H. Carleston, District Collector, Visakhapatnam, to the Secretary to the Board of Revenue, Madras, 16 March 1944.

[43]  TNA, Public Works Department, File No. PWD Letter 1178, 22-4-1944, Resolution of the Board of Revenue, Madras, 17 April 1944.

as the cost of living rose dramatically.[44] By the beginning of May 1942, reports of widespread unemployment and groups of disaffected evacuees joining political demonstrations filtered back from the districts to the provincial government in Madras.[45] In response, the Madras government instituted relief programmes designed to provide employment for evacuees and a limited loan programme for those who were unable to work.

Providing suitable employment to evacuees posed a challenge since they represented a range of occupations, including cooks, electricians, sweepers, merchants, shopkeepers, sellers of vegetables and rice, employees of companies such as the Burmah Oil Company (BOC) as well as tailors, drivers, scavengers, cultivators and students. By far, however, the most common occupation reported by evacuees was manual labour.[46] The government, finding itself with a large labour force on its hands, made some efforts to match 'skilled' workers with jobs similar to those they had performed in Burma. The provincial government would circulate lists from one department to another, including the names, addresses and qualifications of evacuees looking for work. For instance, one Y. Narayadu, resident of Ichchapuram, was around 40 years old and had been 'working in Rangoon Saw Mills getting Re. 1 As. 2 [per day] on average. Wants any job.'[47] These employment opportunities, however, were limited to evacuees meeting certain training or education standards and only open to a small percentage of the displaced populations overall.

For 'unskilled' evacuee labourers, the government ran a series of work camps for road-building, irrigation works and other construction projects. These were designed and implemented according to the guidelines of the Madras Famine Code, 1927. In May 1942, the provincial government ordered Visakhapatnam's district collector to follow the guidelines of the Madras Famine Code and start test works. These were work projects that colonial administrators used to assess the distress levels of workers by offering difficult work and low wages to determine whether the evacuees 'and other unemployed persons are actually in need of

---

[44] Brennan (1988), p. 542.

[45] APSARI, Public Works Department, File No. GO 2806, 21-12-1943, Report from C. H. Masterman to the Board of Revenue, Madras, 5 July 1942.

[46] In a sample of 265 entries of evacuees traveling to Visakhapatnam district, 156 (58 per cent) were listed as coolies, menials, labourers or bearers. See Sharpe (1943), pp. A2–S20.

[47] TNA, Public Works Department, File No. GO 140, 20-1-1943, Letter from J. A. Limaye to the Secretary to the Government of Madras, Public Works Department, 5 July 1942.

work and are willing to work'.[48] The test works would continue until they either 'proved' or 'disproved' the existence of famine in the locality. If needy workers continued to frequent them in large numbers despite the harsh conditions, the government officials would consider 'proof' that the workers were suitably desperate to justify converting the test works into relief works, which were work projects that paid higher wages and were outfitted with more amenities, including kitchens.[49]

In early June 1942, the Visakhapatnam collector, C. H. Masterson, provided a list of works located in the taluks of Ichchapuram, Tekkali and Sompeta, where thousands of evacuees were residing. These included tasks such as 'building up the flood bank of Bahuda River' in Ichchapuram taluk, repairs to the Nalla and Bhagiradhi tanks, mending the road between Kaviti and Rajapuram and laying out a new road between Kaviti and Manikyapuram.[50] Over the next several years, these initial test works were converted into famine camps and new camps were founded throughout the district. By the end of May 1943, test works had been started in several places and had been converted to 'relief works under the Famine Code' in Venkatapuram, Paravada, Mantripalem, Ampuram and Kaviti. Together, these five famine camps employed approximately 20,000 workers on a regular basis, while test works stationed throughout the district would have engaged thousands more.[51] By April 1944, the number of famine camps operating throughout the district had further increased (Table 13.1).

The few accounts of 'relief' offered at the test and famine camps agreed that conditions were gruelling. In July 1942, N. G. Ranga, an Indian politician from Guntur district who worked as a proponent of the Burma evacuees, lodged a complaint with the Madras government regarding the inadequacy of aid offered at test works:

---

[48] APSARI, Public Works Department, File No. PWD GO 2806, 21-12-1943, Memorandum from Revenue Department, Government of Madras, to the Collector of Visakhapatnam District, 2 May 1942.

[49] The famine protocol applied to the Burma evacuees was iterated in the 1927 Madras Famine Code. Between its inception and the arrival of the evacuees in 1942, this version of the Code was updated and corrected through a series of government orders in 1936, 1937, 1938 and 1943. See *Famine Code, Madras Presidency* (1927).

[50] APSARI, Public Works Department, File No. GO 2806, 21-12-1943, Letter from C. H. Masterman to Secretary to the Board of Revenue, Madras, 9 June 1942.

[51] APSARI, Public Works Department, File No. PWD GO 2806, 21-12-1943, Letter from District Superintendent of Police, Visakhapatnam, to the Inspector General of Police, Madras, 31 May 1943.

As the work is too arduous i.e., stone-breaking in red hot sun or in rainy weather and the wage is not at all enough owing to higher prices of food etc., and scarcity of drinking water, many of the Evacuees are obliged to abandon the Relief works and go back to their villages there to beg or starve or anyhow live a less troubled life.[52]

Despite such criticisms, work camps designed under the Madras Famine Code continued to be the central means of 'relief' offered to Burma Indian evacuees during the war years.

The second major wing of aid offered to evacuees in Visakhapatnam during the war consisted of loans classified as 'gratuitous relief' under colonial famine policy.[53] Beginning in mid-1942, the government of India began issuing loans to

**Table 13.1**  Evacuees and dependents employed at famine camps in Visakhapatnam district, April 1944

| Name of charge | Number of evacuees | Number of dependents |
| --- | --- | --- |
| Khojiria (Ichchapuram taluk) | 3,890 | 444 |
| Ichchapuram (Ichchapuram taluk) | 2,441 | 462 |
| Korlam (Sompeta taluk) | 2,430 | 596 |
| Palasa (Tekkali taluk) | 1,230 | — |
| Mantripalem (Anakapalli taluk) | 3,727 | 1,012 |
| Venkatapuram (Yellamanchili taluk) | 1,749 | 499 |
| Paravada (Anakapalli taluk) | 4,658 | 1,382 |
| Kaligotla (Chodavaram taluk) | 827 | — |
| [Visakhapatnam] labour camp (Visakhapatnam taluk) | 1,397 | 408 |
| **Total** | 22,349 | 4,803 |

*Source*: Tamil Nadu Archives (TNA), Public Works Department, File No. PWD, Letter 1178, 22-4-1944, Letter from R. Galletti, Board of Revenue, Madras, to J. B. Brown, 17 April 1944.

---

[52]  APSARI, Public Works Department, File No. PWD GO 2806, 21-12-1943, Letter from N. G. Ranga to G. S. Bozman, 6 July 1942.

[53]  For those unable to labour who did not have family or other connections to support them, there were limited options, including local charitable houses that took in homeless or sick evacuees. Since these institutions housed a relatively small percentage of evacuees in the region, they will not be covered in this chapter.

individuals and families who had been left destitute by the war. For households dependent on one earner or remittance, the allowance was not supposed to exceed either 75 per cent of the normal income of the household or 350 rupees per month, whichever was less. District collectors and the protector of emigrants in Madras were authorised to grant allowances up to these limits. *Tahsildars*, or local revenue collecting officials, could grant allowances up to 15 rupees per month, and revenue divisional officers were authorised to give out allowances up to 30 rupees.[54]

Despite these stated guidelines for loan disbursal, government officials' suspicions about evacuees misusing the loan system severely hampered the distribution of funds. The Madras provincial government instructed officers to be careful in distributing loans to make certain that allowances were not given 'to evacuees who have obtained employment or have refused employment offered to them'.[55] In addition, many of the officials involved in the loan-granting scheme refused to grant evacuees the full amount they had been sanctioned, citing fears of creating a 'dole mentality'. In March 1943, E. Ramanathan, an assistant refugee officer of the Southern Zone, toured the districts of East Godavari and Visakhapatnam after receiving reports from evacuees about the 'deplorable conditions prevailing' in these two districts. He found that the district officials 'were not prepared to encourage dole mentality and continue allowance though it was granted by Government of India'. Furthermore, the district officers who did disburse loans would regularly underpay evacuees, giving two to five rupees rather than the 15–30 rupees that they had been instructed to give. When Ramanathan questioned the *tahsildar* officers about this practice, they cited an unwillingness to promote dependence on the dole as well as a belief that 'these people' (that is, the evacuees) could easily survive on five rupees per month. As for the latter claim, Ramanathan doubted that evacuees could live on such a small amount, especially given the prevailing food shortages and inflated prices due to the war. In his report, Ramanathan noted that the practice of withholding loans had the largest impact on the 'labouring classes who are practically under starved conditions, and they have not seen the lighted day of any relief worth mentioning'.[56] No improvements were reported later that year, in November 1943, when C. Krishnaswamy, another

---

[54]  TNA, Public Works Department, File No. PWD GO 44, 6-1-1943, File insert, n.d.

[55]  TNA, Public Works Department, File No. PWD GO Ms. 94, 11-1-1943, File insert by D. D. Warren, Secretary to Government, n.d.

[56]  APSARI, Public Works Department, File No. PWD GO 788, 11-5-1943, Report of the Assistant Refugee Officer, Southern Zone, (Mr. E. Ramanathan) of his tour of Cocanada and Vizagapatam from the 7th to the 13th March 1943.

assistant refugee officer, toured several taluks in southern Visakhapatnam district. In his report to the provincial government, he claimed to have interviewed 5,000 evacuees:

> Most of these evacuees were women, and they had received allowances mostly only once from the time of their arrival into the District till now. Some of them received twice and a very small number received thrice. They were all in very pitiable circumstances, practically clothed in rags, emaciated and hunger-stricken in appearance.[57]

Though the loan programme would expand in subsequent years, it remained a supplementary and irregular source of support for evacuees.[58]

## Evacuee Resistance

The evacuee subjects of colonial 'relief' programmes criticised their design and implementation and called for expansions to government aid. Many evacuees organised associations to publicise their plight and to tend to the needs of their communities. Several evacuee associations formed throughout the Madras Presidency, and in Visakhapatnam district the taluks of Anakapalli, Yellamanchili, Visakhapatnam, and Sompeta all had active associations. These organisations held meetings and put together marches, hunger strikes and other public demonstrations to attempt to improve the poor living and working conditions for their members.

At the worksites that composed the core of the government's 'relief' efforts, evacuees and other relief workers showed their displeasure with arrangements through a series of actions, including walk-offs, migrations from one famine charge to another and small-scale strikes. On the early test works set up in the northernmost reaches of Visakhapatnam district, government officials reported multiple instances of workers arriving onsite and subsequently refusing to work. Labourers on test works in Sompeta were out on strike on 24 June 1942, followed by a separate strike on the next day in Ichchapuram. The next week, the charge officer at Tekkali testified that approximately 300 workers came to the local test works on 30 June 1942 but subsequently left after a dispute over wages. As the district collector, C. H. Masterman, stated about these incidents, 'The coolies

---

[57] TNA, Public Works Department, File No. PWD GO 337, 4-2-1944, Report of Mr. C. Krishnaswamy, Assistant Refugee Officer, 12 November 1943.

[58] TNA, Public Works Department, File No. Letter No. 1178, 22-4-1944, Statement No. II, Maintenance Allowances, 17 April 1944.

attending the works seem to be somewhat unruly and on some days have been on strike on the context that they are not being paid full wages irrespective of the out-turn.'[59]

Although Masterman downplayed these events as isolated disruptions, contemporaneous evacuee conferences and demonstrations also raised the issues of fair wages for displaced workers and conditions in government-run test works, along with a range of other matters related to relief for evacuees. Less than a month after the work-camp strikes, the Andhra Provincial Evacuees' Committee brought together evacuees from across the Telugu-speaking districts of the Madras Presidency for a meeting at Baruva, Visakhapatnam district, on 21 July 1942. Conference attendees named prominent labour leader and former Burma Indian legislator Avatapalli Narayana Rao, who had evacuated from Burma himself, as the head of the committee. Evacuees at the Baruva meeting also chose N. G. Ranga, an Indian politician and proponent of farmers' and labourers' rights, to represent them. The conference leadership, which joined evacuees and politically influential non-evacuee Indians, formed a list of grievances and demands for Burma Indian evacuees settled in the region. A written account of the conference's proceedings, which was submitted to the colonial government, contained the following lines condemning the government's attempts at relief:

> This conference, while appreciating the starting of Relief works in Vizag District, *is constrained to complain against* the heartless and unimaginative application of the inhuman provisions of the Famine Code to these Evacuees and the imposition of the brutal Test Works with their starvation wages etc. and *to demand* that the sooner Government revises its attitude and starts *paying more humane and adequate wages* than are provided for in the Famine Code, the better it will be for the starving Evacuees and also for the good name of the Government.[60]

In addition, evacuees in attendance developed a detailed list of more than 30 requests, including higher wages paid to evacuee labourers employed on government works, adequate quinine stores supplied to local hospitals for the treatment of evacuees

---

[59]  APSARI, R2 Section, Public Works Department, File No. PWD GO 2806, 21-12-1943, Letter from C. H. Masterman to the Secretary to the Board of Revenue, Madras, 24 July 1942.

[60]  According to notes in the file's margins, the italicised parts – originally underlined – had been points stressed by Ranga when he presented the conference proceedings to the government. TNA, Public Works Department, File No. PWD GO 3910, 27-10-1942, Proceedings of the Andhra Provincial Evacuee's Conference, n.d.

with malaria, a moratorium on debts owed by evacuees engaged in agriculture and the founding of orphanages for those who had lost their parents in the war.[61]

By the following year, evacuees honed these wide-ranging demands into a central platform at a second conference, which was held in Razole, East Godavari district, on 25 September 1943. More than 6,000 evacuees attended the event, and attendees produced eight resolutions that they presented to the colonial government. Among their demands, evacuees called for loans or advances to be paid to 'the poorer classes of evacuees' in a timely fashion, an eight-hour work day and a raise of wages on test works, especially given the 'increasing prices of food stuffs and other necessaries of life' in the region. They also asked that shops be opened near the famine camps to provide 'clothes, food stuffs, vegetables and other necessaries of life ... at cost price so that the worker could obtain wholesome and nourishing food'. The final three resolutions reiterated demands made in Baruva the previous year – that previous uncultivated lands be granted to evacuees for agricultural pursuits, that the government establish cottage industries among evacuees in rural areas and that evacuees owing money receive a moratorium on their debts.[62] Conferences such as these two allowed evacuees to come together, communicate their common grievances and propose changes to existing policy. Most notably, the evacuees were not passive subjects of government aid programmes. Their criticisms of government aid's limitations and demands for its expansion show that evacuees were actively involved in the shaping of 'relief' during the late colonial period.

## Post-War Adjustments

Though the Burma evacuees had spent the war years in India, the end of hostilities in 1945 opened a new period of uncertainty for displaced communities throughout South Asia and Southeast Asia. While migration pathways briefly reopened in the post-war period and plans to repatriate half-a-million evacuees to Burma began to take shape by the end of 1945, evacuees soon found that there would be no going back to the Burma they had known. Though they tried to recreate the patterns of movement that had characterised the early twentieth century, circumstances in the post-war era heavily constrained their efforts.

---

[61] TNA, Public Works Department, File No. PWD GO 3910, 27-10-1942, Proceedings of the Andhra Provincial Evacuee's Conference, n.d.

[62] NAI, Department of Indians Overseas (Evacuation Branch), File No. 115-6/43-O.S., Letter from the Andhra Provincial Burma Evacuees' Relief Committee to G. S. Bozman, Secretary to the Government of India, 8 October 1943.

After the Allied forces reclaimed Burma in May 1945, many evacuees hoped to return to Burma to resume employment there, check on homes and properties they had left behind or seek news of family members who had stayed in Burma during the war.[63] Representatives of evacuee associations and officials from the governments of Burma and India repeatedly met to discuss the possibility of the evacuees' return. Related topics of debate included the role that Indian communities would play in Burma's reconstruction, the possibility of 'minority' communities attaining citizenship in independent Burma, the protection of Indian properties and financial interests and the shape of Burma's immigration policies, which included revisiting the Indo-Burma Immigration Agreement from 1941.[64] Though the Indian government maintained its conviction that all evacuees should be allowed to return to Burma, politicians and administrators from both sides of the Bay of Bengal shared concerns about the strain that large-scale repatriations would place on the overburdened transportation network and the weakened Burmese infrastructure.[65] In addition, many Burmese nationalists were unenthusiastic about the prospect of returning to the pre-war status quo, when Indian communities had been both numerous and influential in Burma.[66] Despite multiple rounds of negotiations, little in the way of a lasting agreement emerged.[67]

Without any new guiding policies, dynamics of labour supply and demand shaped post-war migrations. Though the highly unpopular Indo-Burma Immigration Agreement remained in place, including the ban on 'unskilled' labour immigration, the military and civil administrations that took control of the colony between 1945 and 1946 recognised that Burma's post-war reconstruction could not move forward without a substantial influx of immigrant workers. Attempts to reopen Burma's factories and repair its rice industry created a strong

---

[63]  Bayly and Harper (2004), pp. 435–438.

[64]  NAI, Indians Overseas Department (Overseas Section), File No. 5.115-10/43-O.S., Letter from G. S. Bozman to unknown, 3 December 1943.

[65]  NAI, Commonwealth Relations Department, Overseas Section (II), File No. 50-2/44-O.S., Report of the Sub-Committee Appointed to Examine Proposals of the Government of Burma on Indian Immigration into Burma, n.d.

[66]  BL, IOR, File No. IOR L-PJ-8-214, Secret Dispatch from Terence E. Shone to the Office of the High Commissioner for the United Kingdom, 3 July 1947.

[67]  The final round of negotiations before the war's end took place between R. N. Banerjee, secretary to the Government of India, Department of Commonwealth Relations, and U. Tin Tut, a Burmese barrister and ICS officer, on 23–24 May 1945. Their agreement, however, was not ratified. See BL, IOR, File No. IOR L-PJ-8-214, Enclosure, R. N. Banerjee to His Majesty's Under Secretary of State for India, 18 October 1945.

demand for labour.[68] A few thousand Indians had accompanied the Indian army as auxiliary support in 1945. In addition, the Civil Affairs Service Branch (CASB) of Burma's military administration brought in an estimated 200,000 Indian workers, many of whom had lived in Burma prior to the war, to conduct tasks related to reconstruction.[69] In Visakhapatnam district, the local CASB depot recruited nearly 16,000 workers before it shut down in March 1946. These individuals (who included both evacuees and non-evacuees) travelled to Burma to work under firms and organisations such as the port commissioners, the Rangoon municipal corporation and the Bombay Burmah Trading Corporation (BBTCL).[70] By the end of 1945, an official in the Ministry of External Affairs and Commonwealth Relations in New Delhi commented that Indian labourers in Burma were already working 'at docks, on rice fields, in saw mills, in oil refineries, in the Public Works Department, in Railways [and] as rickshaw coolies'.[71]

Aside from the thousands brought in to work, the government of India arranged a separate repatriation programme exclusively for evacuees that began in December 1945. The Indian government required evacuees to register themselves by applying for evacuee identification cards. Each evacuee family was to fill and resubmit a set of forms that would provide the Indian government with information about how many evacuees intended to return and their reasons for doing so. By late 1945, the government of India announced that those who had left behind families in Burma would have top priority, followed by landholders and merchants wanting to look after their possessions.[72]

Despite an extensive planning phase, the repatriation programme never fully launched. The lack of shipping facilities after the war meant that passage to Burma was extremely limited. Furthermore, the news coming out of Burma was not promising. In March 1946, the Indian government publicised 'the fact that the cost of living in Burma was reported to be very high and that there was acute shortage of accommodation and transport'.[73] Burma's ability to support an influx of evacuees was doubtful. From the second half of 1946 onwards, India and

---

[68] Chakravarti (1971), pp. 175–177.

[69] Chakravarti (1971), p. 185.

[70] BL, IOR, File No. IOR M-4-1222, Extract from the Official Report of the Legislative Assembly Debates, 14 February 1946.

[71] Amrith (2013a), p. 215.

[72] 'Return of Burma Refugees: Plans to Repatriate Half a Million', *Times of India*, 26 October 1945, p. 10.

[73] BL, IOR, File No. IOR M/4/1222, Official Report of the Legislative Assembly Debates, n.d.

Burma began to selectively restrict the return of evacuees. There were no official limitations placed on the entry of Indians into Burma, but, as Jawaharlal Nehru (who was then serving as member for commonwealth relations) stated, 'evacuees have been advised that only those of them who own land or house property in Burma or are businessmen who have their own arrangements for accommodation, food, etc., should go at present'.[74] In other words, evacuees who did not require government assistance to travel and who could prove they had some material holdings in Burma could freely pass across the Bay of Bengal.

For evacuees from the 'labouring classes', making the return journey quickly became more complicated as the governments of India and Burma began restricting the return of evacuee labourers by August 1946. Two months later, they announced that 'skilled' evacuee labourers only would be allowed to emigrate if they could produce a contract showing that they had secured a livelihood that would provide a wage and a living allowance.[75] Though a considerable number of evacuees did return to Burma after the war, their numbers were less than half of the full number who had fled to India in 1942.[76] Partial counts of Burma Indian evacuees made in Visakhapatnam district in the early 1950s show that approximately 59 per cent still lived in the district, 2 per cent were deceased and the remaining 39 per cent were 'unable to be traced'. How many of the evacuees in the 'unable to be traced' category went to Burma is unknown.[77]

For evacuees who remained in India, those who had relied on government aid schemes to survive during the war found that continued support was not guaranteed. Though pared-down aid programmes functioned between 1945 and the end of 1947, the government of India gradually reduced its expenditure on relief. Especially after Indian independence in August 1947, the enormous task of resettling millions of partition evacuees stretched thin the Indian government's resources.[78] In a final stroke, all Burma evacuee aid programmes closed at the end of February 1948, a little more than six years after the first evacuees had arrived in India.

---

[74] BL, IOR, File No. IOR M/4/1222, Official Report of the Legislative Assembly Debates, n.d.

[75] Mohan (1955), p. 169; BL, IOR, File No. IOR L-PJ-8-214, Extract from the Official Report of the Legislative Assembly Debates, 29 October 1946.

[76] Amrith (2011), pp. 246–250.

[77] These estimates were generated from approximately 5,000 entries in multiple ledgers in the Visakhapatnam Regional Office of the Andhra Pradesh State Archives. These ledgers were generated by the Revenue Department, Visakhapatnam Collector's Office, between 1951 and 1953.

[78] U. B. Rao (1967).

Although Burma had been an extremely important destination for Indian migrants, the inauguration of the Indo-Burma Immigration Agreement and the arrival of the Second World War in the Bay of Bengal in 1941 disrupted the lives and migration patterns of Burma Indian communities. During the war years, approximately half-a-million refugees sought safety in India. However, the evacuation was not the end of their story. In the months and years after their arrival in India, these evacuees became the subject of colonial-era 'relief' programmes, followed by an abortive attempt at 'repatriation' to Burma starting in 1945. While the post-war years initially held great promise, they did not usher in a return to the days of unfettered migration and comparatively higher wages that had been available in the early decades of the twentieth century. Instead, the evacuees from Burma faced further restrictions on migration, increased debates over who had a claim to Burma's future and the conclusion of evacuee relief programmes in India.

## Bibliography

Adas, Michael. 2011. *The Burma Delta: Economic Development and Social Change on an Asian Rice Frontier, 1852–1941*. Madison, WI: University of Wisconsin Press.

Amrith, Sunil S. 2011. 'Reconstructing the "Plural Society": Asian Migration between Empire and Nation, 1940–1948'. *Past and Present* 11(6): 237–257.

———. 2013a. *Crossing the Bay of Bengal: The Furies of Nature and the Fortunes of Migrants*. Cambridge, MA: Harvard University Press.

———. 2013b. 'South Indian Migration, c. 1800–1950'. In *Globalising Migration History: The Eurasian Experience*, edited by Leo Lucassen and Jan Lucassen, pp. 122–148. Leiden: Brill Publishers.

Andrew, E. J. L. 1933. *Indian Labour in Rangoon*. Oxford: Oxford University Press.

Basu, Subho, Sanjoy Bhattacharya and Robert Keys. 1999. 'The Second World War and South Asia: An Introduction'. *Social Scientist* 27(7–8): 1–10.

Baxter, James. 1941. *Report on Indian Immigration*. Rangoon: Government Printing and Stationery.

Bayly, Christopher, and Timothy Harper. 2004. *Forgotten Armies: The Fall of British Asia, 1941–1945*. London: Allen Lane.

———. 2007. *Forgotten Wars: Freedom and Revolution in Southeast Asia*. Cambridge, MA: Belknap Press.

Brennan, Lance. 1988. 'Government Famine Relief in Bengal, 1943'. *Journal of Asian Studies* 47(3): 542–567.

Brown, Ian. 2005. *A Colonial Economy in Crisis: Burma's Rice Cultivators and the World Depression of the 1930s*. London: Routledge.

Chakravarti, Nalini Ranjan. 1971. *The Indian Minority in Burma: The Rise and Decline of an Immigrant Community*. London: Oxford University Press.

*Famine Code, Madras Presidency*. 1927. Madras: Superintendent, Government Press.

Gandhi, Mohandas K. 2000–2001. *The Collected Works of Mahatma Gandhi*, vol. 81. New Delhi: Publications Division, Ministry of Information and Broadcasting, Government of India.

Jaiswal, Ritesh Kumar. 2014. 'Indian Labour Emigration to Burma (c. 1880–1940): Rethinking Indian Migratory Patterns'. *Proceedings of the Indian History Congress* 75: 911–919.

Khan, Yasmin. 2015. *India at War: The Subcontinent and the Second World War*. New York: Oxford University Press.

Leigh, Michael D. 2015. *The Evacuation of Civilians from Burma: Analysing the 1942 Colonial Disaster*. London: Bloomsbury.

———. 2018. *The Collapse of British Rule in Burma: The Civilian Evacuation and Independence*. London: Bloomsbury Academic.

Manikumar, K. A. 2003. *A Colonial Economy in the Great Depression: Madras (1929–1937)*. Hyderabad: Orient Longman Private Limited.

McKeown, Adam. 2004. 'Global Migration, 1846–1940'. *Journal of World History* 15(2): 155–189.

Meyer, Emma C. 2020. 'Resettling Burma's Displaced: Labor, Rehabilitation, and Citizenship in Visakhapatnam, India, 1937–1979'. PhD dissertation, Emory University, Atlanta, GA.

Mohan, Radha. 1955. 'Immigration Policy of Burma in Relation to India: A Brief Survey'. *Indian Journal of Political Science* 16(2) (April–June): 165–170.

Prakash, Gyan, Nikhil Menon and Michael Laffan (eds.). 2018. *The Postcolonial Moment in South and Southeast Asia*. New York: Bloomsbury Academic.

Rao, A. Narayana. 1933. *Indian Labour in Burma*. Madras: Kesari Printing Works.

Rao, U. Bhaskar. 1967. *The Story of Rehabilitation*. Delhi: Department of Rehabilitation, Government of India.

Satyanarayana, Adapa. 2002. '"Birds of Passage": Migration of South Indian Laborers to Southeast Asia'. *Critical Asian Studies* 34(1): 89–115.

Sharpe, Eileen K. 1943. *Register of Evacuees from Burma*, vol. 2. Calcutta: Evacuee Enquiry Bureau.

Tinker, Hugh. 1975. 'A Forgotten Long March: The Indian Exodus from Burma, 1942'. *Journal of Southeast Asian Studies* 6(1): 1–15.

# 14

## Opposing the Group Areas Act and Resisting Forced Displacement in Durban, South Africa

*Brij Maharaj*

The implementation of apartheid in South Africa centred to a large extent on the control of residential location.[1] One of the cornerstones of apartheid and one of the few areas in which the policy has been effective was in the provision of separate residential areas for the different race groups.[2] This spatial segregation and segmentation of residential areas for whites, Coloureds, Indians and Africans expressed the impact of apartheid most acutely.[3] The Group Areas Act (GAA), 1950, was one of the key instruments used to reinforce the ideology of apartheid and emphasised separate residential areas, educational services and other amenities for the different race groups.

The major impact of group area dislocations has been borne by black communities, particularly Coloureds and Indians.[4] According to Johannes T. Schoombee, 'the actual legislative model taken for group areas has been the string of legislative measures starting in the 1880s directed against "Asiatics" [particularly Indians] in the Transvaal and later, Natal'.[5]

Indians represent the smallest proportion of the four population groups in South Africa, numbering about one million. Yet, proportionately, the impact of the GAA 'has been borne most heavily by the Indians, with one in four of them having been resettled'.[6] Indians 'suffered the most from the implementation of

---

[1] Soussan (1984).

[2] Preston-Whyte (1982).

[3] Given its apartheid history, racial terminology in South Africa is a veritable minefield. Any study of the South African social formation cannot avoid reference to race and ethnic divisions. However, the use of such terminology in this chapter does not in any way legitimise racist ideology and doctrine.

[4] Western (1981).

[5] Schoombee (1987), p. 189.

[6] Western (1981), p. 81.

the GAA, either through removals or the inadequate provision of living space'.[7] This was especially so in the port city of Durban, situated on the east coast of South Africa, where indentured labourers from India first disembarked in 1860 and who were followed by traders (or passengers who paid their own way) in the mid-1870s.[8]

This chapter is a continuation of my earlier historical research on the GAA in Durban. The focus of the chapter is on opposition to the GAA and resistance to forced displacement. The reasons for the failure of resistance is also analysed. The chapter is divided into three sections. The background and context are presented in the first section. Opposing the GAA is the theme of the second section. Resisting forced displacement is discussed in the third section, and the sub-themes include the approaches of the Natal Indian Congress (NIC), the Natal Indian Organisation (NIO), the 'All-in-Congress', and the 1958 proclamations and mass action.

The data for this chapter were derived from a variety of primary documentary sources, ranging from official central and local government records and newspaper reports[9] to memoranda prepared by political and civil society organisations.

## Background and Context

Calls for some form of segregation between whites and blacks (Africans, Coloureds and Indians) started in the 1880s with the former expressing fears about being contaminated by the latter who were viewed as carriers of disease – the so-called sanitation syndrome.[10] The solution was to confine blacks to compounds, hostels and locations that served as effective means of control and repression and stifled political or labour action.[11] The Urban Areas Act of 1923 represented the first national attempt to control, manage and segregate urban Africans.[12]

However, the legal segregation of Indians in South Africa preceded that of urban Africans by more than 30 years. The whites of Durban were more concerned about the 'Asiatic menace' than the 'Native problem'. Natives were perceived as a passive threat, but Indians were regarded as a 'sophisticated and active menace

---

[7]  Carter (1987), p. 207.

[8]  Bhana and Brain (1990).

[9]  During the period under study, the following newspapers served the Indian community: the *Indian Opinion*, the *Indian Views*, *The Leader* and *The Graphic*.

[10]  Swanson (1983).

[11]  Rex (1974).

[12]  Rich (1978).

to their own position in colonial society, competing for space, place, trade, and political influence with the imperial authority'.[13] Basically, there was a conflict between white and Indian capital, and this was expressed in racial terms.

In Durban, strategies to curtail Indian access to land as well as the economic activities of trader groups (who followed the indentured Indians) dominated local political debates for the first half of the twentieth century. Amidst intensified anti-Indian agitation in the post-First World War period, the government appointed the Lange Asiatic Inquiry Commission in 1920 to investigate the two burning issues of the period: Indian trading and their acquisition of land.[14] The commission maintained that there should not be any compulsory segregation of Asiatics; rather, there should be a system of voluntary segregation, which, if possible, should be mutually agreed upon. This process would be facilitated if municipalities laid out suitable residential and commercial areas, with satisfactory public services and amenities to attract Indians.[15]

The Class[16] Areas Bill, 1924, was the first attempt to implement some of the recommendations of the Asiatic Inquiry Commission. The main aim of the Bill was to assign separate areas in Natal towns where Indians could trade, live and obtain property without permit or obstruction. The Bill did not reach the statute book because of the impending general election that the Jan Smuts government lost to the National Party. The Areas Reservation and Immigration and Registration (Further Provision) Bill[17] was introduced in 1925 by the new minister of the interior, D. F. Malan. In essence, it constituted a revival of the Class Areas Bill.[18]

On 23 February 1926, Indians throughout the union observed a National Day of Prayer for protection in this hour of danger. A South African Indian Congress (SAIC)[19] deputation was sent to India to inform the government and the public there about the plight of Indians in South Africa.[20] The Bill generated 'consternation and anger throughout the whole Indian world, and for the first

---

[13]  Swanson (1983), p. 404.

[14]  Palmer (1957).

[15]  Maharaj (1995).

[16]  Class 'includes any persons having, in the opinion of the Minister, common racial characteristics, but does not include European persons, persons commonly described Cape coloured persons and natives' (Indian Penetration Commission 1941, p. 6).

[17]  This has also been referred to as the Asiatic Bill.

[18]  The first chapter of the Areas Reservation Bill was almost identical to the Class Areas Bill.

[19]  The SAIC was formed in 1923 and comprised the NIC, the Transvaal Indian Congress (TIC) (established in 1927) and the Cape British Indian Council (Dhupelia-Mesthrie, 1989).

[20]  Palmer (1957).

time the treatment of Indians became a decisive factor in Indian nationalism and British–Indian relations'.[21] The official opposition of the Indian government to the Bill resulted in the second reading being dismissed, and it was referred to a Select Committee.[22]

Allegations of Indian penetration into white areas in Durban – the 'deliberate intention on the part of Indians to intrude into European areas' – continued.[23] This resulted in the establishment of the Broome Commissions, in 1941 and 1943, to investigate the extent of Indian penetration and served as a precursor for the introduction of statutory segregation.

This period was also characterised by a shift in Indian politics. It is important to note that up to 1939, Indian politics was dominated by the trading and commercial elite. The NIC (established by Mohandas K. Gandhi in 1894), for example, served vested commercial interests and was controlled by affluent merchants. The various restrictions in Natal curbed the expansion of the bourgeoisie and threatened the very existence of the petty bourgeoisie. Therefore, although the merchants sometimes included the complaints of the working class in their political representations, they were primarily concerned with protecting their commercial interests.[24] The working class was thus not regarded as an important constituency. Earlier, in 1933, the Colonial Born and Settlers Association (CBSIA) was formed to oppose the elite ideology of the NIC.[25] In 1939, a new generation of more militant political activists began to contest leadership positions in the NIC. As a result, the majority in the NIC and the CBSIA merged to form the Natal Indian Association (NIA). However, the more conservative elements continued to operate under the NIC banner, led by A. I. Kajee.

In an attempt to avert compulsory segregation, both the NIC and the NIA had adopted accommodationist strategies of negotiating with the state to protect their commercial, residential and investment interests. The NIA had served on the Lawrence Committee, and the NIC was party to the abortive Pretoria Agreement, adopted in April 1944. Significantly, both attempts at voluntary segregation and cooperation were destroyed by the local state of Durban.[26]

The NIC and the NIA merged to form a newly constituted NIC in 1943 to unite opposition to the Pegging Act, 1943. In terms of the Pegging Act, Indians

[21]  Calpin (1949), p. 60.

[22]  'Natal India Association (NIA), A refutation of the European Agitation against "Indian Penetration"', Supplement to the *Indian Opinion*, 16 April 1943, para. 72.

[23]  Calpin (1949), p. 102.

[24]  Ginwala (1974), p. 1830.

[25]  Padayachee, Vawda and Tichmann (1985), p. 142.

[26]  Maharaj (2003).

were allowed to retain properties purchased up to March 1943, and thereafter it was illegal to acquire or occupy premises in predominantly white areas in the Durban municipal area. The Act was to operate for three years, and within this period it was envisaged that a solution to the problem would be found.[27]

The Pegging Act was due to expire in March 1946. After the abortive Pretoria Agreement, prime minister Jan Smuts announced on 21 January 1946 that the Asiatic Land Tenure and Indian Representation (Ghetto) Act would replace the Pegging Act.[28] The Asiatic Land Tenure Act covered two main issues which affected Asians: ownership and occupation of land and the franchise.[29] After a great deal of grassroots mobilisation of working-class Indians, the radicals ousted the accommodationists and took control of the NIC in October 1945, and George Naicker was elected as president. With a more radical leadership, the NIC embarked on a massive passive resistance campaign to protest against the Ghetto Act. The campaign was launched on 13 June 1946 and suspended on 31 May 1948. Resistance took the form of occupying properties in defiance of the Act. The state responded by arresting the resistors, and many prominent Indian leaders were sent to prison. The state also auctioned the properties of passive resistors to defray fines.[30]

However, there was very little evidence of mass working-class support for the passive resistance campaign, as this group was not immediately affected by the Ghetto Act. The Act seriously affected wealthy Indians who could afford to buy land in white areas. It did not directly affect the majority of Indians who were poor and could not afford to live outside their existing slums.[31]

By 1945, political organisations were only beginning to address working-class issues such as exploitation, poverty, inadequate housing, and so on. Under these circumstances, 'to have expected any greater empathy or committed support for these political struggles from the newly proletarianised and poorly educated working class ... would surely have been unreasonable'.[32]

In 1947, the accommodationists, under the leadership of A. I. Kajee, formed the NIO. Its membership consisted largely of businessmen, attempting to obtain concessions from the government by 'constitutional' and

---

[27]  Maharaj (1995).

[28]  Singh (1946).

[29]  The Act conferred a form of communal franchise to Indians in terms of which they could elect two Europeans to represent them in the Senate and three Europeans in the House of Assembly. For more information, see Pachai (1971).

[30]  *Report of the Passive Resistance Council* (1947).

[31]  Johnson (1973).

[32]  Padayachee, Vawda and Tichmann (1985), p. 156.

'legitimate' means.[33] While opposing segregation, it was also against the more militant strategies of the NIC.

In 1948, the National Party won the general election, and given its previous support for stringent segregation policies, there was little doubt about what was in store for Indians. The Ghetto Act of 1946, in fact, laid the foundations of the GAA, which followed in 1950.

## Opposing the Group Areas Act

The GAA was an intricate and lengthy piece of legislation, couched in technical and legal terminology that was often difficult to understand. The 'definitions' alone comprised five pages. The GAA comprised of 39 clauses that were extensively amended.

The maxim underlying the GAA was the division of land among the different race groups. The GAA was a powerful tool for state intervention in controlling the use, occupation and ownership of land and buildings on a racial basis. The state also controlled all interracial property transactions. Complex machinery was set up for the establishment of group areas.[34] The GAA was the most far-reaching apartheid proposal to sustain the separation of the races and served as an instrument of oppression.

It was evident from an analysis of the legislation, parliamentary debates and statements by various politicians that the GAA was a culmination of the anti-Indian measures, restricting access to land and trade for almost a century. The local state in Durban played a significant role in the development and promulgation of the GAA, which it regarded as a lifeline by which a 'European' city could be preserved and worked in close collaboration with the central state. The National Party claimed that the GAA was in response to calls from Durban to act against Indian penetration.[35]

The general reaction of the Indian community to the GAA was one of shock, dismay and anger. The different political and civic organisations were unanimous in their rejection and condemnation of the legislation as well as in their analysis of its impact. There was also an agreement that the legislation was intended to ruin the Indians economically and force them into ghettoes.[36]

---

[33] Johnson (1973).

[34] Pirie (1984).

[35] Maharaj (1992).

[36] NIC Agenda Book, Fifth Annual Provincial Conference, Durban, 29 September–2 October 1951, p. 31.

According to the NIC, in terms of the GAA, the central and local state had the backing of the law to uproot settled Indian communities, disrupt their commercial and economic activities and force them to the undeveloped urban periphery to start afresh. The process represented a vicious cycle, for as urban expansion occurred, Indian property would once again be expropriated for European benefit. Ultimately, it was envisaged that through oppression and persecution, the Indian would be forced out of South Africa.[37]

The NIC maintained that the aim of the GAA was to ruin the Indians economically and to make their lives so unbearable and unpleasant that they would be forced to return to India.[38] More specifically, the intention of the state was to (*a*) deprive the Indian people of their long-established ownership and occupation of land and homes, (*b*) facilitate the uprooting and expatriation of South African citizens of Indian origin, (*c*) ruin the Indian people economically and (*d*) confine them to ghettoes as a source of cheap labour.[39]

The NIO contended that the GAA was 'the most devastating legislation that human ingenuity could have conceived, and its administration would bring complete ruin to Indian and non-European people'.[40] At numerous protest meetings, the NIO resolved that the GAA was sinister in its design because (*a*) it imposed compulsory segregation on Indians throughout the country, which would result in the sequestration of all properties owned by Indians outside their group areas, (*b*) it would destroy Indian businesses and agricultural activities outside their group areas as the issuing of licences would be controlled, (*c*) the arbitrary powers of the inspectors and police would turn South Africa into a police state, (*d*) the natural development of the Indian community in South Africa would be stultified, who would become helots within the Commonwealth of Nations, and (*e*) it represented a violation of human rights.[41]

## Resisting Forced Displacement

Given its support for compulsory racial residential segregation, Durban was the first pioneering city to plan for group areas zoning and established a Technical

---

[37] NIC Agenda Book, Fourth Annual Provincial Conference, Durban, 30 September–2 October 1950, p. 32.

[38] 'An Urgent Call to all Branches', NIC pamphlet, 25 April 1950.

[39] Memorandum of NIC, 18 February 1953, op. cit., para. 7.

[40] Telegram from the NIO to the Hon. N. C. Havenga, House of Assembly, Cape Town, 26 May 1950.

[41] Maharaj (1992).

Sub-Committee (TSC) for this purpose in November 1950.[42] The first racial plan of the TSC allocated the Central Area, Lower Berea, Durban North, Riverside, Prospect Hall and Cato Manor to whites. The Main Line suburbs (Sea View, Hillary and Bellair) were zoned for Indians (Figure 14.1).[43] According to the TSC plan, about 119,249 blacks out of a total population of 145,744 would be dispossessed, with the future of the remainder uncertain. Indians would be evicted from the mixed neighbourhoods in the Old Borough of Durban, as well as in Sydenham, Springfield and Cato Manor, areas they established as pioneers almost a century earlier.[44] In comparison, the TSC plan would require the removal of 7,000 to 12,000 whites.[45]

Indian political and community organisations argued that the implications of the TSC's plans were far-reaching in that it envisaged the ultimate exclusion of all Indians from the city. Consequently, Durban would become a white group area, with the other race groups being located outside its boundaries. Concern was expressed that the Durban City Council (DCC) in taking the lead with regard to the implementation of the GAA would influence other town councils with their unjust ideas.

The NIC contended that the TSC did not even make any charade at objective planning in response to the needs of the different groups. Its proposals were regarded as a calculated effort to seize Indian homes, properties, businesses and other economic interests in Durban. Millions of pounds worth of property acquired over 90 years of hard labour would be forfeited under the guise of racial zoning.[46]

The NIO argued that an evaluation of the TSC report revealed that its primary objective was to serve and entrench the white interests in Durban at the expense of Indians. The white protest at the zoning of Sea View, Hillary, Bellair and Malvern for Indians would ultimately be heard because they had the vote.[47] The vociferous resistance of whites to the zoning proposals of the TSC, the NIO maintained, emphasised an important factor neglected by the TSC: 'the deep-rooted attachment which human beings have for their homes and established areas, in this case the Europeans who live in the Main Line suburbs'.[48]

---

[42]  DCC minutes, 20 November 1950.

[43]  Technical Sub-Committee on Race Zoning (1951).

[44]  Maharaj (1997).

[45]  *Natal Mercury*, 11 November 1951.

[46]  Resolution adopted at the Fifth Annual Provincial Conference of the NIC, 29–30 September–1 October 1951, Durban.

[47]  *Indian Views*, 28 November 1951.

[48]  NIO Memorandum to the Land Tenure Advisory Board (LTAB), 19 February 1953.

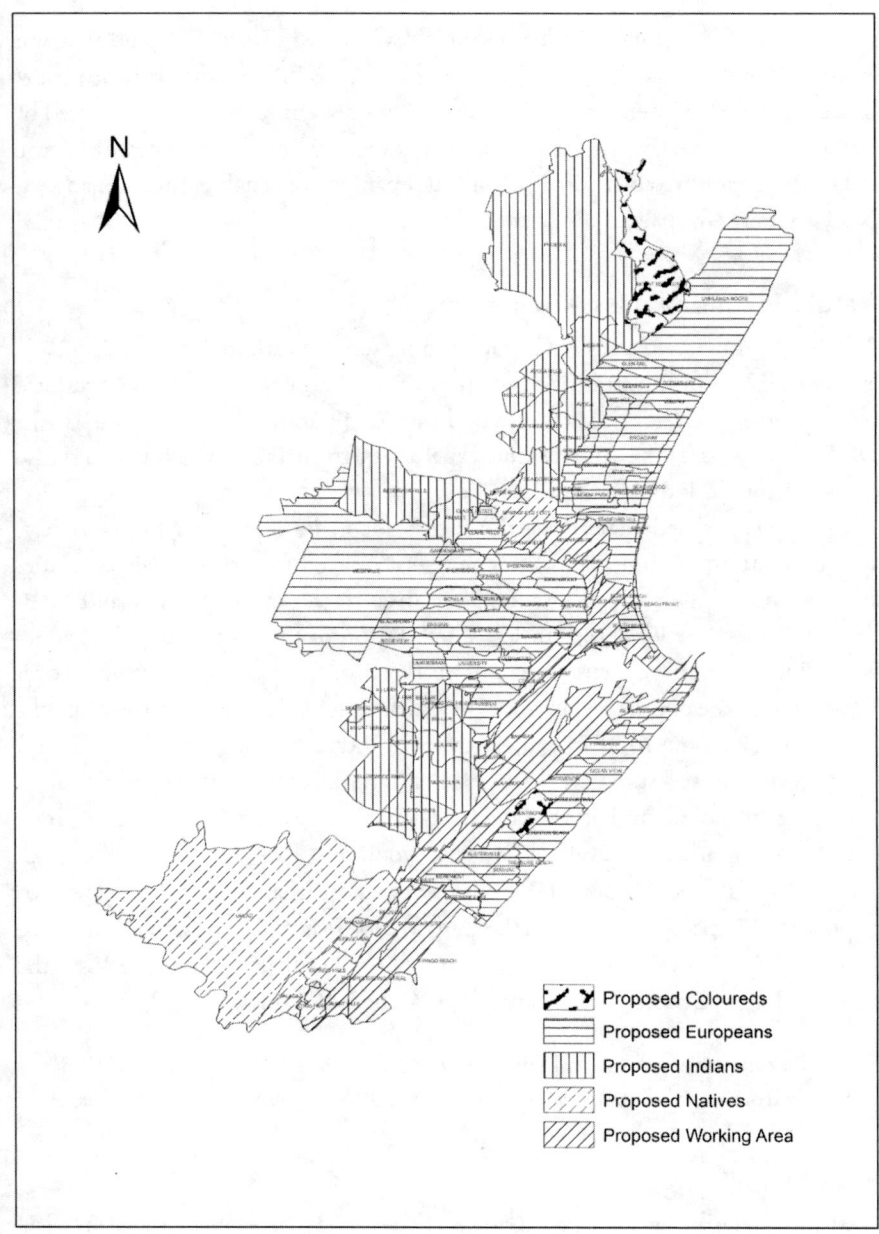

**Figure 14.1** The Technical Sub-Committee's proposals for Durban group-area zoning, 1950

*Source*: Adapted from Maharaj (1992), p. 314.

The only change in the initial race plan submitted by the TSC and that was approved by the DCC in May 1952 was that the Main Line suburbs (Sea View, Hillary and Bellair) were zoned for whites. The concerns and objections raised by Indian political and civic organisations were ignored. There was difference between the strategies adopted by the main political organisations, such as the NIC and the NIO, to resist group areas displacement.

## Natal Indian Congress – Repeal the Act

The NIC condemned the DCC's race-zoning scheme accepted in May 1952 as a 'sinister plan to uproot thousands of non-European people from areas occupied by them for generations'. It represented the culmination of the attempts by the DCC to dispossess the Indians and expel them from the city. This would also displace thousands of Africans.[49]

The NIC argued that as the GAA did not make provisions for alternative accommodation, and municipalities were not obliged to provide civic amenities and services in the relocation zones, the disenfranchised Indians would be at the mercy of white local authorities. The location of the proposed Indian zones would increase transport costs and add to the burden of a community where over 70 per cent of the population lived below the breadline. According to the NIC, the DCC was 'notorious for its criminal neglect of Indian housing needs'.[50]

A conservative estimate by the NIC indicated that about 72,869 Indians would be uprooted from their homes. This would exceed 100,000 if accurate population figures were available. If Clairwood and Rossburgh were included, the total would exceed 130,000.[51] Moreover, more than half of the displaced population (54 per cent) was from the Cato Manor–Mayville–Sydenham complex. Large proportions were also displaced from Sea View–Bellair (9 per cent) and the Prospect Hall–Riverside (8 per cent) areas.[52] The NIC concluded:

Only a callous central or local authority can contemplate the shifting of 100,000 people from their homes in the interests of race discrimination. A large number of

---

[49] *Indian Opinion*, 16 May 1952.

[50] Memorandum submitted by the NIC to the LTAB on the Proposed Proclamation of Group Areas in Durban, 18 February 1953.

[51] Memorandum submitted by the NIC to the LTAB on the Proposed Proclamation of Group Areas in Durban, 18 February 1953, paras. 20–21.

[52] Memorandum submitted by the NIC to the LTAB on the Proposed Proclamation of Group Areas in Durban, 18 February 1953, para. 20.

African are to be displaced by these plans. If the Act can cause the displacement of non-Europeans on such a large scale in one municipal area alone, how grim a picture will the country as a whole present?[53]

In terms of the DCC's plans, Indians would lose 7,741 dwellings, valued at 7,778,640 pounds.[54] Also, Indians would lose 9,737 acres of land, valued at 15,683,765 pounds.[55] The NIC estimated that providing for the homeless and the natural population increase (excluding the displaced) would require 8,000 houses for the five-year period ending 1956. This figure excluded thousands of Indians who were living in slums. Therefore, the NIC concluded that the basic problem facing Durban was to provide more housing, rather than reducing this commodity by the creation of racial zones that would cause chaos and suffering. The NIC resolved not to cooperate with the local or central government in the implementation of the GAA.[56]

The DCC's response was that it would achieve its objectives with regard to the GAA with or without the cooperation of the NIC. In a letter to the NIC, the town clerk stated that the General Purposes Committee of the DCC 'notes your Congress' resolve not to cooperate with the City Council in securing the most advantageous application of the GAA to this City.... The Committee has no doubt that the City Council will achieve its objective nevertheless'.[57] In contrast to the NIC, the NIO adopted a more conservative approach.

## The Natal Indian Organisation's 'Situational' Approach

The NIO asserted that it was opposed to the GAA in principle and that its ultimate aim was to achieve the repeal of the legislation by legitimate and constitutional means. In the interim, it had no option but to submit, under duress, alternate race-zoning proposals for Durban.[58] The plan advocated by the NIO envisaged that

---

[53] Memorandum submitted by the NIC to the LTAB on the Proposed Proclamation of Group Areas in Durban, 18 February 1953, para. 22.

[54] Memorandum submitted by the NIC to the LTAB on the Proposed Proclamation of Group Areas in Durban, 18 February 1953, para. 24.

[55] Memorandum submitted by the NIC to the LTAB on the Proposed Proclamation of Group Areas in Durban, 18 February 1953, para. 26.

[56] Memorandum submitted by the NIC to the LTAB on the Proposed Proclamation of Group Areas in Durban, 18 February 1953, para. 23.

[57] Southworth (1991), p. 12.

[58] Memorandum submitted by the NIO to the LTAB, 19 February 1953, paras. 1–2, 34.

the maintenance of the status quo in long-established [Indian] areas, and coupled with it the provision for the future needs by the allocation of land large enough for immediate occupation and development and for expansion.[59]

It argued that these twin principles could be applied in Durban fairly rapidly because there would be no forced removals, no insurmountable demands upon the public exchequer and no pressure upon the present administrative resources of the city.[60] According to P. R. Pather, it was necessary for the Indian to fight to protect his property and commercial interests and his case had to be presented to the government under duress. He contended that under these circumstances no one could be accused of collaborating with the implementation of the Act.[61]

More specifically, the NIO recommended that the following predominantly Indian areas should be zoned for this group: Riverside and Prospect Hall (north of the Umgeni River; Cato Manor and Merebank and Wentworth). According to the NIO, these proposals would avert the displacement of 30,000 Indians.[62] The President of the NIO, Pather, referred to this as a 'situational' approach: 'In other words, to seek ways in which something can be saved from the wholesale schemes designed to dispossess Indians of their ownership and occupation.'[63]

The difference in strategies adopted by the NIC and the NIO increased the tensions between these organisations. Doctor Theophilus Ebenhaezer Donges had stated in the parliament that a section of the Indian community was prepared to make the GAA work. This was taken to refer to the alternate zoning proposals submitted by the NIO.[64] To the NIC, the NIO was attempting to safeguard the vested interests of the commercial elite. G. M. Naicker, the President of the NIC, stated:

We must not live in a fool's paradise and believe that with this danger facing the entire community a few will be able to save themselves. We must expose those in our community who are thinking in terms of saving their own commercial interests at the expense of the rest.[65]

---

[59] Memorandum submitted by the NIO to the LTAB, 19 February 1953, para. 37.

[60] Memorandum submitted by the NIO to the LTAB, 19 February 1953, para. 37.

[61] *The Leader*, 7 May 1954.

[62] *The Leader*, 7 May 1954.

[63] *The Graphic*, 8 August 1953.

[64] *The Leader*, 4 June 1954.

[65] *The Leader*, 4 June 1954.

However, the NIC was also representing middle-class interests. According to Naicker, '[e]very property owner, big and small, is seriously affected' by the GAA.[66] The NIC concluded that the NIO's actions were harmful to the community as this implied that it had accepted the principle of racial segregation. Consequently, Debi Singh, the secretary general of the NIC, maintained that the difference between the NIO and the government was one of degree only, as the former had submitted plans which would also uproot people, regardless of how few.[67]

The NIO summarised the NIC's policy as 'we shall object to any zoning proposals, we shall accept no areas, but if areas are forced upon us and if we are compelled to shift, we shall do so. Such a stand means that the interests of the people must be sacrificed at the altar of vaunted principles'.[68] However, the apartheid government disregarded the submissions of the NIO.

In an editorial comment, *The Graphic* maintained that there were dangers in the strategies of both the NIO and the NIC:

> The NIO policy may be interpreted by the authorities as an indication of willing co-operation in an Act that is fundamentally alien to Indian interests, and they have been so accused by their opponents. On the other hand, the NIC policy is such as to alienate any sympathy for the Indian case. We cannot afford either.[69]

The NIC was concerned about Indian apathy and was aware of the need to engage in more broad-based community mobilisation at grassroots level against the GAA.

## Mass Action: 'All-in-Conference'

Monty Naicker, the President of the NIC, in November 1955, called for an urgent 'All-in-Conference' so that the entire Indian community could discuss the far-reaching implications of the GAA and its various amendments since 1950. There was an evident need to mobilise the community, and Naicker urged that an alliance of

> Congress branches, trade unions, traders' organisations, ratepayers' associations, sport and religious societies and all other Indian bodies should meet together to formulate plans to oppose the Group Areas Act, which is being implemented to strangle the Indian people economically.[70]

---

[66]  *New Age*, 24 November 1955.

[67]  *New Age*, 24 November 1955.

[68]  *The Leader*, 5 March 1954.

[69]  *The Graphic*, 22 August 1953.

[70]  Reddy (1991), p. 25.

In May 1956, the NIC convened such a conference to discuss the different aspects and implications of the GAA. NIC branches, the African National Congress (ANC), the Labour Party, the Liberal Party, trade unions, trader organisations and ratepayers' associations were represented at the conference. The most important resolution of the conference was the need for all organisations to rally the blacks to oppose the GAA at all levels. In order to do this, vigilance committees were to be formed in all provinces. Although an invitation was extended to the NIO, it was not represented.[71]

While there was some collaboration between the NIC and ANC leaders, a telling indictment against the political leadership of the period was their elite tendencies and the failure to mobilise across racial barriers at the grassroots level:

> A study of the working class areas of Durban would surely reveal that even by the 1930s there was a considerable intermingling of African and Indian workers. Much of this was superficial – on the race track, in the cinema, or in the bus – but some was more durable, in terms of worker or home relationships. This urban intermingling might have become the basis for a political movement, if the Indian leaders had not remained so completely middle class, whether they were moderates or radicals in their ideology.[72]

While the May 1956 conference was successful in the sense that it was educational and informative, the *Indian Opinion* criticised it for not discussing a mode of action: 'That is to say what action were those victims of the obnoxious Group Areas Act were to take if they were asked to move out?' It pointed out, ominously, the views of the layman:

> Today the general opinion of the layman is that if the Government gives them a nice new home at a nominal sum why shouldn't they move. On the other hand they are told that they should not identify themselves with the Government's plans but should fight for freedom. They reply: 'Why should we join the Congress? What have they to offer us when our life possessions are in jeopardy? While we stand to gain by doing as the Government wants us to do.' That is the trend in which the ordinary laymen thinks.[73]

The class divisions in the Indian community were once again being highlighted. The failure of mass mobilisation against the GAA at grassroots level was due to the

---

[71]  *Indian Opinion*, 11 May 1956.

[72]  Tinker (1973), p. 525.

[73]  *Indian Opinion*, 11 May 1956.

fact that the landowners faced the greatest losses as a result of the legislation. It was possible that low-income groups would benefit by moving into public housing in the relocated areas, in contrast to their present slums. In the mid-1950s, about 33 per cent of Indian families lived in one room and 42 per cent in overcrowded houses.[74]

Furthermore, there was also a high level of unemployment among Indians. It was estimated that 70 per cent of the Indians lived below the poverty datum line. According to the Social and Economic Planning Council, the income of 50 per cent of Indian households was too low to enable them to purchase low-cost diets.[75] Councillor J. J. Higginson, the chairman of the DCC's Housing Committee, drew attention to the 'unemployment, poverty and shocking living conditions' that were the plight of over 125,000 Indians living in and around Durban. He estimated that 25 per cent of the Indians were unemployed.[76]

Moreover, Indian activists in political organisations were under constant surveillance by the security apparatus of the state.[77] Under these circumstances, Indians were less likely to support militant mass action, which, with the possibility of police arrests and imprisonment, would jeopardise their already precarious positions.

Emanating from the resolution of the Group Areas Conference, the Natal Provincial Vigilance Committee was formed in June 1956. It comprised of representatives of the NIC, the ANC, the Liberal Party, the Congress of Democrats, the Liberal Party, the Durban Combined Ratepayers' Association and the South African Congress of Trade Unions. The function of the committee was to 'safeguard the existing rights of the people and dissemination of propaganda written and spoken particularly to acquaint the European public with the inequities of the Group Areas Laws'.[78] Successful meetings were held in various parts of Natal. Archie Gumede, the ANC representative on the committee urged the Indian community not to be apathetic or 'all that they worked for over generations' would be lost.[79]

---

[74]   *Century of Indians* (1960), p. 180.

[75]   *Century of Indians* (1960), p. 180.

[76]   *The Graphic*, 7 July 1961.

[77]   See Memorandum from the South African Police Re. Indian Political Movements in South Africa, to the Secretary for External Affairs, Pretoria, 30 January 1948.

[78]   *Indian Opinion*, 8 May 1956.

[79]   *New Age*, 30 September 1956.

However, the effectiveness of the committee was impeded when its chairman, G. Hurbans (NIC), and joint secretaries, N. T. Naicker (NIC) and P. H. Simelane (ANC), were arrested to face trial for high treason.[80]

## The 1958 Proclamations and Mass Action

The 1958 group-area proclamations in Durban basically confirmed the recommendations of the TSC in 1952, as amended by the DCC in May 1952 and submitted to the government in 1954. The proclamations distinguished between group areas for immediate ownership and occupation, and for ownership and future (undated) occupation (Figure 14.2).

The areas for immediate (within a year) white ownership and occupation were the Beachfront, Berea, Sherwood, Woodlands, Montclair, the upper white sections of Rossburgh, Hillary and Sea View, Durban North and the Bluff.[81] The following areas were intended for ownership and future occupation by whites: Fenniscowles, the low-lying areas of Rossburgh, Sea View and Bellair, Cato Manor, Mayville, Sydenham (Overport), Riverside and Prospect Hall (Figure 14.2).

Indian areas for immediate ownership and occupation were the Springfield Housing Scheme, Reservoir Hills and Umhlatuzana Township. Merebank, Clare Estate and the area between the Umhlatuzana and the Umlaas Rivers (Chatsworth) were proclaimed for future Indian ownership and occupation. The only Coloured area for ownership and future occupation was Wentworth. The largest proportion of the residentially developed area of Durban was proclaimed for whites. However, in many of the proclaimed group areas for whites, Indians made up more than 50 per cent of the population.[82]

The Indian community was devastated by the proclamations. They would lose property valued millions of pounds. Based on the 1951 census, it was estimated that 1,000 whites, 75,000 Indians, 8,500 Coloureds and 81,000 Africans would have to move as a result of the 1958 proclamations.[83] These figures, the NIC argued, drew attention to the immense human suffering involved, the magnitude of the economic loss and the impossible tasks facing the authorities of providing sufficient and suitable accommodation for those to be displaced.[84] According to

---

[80]   *The Leader*, 13 June 1958.

[81]   Horrell (1958).

[82]   Schlemmer (1967).

[83]   Hansard, col. 1472, 5 August 1958.

[84]   *The Graphic*, 4 July 1958.

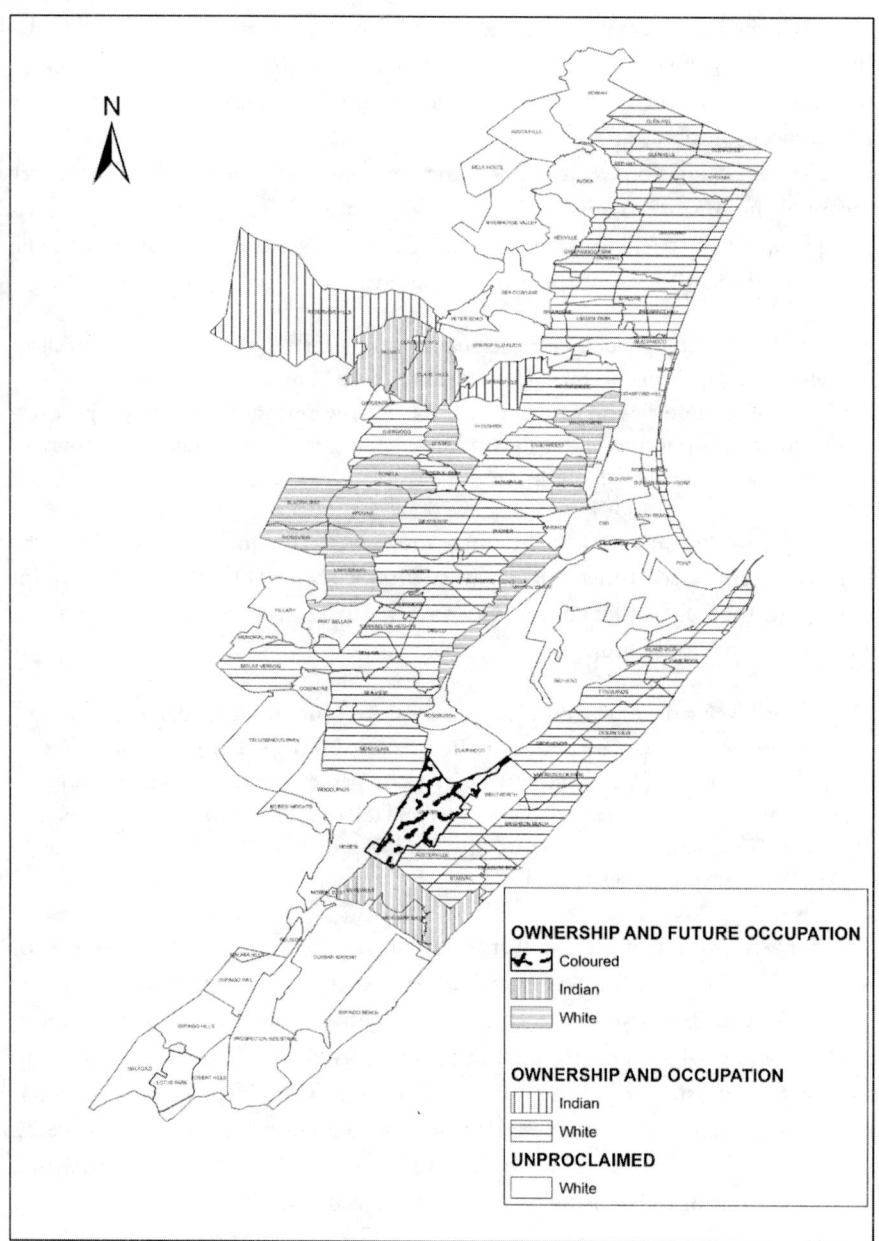

**Figure 14.2**  The group-area proclamations, 1958

*Source*: Adapted from Maharaj (1992), p. 367.

the NIC, the mass dispossession envisaged in these proclamations exemplified a flagrant infringement of human freedom and represented 'a heartless attack in the name of racialism, on a voteless people. Its aim is to render the Indian people economically impotent'.[85]

The proclamations galvanised the various political and community organisations into recognising the need for a united front, transcending class and ideological barriers, in opposing the GAA. This move was initiated by the President of the NIC, G. M. Naicker, who said:

> In the face of the grave dangers which face our people, I call upon all Indians, in all walks of life, to come together as never before in the history of our people, to meet the challenge unitedly and with one voice. Now is the time for the Indian people to declare to the authorities and to the world, in the clearest possible language that they are totally opposed to the Group Areas Act.[86]

The major bodies involved in the unity move were the NIC, the NIO and the Durban Combined Indian Ratepayers' Association (DCIRA). In a joint statement, they urged the community to participate in mass protest action and emphasised the need for unity:

> The crisis facing the Indian people under the GAA is unprecedented in the history of our people. In this grave hour let us in a dignified way speak with a united voice condemning the GAA and the injustice it seeks to perpetuate in its implementation. With calm and dignity we want the country and the world to know the plight of our people. We ask every Indian to participate in this protest against the recent Group Area Proclamations in Durban.[87]

Three mass protest meetings were held in Durban within three weeks of the proclamations. A protest meeting convened by the Riverside–Briardene District Indian Ratepayers' Association on 15 June 1958 was attended by about 2,000 residents. The meeting unanimously resolved to call upon the DCC to request the minister of the interior to deproclaim Riverside, Prospect Hall and Briardene, where Indians had settled and owned property for over 90 years. The DCC was also urged to allow Indians to develop their properties, as this would help meet some of the housing needs of the community. The meeting emphasised the need for unity in protest action against the GAA and its proclamations.[88]

---

[85]  *Indian Opinion*, 20 June 1958.

[86]  *Indian Opinion*, 20 June 1958.

[87]  *The Graphic*, 20 June 1958.

[88]  *The Graphic*, 20 June 1958.

On 22 June 1958, a mass protest meeting was held in Mayville, Cato Manor, which endorsed the call for united protest and opposition to the proclamations.[89] The call for mass protest action culminated in a rally held at the Curries Fountain ground on 26 June 1958, convened jointly by the NIC, the NIO and the DCIRA (which was referred to as the Sponsors' Committee) and attended by over 20,000 people. Thousands heeded the call to stay away from work and school, and Indian businesses and shops closed for the afternoon. The meeting was addressed by representatives from the three main conveners, as well as priests from the different religions. The meeting declared:

> We would like to make it clear that we who have had no say in the making of this barbaric law and are totally opposed to the Act and the principles and aims of its originators, will not at any stage, acquiesce in its implementation. Our stand is based on fundamental principles and truths. We believe in the right of every man to choose his abode according to his means without any racial restriction. We believe in the sanctity of our homes and cannot tolerate any interference from authorities who have not the slightest regard for our feelings. Nowhere in the world would thinking people permit their Government to stampede thousands of its settled communities from their hearths and homes, and allow them to build in the bare veld.[90]

A significant feature of the protest meeting was the involvement of Europeans who also opposed the proclamations. Hansi Pollak, the chairperson of the Natal Coastal Region of the South African Institute of Race Relations (SAIRR), stated that many Europeans were also shocked at the proclamations. Alan Paton of the Liberal Party, questioned whether those who created such evil laws or those who protested against them were responsible for racial conflict.[91]

At the meeting, an impassioned appeal was made to Europeans to become more aware of the havoc inflicted by the proclamations. An extract from the appeal read as follows:

> It was 93 years ago that we founded such settlements as Prospect Hall and Riverside. In other places we have been living for 50, 60 or 70 years. The vast majority of us have put all our savings into our homes. Now under the GAA, 60 000 of us are to be removed. Our properties, so valuable to us, have nothing like the same value for white purchasers. We expect to suffer grievous losses, much heavier than most of us will be able to bear. Most of us are humble working people and to buy land and

---

[89]   *The Graphic*, 27 June 1958.

[90]   *The Graphic*, 4 July 1958.

[91]   *New Age*, 3 July 1958.

build houses in the new areas will be beyond our means. Those who are in business in these proclaimed areas will receive no compensation at all.[92]

A group of 36 prominent concerned European citizens, including members of the parliament, churchmen and academics, signed a statement that declared that they shared the distress of those who would be uprooted by the GAA:

> We the undersigned, have read and have been deeply moved by the appeal of the Indian community to the white citizens of Durban. We are confident that many will share their distress at the present Group Areas proclamations, which will ultimately uproot 100,000 of Durban's citizens from their homes and settled communities. Sympathy must be extended to all affected persons, whether they be European or non-European. We are sure that the community's sense of justice and humanity will be shocked by the inequality of the sacrifice falling upon the Non-European citizens of Durban. We respond to the Indian appeal and commend it to our fellow citizens.[93]

The mass meeting adopted the following resolutions:

1. Call upon the government 'in the name of human decency and justice' to withdraw the proclamation of June 6 so that tens of thousands of people would be saved from uprooting.
2. Request the DCC to make a similar call to the government for deproclamation.
3. Appeal to all South Africans who believed in justice and human dignity to support the clamour for the repeal of the GAA.
4. Call upon the international community for moral support.
5. Emphasise the need for the Indian community to be united in their opposition to the proclamations.
6. Embark on a mass petition campaign to draw the attention of the parliament to the implications of the proclamations and to request immediate redress.[94]

Commenting on the meeting, *The Graphic* stated that although 'there was no challenge to authority, no resistance advocated, the meeting itself was the greatest possible challenge to the conscience of the White citizens of Durban and elsewhere'.[95] However, the period after the mass protest meetings of June 1958 was characterised by a general lull.

---

[92]  *The Graphic*, 27 July 1958.

[93]  *The Graphic*, 2 July 1958.

[94]  *Indian Opinion*, 4 July 1958.

[95]  *The Graphic*, 4 July 1958.

There was a failure to capitalise on the awareness associated with the mass mobilisation following the proclamations of 6 June 1958. The main form of protest supported by the NIC was a door-to-door campaign to petition the parliament about the injustices of the GAA and its proclamations. The effectiveness of this action was, however, very limited:

> In fact, public petitions, except when part of a carefully organised parliamentary campaign, appear to be little but a waste of money and energy on the part of the petitioners. The House itself will not, in fact cannot, do anything about them, and their only useful purpose is to serve as an indication of public opinion.[96]

Concern was expressed about the ageing, bankrupt leadership and lack of direction and poor organisation.[97] *The Leader* called for greater action and militancy.[98] It maintained that 'the militants [NIC] appear to have sold out to the moderates [NIO], and in the name of unity have completely forgotten their militancy'. The NIC attempted to justify the apparent ambiguity in its position at its 11th Annual Provincial Conference in November 1958:

> A distinction must be drawn between the principled opposition to the Group Areas Legislations ... and the broader united front formed for the specific purpose of opposing the Proclamation of June 6th.... In respect of the Proclamations of June 6th [the] primary function was to demonstrate to the Union Government and to the world the unanimous rejection of the devastating Proclamations. Besides this primary function Congress has another vital function to fulfil in respect of its policy and programme and that is to take its independent policy of total opposition to the people as a whole. There should be no room for confusion in regard to these dual functions of working within the united front and yet boldly putting forth to the people our independent line of action.[99]

There were accusations that the NIC had 'reverted to opposition tactics that would have been approved by its NIO rival'.[100] The NIC did not consider using passive resistance to oppose the group-area proclamations. According to Robert E. Johnson, the NIC's restrained response to the Durban proclamations was related to the inability to maintain a sense of urgency among Indians:

---

[96] *The Leader*, 1 August 1958.

[97] *The Graphic*, 19 September 1958.

[98] *The Leader*, 1 August 1958.

[99] NIC Agenda Book, 11th Annual Provincial Conference, Durban, 21–23 November 1958, p. 28.

[100] Johnson (1973), p. 145.

This had been cited as a problem by NIC organiser George Singh in 1946, and the situation had not changed by 1958. Only thirty-five Indian property owners were required to immediately vacate their homes by the 1958 proclamation, and even these were permitted to retain ownership. An immediate resistance effort would therefore have been impractical, even if the NIC had been prepared to wage one.[101]

There was also a decline in the active membership of the NIC. The branches considered active by the general secretary of the NIC were reduced by more than half from 28 in 1947 to 12 in 1959. 'Lethargy' and 'inactivity' appeared to characterise the attitude of most members. The main problem experienced by the NIC was poor organisation, inherited from the pre-1945 period, and ultimately it was dominated by an elite group.[102] It is pertinent to note that many in the leadership hierarchy of the NIC, including its president, G. M. Naicker, were facing trial for high treason during this period, and they were pre-occupied with this issue rather than the GAA.

## Conclusion

In apartheid South Africa, the GAA was the most glaring example of the role of the state in the social engineering of space in order to realise ideological and political ends. It was a culmination of the anti-Indian measures, restricting access to land and trade for almost a century, and was significantly influenced by the DCC. The nature of the resistance to the dispossession wrought by the GAA and the reasons for its failure were discussed in this chapter.

Indian political organisations were vociferous in their condemnation of and opposition to the GAA and racial residential segregation, which was intended to ruin the community economically and force them into ghettoes. They resolved to mobilise their resources, to use every available avenue of protest to oppose the implementation of the GAA and to defy the unprecedented assault on basic human rights.

While the NIC and the NIO claimed to represent the Indian community, there was very little evidence of mobilisation of the working class and the poor, whose interests were neglected by elite political leaders. Political action consisted mainly of petitions, letters and delegations to the South African government authorities and the occasional mass meeting. These organisations were, however, primarily

---

[101] Johnson (1973), p. 146.

[102] Johnson (1973).

concerned with protecting trading and middle-class property interests.[103] Hence, while 'they protested against white discrimination against Indians (hence their claim to represent the entire "community") they protested from a class rather than a national or racial position'.[104]

In an atmosphere of increasing hostility and intolerance, they utilised every peaceful measure to expose the injustice and violation of human rights in South Africa. This included passive resistance, recourse to the law and appeals to the government. However, the differences between the NIC and the NIO were in terms of strategy rather than principle and marred united opposition to the implementation of the GAA. The 'collaboration' between the conservative and numerically smaller NIO, which represented powerful economic and business interests, and the apartheid government did not yield any concessions in terms of the implementation of the GAA.

In spite of strategic differences, the 1958 Durban proclamations galvanised the various Indian political and civic bodies into recognising the need for a united front in opposing the GAA. Opposition took the form of futile mass protest meetings and rhetorical outbursts. There was an obvious lack of effective leadership to strengthen the non-racial alliances that developed in June 1956 and to mobilise mass opposition to the group-area proclamations.

The main reason for this was that segregation affected the different classes of the Indian community dissimilarly. It reduced opportunities for investment and commercial expansion for the wealthy, who would also suffer financial losses. Segregation represented a double-edged sword for the underclasses – with increasing rents and slum clearance, some would become homeless, while others could possibly be housed in municipal housing schemes.[105] In fact, the question of housing for the underclasses was not raised forcefully by the NIC or the NIO 'since elements within the Indian merchant class were extensively involved in rack-renting to the Indian and African working class'.[106]

Above all, the coercive apparatus of the apartheid state, as represented by the army and the security branch police force, was very strong. Indians struggling to eke out a living were unlikely to court arrest and imprisonment. The apartheid state was keen on consolidating its power and was 'constantly on the defensive against

---

[103]  Hemson (1977).

[104]  Swan (1987), p. 192.

[105]  Swan (1987).

[106]  Bailey (1987), p. 48.

the threat of destabilisation through popular unrest'.[107] The fledgling apartheid state of 1948 and its repressive apparatus was firmly in control by the late 1950s, and it refused to acquiesce to the most reasonable demands of a disenfranchised, minority community.

## Bibliography

Bailey, D. E. 1987. 'The Origins of Phoenix, 1957–1976: The Durban City Council and the Indian Housing Question'. MA thesis, University of Natal.

Bhana, Surendra, and Brain, Joy B. 1990. *Setting Down Roots: Indian Migrants in South Africa 1860–1911.* Johannesburg: Witwatersrand University Press.

Calpin, G. H. 1949. *Indians in South Africa.* Pietermaritzburg: Shuter and Shooter.

Carter, G. M. 1987. 'The Coloured and the Indians'. In *The Anti-Apartheid Reader: South Africa and the Struggle against White Racist Rule*, edited by David Mermelstein, pp. 203–208. New York: Grove Press.

*Century of Indians.* 1960. Durban: Cavalier Publications.

Dhupelia-Mesthrie, Uma. 1989. 'Indian National Honour versus Trader Ideology: Three Unsuccessful Attempts at Passive Resistance in the Transvaal, 1932, 1939 and 1941'. *South African Historical Journal* 21(1): 39–54.

Ginwala, F. N. 1974. 'Class, Consciousness and Control: Indian South Africans 1860–1946'. Unpublished PhD thesis, Oxford University.

Hemson, David. 1977. 'Dockworkers, Labour Circulation and Class Struggles in Durban, 1940–59'. *Journal of Southern African Studies* 4(1): 88–124.

Horrell, Muriel. 1958. *A Survey of Race Relations: 1957–58.* Johannesburg: South African Institute of Race Relations (SAIRR).

Indian Penetration Commission. 1941. *Report of the Indian Penetration Commission.* Pretoria: Government Printer.

Johnson, Robert E. 1973. 'Indians and Apartheid: The Failure of Resistance'. PhD thesis, University of Massachusetts Amherst.

Maharaj, Brij. 1992. 'The Group Areas Act in Durban: Central–Local Relations'. PhD thesis, University of Natal.

———. 1994. 'The Group Areas Act and Community Destruction in South Africa: The Struggle for Cato Manor in Durban'. *Urban Forum* 5(2): 1–25.

———. 1995. 'The Local State and Residential Segregation: Durban and the Prelude to the Group Areas Act'. *South African Geographical Journal* 77(2): 33–41.

———. 1997. 'Apartheid, Urban Segregation and the Local State: Durban and the Group Areas Act in South Africa'. *Urban Geography* 18(2): 135–154.

---

[107] Posel (1991), p. 220.

———. 2003. "'Co-operation ... Consultation and Consent': The Failure of Voluntary Residential Segregation in Durban in the 1940s'. *South African Geography Journal* 85(2): 134–143.

Pachai, Bridglal. 1971. *The South African Indian Question 1860–1971*. Cape Town: C. Struik.

Padayachee, Vishnu, Shahid Vawda and Paul Tichmann. 1985. *Indian Workers and Trade Unions in Durban, 1930–1950*. Durban: Institute for Social and Economic Research, University of Durban-Westville.

Palmer, Mabel. 1957. *The History of Indians in Natal*. Cape Town: Oxford University Press.

Pirie, G. H. 1984. 'Race Zoning in South Africa: Board, Court, Parliament, Public'. *Political Geography Quarterly* 3(3): 207–221.

Posel, Deborah. 1991. *The Making of Apartheid 1948–1961: Conflict and Compromise*. Oxford: Clarendon Press.

Preston-Whyte, E. 1982. 'Segregation and Interpersonal Relationships: A Case Study of Domestic Service in Durban'. In *Living under Apartheid*, edited by David M. Smith, pp. 164–182. London: George Allen and Unwin.

Reddy, Enuga Sreenivasulu. 1991. *Monty Speaks: Speeches of Dr GM Naicker 1945–1963*. Belville: Mayibuye Books.

Rex, J. 1974. 'The Compound, the Reserve and the Urban Location: The Essential Institutions of Southern African Labour Exploitation'. *South African Labour Bulletin* 1(4): 4–17.

*Report of the Passive Resistance Council*. 1947. Durban: NIC Agenda Book.

Rich, P. B. 1978. 'Ministering to the Needs of the White Man: The Development of Urban Segregation in South Africa 1913–1923'. *African Studies* 37(2): 177–191.

Schlemmer, L. 1967. 'The Resettlement of Indian Communities in Durban and Some Economic, Social and Cultural Effects on the Indian Community'. In 'The Indian in South Africa', papers presented at a conference organised by the South African Institute of Race Relations (SAIRR), Durban.

Schoombee, Johannes Theodorus. 1987. 'An Evaluation of Aspects of Group Areas Legislation in South Africa'. PhD thesis, University of Cape Town.

Singh, George. 1946. *The Asiatic Land Tenure and Indian Representation Act of South Africa: A Brief Survey of Its Background, Terms and Implications*. Durban: Council for Human Rights.

Soussan, John. 1984. 'Recent Trends in South African Housing Policy'. *Area* 16(2): 201–207.

Swanson, Maynard W. 1983. '"The Asiatic Menace": Creating Segregation in Durban, 1870–1900'. *International Journal of African Historical Studies* 16(3): 401–421.

Southworth, Hamilton. 1991. 'Strangling South Africa's Cities: Resistance to Group Areas in Durban during the 1950s'. *International Journal of African Historical Studies* 24(1): 1–34.

Swan, Maureen. 1987. 'Ideology in Organised Indian politics, 1891–1948'. In *The Politics of Race, Class and Nationalism in Twentieth Century South Africa*, edited by Stanley Trapido and Shula Marks, pp. 182–208. London: Longman.

Technical Sub-Committee on Race Zoning (1951). *Methods of Implementing Race Zoning Report*, part 2, June. Durban: Durban City Council.

Tinker, Hugh. 1973. 'The Politics of Racialism: South African Indians'. *Journal of African History* 14(3): 523–527.

Western, J. C. 1981. 'Outcast Cape Town'. In *Outcast Cape Town*. Sydney: Allen & Unwin.

# 15

## Indo-Fijians

### From Agency to Abjection

*Brij V. Lal*

Indo-Fijians are descended from the 60,000 Indian indentured immigrants brought to Fiji between 1879 and 1916 and from a smaller number of free migrants who began arriving there from the 1920s onwards. Once their five-year contracts expired, the majority of the indentured labourers chose to remain in Fiji, with only about 24,000 returning to their homeland. In time, the descendants of these immigrants became, as growers and labourers, the backbone of Fiji's sugar industry for which they had been brought to Fiji in the first place.[1] Now that industry is in severe decline with the expiry of the preferential access to the European market and the vagaries in global sugar prices. Once nearly half the total Fijian population, Indo-Fijian numbers declined substantially to around 30 per cent of the total by 2020 and are still declining due to emigration and a low birthrate. Indo-Fijian history may in the future be a history of immigration to emigration from Fiji. Now, the Indo-Fijians, diminished and declining, stand at crossroads, unsure of their present prospects and apprehensive about their future. Once active agents and proponents of progressive change, they are increasingly its passive recipients. To discuss how this came about is the purpose of this chapter.

The Indo-Fijian quest for equality and acceptance was fraught from the very beginning. The colonial government created a racially compartmentalised society of often conflicting interests and expectations without, for its own survival, providing the conditions of common citizenship. Fiji under the British remained a colony of separate and unequal citizens. The powerful European elite, controlling all the levers of the economy, would not countenance equality with Indo-Fijians whose proper station in the colony, they asserted, was as tillers of the soil who should know their proper place in the larger order of things. 'We have the Indians

---

[1] Gillion (1962).

here and we have to make the most of it. We are the Colony, not the Indians,'
said the prominent European leader and member of the Executive Council Henry
Scott.[2] The Europeans justified their disproportionate legislative power and
influence because of their self-assumed role as the 'trustees' of the Fijian 'race'.
Preserving the status quo became their major cause. Indigenous Fijian leaders
always wanted their position to be paramount, not only in the management of
their own internal affairs but also in the affairs of the country.[3] They were the
iTaukei, owners of the land, and Indians were *vulagi*, guests, who by the very
definition of these terms could not ever aspire to equality.[4] They would accept
the paraphernalia of democracy – political parties, elections, and so on – with a
key precondition: that the verdict of the ballot should always return Fijians to
power. Democratic principles and practices, by which the Indo-Fijians put so
much store, was for the Fijians a foreign flower unsuited to the Fijian soil.[5] For
their part, Indo-Fijians demanded parity with other British subjects resident
in the colony on account of official assurances and their own contribution
to the economy.[6] The tragic truth for Indian people in Fiji was that they were
destined to remain forever the eternal 'Other' in the land of their birth, separate
and unequal.

Fiji was paraded before the world as the United Kingdom's (UK) model
colony where three different ethnic groups played their assigned roles in
harmonious concert with a benevolent colonial state as an impartial arbiter of
the national interest.[7] However, this was little more than a feel-good metaphor
for the colonial state. None of the three groups were socially homogenous, and
they all, in varying degrees, resisted the demands and impositions of the colonial
government and European commercial interests. The colonial state itself was
caught in a web of competing and internally contradictory promises to each of
the different communities: privilege for Europeans, paramountcy for Fijians and
parity for Indians. Balancing these between the three ethnic groups would be
the major challenge for both the colonial government as well as the government
of independent Fiji. In this chapter, our concern is the response of the Indian
community to these issues.

---

[2]  Lal (1997), p. 1.

[3]  Scarr (1980).

[4]  Ravuvu (1991).

[5]  Larmour (2005).

[6]  Lal (1997).

[7]  Scarr (1984).

## The Foundations to 1939

The foundations of modern Fiji, which determined the growth and direction of the Indian community in Fiji, were laid at the time of the cession of the islands to the UK in 1874, especially by its first substantive governor, Arthur Gordon.[8] Among his most important initiatives was his 'native policy'. Fearing the gradual destruction of the native Fijians from exposure to the corrosive forces of the modern world, especially European demand for cheap Fijian land and labour, he prohibited the commercial employment of Fijians on European-owned plantations, legislated against future alienation of all native land, promulgated legislation that would retain fully 83 per cent of all land in native hands (now around 90 per cent following the reversion of Crown land to native land in the early 1990s) and implemented other policies designed to keep Fijians in their subsistence lifestyle under the tutelage of Fijian chiefs. This system of 'native administration' remained in place for nearly a century. Distortions inevitably occurred from the imposition of a uniform code of practice across a fluid and contested field, but at least further population decline was halted, and the Fijian way of life was preserved[9] but preserved, or rather ossified, when the world around had changed dramatically.

To develop the nascent economy of a reluctant colony, Gordon adopted the plantation system that he had observed in Trinidad and Mauritius, where he had been governor before coming to Fiji. Cane sugar would be the crop of choice. Looking beyond the impecunious local planters suffering from the collapse of the cotton boom following the end of the American Civil War, he invited the Colonial Sugar Refining Company (CSR), an Australian company, to start Fiji's sugar industry, which it did in 1882, remaining in Fiji until 1973, three years after Fiji gained its independence.[10] For nearly a century, sugar exports accounted for nearly two-thirds of the country's foreign exchange, giving the CSR a preponderant influence in colonial affairs. To provide the projected large-scale labour supply for the industry, Gordon turned to India, which had been supplying indentured labour to the British colonies since 1834 – first to Mauritius and subsequently to the West Indian colonies.[11] The system was state-regulated, but there was much discrepancy between what was promised and what transpired on the ground.

---

[8]  Chapman (1964).

[9]  France (1969).

[10]  Moynagh (1981).

[11]  Tinker (1974).

Indian indentured emigration ceased in 1916, and the indenture system itself was abolished on 1 January 1920.[12]

The agreement (*girmit*) under which Indian indentured labourers came to Fiji (and went elsewhere) specified their terms and conditions of service, including the provision of a free return passage to India at the end of ten years of 'industrial residence' in the colony or after five years at their own expense. The majority opted to stay on in Fiji. The colonial government actively encouraged this development of a local pool of labour to supply the needs of the plantations, but no thought was given to what political rights and privileges the new resident Indians would have as free British subjects. The Salisbury Dispatch of 1875,[13] which predated Indian emigration to Fiji, envisaged equal status for the new immigrants. This was never formalised in law, although its spirit was never disavowed. Indeed, in 1921, the Fijian colonial government drafted a bill with this provision as a precondition for renewed Indian emigration to Fiji. When the Great Council of Chiefs, the umbrella organisation of the indigenous Fijians, established in 1875, raised concerns about the implications of the growing numbers of Indians in their midst and their future place in Fiji, the colonial government assured them that the new immigrants would 'remain working men and nothing more'.[14] During the period of indenture, the interests and concerns of the Indians were represented in the legislative council by the agent general of immigration, a senior public servant. In 1917, in response to pressure from the Indian community, the government nominated an Indian, Badri Maharaj, to the legislative council, but not the preferred candidate of the community, Manilal Maganlal Doctor, who had the reputation of being a fearless defender of Indian rights in Fiji. He had been invited to come to Fiji from Mauritius by Indo-Fijians in 1912 to represent them in the courts and to colonial officialdom. He was Fiji's first Indian lawyer, and he had come with Mohandas K. Gandhi's blessing.

With the abolition of the indenture system, the question of the political representation of Indians came to the fore for the first time, spurred by a labour strike in Suva that year and one in the sugar industry a year later.[15] The Indo-Fijian population, numbering 60,634, out of a total population of 157,266 in 1921, were a far cry from their more subdued and dependent indentured forebears. Confident and determined, they demanded elected representation in the affairs of the colony. Their cause was championed by the government of India

---

[12]  Gillion (1962); Lal (1983).

[13]  Gillion (1962); Lal (1997).

[14]  Saunders (1984), p. 147.

[15]  Gillion (1977).

that called for equal and non-racial representation for the community. The equality of status of Indians with other groups in Fiji, India reminded the Fijian government, explicitly underpinned its approach to the emigration of its subjects: 'that the position of Indian immigrants in their new homes would in all respects be equal to that of any other class of His Majesty's subjects resident in Fiji'.[16] The Indians should be enfranchised along the same lines as Europeans – that is, with property qualifications that would continue to apply. No special concessions were asked for. The government of India merely asked that communal franchise should be replaced by a non-racial common roll franchise (of one person, one vote and one value). In response, the colonial government argued, not for the last time, that enfranchising Indians might jeopardise their commitment in the Deed of Cession to protect Fijian interests, avoiding the obvious question that if European enfranchisement did not jeopardise Fijian interests, how would the enfranchisement of Indians do that? The European response was that they were 'the trustees' of the Fijian people. Nonetheless, as a result of negotiations between Delhi, London and Suva, Indians received a franchise with three communal seats in Fiji's legislative council. The Fijians got three seats, all nominated by the Great Council of Chiefs, and five seats were given to Europeans.

Upon being elected to the legislative council in 1929, the Indian members boycotted it, demanding a common roll. In a memorandum to governor Murchison Fletcher on 29 December 1929, a group of prominent Indian leaders argued:

> The claim for a common franchise is a matter of principle to us and it is based on a sincere and earnest desire of the Indian community to work in amity and harmony with other sister communities living in the Colony. We are of the opinion that the present franchise on communal basis is bad in principle and harmful in working and intends to perpetuate the racial distinctions and bickering so much evident today in the Colony. Against the present franchise denotes to our mind an inferiority of political status which is not consonant with pledges and deliberations made on high and solemn authority regarding the equal political status, rights and privileges to Indian British subjects domiciled in various Crown colonies.[17]

Their protest failed, but the principle of non-racial electoral franchise would underpin Indian political discourse and demands for the next half-century. The demand for a common roll was the refrain of overseas Indian communities

---

[16] 'Report of British Guiana and Fiji Colonisation Committee Appointed with Reference to the Resolution of the Legislative Council on the 4th February, 1920', para 4, *United Provinces Gazette*, 22 May 1920, p. 211.

[17] Lal (2012), p. 5.

in the 1920s, but many Europeans argued that the common roll campaign was directed from abroad and that local Indians were content with their status. Equally, they felt that the principle of a common roll mattered less to Indians than equality with European rights. This contention fundamentally misread the situation at the time. Indians were no longer solely the tenants of the CSR but were branching out into independent commercial cultivation of their own and making steady inroads into trading in rural areas and in urban centres as well. The demand for a common roll and for equality was the outcome of a resurgent Indian community finding its feet in Fiji, and the challenge to European dominance was a by-product, not the cause of Indian political agitation.

European resistance to the Indian demands is understandable. An enfranchised community, confident and growing, would represent a challenge to their privileged position and continuing economic dominance. The demand for greater democracy in electoral representation also posed a challenge to the privileged position of Fijian chiefs who represented their people in the legislature. Responding to the Indian demand for a common roll and equal representation, the pre-eminent Fijian leader, Ratu Sir Lala Sukuna, an Oxford graduate and a soldier, made a speech in the legislative council in 1933 that had a long-term effect on Fiji's political development:

> Listening to the democratic clamour of the past months, one question repeatedly comes up in our minds, for what did our fathers cede this country? They did so in order to secure for themselves, their people and posterity forms of government that would ensure peace and happiness, justice and prosperity. Systems or institutions that fail in human experience to produce these things are not for us. For after all, the moral justification of representative government lies in its power to do good, and to achieve something of this the elements that contribute must all be present. We have come to the parting of the ways and, and, looking ahead in the light not only of our interests but also of those to whom we handed over this country, we choose, with the full support of the native conservative and liberal opinion, the system of nomination believing that along this road, and along it alone, the principle of trusteeship of the Fijian race can be preserved and the paramountcy of native interest secured.[18]

The colonial government was caught in a bind. The colonial office rejected governor Fletcher's recommendation to replace the elective system with nomination. That would go against the grain of its wider colonial policy, gradually empowering its colonial people to accept a role, albeit a restrictive one, in the governance of the colonial territories, and the government of India would almost

---

[18]  Lal (1992), p. 93.

certainly object. Similarly, Fletcher's bizarre proposal to introduce a modest number of Chinese immigrants to counteract the influence of the Indians was rejected as adding a further complication to an already complicated demographic and political situation.[19] In 1937, the colonial government adopted a new Letters Patent that provided for five members of the Indo-Fijians and Europeans in the legislative council, two each nominated and three elected on restricted franchise. All five Fijian representatives were nominated by the governor upon the advice of the Great Council of Chiefs. One of the two nominated Indo-Fijian members would always be a Muslim. They had been demanding separate Muslim representation since the 1920s and would continue to do so throughout the twentieth century.[20]

Debates over constitutional reform would continue to surface periodically for the next two decades concerning the merits or otherwise of the dominance of official majority in the legislative council, the merits of nomination and the elective principles of representation. However, two factors played a critical role in stalling change. One was the fear of 'Indian dominance' following the rapid expansion of the Indo-Fijian population, which exceeded that of the indigenous Fijians by the 1940s. The racial fears and phobias of the 1950s had a palpable effect on political attitudes leading to suggestions to deport Indo-Fijian boys and girls to the highlands of New Guinea and even the desolate Marquesas in eastern Polynesia to deal with the problem.[21] The other factor stalling change was the enthusiastic Fijian participation in the Second World War and in the Malaya campaign in the 1950s to demonstrate Fijian loyalty to the British Crown. By contrast, Indo-Fijian responses to the war effort were more muted, not the least because of pressure from the CSR discouraging recruitment of its tenant farmers and farm workers. The government appreciated the expression of Fijian loyalty and invoked the Deed of Cession and the United Kingdom's 'Trusteeship' guarantees to the Fijian people to thwart changes in any shape or form. The mantra of the deed became a millstone on the prospects of political progress.

The foundations of the colonial empire were shaken from the late 1940s, beginning with the independence of India in 1947 and the African colonies in the 1950s. British prime minister Harold Macmillan's 'Winds of Change' reached the Pacific by the early 1960s with Western Samoa (present-day Samoa) leading the way when it became an independent nation in 1962, followed by the Cook Islands in 1965. Reluctantly, the Fijian government presented a new

---

[19]  Lal (1992), p. 65.

[20]  Ali (1980).

[21]  Lal (1992).

Letters Patent in 1961 that enlarged the colonial legislature, removed property qualification for franchise and enfranchised women as well as commoner Fijians who had hitherto been represented by chiefs appointed by the governor on the recommendations of the Great Council of Chiefs. The reaction to these proposals followed a predicable path. Fijians and Europeans rejected outright independence and, even more, the idea of internal self-government. Ratu Kamisese Mara, the emerging Fijian leader and the country's first prime minister, said in 1961, 'We are not as stupid as that [to ask for independence]. What would we get out of it? We can't even pay for our own food. We would have to pay for everything, there would be no advantage in independence.'[22] Ratu Penaia Ganilau, who would be Mara's long-time deputy, saw in the proposal a betrayal of British promises to the Fijian people to always protect them. However, if Fiji was to be granted independence, he said, the islands should be returned to the Fijian people alone who had ceded them to the UK in the first place. The Indian leaders disagreed. A. D. Patel said, 'Who does not want independence? Even birds and animals want independence.[23] If the tiny islands of Western Samoa could become independent and self-sustaining, so could Fiji. Independence would come to Fiji sooner rather than later. The real question was whether it would come as Lakshmi, the goddess of wealth, or as Durga, the goddess of destruction.'

The other issue that caused great controversy in the 1960s was the method of election to the legislative council. Fijians and European leaders steadfastly stood by the communal roll. For them, this was natural and practical – their people would only trust one of their own kind to faithfully represent their interests, and they were perplexed why Indian leaders favoured a common roll. They saw in that demand sinister motives designed to dominate the politics of the country. For the Indian leaders, their cause was ideological. It was only through 'making one nation out of Fiji that we can achieve the sort of future we want for everybody', said Patel.[24] A common roll would encourage the development of a common citizenship and common consciousness rather than divided ethnic loyalties. It would encourage the development of genuine parliamentary democracy. It was the system of representation in most of the newly independent countries.[25] However, minds were already made up, and the prospects for progress on this would prove elusive for the rest of the twentieth century.

---

[22]  Lal (1992), p. 164.

[23]  Lal (1997), p. 159.

[24]  Lal (1997), p. 50.

[25]  Lal (1997), p. 192.

When it became clear that simple opposition to any constitutional change was untenable, Fijian leaders, with the support of their European counterparts, demanded the fulfilment of certain conditions before they would entertain any further proposals for constitutional development. These were articulated in the 'Wakaya Letter' that demanded the retention of the 'special relationship' between the Fijian people and the British monarchy, preferably along the lines of the relationship the Channel Islands enjoyed with the UK. Any change would have to embody the 'spirit and substance of the Deed of Cession', including the promotion of Christianity in the islands, the protection of Fijian landownership and a 'balance of races' in the civil service.[26] The Wakaya Letter was a powerful negotiating document for the Fijian position. However, constitutional change could not be stalled, especially as the United Nations (UN) Committee on Decolonisation was keeping a watchful eye on Fiji. When the UK government announced a constitutional conference in London in July 1965 to formulate a new constitution for the colony, the three groups articulated their views in contrasting terms. Patel told the conference:

> Political liberty, equality and fraternity rank among the good things of life and mankind all over the world cherishes and holds these ideals close to its heart. The people of Fiji are no exception. We in Fiji, as in other underdeveloped countries of the world, are faced with the three most formidable enemies of mankind, namely poverty, ignorance and disease. We need political freedom to confront these enemies and free our minds, bodies and souls from their clutches. When I refer to political freedom, I mean democracy under the rule of law, the sort of freedom that the British people and people of the United States enjoy. We need freedom which will politically, economically and socially integrate the various communities in Fiji and make out of them one nation deeply conscious of the responsibilities and tasks which lie ahead.[27]

Colonialism, Patel said, 'was a system of government universally condemned in the modern world'. For their part, Fijian and European leaders completely repudiated any severance of ties to the British monarchy at all. They saw no reason to. On the contrary, Ratu Mara celebrated Fiji's warm affection for the UK and saw no reason to 'attenuate, let alone abandon a historic and happy association'. The European delegation, led by J. N. Falvey, who was also an advisor to the Fijian delegation, echoed identical views to Mara's. The idea of independence, he said, was alien to most people in Fiji.[28]

---

[26]  Lal (1992), p. 189.

[27]  Lal (2006), pp. 242–243.

[28]  Lal (1997), p. 184.

The conference produced a constitution that had a happy outcome for Fijians and Europeans. An expanded legislature comprised twelve Fijian and Indian and eight European seats, of which the majority (nine each for Fijians and Indians and five for Europeans) would be communal seats, and the remaining three seats for each group would specify the candidates' ethnicity but would be elected by registered voters of all ethnic groups. They would be known as cross-voting seats. For the first time, the Great Council of Chiefs would have two members in the legislature nominated by itself that negated the principle of parity between the two groups. Further, Rotumans and other Pacific islanders would join the Fijian roll, and Chinese and part-Europeans would join the European roll. Only the Indians would not share seats with any ethnic group. Their political isolation was complete, which this was consistent with the UK's privately canvassed plans to devise a structure that would keep the status quo alive.

The Indo-Fijians rejected the constitutional outcome as 'iniquitous and undemocratic' and boycotted the legislative council after a year to force reconsideration of the constitution. The by-elections of 1968, which returned the National Federation Party (NFP)[29] with increased majority in its nine communal seats, signaled the need for a new constitution. A year later, negotiations between the two parties took place, but by then, Patel, the tireless campaigner for a common roll, had died, and with his death went the cause of a common roll. The new leader, S. M. Koya, proved ambivalent on an issue that had formed the cornerstone of his party's political platform and accepted 'race' as a political reality of life in Fiji. The independence constitution was, for all practical purposes, an extension of the 1966 constitution over which the NFP had fought a bitter by-election. It provided for a 52-seat lower house comprising of 27 racially reserved seats (12 each for Indo-Fijians and Fijians and three for general electors) and 25 national seats with racial reservation. The Great Council of Chiefs' nominees in the senate enjoyed the power of veto over all legislation relating to specifically Fijian issues. The NFP knew that under the new constitutional dispensation, the Fijians would always remain in power provided they remained united and had the solid support of the general electors, who were variously aligned by blood and history to the Fijians anyway. That was the unspoken 'time bomb' that lay hidden in the independence constitution, as Fiji's last governor, Robert Foster, informed London in his final despatch. He meant by this that the deep cracks about contentious issues – about

---

[29] The NFP was registered in 1964 from a loose 'Citizens Federation' formed during the sugar strike of 1960. Non-racial in political philosophy, its principal base was the Indo-Fijian community. The Alliance Party of Fijians, Europeans and a small group of Indo-Fijians was formed in 1965.

power sharing between the communities and the values and assumptions that underpinned the political settlement arrived at in London – were never really properly addressed nor faced in a hurry to get a smooth transition to independence. The constitution was negotiated behind closed doors and never subjected to a national referendum. Ideologically, the NFP and the ruling Alliance Party (henceforth, the Alliance; widely seen as a political vehicle of the traditional Fijian chiefs) became virtually indistinguishable from each other. The party's capitulation to a racialised view of politics in Fiji was also an unspoken acknowledgement of their limited space for action in view of the Fijian determination to remain in harness. The Indian leadership broke away from its era of agency and entered an era of acquiescence.

## Independence: From Agency to Acquiescence

Clearly, the 1970 constitution was not a new and imaginative charter for the nation laying the foundations of a fair and equitable society but a reaffirmation of the old order of racial compartmentalisation. The assumptions and understandings that underpinned it would be challenged and eventually undermined in the years following independence. The commitment to genuine multiracialism and power sharing suffered a major blow. The ideal of Fijian political unity on which Fijian power rested fractured over criticism of the dominance of chiefs from eastern parts of Fiji, the perception of neglect of certain regions in favour of others and the non-recognition of the rights of Fijians from western parts of the group in the traditional power arrangements. The Alliance lost the April 1977 elections when 25 per cent of Fijians voted against the ruling Fijian party. However, the governor general, who was also Fiji's highest-ranking chief, reappointed the defeated Alliance to power after the NFP was found to be divided over its leadership (and candidate for post of the prime minister). The delay of a few days gave the governor general the perfect excuse to restore the status quo. He had arrogated a right, the choice of a new government, which was the parliament's to exercise. A clearly divided NFP refused to challenge the governor general's decision. Ratu Mara's return to power had brought a sigh of relief to the country. There was also a general fear that continued political turbulence might bring with it strife and instability. The Fijian desire to retain power was clear, and it was also clear that Koya and his colleagues lost their nerves at a critical moment in post-colonial Fiji.[30]

In hindsight, April 1977 was a significant date in Fiji's post-colonial history. It was a temporary loss for a political party, but something more

---

[30]  Lal (1992).

profound occurred: it was the loss of a vision for a genuine multiracial future for Fiji. To win back power, Mara realised that he would have to bolster his indigenous base without which power would elude him. To that end, he marshalled all the resources at his command to cut the ground from under the Fijian nationalists. He succeeded. The Fijian Nationalist Party became a spent force by the late 1970s because its essential goals were silently appropriated by the ruling party. The nationalists' essential platform would be revived by small regional parties but without conviction or effect. The emphasis changed from trying to deport the Indians – an unattainable prospect anyway – to enduring that they knew their place in Fiji: they could make as much money as they wanted, but they should not aspire for political governance. That became the unspoken truth about Fijian politics hidden behind the paraphernalia of electoral processes.

To placate its Fijian constituency, the government adopted further measures. Among them was the reservation of Crown Schedule A and B lands.[31] These lands became Crown property because they were either unoccupied at the time of cession or had no recognised owners. As Crown land, they were to be used by the government for national purposes. Indeed, throughout the colonial period, the government had not touched the status of Crown land. But Mara was adamant. He clearly understood that land was power – Fijian power – and he intended to use it to full political advantage, reminding the country of the generosity of the Fijian people in sharing their land with others in the first place. The opposition Indian leaders reminded the government of their broader national responsibilities, including to Indo-Fijian tenants whose leases to Fijian landowners had expired and who were facing a dire future. The reservation of Crown land, according to Jai Ram Reddy, the opposition leader, was

> an act calculated to make the life of [Indo-Fijian tenants] more difficult in this country. This single decision more than any other in the ten years since independence will help ruin the kind of race relations we would like to develop in this country.[32]

However, there was no vote for the Alliance among displaced Indo-Fijian tenants whose problems were ignored. This issue deepened the rift between the two political parties and the two communities. Around this time, the expression 'blood will flow' if Fijian rights and sensibilities were not respected entered public discourse. What was intended to be understood was that the Fijian leadership of the country should not be challenged.

---

[31]   Lal (2009).

[32]   Lal (2009), p. 201.

Another pro-Fijian approach adopted by the government was the rapid promotion of a disproportionate number of indigenous Fijian civil servants to its upper echelons. In 1977, only 6 of the 31 permanent heads of departments were Indo-Fijians.[33] This was a major departure from the time of independence when the principle of parity was generally observed in public service appointments and promotions. By the late 1970s and the early 1980s, the promises of independence had gone. The culture of patronage and ethnic preferencing was visible for all to see. Once Indo-Fijians were safely ensconced in the civil service and proven to be dependable (they would all contest future elections under the Alliance banner), they were promoted upon transfer to other sections of the service until they reached the top. A classic example was Filipe Bole, a high school teacher from Mara's own province, promoted to the Education Department, appointed Fiji's permanent representative to the UN, appointed the permanent secretary of education, and then selected as a candidate for elections. He would later serve in the coup cabinets of both Sitiveni Rabuka and Frank Bainimarama. Bole, though, was not the only beneficiary of ethnic preferencing under the Alliance government.

A bigger national crisis erupted in 1975 when the indigenous Fijian leader Sakeasi Butadroka, formally of the Alliance, moved an astonishing motion in the parliament to have the Indian people of Fiji deported to India. The deputy prime minister, Ratu David Toganivalu, acknowledged the abhorrence of the sentiment but added that, in their darkest moments, many Fijians felt the same way. That assessment came as a deep shock to the Indo-Fijians, whose parliamentary leaders wanted an immediate and unequivocal repudiation of the motion. Ratu Mara moved a counter-motion acknowledging the contribution of all immigrant communities in Fiji. Whatever the logic behind this assessment, the ripple of fear and disillusionment was palpable in the Indo-Fijian community. The late 1960s and the early 1970s were a fraught time for Indian communities in many other parts of the world as they faced marginalisation and exclusion. The Indians in Trinidad and Tobago felt the wrath of the Black Power movement; Forbes Burnham's racist socialism took its toll on the Indians in Guyana; the plantocracy of French descent were making demands in Mauritius; there was apartheid in South Africa and the expulsion of Asians from Uganda in 1974. The timing of the Butadroka motion could not have been more inauspicious.

The promise of equality and partnership was visibly disappearing. All the former leading Indo-Fijian members of the Alliance – indeed its founding members, such as Vijay R. Singh and James Shankar Singh, both former cabinet

---

[33]  Lal (2009), p. 199.

ministers – left for the NFP, as did the party's lower-level functionaries. The ethnic divide in politics was nearly complete. When the NFP came within a whisker of winning the 1982 general elections, Fijian anger erupted. At the Great Council of Chiefs meeting on the historic island of Bau attended by Queen Elizabeth, Fijians threatened retribution against Indians for not voting for the Alliance in the general elections, by not reserving their agricultural leases, by reserving 75 per cent of the seats in parliament for indigenous Fijians and by warning against the *kaitanii* (foreigners) dividing the indigenous community. It was not the last naked threat of violence against the Indian community, and the silence of the leading chiefs was deafening. The expression 'blood will flow' entered the Fijian political discourse and began to be repeated widely as a warning to the Indo-Fijian community to respect the protocols of Fijian culture and, in effect, to accept the legitimacy of Fijian political rule.

Having won a closely fought election, the Alliance government embarked upon a series of austerity measures recommended by the International Monetary Fund (IMF). These included a 25 per cent wage reduction and a cutback in the intake of graduate teachers trained on government scholarships. Further, it dismantled the Tripartite Forum in which the government, the employers and the trade unions were party to the negotiation of wages and salaries and other conditions of employment. The ire of the hitherto non-political trade union movement was aroused, which led it to form the Fiji Labour Party (FLP) in July 1985. It was a modest movement towards the emergence of multiracial politics. The leader of the new party was an indigenous Fijian, Timoci Bavadra, and its other leaders were prominent members of the Fijian labour movement. The symbolism of multiracial cooperation represented by the FLP was threatening to the ruling Fijian elite whose long-standing mantra was that 'race is a fact of life'. They had been in power continuously for a generation (21 years) and regarded this as part of the natural order of things, a fulfilment of the promise of Fijian paramountcy that they believed emanated from the Deed of Cession.

When the FLP formed a coalition with the predominantly Indo-Fijian NFP and narrowly won the 1987 general elections, the wrath of the Fijian establishment was unleashed. The new government was buffeted by angry protest marches across the country, organised by militant Fijian nationalists determined to derail the new government. On 14 May 1987, a military coup finally deposed the Labour coalition government. The Fijian military is overwhelmingly indigenous both by design as well as necessity as the bulwark of indigenous Fijian power. Initially the coup was portrayed as a simple racial contest between an indigenous group trying to protect its rights against a grasping immigrant community intent on dispossessing them.[34] However, for all its sensationalism, it was a superficial explanation for a complex problem. Race was used as a scapegoat for other interests and agendas: a ruling chiefly elite reluctant to relinquish power, individuals without skills outside of politics, individuals with dynastic ambitions, others scared by the possible reconfiguration on the basis of traditional power arrangements in indigenous society and the reluctance of indigenous Fijians to accept the verdict of the ballot box if it did not deliver an outcome acceptable to them.[35] Racism and bigotry raised their ugly heads to extract Indo-Fijian acquiescence to the plans of the indigenous nationalists. The Taukei Movement, a loose coalition of various Fijian groups opposed to the coalition, demanded constitutional change to enshrine Fijian political control in perpetuity. Indo-Fijian tenants were threatened with the non-renewal of their agricultural leases if they refused to accept Fijian dominance. The Methodist church, to which most indigenous Fijians belonged, and which actively supported the coup and the cause of Fijian nationalism, demanded the declaration of Fiji as a Christian state. A strict observance of the sabbath was enforced and abandoned only when it was found to be particularly harmful to indigenous Fijians themselves, who were unable to access public transport, buy essential items from shops or indulge in their favourite pastime of weekend sport.

For their part, the Indo-Fijian community passively resisted the provocations and threats of violence and sought to raise their concerns in the international fora, more out of necessity than choice because all the guns were on the other side. In the Pacific region, criss-crossed by blood and kinship ties, especially in Polynesia, there was much sympathy for the 'Fijian cause' as they perceived it. For them, Fiji was a Fijian country, and democracy was merely a foreign flower unsuited to the Pacific soil anyway. Australia and New Zealand applied short-lived sanctions, and the Commonwealth Secretariat urged caution and a constitutional path to resolve political difficulties. However, all this counted for little with the rampant nationalists, and Indians had little leverage to extract meaningful political concessions from them.

In 1990, a new constitution was decreed that effectively encapsulated the Fijian nationalist agenda and disenfranchised the Indo-Fijian community altogether. It provided for a parliament elected exclusively on separate racial rolls, extinguishing the common roll from Fiji's political agenda. Of the 71 seats, indigenous Fijians were allocated 37, Indo-Fijians 27, 'Others' (Europeans, part-Europeans, Chinese

---

[34] Scarr (1988).

[35] Lal (1988).

and Pacific Islanders) five, and the tiny island of Rotuma one. This allocation was completely at odds with the ethnic composition of the population in which Indo-Fijians were nearly half the total population. Rural Fijian areas, where traditional chiefs held sway, were grossly over-represented in comparison to Fijians in urban areas, where nearly half of them lived, because the political 'loyalty' of urban Fijians to the traditional order could not be trusted. The government's pro-Fijian affirmative action policies were placed beyond the purview of parliamentary scrutiny. To top it all, all the most important offices of the state were reserved for indigenous Fijians – president, prime minister, chief justice, commander of the military forces and commissioner of police – as well as the heads of important statutory organisations such as the Public Service Commission. The programme of excluding Indo-Fijians from the governance of the country was complete. However, it was a pyrrhic victory for indigenous nationalists, for no sooner was the constitution decreed than divisions emerged among the indigenous Fijians. The incontrovertible fact was thus laid bare that the Fijian people were as divided by ancient greed and modern prejudices along class and regional lines as other communities and that only the real and manufactured threat of the Indo-Fijians had helped maintain a facade of indigenous Fijian unity.

Indo-Fijians unsurprisingly rejected the 1990 constitution and sought its revocation through constitutional means. To that end, they joined a bipartisan parliamentary committee to seek an independent review of the constitution. This was done by a three-person commission chaired by Paul Reeves, the former governor general of New Zealand, with an indigenous Fijian member, Tomasi Vakatora, and an Indo-Fijian, Brij V. Lal, the author. After exhaustive consultation throughout the country, the commission produced a report whose most important recommendations were for the country to gradually but decisively jettison the path of racial politics and to embrace the idea of democratic multi-ethnic governance based on the principles of inclusion and equality in the allocation of state resources.[36] It was a monumental achievement of reconciliation at a time of unpresented rancour and division.

A new constitution unanimously approved by the parliament endorsed the commission's recommendations for non-racial, open and transparent governance, but modified its recommendation for the majority of seats to be non-racial with the provision of a 71-seat parliament in which 46 seats would be racially reserved for the different communities in proportion to their population size and 25 would be open, that is, common roll seats. It was proposed that the racially reserved seats

---

[36]  Reeves, Vakatora and Lal (1996).

would be gradually reduced over time as citizens embraced the idea of non-racial politics. The 1997 constitution was a spectacular achievement in the circumstances, given the coup-scarred environment in which it took place. It was the handiwork of two men: Sitiveni Rabuka, the maker of the 1987 coup, and Jai Ram Reddy, the Indo-Fijian leader who was the principal target of the coup makers. It was his 'sincerity of purpose', as he put it, that won Rabuka over. In an address to the Great Council of Chiefs, a body of men and women who had endorsed the coup, Reddy gave a speech that laid out Indo-Fijian feelings to assuage their fears and doubts.[37] He spoke of history and memory. His ancestors had not come to Fiji to conquer or colonise, 'and we, their descendants, have no wish, no desire, to usurp your ancient rights and responsibilities'. Fiji was the home of the Indo-Fijian people: 'We have no other. We want no other.' He implored the chiefs gathered at the meeting to be chiefs not only of Fijians 'but for all the people of Fiji'. He reaffirmed his pledge to 'honour your place, and the place of your people as the first inhabitants of Fiji'. He spoke about the fears of his people, about being second-class citizens 'condemned to perpetual insecurity in the land of their own birth, doomed to be the eternal *vulagi* [guest]. I reach out to you today and seek your blessings for a better way of life.' Fijian interests were securely protected. There was nothing to fear on that count, and he called for courage to respond to the call of history to loosen the shackles of the past and embrace a united future. It was a remarkable moment of reconciliation.

The stability and harmony the new constitution promised soon proved illusory. A government elected under the 1997 constitution and led by an Indo-Fijian, Mahendra Chaudhry, was deposed in a putsch in 2000, a year after the elections. The main reason for derailing the government was the unwillingness of Fijian nationalists to accept the legitimacy of Chaudhry's government and especially his own occupation of the office of prime minister. Race was, once again, given as the reason for the ouster of the government, although the real reasons had more to do with the dynamics of traditional Fijian politics. George Speight was the frontman, but the names of the real players behind the scenes never came to light after the putsch failed, and Speight was jailed for life for his attempted treason. The shadowy figures behind it have remained in the shadows. The president, Ratu Sir Kamisese Mara, refused to defend the constitution and accepted Chaudhry's ouster as fait accompli, as a political necessity to resolve the impasse. The Great Council of Chiefs that had unanimously endorsed the 1997 constitution asked for its replacement by a more pro-Fijian one. Many of the Fijian leaders who

---

[37]  Lal (2009), pp. 633–639.

had voted for the constitution barely five years back turned their backs on it and endorsed the coup. 'Right cause, wrong method,' many of them said. A Fijian party, Soqoqo Duavata ni Lewenivanua, elected in the 2001 elections reintroduced pro-Fijian measures through a 'Fijian blueprint' with a vengeance.

These developments starkly underlined the vulnerability of the Indo-Fijian community. The promises of reconciliation contained in the achievement of the 1997 constitution receded over the horizon. The non-renewal of agricultural leases pushed long-term Indo-Fijian farmers into mushrooming squatter settlements around urban and peri-urban areas, forcing them to start all over again in the circumstances of great adversity that was common to their ancestors. However, they had nowhere else to go, and none would have them. Often, they lived on the sufferance of indigenous landowners on whose property they squatted. Increasingly, they became victims of burglaries and harassment. Many lived in the hope that the squatter settlements would not be their destination. Many entertained the hope that their children would acquire enough education to be able to emigrate. Emigration had been on the rise since 1987, and by the early years of the twenty-first century, over 120,000 had migrated mostly to Australia, New Zealand and North America. It is no exaggeration to say that Fiji's best and the brightest have left, mostly the professional classes, and the torrent is unlikely to subside anytime soon. With the significant decline in Indo-Fijian population, estimated to become less than 30 per cent within a few years, the fear of Indian domination that had so profoundly affected the texture of political life in Fiji has disappeared. Those who have remained in Fiji are often resigned to their fate as a minority community dependent on the goodwill of others.

## The 2006 Coup: Indo-Fijians between a Rock and a Hard Place

On 5 December 2006, Commodore Frank Bainimarama executed Fiji's fourth coup and removed a multiparty government headed by an indigenous Fijian, Laisenia Qarase.[38] He justified the military takeover as a 'clean-up campaign'. By that he meant cleaning the country of corruption, a claim he found difficult to prosecute in the courts. The coup by any other name was still a coup. It was not about saving the nation but, in truth, about saving Bainimarama's bacon. He had fallen out of favour with the elected government, which was determined not to renew his contract and had planned to reform the top-heavy Fijian military. Bainimarama struck before he was struck down and he proceeded methodically to entrench his position in the country through force and fear and a deluge of draconian decrees

---

[38]  Lal (2019).

that severely curtailed the freedom of speech and association, disabled rival centres of power, such as the trade union movement, the Sugar Cane Growers Council and the city and municipal councils, and, finally, cowed the judiciary. Censorship and self-censorship became travelling companions. Fear of retribution was real and interrogations at the military barrack well publicised.

Indo-Fijian reactions to the coup were mixed. Some political leaders and trade unionists stood up for the values of democracy and the rule of law, but the majority threw their support behind Bainimarama. Pragmatism rather than principle determined the overall reaction of the Indo-Fijian community. They had been victims of previous coups and targets of indigenous Fijian nationalism and quietly applauded the fact that these previous perpetrators were now tasting their own medicine, as the local expression goes. Revenge and retribution weighed heavily with them. Many Indo-Fijians living precariously in the squatter settlements and others languishing in the lower rungs of the socio-economic order saw promise and hope in Bainimarama's rhetoric and threw their support behind him. The Indo-Fijian business community were early supporters and financiers of Bainimarama, and so they have remained rewarded with diplomatic and lucrative appointments on the boards of statutory organisations. Many Indo-Fijian academics and former civil servants living abroad also saw in Bainimarama's intervention and in his incoherent effort to forge a path forward an opportunity to restructure Fijian society by presenting the coup leader with a template for a perfect democracy. One such example was a so-called 'Peoples Charter' that sought to prescribe a template for the governance of the country. Bainimarama would eventually disregard all this advice, but these efforts gave the appearance of public consultation and bought him valuable time to consolidate his hold on power.

Most surprising of all was the endorsement of the coup by Mahendra Chaudhry, the former prime minister, who himself had been a victim of the coup in 1987, when he was the finance minister in the coalition government, and in 2000, when he was the prime minister. In 2007, a month after the military takeover, he joined the Bainimarama regime as its finance minister. His decision dismayed many and hobbled opposition to the military regime. Chaudhry justified his participation as being in the national interest to stabilise the economy of the country, but it was more likely that, as the country's most experienced politician, he thought he would be the tail which would wag the dog. Bainimarama, though, had the last laugh. Eight months later, Chaudhry would leave the government and subsequently prosecuted for foreign exchange violations and prohibited from standing for elections for eight years. Used and discarded, Chaudhry would become a bitter critic of a government to which he had lent credibility at a crucial time.

Chaudhry's decision to participate in the Bainimarama regime was a monumentally flawed decision – not the least because it alienated the Indo-Fijian community from the indigenous Fijians, many of whom opposed the coup, and this severely affected race relations between the two communities.

In 2013, the Bainimarama regime decreed a new constitution after unceremoniously disregarding a draft prepared by a committee headed by the eminent constitutional lawyer Yash Ghai. That draft provided for a path back to meaningful representative democracy that required, among other things, an acknowledgement of the complicit role of the security forces in the coup before being granted immunity. The decreed draft rejected that and other recommendations. Some of the provisions of the new constitution were novel. It provided for a 52-seat parliament (instead of 71 seats), removed constituency-based elections in favour of making the whole country a single constituency, abolished race-based franchise altogether, discontinued any role for the Great Council of Chiefs in matters of particular indigenous concerns and gave all of Fiji's citizens a common name, Fijian, a word which since cession in 1874 had been associated exclusively with the indigenous community. The principle of Fijian political paramountcy that had underpinned Fiji's political discourse throughout the twentieth century was abolished. Many Indo-Fijians welcomed the 2013 constitution's equal citizenship provisions as fulfilling a dream they had held for a long time.

However, certain provisions of the constitution that have the potential to wreak havoc in the future escaped the Indo-Fijians. One is the truth that the constitution is virtually impossible to change. For that to take place, it would need 75 per cent of the votes of the parliament and an equal percentage of votes of all the registered voters. In these circumstances, the only way to change it would be to abrogate it and draft a new one. This course of action has precedence in Fiji's post-colonial past (in 1987 and 2006). A more ominous provision is Article 131, which gives the military the overall responsibility for the 'security, defense and wellbeing' of the nation. In effect, the military enjoys a guardian role over the constitution. It will be the military that will interpret and enforce the constitution, not the parliament. In other words, no change will be possible without the assent of the military. The Fijian military, it should be remembered, is virtually entirely ethnic Fijian.

In the 2014 and 2018 general elections, 80 per cent to 90 per cent of Indo-Fijians voted for Bainimarama's FijiFirst party. It is clear that the majority of Indo-Fijians regard Bainimarama and not any Indo-Fijian as their leader, and they show their feelings of respect and gratitude towards him in abasing ways: schoolchildren ceremoniously washing his feet as a sign of welcome and respect, doing *arti* (a Hindu lamp-burning ritual) for him in his presence and inviting him to give political speeches at temples. They see him as a saviour standing between them and the Fijian nationalists. Seventeen of the twenty-seven members on the government benches are Indo-Fijians, while the opposition benches are occupied by indigenous Fijians and a lone Indo-Fijian who is also the leader of the NFP. It is a curious sight indeed, full of irony, but in truth Indo-Fijians on the government's side are small figures with no independent record of public service or other noticeable accomplishments. Bainimarama has placed his men in strategic positions in the police force, the military and in charge of prisons: Brigadier General Sitiveni Qilino is the commissioner of police, Lieutenant Colonel Ben Nalluva and Major Asaeri Rokouso, Bainimarama's former personal guards, occupy senior positions in the military, and his brother-in-law, Francis Kean, is the commissioner of corrections services. He is safe for the moment, but what happens when he goes? This is the dilemma facing the Indo-Fijian community. They are caught between a rock and a hard place. They have burned their bridges with the indigenous Fijians, and they have no option but to stick with Bainimarama. However, the larger question looms: what after Bainimarama?

## Where to from Here?

Indo-Fijians in the early decades of the twenty-first century are a far cry from their counterparts on the eve of independence. Then they were half the population, confident and optimistic. They had taken on the mighty CSR Company and forced its departure from Fiji after its 90 years of domination of the economy of the country. They had branched out into farming as well as the retail and service sectors of the urban economy, in which they were becoming pre-eminent. Their health and literacy levels were all exceptional by the standards of other Pacific Islands nations. With their new-found confidence, they drove the pace of political change against the combined opposition of Fijians and Europeans. They presented an alternative vision for the country. They demanded parity of political representation and a fair representation in the public sector. Most saw no alternative but to live in Fiji and secure a future there. The country had their commitment of heart and mind. However, all that is in the distant past. Now, uprooted and on the margins, everyone who can emigrate is emigrating. The safety valve of emigration has been an important factor in shaping the community. The decline of the sugar industry and the general unattractiveness of rural life with its absence of jobs and employment opportunities have forced people into urban and peri-urban areas and often into low-paying employment. Economic and physical security is a topmost priority in the minds of most Indo-Fijians, which is why they are prepared to trade rights and freedoms to achieve it. Freedom of speech exists on paper, but censorship and self-censorship are the order of day. The limits and limitations are obvious and quietly acknowledged but are seen as the reality of life in Fiji. A sense of powerlessness is palpable. Bainimarama is often paraded as a demigod beyond reproach even when (as late as 2019) he freely abuses and assaults opponents within the precincts of the parliamentary complex. The person he assaulted was a former soldier and now the president of the NFP and a member of parliament, Pio Tikoduadua. He needs public adulation for self-affirmation, and Indo-Fijians provide him that in ample measure, both out of appreciation as well as opportunism. The preference for rule by a strongman rather than the rule of law has its perils. Indo-Fijians have become a minority in numbers and diminished in influence and stature, destined to live on the grace and goodwill of others. Immigration to emigration may, indeed, come to be the epitaph of the Indo-Fijian people.

## Bibliography

Ali, Ahmed. 1980. *Plantation to Politics: Studies on Fiji Indians*. Suva: Fiji Times.
———. 2007. *Fiji and the Franchise: A History of Political Representation, 1900–1937*. New York: iUniverse.
Brij V. Lal. 2012. *Chalo Jahaji: On a Journey through Indenture in Fiji*. Canberra: Australia National University Press.
Chapman, J. K. 1964. *Career of Sir Arthur Hamilton Gordon, First Lord Stanmore*. Toronto: University of Toronto Press.
France, Peter. 1969. *Charter of the Land: Custom and Colonisation in Fiji*. Melbourne: Oxford University Press.
Fraenkel, Jon, Stewart Firth and Brij V. Lal (eds.). 2009. *The 2006 Military Takeover in Fiji: A Coup to End All Coups*. Canberra: Australian National University Press.
Gillion, K. L. 1962. *Fiji's Indian Migrants: A History to the End of Indenture in 1920*. Melbourne: Oxford University Press.
———. 1977. *Fiji Indians: Challenge to European Dominance, 1920–1946*. Canberra: Australian National University Press.
Lal, Brij V. 1983. *Girmitiyas: The Origins of the Fiji Indians*. Canberra: Fiji Institute of Applied Studies.
———. 1988. *Power and Prejudice: Making of the Fiji Crisis*. Wellington: New Zealand Institute of International Affairs.
———. 1992. *Broken Waves: A History of the Fiji Islands in the Twentieth Century*. Honolulu: University of Hawaii Press.
———. 1997. *A Vision for Change: AD Patel and the Politics of Fiji*. Canberra: National Centre for Development Studies.
——— (ed.). 2006. *Fiji: British Documents on the End of Empire*. London: The Stationery Office.

———. 2009. *In the Eye of the Storm: Jai Ram Reddy and the Politics of Postcolonial Fiji*. Canberra: Australian National University Press.

———. 2019. *Levelling Wind: Remembering Fiji*. Canberra: Australian National University Press.

Larmour, Peter, 2005. *Foreign Flowers: Institutional Transfers and Good Governance in the Pacific*. Honolulu: East West Center.

Milne, R. S. 1981. *Politics in Ethnically Bipolar States: Guyana, Malaysia, Fiji*. Vancouver: University of British Columbia Press.

Moynagh, Michaël. 1981. *Brown or White? A History of the Fiji Sugar Industry 1878–1973* (Australian National University Pacific Research Monograph Series, no. 5). Canberra: Australian National University.

Ravuvu, Asesela D. 1991. *Façade of Democracy: Fijian Struggle for Political Control, 1830–1987*. Suva: South Pacific Books.

Reeves, Paul, T. R. Vakatora and Brij V. Lal. 1996. *Towards a United Future: Report of the Fiji Constitution Review Commission* (Fiji Parliamentary Paper, no. 34/1996). Suva: Fiji Constitution Review Commission.

Saunders, Kay (ed.). 1984. *Indentured Labour in the British Empire, 1934–1920*. London: Croom Helm.

Scarr, Deryck. 1980. *Ratu Sukuna: Soldier, Statesman, Man of Two Worlds*. London: Macmillan Publishers.

——— (ed.). 1984. *Fiji: A Three-Legged Stool: Selected Writings of Ratu Sir Lala Sukuna*. London: Macmillan Publishers.

———. 1988. *Politics of Illusion: Military Coup in Fiji*. Kensington, NSE: University of New South Wales Press.

Tinker, Hugh. 1974. *A New System of Slavery: Export of Indian Labour Abroad, 1834–1920*. London: Oxford University Press.

———. 1977. *Separate and Unequal: India and the Indians in the British Commonwealth, 1920–1950*. St Lucia, Brisbane: University of Queensland Press.

# 16

## New and Old Diasporas of South South Asia

### Sri Lanka and Cyber-Nationalism in Malaysia*

*Darini Rajasingham-Senanayake*

Having been borne across the world, we are translated men. It is normally supposed that something always gets lost in the translation; I cling, obstinately, to the notion that something can also be gained....

[W]e will not be capable of reclaiming precisely the thing that was lost; we will, in short, create fictions, not actual cities or villages, but invisible ones, imaginary homelands, Indias of the mind.

—Salman Rushdie[1]

Introduced following the official abolition of the slave trade in the British Empire in 1833, Indian indentured labour migration in turn came largely to an end by the end of First World War. By the time of its abolition, millions from the Indian subcontinent had shipped across the Indian Ocean and around the globe. Many were 'free migrants', or so-called passenger Indians, but others had signed an agreement to perform contract labour as indentured workers for three to five years in colonial plantations, on railways or roads, or in construction work.[2] Whether in neighbouring Ceylon (present-day Sri Lanka) and Malaya (present-day Malaysia) or further afield in Fiji, Africa or the Americas, from Jamaica to Trinidad and Tobago in the Caribbean, to Surinam in South Africa, Kenya,

---

* A previous version of this chapter was originally published as an article titled 'Of Cyber-Nationalism & Tea Parties: New & Old Diasporas of South–South Asia' in the *Colombo Telegraph* on 23 October 2017, https://www.colombotelegraph.com/index.php/of-cyber-nationalism-tea-parties-new-old-diasporas-of-south-south-asia (accessed on 3 August 2022). All rights reserved. Reproduced with the permission of the *Colombo Telegraph*.

1 Rushdie (1992).

2 *Girmit* referred to the 'agreement' of the British government with the Indian labourers which determined their length of stay overseas and when they would be allowed to go back to India.

Uganda and Mauritius, first-generation 'coolies' – the name given to bonded labour migrants and those recruited under the *kangani* system (where free migrants were recruited by Indian intermediaries) – courageously journeyed for the larger part of a century, first by sail and then by steamship, to live and labour in far-off lands.

Indentured and free labour migrants from India and their descendants, who worked in the lucrative sugar, rubber, cotton, coffee, cocoa and tea plantations in the tropics of the world, played an essential role in the development of the modern world and the functioning of global capitalism, as Crispin Bates, Adam Mckeown and Sunil Amrith have noted.[3] Yet the oral history and literary record of generations of Indian indentured diasporic communities echo narratives of social suffering. They describe the struggle for agency against victimhood within the colonial plantation economies. Their literature and songs detail loss and longing for an increasingly 'imaginary homeland', similar to those portrayed in the writings of African American descendants of the transatlantic slave trade.[4]

In academic writing and ethnography, indentured migration from India has been viewed mainly as a process of cynical exploitation of passive labour under colonialism, while migrants and their descendants were seen as victims who had little control over the decision to cross the *kala pani* (the black seas that some believed stripped the elite of their caste status) and the outcomes of their migration.[5] These imbalances in the representation of Indian overseas migration are being redressed in research that explores the diverse forms of mobilisation, agency and resistance amongst Indian migrants.[6] At the same time, the south Indian, or Dravidian, labour diaspora that includes Tamil, Telugu, Malayalee and Kanada migrants has remained marginal in studies of the Indian diaspora with a few notable and recent exceptions.

Until recently, diasporic descendants of south Indian indentured labour were largely ignored by the Indian state, even as it reached out to Silicon Valley non-resident Indians (NRIs). Remarkably, it was only in May 2017 that an Indian prime minister chose to visit and acknowledge the Hill Country descendants of

---

[3] Bates (2017); McKeown (2004); Amrith (2013).

[4] The everyday social suffering and precarious residency status of Indian indentured labour communities within the confines of the ultra-exploitative colonial plantation economy echo in the writings of members of the Girmitiya diaspora and their descendants, as much as in social science and historiographic accounts of these communities.

[5] See Tinker (1974). The idea of Indian fears of the *kala pani* is now widely regarded as an exaggerated orientalist trope, with the exception of its application to political prisoners transported to the Andaman Islands, for whom it had a special meaning. See Bates and Carter (2021).

[6] See, for example, A. Kumar (2017).

south Indian indentured labour in Sri Lanka. However, on 3 September 2016, nearly 100 years after the abolition of indenture, a group of Malaysians, mainly of south Indian indentured migrant origin, held demonstrations in Kuala Lumpur (KL) where they tried to assault the chief monk of the Sri Lankan Buddhist temple in Sentul. They were protesting against the visit of the former war-winning Sri Lankan president, Mahinda Rajapaksa, to Malaysia to attend the ninth International Conference of Asian Political Parties, convened at the Putra World Trade Centre in KL, and his reception as a VIP by the Malaysian state. The group of about 50 protesters had gone to the Sentul Buddhist temple when rumours of Rajapaksa's visit began to spread. The protests gained coverage in the national press, both in Malaysia and Sri Lanka.[7]

Why were diasporic Indians in Malaysia protesting before a Buddhist temple patronised by a former prime minister of Sri Lanka? What were the motives for the attempted assault? The three-decades-long armed conflict (1983–2009), waged by the Liberation Tigers of Tamil Eelam (LTTE) for a separate state for the Tamil minority in north-east Sri Lanka, had ended in 2009 amidst allegations of war crimes committed by both the Sri Lankan state and the LTTE. Why had it elicited such broad-based support from south Indian overseas communities throughout the world? The September 2016 protests in KL were reminiscent of other protests by the Tamil diaspora, held in the spotlight of the international media in major world capitals, ranging from New Delhi to London, Toronto and Washington, in May 2009, during the last days of the war in Sri Lanka. The protests then were in response to the LTTE being destroyed by the island's military. A troubled 'peace' has since dawned on the island.

This chapter explores the political economy of 'cyber-nationalism' among south South Asia's new and old diaspora communities and traces the emergence of a global Tamil 'ethnoscape'. It suggests that the 'Tamil national question' in Sri Lanka, during the LTTE's search for Tamil Eelam, reconfigured and boosted the diasporic identities and activism of significant groups of descendants of indentured south Indian migrant communities, many of whom constitute an emergent global 'precariat', even as the Tamil Eelam morphed into an 'imaginary homeland' seemingly inclusive of an older south Indian diaspora in Malaysia and beyond.[8] This was arguably due to the insecure and precarious economic and political status of many south Indian diasporic communities that constitute 'minority groups' with diminished citizenship, economic rights and cultural entitlements in

---

[7]   K. Kumar (2016).

[8]   Standing (2011). Standing distinguishes the precariat from the salaried, proletariat and lumpen underclass.

post-colonial states such as Malaysia and Sri Lanka. Chelva Kanaganayakam has noted the burgeoning of creative writing during the three decades of political struggle in the island in what we may term a global Tamil ethnoscape.[9] Simultaneously, diasporic descendants of Indian indentured labour migrants seemed to emerge as a 'new dangerous class', even as their ancestors may well be viewed, retrospectively, as archetypal precursors of the contemporary global precariat.[10]

Guy Standing termed the precariat 'an emerging global mass class', characterised by precarious employment, debt and insecurity.[11] Members of the precariat, potentially the democratic majority as well as the 'new dangerous classes', are diverse: immigrant Uber drivers, millennial interns, part-time lecturers, temporary factory workers, and the cleaners and couriers of the 'gig economy' – the old working class, forced into temporary and casual labour. Many protestors at the Sentul Buddhist temple were descendants of indentured labour communities that had been ghettoised in British rubber plantations in Malaysia, where they were segregated from wider society and treated as second-class citizens. Many had subsequently managed to migrate to urban areas, where they were free from the strictures of the colonial plantation economy and were simultaneously upwardly mobile. Nevertheless, they were still treated as non-*bhumiputra* (sons of the soil) members of an Indian-origin ethnic minority in Malaysia. They belonged to a class that lived precarious lives in the urban post-colony; having escaped the stigma of coolie labour in the plantation economy, they still remained trapped in precarious jobs and urban poverty. In a sense, they were and are the 'inheritors of loss', the losers of (neo)liberal globalisation and the contemporary economic restructuring of labour. Some were members of the Hindu Rights Action Force (HINDRAF) movement for Malaysian Indian minority rights, which exploded onto the political scene with a mass rally in KL in 2007.[12] Their activism and resistance to the long-sustaining structures of economic inequality and political marginalisation were later on increasingly visible in other resistance movements opposed to the ongoing structural adjustment of labour regimes.

The group that attacked the Sri Lankan Buddhist temple was comprised of members of the Malaysian Indian Progressive Association and the Malaysian

---

[9]   Kanaganayakam (2009), p. 81.

[10]  Standing (2011) outlined the political risks that the precariat might pose and what might be done to diminish inequality and allow such workers to find a more stable labour identity. His concept and conclusions have been widely taken up by thinkers from Noam Chomsky to Zygmunt Bauman, by political activists and policymakers.

[11]  Standing (2011).

[12]  Kaur (2017).

Indian Education Transformation Association (MIETA). They began to burn an effigy of Rajapaksa in front of the temple. When the chief monk, Sri Saranan, came out of the temple, some individuals questioned him about Rajapaksa's arrival and then abused and punched him. The Sentul police prevented the crowd from further attacking the monk. The MIETA chairman, A. Elangovan, later entered the temple along with the police and apologised to the monk. Subsequently, the police told reporters that members of the Light Strike Force and some officers would be stationed at the temple to ensure peace as certain people could turn up with sticks and stones. M. Shammuga, the leader of another group, had said that a vigil would be kept to ensure that Rajapaksa did not make an appearance: 'Once he [Rajapaksa] comes here, we are going to demonstrate against him so that he will not enter the temple.'[13]

Under Rajapaksa as president, the Sri Lankan military had defeated the LTTE, even as his regime was accused of war crimes. More significantly, Rajapaksa had destroyed the dream of an 'imaginary homeland' that many in the global Tamil diaspora had begun to identify and empathise with in order to restore a victim community with pride, dignity and self-respect. Nationalist pride as well as the circulation of narratives of collective social suffering and victimhood are two sides of a coin. The LTTE's nationalist struggle for 'Tamil rights' became a cause célèbre and a lightning rod for resistance, agency and 'long-distance cyber-nationalism'. The struggle was structured by the complex play of home- and host-country dynamics of inherited exclusion among diasporic descendants of indentured labourers across generations and aided by social media and new information and communication technologies. It was the existential insecurity of precarious or second-class citizenship in 'host' countries as much as the strength of descendants of the south Indian indentured migrant diaspora that the LTTE had been able to mobilise, posing a formidable challenge to the Sri Lankan state.

Much ink has been spilt on the question of nationalism, including cyber-nationalism: Would it die out with globalisation, the migration of peoples, ideas and things? Or would it take new forms? The case of the descendants of the indentured south Indian labour diaspora's support for the armed struggle of the LTTE and Ceylonese Tamils suggests that both propositions seem to be true, depending on local context, patrimonies of precarious work, inequity and citizenship. Expanding global patterns of inequality and advances in new communication technologies that enable labour and diasporic networking and activism must also be taken into account. At the same time, the cyber-activism of precariat groups is increasingly

---

[13]  Tan (2016).

conflated by national-security states threatened by ISIS recruitment from the Middle East and North African diasporas in Europe.

## Malaysia 2016: The Afterlife of Empire

A day after the events at the Putra World Trade Centre and Sentul, Ibrahim Sahib Ansar, the Sri Lankan envoy to Malaysia, was assaulted by a group of people at the Kuala Lumpur International Airport (KLIA). He was there to see off the visiting Sri Lankan minister, Daya Gamage, and deputy minister, Anoma Gamage. Fearing for his safety, Ansar later requested the court to move the trial on his assault from the court in Sepang District to the capital city of KL. He believed that his safety could not be guaranteed if he were to attend the trial in the Sepang Sessions Court as witness because large groups of Tamils had gathered there during the last two case managements. Tamil businessmen of Indian origin – A. Kalaimughilan (26), V. Balamurugan (33) and V. Ragunathan (38) – had claimed the right to trial in the Sepang Sessions Court the previous year on charges of assaulting Ansar. The high commissioner said he was still traumatised by the brutal attack on him at KLIA, a public area, that ought to have had tight security measures. Remarkably, none of the attackers were of Ceylonese or Sri Lankan origin, as a debate on the incident in the Sri Lankan parliament revealed, with Tamil National Alliance leader, R. Sambanthan, being at pains to stress that Sri Lankan Tamils (including the Sri Lankan diaspora) were not returning to violence against the Sri Lankan state and its overseas representatives.

The passions that the conflict in Sri Lanka raised among Malaysians of Indian origin had much to do with a sense of marginalisation within the Malay polity. This was translated into sympathy towards real and perceived discrimination experienced by fellow Tamils of Sri Lanka. A sense of pan-Tamil linguistic nationalism and the play of ethnic identity politics in Malaysia also played its part. Indians form the third-largest ethnic group in Malaysia after the Malays and the Chinese. Malaysia is home to one of the largest populations of overseas Indians, constituting of 7 per cent of the Malaysian population, 90 per cent of whom are Tamils. Often, they materially supported the violent armed struggle of the LTTE. The head of the LTTE's international wing was arrested in Malaysia, where he had lived for many years, deported to Sri Lanka and placed under house arrest.

Ironically, rather than joining the LTTE's struggle for a separate state, the leadership of the Tamil indentured labours in the hills of Sri Lanka have consistently struggled to belong in the Sri Lankan state ever since they were initially disenfranchised in 1948.[14] It was the indigenous Ceylonese Tamils of Lanka – whose formal citizenship and belonging in the post-colonial state was less obviously in question – who rejected the state because of real and perceived discrimination by the ethnic majority Sinhala Buddhists and launched a struggle for a separate state in north-east Sri Lanka. On the other hand, Indian indentured migrants – called Hill Tamils, or Malayakam, in Sri Lanka (who were disenfranchised by the post-colonial state's infamous Ceylon Citizenship Act of 1948 on the grounds that they were Indian, but were later granted citizenship on the intervention of India under the Sirima–Shastri Pact) – steadfastly struggled for acceptance, national belonging and full citizenship in the post-colonial state of Sri Lanka (like their kin in Malaysia) rather than rejecting the state and struggle for the creation of an independence state (Tamil Eelam). The political leaders of Indian labour migrants in Sri Lanka, such as Arumugam Thondaman of the Ceylon Workers' Congress (CWC), refused to join the struggle for Tamil Eelam, preferring to engage with the state to broaden the citizenship rights of Indian-origin Tamils of Sri Lanka. This was partly because the indigenous Ceylonese Tamils had worked with the Sinhala majority to pass the Act of 1948 and the Indian–Pakistani Citizenship Act of 1949 to disenfranchise the Malayakam due to a fear of the influence of Marxist and leftist ideologies on plantation communities. This was also because of the history of caste and class discrimination by Ceylonese Tamils against indentured Indian Tamils settled in the British plantations of the central hills.

During this 30-year war, Tamil refugees and migrants from north-east Sri Lanka, or Ceylon Tamils, turned to already established communities and the religious institutions (Hindu *kovils*) of the older south Indian indentured labour diaspora throughout the world for assistance and received ready support, as they did from Tamil Sangams. The LTTE's struggles for Tamils in Sri Lanka tapped into a reservoir of sentiment among Malaysians in the Indian indentured labour diaspora because of their shared historical experiences of marginalisation, both by the colonial and post-colonial state. Tamil refugees from Sri Lanka from 1980 to 2009 also found common cause and shared patterns of Hindu worship with the descendants of Indian indentured labour communities in Malaysia and other parts of the world where they joined the precariat and shared in its common culture. The present forms of labour and modern forms of 'precarious citizenship' and their resonance with the struggles of other overseas south Indian communities in their host countries were evident in the sympathy and support that Sri Lankan Tamils and the LTTE garnered from significant organisations and groups in the

---

[14]  Bass (2013).

global Tamil diaspora. Many migrants of south Indian origin from Malaysia and Indian-origin twice-migrants domiciled in North America, Europe and Australia – displaced from South Africa, Kenya, Uganda and Tanzania – tended to identify with the LTTE's project of a separate state for Tamils. This arguably displaced some of the sense of marginalisation and frustration that they experienced in their respective host or home countries.

The members of the LTTE, which promoted the out-migration and resettlement of refugees, found sympathy and support from the descendants of south Indian Tamil indentured labourers who continued to be marginalised because of the structure of the plantation economy and their ethnic minority status in Malaysia. Thus, in a time of emergency, caste and regional differences that existed between the Ceylonese Tamils and the Malayakam in Sri Lanka were blurred when in the diaspora. In Sri Lanka, too, there was a movement by the plantation communities displaced by conflict to the north-east of the island to areas where the Ceylonese Tamil community constituted a majority.

Arguably, post-colonial Tamil migration from Sri Lanka during war in that country was both a distraction from more local discrimination in countries such as Malaysia and a cause célèbre for agency and activism for many Malaysians of south Indian origin who had felt the weight of Malay *bhumiputra* nationalism. Thus, we may track how the global Tamil diaspora, the majority with roots in south India's Tamil Nadu, became activists for Ceylonese or Sri Lankan Tamils as a result of successive 'displacements' – mental and material.

Contemporary Tamil and Dravidian diasporic identity politics in Malaysia and elsewhere were displaced onto questions of citizenship and the national belonging of Tamils in the post-colonial state of Sri Lanka. The precarious situation of minority Tamils in Sri Lanka resonated with the insecure precariat conditions of many ethnic-minority south Indians in Malaysia and enabled a shared search for a separate state or 'imaginary homeland' for Tamils in north-east Sri Lanka. Many in the global south Indian indentured labour diaspora, mainly Tamil- and Telugu-speaking communities, had identified with the dream of Tamil Eelam destroyed by Rajapakse. Thus the reason adduced for the attack by protestors at Sentul was that they were protesting 'war crimes' committed in Sri Lanka during the war against the LTTE, listed at that time as one of the most dangerous terrorist groups in the world by the Rajapaksa regime, which lost power in January 2015.

## Neoliberalism and the Sense of Loss

Significant groups of south Indian descendants of the indentured labour diaspora in countries such as Malaysia, who found common cause and voice in the post-colonial Sri Lankan diasporic struggle for Tamil Eelam, were the losers of neoliberal economic globalisation. They were the inheritors of loss before, during and after the birth of the modern nation state in the Afro-Asian post-colony. Characterised by precarious citizenship and exploitative work and living conditions in the plantations' paternalistic set-up, on the edge of debt insecurity and inequality, they joined the precariat as they moved beyond the confines of the plantation. Such conditions increasingly fuelled the political activism of dangerous classes in the global precariat among communities with shared histories of precarity across continents, as the support in modern times garnered by the Sri Lankan Tamil struggle from Malaysian Tamils of Indian origin would indicate.

The south Indian indentured labour diaspora in Malaysia constitutes an ethnic minority community (like their kin in Sri Lanka) and identifies with post-colonial Tamil cyber-nationalism in Sri Lanka promoted by the LTTE, giving rise to new forms of agency and activism, political organisation and networking in the context of new social media and information technologies. It is debatable that a distinct south South Asian diaspora, which encompasses south India and Sri Lanka, emerged via a pan-Dravida and subaltern, or Dalit (caste), struggle of the descendants of indentured labourers, who shared a common sense of belonging with the post-colonial precariat and found pride and dignity in the Tamil nationalism of the LTTE struggle.

Old and new diasporic communities appear to be drawn to long-distance ethno-religious cyber-nationalism, as they live lives of marginalisation and existential insecurity enforced by the state. Sometimes they indulge in 'days of rage' and protest, even as they are made increasingly insecure by states that tend to distrust minorities, refugees, migrants and diasporas. The notion of 'precarious citizenship' that encompasses both economic and political marginalisation and exclusion may explain the enormous support for post-colonial Sri Lankan Tamil cyber-nationalism and a separate state or territory for Tamils in the Global South: a South Asian indentured labour 'post-colony' (akin to the attraction of Palestine or Israel to the besieged European Jew). Shadow lines and histories of sometime mutually reinforcing exclusion and marginalisation (along caste, class, gender and ethno-religious lines) were, in different ways, constitutive of the attraction of Tamil Eelam cyber-nationalism for communities, which for generations had remained economically, politically and culturally marginalised, given the structure of the post-colonial plantation economy and the rise of post-colonial majoritarian nationalism in countries such as Malaysia and Sri Lanka. Here, Indian-origin indentured labour descendants were twice marginalised by Sinhala Buddhist nationalism and Malay *bhumiputra*-ism, with affirmative action or positive discrimination policies for Malays and the majority community. Hence, it is through lineages of dispossession as well as shared cultural factors that we may map an emergent community of the South Asian diaspora in the Global South in Malaysia, Sri Lanka and beyond.

## Conclusion: Traversing the Local and the Global

There were many migrations back and forth across the Bay of Bengal and the Indian Ocean Rim countries from South Asia to Southeast Asia prior to, during and after the British Raj and the arrival of the modern nation state in the Indian Ocean region. So too were there divergent patterns of struggle for citizenship, accommodation and labour rights in host communities – that is, home countries. In colonial times, Ceylonese Tamil migrants to Malaya (including Singapore) tended to be of the professional classes and higher castes who lived in urban centres and did not often associate with communities of Indian indentured Tamil labour from south India, who tended to be confined within the plantation political economy. Thus, in 2017, on a state visit to Sri Lanka, the Singaporean foreign minister, Vivian Balakrishnan, after visiting Jaffna – the cultural homeland of Sri Lankan Tamils and meeting with Northern Provincial Council officials – noted that Jaffna held special significance for Singapore, given strong cultural and people-to-people ties. He said that the relationship had evolved from the early days of government administrators to fit with present-day institutions, such as the Singapore Ceylon Tamils' Association. The deputy prime minister of Singapore at this time is of Ceylonese Tamil descent, even though Sri Lanka has never had a head or a deputy head of state from its Tamil minority communities. 'Some of our pioneering leaders in politics, education and medicine have hailed from Jaffna. Today, we are here to strengthen these enduring ties and give back to Jaffna,' said Balakrishnan.[15]

While many Indian indentured migrants and their children assimilated and joined the professional classes and prospered in host countries, other groups and individuals from the indentured labour diaspora had different and negative experiences. These were particularly because of the social and spatial segregation of plantations where the majority were ghettoised due to the legal and administrative structure of the plantation economy of the British Raj and the lack of social capital resulting from caste and class marginalisation in their home countries. Moreover, the structure of exclusion in the plantation economy of the Raj persisted in the post-colony when plantations were transferred to majoritarian states or local elites.

---

[15] *Straits Times* (2017).

The agency, activism (including long-distance cyber-nationalism) and identity politics of succeeding generations of descendants of south Indian indentured labour migrants, many of whom constitute a modern precariat diaspora in the countries where their ancestors settled and gained citizenship, have been long shadowed in the violence and despair of their ancestors' original displacement. So too have their struggles for acceptance, belonging, citizenship and labour rights in the countries in which they worked and settled, mainly in tea, rubber or sugar plantations. Hence, this chapter has attempted to explore the spaces of political and economic agency of migrant or refugee communities and traced the manner in which new migrants may provide new languages of cultural and political agency, activism and empowerment for the descendants of old indentured migrant communities, many of whom were rendered precarious citizens in some of the post-colonial nation states where they settled. Of course, the LTTE, with its overseas diasporic organisational reach, was a hidden signifier in the regeneration of a south South Asian diasporic cultural identity and political agency among the Indian-origin precariat in Malaysia.

In the final analysis, there is a need to move beyond traditional 'identity politics'. The ethno-religious cultural analysis of new and old diasporas may blur the inherited economic inequalities that are at the root of diasporic activism and cyber-nationalism, given a ready market for ethno-religious identity politics in the context of the 'clash of civilisations'. The study of diasporic long-distance cyber-nationalism has suffered from too much historical and cultural analysis and an inadequate analysis of its economic roots. This chapter has attempted to bring into the same frame the political and economic dynamics of apparently ethno-religious identity conflict by locating the attack on the Sri Lankan Buddhist Temple in KL in the dynamics of precariat life and the search for an 'imaginary homeland' where political, economic and cultural rights may be restored. In this manner, we may trace parallel and intertwined histories of inherited economic and political exclusion, indeed the 'inheritance of loss' across generations, whence the modern global precariat may be seen to be produced – locally and culturally.

Clearly, the diaspora and citizenship are two sides of a coin, and diasporic identities and associated forms of long-distance nationalism tend to wax and wane inversely to the quality of citizenship rights and entitlements, or lack thereof, of members in both home and host countries, as I have argued elsewhere.[16] The LTTE's cyber-nationalism and search to secure a separate state, or 'imaginary homeland', for Tamils was a surrogate for feelings of displacement and insecurity

---

[16]  Rajasingham-Senanayake (2003).

of the Indian-origin diaspora in Malaysia and other parts of the world where Asian immigrants are being increasingly rendered insecure.

With a few notable exceptions, academic studies of Indian indentured labour diasporas have tended to focus on north Indian rather than south Indian indentured labour migrations. This chapter has sought to locate the experience of south Indian indentured labour migrants and their descendants who occupy a particular (Dravidian) racialised and caste-inflected location in the field of diaspora studies. This is in the wider context of migration and refugee flows in the post-colonial period from Sri Lanka, which resulted in the emergence of a 'south South Asian diaspora' identity that encompasses Tamil, Telugu, Malayalee, Kannada and other Dravidian migrants from both India and Sri Lanka. At the same time, an attempt has been made to contextualise global Tamil nationalism and diaspora activism within labour studies and the global precariat.

I have sought in my argument to bring into the same frame different migrations and transnational flows of migrants from south India and Sri Lanka while following their intersecting organisational networks (Tamil Sangams, Hindu *kovils*, and so on) and tracing how Indian-origin colonial indentured labour migrant diasporas connected and identified with post-colonial Sri Lankan Tamil diasporic networks. Diasporic descendants of indentured labour migrants from south India found common cause with Sri Lankan Tamil refugees with whom they shared cultural, linguistic and religious affinities. Simultaneously, diverse struggles for the dignity of labour, as well as Tamil and Dalit caste identity, found pride and voice in the LTTE's nationalist project of Tamil Eelam. The LTTE struggle for a homeland held out the prospect of dignity and respect for Malaysia's precarious citizens.

In order to understand transnational migrant communities it is important to think before, through and beyond the 'methodological nationalism' that renders natural the modern nation state and related 'territorial nationalisms', by locating south India and Sri Lanka in a common post-colonial analytical frame. Arguably, it is methodological nationalism that configures a scholarly culturalist bias that reinforces the binary analysis of cyber-nationalism as either good or bad. By and large cyber-nationalism has been viewed as negatively promoting nationalism and is thus increasingly securitised. This binary logic may be undone by bringing into the frame both the sending and the receiving countries and multiple diasporic imaginations of homelands and tracing how both home- and host-country dynamics of economic inclusion and the exclusion of minority cultural groups impact diaspora identity politics and cyber-nationalism.

The networking and interaction of old and new and colonial and post-colonial migrations bring into view the emergence of what may be termed a new community of the South Asian diaspora in the Global South, even as we map differences in these struggles for full citizenship in their host countries. While many migrants have assimilated into host countries and have become entirely successful immigrants, transcending the challenges and even the stigma of foreignness, others, often twice-migrants, continue to struggle for citizenship and belonging, living precarious lives mired in debt and insecure labour on the peripheries of cities. It is in this space of struggle that 'imaginary homelands', such as Tamil Eelam, may be reborn as cyber-nationalism, enabled by social media and the development of new information and communication systems.

If India and Indian politics remain central to the 'imaginary homeland' of descendants of the global south Indian indentured labour diaspora created by the colonial plantation economy, the war in Sri Lanka enabled the (re)generation of a common post-colonial south South Asian Dravidian diasporic cultural identity broadly inclusive of Indian and Sri Lankan Tamils as well as new forms of political agency, activism and organisation in the context of diverse yet continuing post-colonial locations of economic exclusion and precarious citizenship. The agency of south Indian and Dravidian descendants of indentured migrants in Malaysia and beyond was thus reshaped and boosted by Sri Lankan Tamil nationalism in the past three decades, and the emergent 'dangerous classes' of the Malaysian Indian minority precariat temporarily embraced the LTTE's cyber-nationalism. Thus, a series of displacements – mental and material – significantly enabled by social media and new information and communication technologies, facilitated South Asian networking in the Asian community and the imagination of entirely new forms of solidarity and identity.

## Bibliography

Amrith, Sunil S. 2013. *Crossing the Bay of Bengal: The Furies of Nature and Fortunes of Migration*. Cambridge, MA: Harvard University Press.

Bass, Daniel. 2013. *Everyday Ethnicity in Sri Lanka: Up-Country Tamil Identity Politics*. Colombo: Social Scientists Association.

Bates, Crispin. 2017. 'Some Thoughts on the Representation and Misrepresentation of the Colonial South Asian Labour Diaspora'. *South Asian Studies* 33(1): 7–22.

Bates, Crispin, and Marina Carter. 2021. 'Kala Pani Revisited: Indian Labour Migrants and the Sea Voyage'. *Journal of Indentureship* 1(1): 34–62.

Desai, Kiran. 2006. *The Inheritance of Loss*. New York: Grove Press.

Kanaganayakam, Chelva. 2009. 'Configuring Space and Constructing Nations'. In *Pathways of Dissent: Tamil Nationalism in Sri Lanka*, edited by R. Cheran, pp. 81–92. New Delhi. SAGE Publications.

Kaur, Arunajeet. 2017. *Hindraf and the Malaysian Indian Community*. Kuala Lumpur: Silverfish Books.

Kumar, Ashutosh. 2017. *Coolies of the Empire: Indentured Indians in the Sugar Colonies, 1830–1920*. Cambridge, UK: Cambridge University Press.

Kumar, Kamles. 2016. 'At PWTC, Indian Malaysians Protest against Sri Lanka's Visiting Rajapaksa (Video)'. *Malay Mail*, 2 September. https://www.malaymail.com/news/malaysia/2016/09/02/at-pwtc-indian-malaysians-protest-against-sri-lankas-visiting-rajapaksa-vid/1197183. Accessed on 15 April 2023.

McKeown, Adam. 2004. 'Global Migration 1846-1940'. *Journal of World History* 15(2): 155–189.

Munck, Ronaldo. 2013. 'The Precariat: A View from the South'. *Third World Quarterly* 34(5): 747–762.

Picketty, Thomas. 2014. *Capital in the Twentieth Century*, translated by Arthur Goldhammer. Cambridge, MA: Harvard University Press.

Rajasingham-Senanayake, Darini. 2003. 'Diaspora and Citizenship: Forgotten Routes of Identity in Sri Lanka'. In *Culture and Economy in the Indian Diaspora*, edited by Bhikhu Parekh, Gurharpal Singh and Steven Vertovec, pp. 93–113. London: Routledge.

Raghuram, Parvati, Ajaya Kumar Sahoo, Brij Maharaj and Dave Sangha. 2006. *Tracing an Indian Diaspora: Contexts, Memories, Representations*. New Delhi: SAGE Publications.

Rushdie, Salman. 1992. *Imaginary Homelands: Chapters and Criticism, 1981–1991*. London: Granta Books.

Standing, Guy. 2011. *The Precariat: The New Dangerous Class*. London: Bloomsbury Publishing.

*Straits Times*. 2017. 'Jaffna Holds Special Significance for S'pore, Says Vivian Balakrishnan'. 19 July. https://www.straitstimes.com/asia/south-asia/jaffna-holds-special-significance-for-spore-says-dr-balakrishnan. Accessed on 15 April 2023.

Tan, Tarrence. 2016. 'Buddhist Monk Assaulted at Anti-Rajapaksa Protest'. *Free Malaysia Today*, 3 September. https://www.freemalaysiatoday.com/category/nation/2016/09/03/buddhist-monk-assaulted-at-anti-rajapaksa-protest. Accessed on 15 April 2023.

Tinker, Hugh. 1974. *A New System of Slavery: The Export of Indian Labour Overseas, 1830–1920*. Oxford: Oxford University Press.

# About the Contributors

**Rochelle Almeida** is Professor of South Asian Studies and Global Cultures in Liberal Studies at New York University. She has taught in universities in the United States (US), the United Kingdom (UK), India and, most recently, in Tashkent, Uzbekistan, on a Fulbright–Nehru Senior Research Fellowship. She is the author of eight scholarly books and numerous peer-reviewed papers in academic journals. She has specialised in ethnographic field research (especially Anglo-Indian ethnography) based on personal interviews and archival examination. She carried out field research in the UK and India and is currently working on a book on the history of Western performing arts in Bombay (present-day Mumbai). An international freelance writer, she divides her time between Connecticut and Mumbai.

**Prinisha Badassy** holds a PhD from the University of KwaZulu-Natal, Durban, and currently lectures in the History Department at the University of the Witwatersrand, Johannesburg. Her research interests include the social medico-legal history of infanticide and abortion in the late-nineteenth- and early-twentieth-century Natal, the study of the domain of the family and childhood, the political economy of reproduction, medico-jurisprudence and gendered discourses of criminality. She has also published on the history of Indian interpreters within the British Empire and the complicated, sometimes lethal, relationship between masters and servants in colonial Natal. She teaches on the historical processes of globalisation, historical transnational flows and networks that give rise to the United States as a superpower, the emergence and historical overview of African urbanism, modern South Africa, theory and methods for historical research and the history of sex. She currently serves as editor of the *South African Historical Journal*, and is a member of the Southern African Historical Society Executive

Council, editorial board member of *Historia* and list editor for the H-Africa Discussion Network.

**Crispin Bates** is Professor of Modern and Contemporary South Asian History at the University of Edinburgh and an Honorary Visiting Professor in the Graduate School of African and Asian Studies, Kyoto University. He completed his PhD at the University of Cambridge, where he was also a junior research fellow. He has held visiting professorships in Paris, Kolkata, Beijing, Kyoto, Tokyo and the National Museum of Ethnology in Japan. He has authored, co-authored and edited a total of 15 books, including a history of South Asia from 1600 to the present, entitled *Subalterns and Raj* (2007), and a series of seven volumes concerning the history of the Indian uprising of 1857, entitled *Mutiny at the Margins* (2013–2017). In 2015–2018, he led 'Becoming Coolies', a project funded by the Arts and Humanities Research Council (AHRC), Swindon, on the origins of Indian overseas labour migration in the Indian Ocean, for which he conducted research in archives throughout the Indian Ocean region.

**Rana Partap Behal** completed his PhD in labour history at Jawaharlal Nehru University, New Delhi, and taught History at Deshbandhu College, University of Delhi. He also held teaching assignments at Cornell University at Ithaca, New York; Syracuse University at Syracuse, New York; and Oberlin College in Ohio, United States. He has been a fellow at the Nehru Memorial Museum and Library, New Delhi; the South Asia Centre, University of Cambridge, in connection with the project 'Work and the Human Life Cycle in Global History' at Humboldt University, Berlin; the Centre for Development Studies, Free University, Berlin; and the Max Weber Center for Advanced Cultural and Social Studies (Max Weber Kolleg), Erfurt. He was also the India coordinator of the 'Labour' module at the International Centre for Advanced Studies: Metamorphoses of the Political (ICAS:MP), Centre for the Study of Developing Societies, New Delhi, and is the author of *One Hundred Years of Servitude: Political Economy of Tea Plantations in Colonial Assam* (2014). He is a founding member and treasurer of the Association of Indian Labour Historians, Delhi.

**Sheetal Bhoola** is Lecturer of Sociology at the University of Zululand, KwaZulu-Natal. Her key research areas are the Indian South African community, lifeways, food security, food and culture (anthropology and sociology), and the anthropology of food, cuisine and tourism, and children's food. She is also affiliated to the Critical Food Studies Research Association (Andrew Mellon Foundation), South Africa. She completed her PhD at the University of KwaZulu-Natal and holds two master's degrees in Sociology. Her first MA degree was a co-badged degree from Albert Ludwig University, Freiburg, and Jawaharlal Nehru University, New Delhi. Her second MA degree was completed at the University of KwaZulu-Natal. She has also been the recipient of several prestigious scholarships and has recently been recognised for her community engagements and academic developments in South Africa.

**Chhanda Chatterjee** is currently Senior Research Fellow at the Indian Council of Social Science Research (ICSSR), New Delhi, affiliated to the Nehru Memorial Museum and Library, New Delhi. Previously she was, for many years, Professor of History and the Director of the Centre for Guru Nanak Dev Studies, Visva Bharati University, Santiniketan, West Bengal. She is the author of *Ecology, the Sikh Legacy and the Raj: Punjab, 1858–1887* (1997), *Punjab and Awadh, 1857–1887: Ideology, the Rural Power Structure, and Imperial Rule* (1999) and *Sikh Minority and the Partition of the Punjab, 1920–1947* (2018), and is the editor of *Literature as History: From Early to Contemporary Times* (2014) and *The Partition of the Indian Subcontinent: Uneasy Borders* (2023).

**Chan E. S. Choenni** was born in Paramaribo, Suriname, in 1953 and emigrated to the Netherlands in 1972. He studied Political Science and Science of Philosophy at the University of Amsterdam. He also qualified as a social researcher and a historian. He received his PhD in 1995 at the University of Utrecht, and his thesis was on conscripts in the Dutch military and integration. In 2010, he was appointed as a professor at Free University of Amsterdam and is now Emeritus Professor at the university. He has published on integration and racism and extensively about the history of 'Hindostanis' overseas.

**Arunima Datta** is Assistant Professor at the Department of History, University of North Texas. She completed her PhD at the National University of Singapore. She has published articles on South and South-East Asian history, labour migration and women's histories. Her first monograph, *Fleeting Agencies: A Social History of Indian Coolie Women in British Malaya* (2021), has been awarded three notable prizes in the field: the Sara Whaley Book Prize by the National Women's Studies Association (2021), the Gita Chaudhuri Prize by the Western Association of Women's History (2022) and the Stansky Prize by the North American Conference of British Studies (2022). Her current research project focuses on

South Asian travelling *ayah*s in Britain. An article based on this work, 'Responses to Traveling Indian Ayahs in Nineteenth and Early Twentieth Century Britain', published in the *Journal of Historical Geography*, was awarded the Carol Gold Best Article Award (2022). She also serves as a co-editor of the journal *Gender and History*, an associate editor of *Britain and the World Journal* and an associate review editor of the *American Historical Review*.

**Nafisa Essop Sheik** completed her PhD at the University of Michigan, Ann Arbor, and currently teaches at the University of Johannesburg. She is part of the transnational Mellon Foundation–funded projects 'Governing Intimacies' and 'Oceanic Humanities for the Global South', based at the Wits Institute for Social and Economic Research (WiSER), University of the Witwatersrand, Johannesburg. She completed a term as Julien and Virginia Cornell Visiting Professor in History at Swarthmore College in Pennsylvania in the United States. She is currently working on a book provisionally titled 'Colonial Rites: Sex, Law and States of Difference in a Nineteenth-Century British South African Colony'.

**Kalpana Hiralal** is Professor of History in the School of Social Sciences at Howard College, University of KwaZulu-Natal. An AfOx Senior Fellow, University of Oxford, and a South African National Research Foundation (NRF)–rated researcher, her two key areas of interest are gender and the South Asian diaspora and gender and resistance in South Africa. She has been the recipient of several research awards including the Nordic Africa Institute's Guest Researchers' scholarship in 2007 and the Inspire Erasmus Staff scholarship 2017. She is the co-editor of *Satyagraha, Passive Resistance and Its Legacy* (2015) and *Gender and Mobility: Borders, Bodies, and Boundaries* (2018), the editor of *Global Hindu Diaspora: Historical and Contemporary Perspectives* (2017), the co-author of *Pioneers of Satyagraha: Indian South African Defy Racist Laws, 1907–1914* (2017), and the author of the first and second volumes of *Sisters in the Struggle: Women of Indian Origin in South Africa's Liberation Struggle, 1900–1994* (2022).

**Yoshina Hurgobin** is a historian of modern South Asia and is currently Assistant Professor of History at Kennesaw State University. Her research interests are related to citizenship, migration and disease. She received her PhD, MA and MPhil in History (South Asia) from Syracuse University's Maxwell School of Citizenship and Public Affairs, Syracuse, New York. At the Maxwell School, the Nelson Blake Prize, Moynihan Challenge grant, Roscoe Martin awards, and Bharati Summer Research grants enabled her to pursue archival work for the writing of her dissertation. She earned her BA in International Studies (focusing on East Asia and social and cultural identity) from the Croft Institute for International Studies at the University of Mississippi, Oxford, Mississippi.

**Brij V. Lal** was Emeritus Professor of Pacific and Asian history at the Australian National University, Canberra. His first pioneering book was *Girmitiyas: The Origins of the Fiji Indians* (1983), followed by more than a dozen books on Fijian and Pacific Islands history, including *Chalo Jahaji: On a Journey through Indenture in Fiji* (2012). He published a similar number of books on Fijian politics and two works of historical fiction, as well as several academic essays and newspaper articles. He played a central role in Fijian public life as an intellectual and through his role in redrafting Fiji's constitution in 1995. He contributed his essay to this volume shortly before he passed away in December 2021.

**Brij Maharaj** is Professor of Geography at the University of KwaZulu-Natal. He has received widespread recognition for his research on urban politics, segregation, local economic development, migration and diasporas, religion and development, and has published over 150 scholarly papers in renowned journals such as *Urban Studies*, the *International Journal of Urban and Regional Studies*, *Political Geography*, *Urban Geography*, *Antipode*, *Polity and Space*, *Geoforum* and *GeoJournal*. He has also co-edited five book collections. He currently serves on the editorial board of the journal *South Asian Diaspora*.

**Emma C. Meyer** completed her PhD from Emory University, Atlanta, with a thesis titled 'Resettling Burma's Displaced: Labor, Rehabilitation, and Citizenship in Visakhapatnam, India, 1937–1979'. Her research, which focuses on histories of forced migration between India and Burma (present-day Myanmar) in the mid-twentieth century, traces the historical development of relief, resettlement and citizenship in modern South Asia.

**Darini Rajasingham-Senanayake** is a social and medical anthropologist with expertise in the political economy of international development. She completed her PhD at Princeton University, New Jersey. She undertook postdoctoral research at Columbia University, New York, and the International Center of Advanced Studies, New York University. She has worked as a gender and social development consultant for various international organisations. She has also worked and taught at the Open University of Sri Lanka, Colombo; the International Centre for Ethnic Studies, Colombo; the Social Scientists' Association, Colombo; and the Institute for South Asian Studies, National University of Singapore. She is a founding member of the Centre for Poverty Analysis, a think tank in Colombo. She recently co-edited *Multi-Religiosity in Contemporary Sri Lanka: Innovation, Shared Spaces, Contestation* (2021).

**Lomarsh Roopnarine** is Professor of Latin American and Caribbean Studies at Jackson State University, Jackson, Mississippi. He has published three books and over three dozen articles on the South Asian diaspora in the Caribbean. His most recent book, *The Indian Caribbean: Migration and Identity in the Diaspora*, was the 2018 recipient of the Gordon K. and Sybil Lewis Book Award by the Caribbean Studies Association.

**Goolam Vahed** is Professor in the Department of History at the University of KwaZulu-Natal. He has published widely in peer-reviewed journals on identity formation, citizenship, ethnicity, migration and transnationalism among Indian South Africans as well as the role of sports and culture in South African society. Some of his recent co-authored books include *A History of the Present: A Biography of Indian South Africans, 1994–2019* (2019), *Colour, Class and Community: The Natal Indian Congress, 1971–1994* (2021) and *Durban's Casbah: Bunny Chows, Bolsheviks, and Bioscopes* (2023).

# Index

cultural traditions as means of,
73–75
domestic servants, 39, 59
European, 346
evacuee, 307–309
everyday, 25–27, 40
impact of, 76–77
return, 151, 157, 168, 170–178, 192,
194, 208*n*28, 253, 266–267,
269–272, 295, 305, 310–313, 321,
342, 344, 351
migration, 7–8, 11, 19, 27, 32, 35,
98, 116–117, 128–131, 142,
144, 146, 152–154, 195
passage, 7, 32, 128–129, 146*n*51,
157, 174–175, 270–272, 344
transports and savings, 133–135
returnee/returnees migrants, 7, 9, 127,
130–146, 168*n*4, 170–171, 176–
177, 193–194
role of, 172–175
returning process, 135–143, 170–171,
177
Réunion, 8–9, 28, 34, 168*n*4, 170,
176–190, 193–194
rubber plantations, 1, 201–205, 208,
210, 365, 367, 374
colonial planters in Malaya, 9
rural–urban, 153–154

Sattara, 176–177
settlement schemes, 157
sex
ratio, 205, 219–220
sexual, 63, 66, 217
abusing of women, 25
arousal, 209
coercion, 64
competition, 226
differences, 223

exploitation of coolie women, 6
jealousy, 202, 206–207
harassment, 69, 72, 82, 207
mores, 228
overtures, 216
relationships of women, 9, 203
rights, 224
sexuality, 236–237
Seychelles, 8, 167–168, 168*n*4, 172,
177–189, 194
Shree Parsuram Darjee Association, 247
Sikhs migrants in Canada, racial
discrimination and political assertion
among
Calcutta and suburbs Sikh residents,
117–118
desire of immigrant revolutionaries
to work together, 120–122
employment opportunities of
aspiring immigrants, 107–108
imperial citizens sharing in
opportunities, 101–102
*Komagata Maru* (Japanese ship),
108–109, 117, 123
local resentment against Sikh
immigrant labourers, 104–105
measures taken by Canadian
government to check
immigration, 105–106
migration from Punjab, 102
opportunities in Canada, 103–104
seditious materials circulation in
Punjab, 118–120
seditious tracts, 111–112
Sikh Educational Conference,
112–113
strategy for exclusion, 106–107
students radicalisation in Canada
and America, 113–115